31 Murders

31 Murders

*Following the Trail
of Serial Sex Killer Earle Nelson*

ALVIN A.J. ESAU

Exposit

Jefferson, North Carolina

ISBN (print) 978-1-4766-9480-1
ISBN (ebook) 978-1-4766-5268-9

Library of Congress and British Library
Cataloguing Data are available

Library of Congress Control Number 2024004585

Front cover images: Earle Nelson mug shot in Winnipeg after his capture in Killarney.
Winnipeg Police File (courtesy John Burchill).
Other images © ArtWell/ Cristina Conti/Shutterstock.

Printed in the United States of America

Exposit is an imprint of McFarland & Company, Inc., Publishers

Exposit

Box 611, Jefferson, North Carolina 28640
www.expositbooks.com

Contents

Part IV—1927: The Gorilla Man Strangler

Acknowledgments

Ironically, this book not only deals with the 31 murders that I think were committed by serial killer Earle Leonard Nelson in the 1925–1927 period, but the book itself took more than 31 years to research and write. Back in 1989 when I was the head of the University of Manitoba Legal Research Institute, the dean of the law faculty, the late Roland Penner, requested that I identify the most famous Manitoba trials for purposes of making some presentation at the 75th anniversary party of the school. I identified nine trials, of which three were murder trials, one of them the trial of the "gorilla man strangler," Earle Nelson, an American serial killer who came to Winnipeg and murdered two women in that city. The late Ken Kehler, then a law student, worked over several summers under my direction gathering materials on various famous trials. He was an outstanding researcher, especially adept at freedom of information applications, and a great deal of material was gathered. Other law students also helped to acquire or organize materials. Special thanks in this regard to Ali Lamont and Michael Styczen.

I eventually took a particular interest in the Nelson case, and from time to time, especially during various sabbaticals and subsequently during my retirement, I would take up further research and writing on it, even while working on other projects and books. I love the research process of traveling to various cities and working in archives and libraries and exploring the sites of the murders. However, the process of writing is much less enjoyable. Indeed, I have often told people that I only write when the agony of not writing exceeds the agony of writing. The length of time that has passed in researching this book has proven to be an advantage in that so much more material has now been digitized and is available via computer databases that can be accessed from your desk at home. For example, instead of the many hours looking through reels of microfilm in libraries, many newspapers are fully searchable on newspapers.com or newspaperarchive.com. Also, my ability to write something about the history of the victims has been enormously improved through the records available on ancestry.com or familysearch.org.

I am grateful to Lisa Camp, executive editor, Sophia Lyons, editorial assistant, and the other good folks at McFarland for their work in bringing this book to fruition. As with my previous books, I am most grateful to Sandra Fowler Esau for reading the drafts and encouraging me to continue with this project. Our four children and their partners provided much needed diversion from the task, as did grandchild Louisa Esau Jordan most recently.

Over the more than three decades during which I have been working on this project, I have received original police files from various officials. Special thanks to Sergeant Kevin Kilkenny for providing the Kansas City police files on the Pace and Harpin cases, Captain Mark Antonio for providing the Buffalo police file on the Randolph case, Rory O'Brian for providing the Chicago police file on the Sietsema case, and John Burchill for providing the Winnipeg police files on Nelson and the Winnipeg murders. Also, thanks to the late Douglas Buhr, city solicitor, who granted my initial freedom of information appeal to view the Winnipeg police file. Other helpful information was provided by Captain Rick Salsedo and Sergeant William Fellers from the Stockton police, Bruce Cuthbertson from the Portland police, Kevin Maiberger from the Los Angeles police, Robert Miller from the Council Bluffs police, Darnell Henry of the Newark police, James Trainum of the Washington, D.C., police, Richelle Goede from the San Jose police, and Officer Bell from the Philadelphia police.

I am also grateful to Sue Keller of the San Francisco Medical Examiner's office for providing autopsy reports and District Attorney Michael D. Schrunk, who granted my freedom of information appeal to access the coroners' reports of the Portland victims.

Various archival staff provided helpful information. Special thanks to Lori Shea Kuechler of the Portland Police Museum who put me in touch with Nancy Salmon, granddaughter of Portland victim Beata Withers. Thanks also to Nancy Salmon for the wealth of information provided to me. Diana Banning and Brian Johnson at the Stanley Parr Archives and Records Center in Portland helpfully provided the police notebooks that I requested. Thanks to Dwight Wallis, records administrator for Multnomah County. The staff at the Bancroft Library and Archives at the University of California, Berkeley, particularly Jack von Euw, provided useful materials. David Baugh, archivist at Philadelphia City Archives, was helpful. Thanks also to Linda Johnson, archivist at the California State Archives. The National Archives in Ottawa and the Provincial Archives in Manitoba provided much of the material that forms the background material for this book. My freedom of information request for the files of the attorney general was approved by Bruce MacFarlane, then deputy attorney general of Manitoba, followed by considerable help from archivist Gordon Dodds.

Much of the research for this book took place at various times over many decades in various libraries. These included the San Francisco Public Library, Toronto Reference Library, Buffalo Central Library, Hatcher Library at the University of Michigan, Hesburgh Library at the University of Notre Dame, Van Pelt Library at the University of Pennsylvania, Chicago Public Library, Regenstein Library at the University of Chicago, Wilson Library at the University of Western Washington, San Diego Central Library, Geisel Library at the University of California, Lied Library at the University of Las Vegas, Suzzallo and Allen libraries at the University of Washington, Portland Public Library, Knight Library at the University of Oregon, Widener Library at Harvard University, Boston Public Library, Detroit Public Library, and New York Public Library. Various staff at these institutions helped me with the often-malfunctioning microfilm readers. Particular thanks to Anita Delaney, reference librarian, at the Palo Alto Library.

I am also grateful to John Eaton and Regena Rumancik of the E.K. Williams Law Library at Robson Hall, University of Manitoba, who were particularly helpful in getting microfilms through interlibrary loan or from the Center for Research Libraries in Chicago. Materials were also provided from the Manitoba Provincial Library. When I moved to Victoria, librarian Ian Baird was pleasant company in the microfilm room at the McPherson Library at the University of Victoria. I also spent a lot of time at the University of British Columbia Koerner Library microfilm area, where the staff were always helpful.

Introduction

The killer was mobile, moving from city to city. The murders were usually linked by various police forces as they occurred because of their similarities. A landlady with a room to rent or a house for sale would be found strangled to death, often with evidence that she had been sexually assaulted after death. Robbery was sometimes a secondary motive as indicated by missing jewelry, clothing or money that had been taken from the scene of the crime. Even though the term "serial killer" was not used in the 1920s, it was clear that the same man was murdering one landlady after another.

The murderer of landladies during the 1925, 1926, and 1927 period was never identified and captured in the United States, although over time various witnesses gave a good description of him. He was called the "dark strangler" because of his dark complexion, but eventually he came to be known by the atavist moniker the "gorilla man strangler." He was not just a coast-to-coast predator but also an international serial killer. In June of 1927 he wandered into Canada and killed a young girl in a rooming house in Winnipeg and then within a few hours murdered a housewife in a different part of the city. After a dramatic manhunt he was captured, he escaped, and then he was recaptured. The "gorilla man strangler" was identified as Earle Nelson from San Francisco, an escapee from a California insane asylum. He was convicted of murder in a jury trial in Winnipeg in November 1927 and hanged in January 1928. I have covered the Canadian side of the story previously in the book *The Gorilla Man Strangler Case: Serial Killer Earle Nelson.*[1]

Part of the reason that I continued my research and writing on Earle Nelson was that I discovered that the existing literature was often riddled with fictional and inaccurate material.[2] People write about serial killers, or create blogs or produce podcasts, without doing any original research. They simply repeat and embellish the often-false information that was published previously.[3] After doing actual research with primary archival materials, it is sobering to see the gap between history based on evidence and "history" that is fantastical rather than factual.

As background to the present book, I provide a summary of the Canadian murders and a biographical sketch of Earle Nelson, but the main purpose of the present book is to cover the American side of the story. Which murders in the United States might be attributed to Earle Nelson? What links, aside from similar *modus operandi*, point to Earle Nelson as the killer? For each of the murders that I think are worthy of examination, I have attempted to reconstruct the murder narratives, utilizing police files when available, as well as the numerous newspaper reports, and I also have attempted in each case to give information as to the history of the victim or victims when there was more than one.

When I was a first-year law student, friends or family might ask, "What's it like?" My reply would be "Just one damned case after another." This book might be thought of as just one murder after another, like a series of cases. However, it should be noted that in addition to the murders that I cover, there is material on suspects falsely arrested, alleged murder attempts, supposed encounters with the strangler, and other materials that tie the individual murders into a somewhat larger narrative.

The police in Winnipeg linked the murder of Mrs. Patterson to the "gorilla man strangler" even before the first murder, that of Lola Cowan, was discovered. But it was only after the discovery of the second body that the local press reported that the suspect was believed to be "the notorious killer wanted for 20 similar murders in the United States."[4] On July 3, 1927, not long after Nelson was arrested, Edward Smith, Jr., wrote an article in *The Sunday Oregonian* containing a list of 22 victims of Earle Nelson starting with Clara Newman in San Francisco and ending with the murders in Winnipeg.[5] The newspaper article included a map of North America with arrows showing the 7,000-mile trail that the strangler had traversed on his killing spree and declared with confidence that Earle Nelson now in a Winnipeg jail had been positively identified across the nation as being the "dark strangler" and "degenerate sadist" responsible for these 22 deaths. This list of murders was said to be based on the work of Detective Archie Leonard of Portland. As the title of this book indicates, I believe that Archie Leonard underestimated the body count of Earle Nelson. It is also ironic that it was a Portland police officer who compiled the "official" list of Nelson murders, given that the Portland police were particularly inept in investigating the murders in Portland, categorizing two of them as suicides and another as a natural death due to heart disease.

Records of the Portland police indicate that Archie Leonard was born in 1879 and was a railroad agent and deputy sheriff before he joined the police force in 1915. He retired in 1946 and died in 1952.[6] Detective Leonard was a graduate of the University of Oregon Law School and was the only detective in the department with a full "civil service rating."[7] To his credit, Leonard did take a special interest in the "dark strangler" murders, as disclosed in the surviving police notebooks in the Portland City Archives.[8] The strangler had allegedly killed four women in Portland in October and November of 1926, and Leonard continued to spend considerable time on these cases, taking work home and following the trail of the strangler long after it was apparent that the fiend had left town.

While the "Leonard list" became the "official" body count list for Earle Nelson, there were other murders on various "expanded" body count lists. For example, one of the most influential books on Earle Nelson was written by Frank W. Anderson in 1974.[9] He deviated from the list of 22 victims by adding five additional killings. He wrote confidently that Nelson started his killing spree with three murders in Philadelphia in 1925, as well as the murders of Mrs. Gallegos in Stockton in August 1926 and Emma Wells in San Francisco in September 1926. We will examine these five murders in due course, because they certainly have enough circumstantial evidence to bring them into the territory of probable victims of Earle Nelson. There seems to have been no good reason for Leonard to have excluded them from the list, especially the Gallegos and Wells murders.

While also adding a layer of fictional reconstruction to the narrative, the most historically reliable book on Earle Nelson is *Bestial* by Harold Schechter, published in 1998.[10] This book reconstructs the "dark strangler/gorilla man" story using the Leonard list of 22 victims. However, Schechter acknowledged that Nelson may well have been responsible for other murders. He mentioned five cases in 1925 (two in San Francisco and three in Philadelphia) where some elements like strangulation, post-mortem rape, or theft of clothing made each of these murders plausible additions to the list of 22. Then Schechter mentioned an additional three murders (one in Boston and two in Newark) that are not as strongly linked but could have been committed by Nelson.[11] As I will subsequently note, I do not think Earle Nelson should be associated with the Boston and Newark murders.

However, there were other murders of landladies during this period which are not found on the Leonard "conventional" list or on the "expanded" list. There are several landlady murder cases that I deal with that have never appeared on previous lists. In addition to the five cases mentioned by both Anderson and Schechter, I have added another four that I think might well be linked to Earle Nelson.

Of course, there were many unsolved murders of women in the United States during the time periods when Earle Nelson was not in jail or in the insane asylum. Linking cases to Earle Nelson cannot be done with any sort of certainty at this stage. Almost a hundred years after the fact, with police records often destroyed or unavailable, the cases are as cold as ice, and we are sometimes left only with newspaper reports of uncertain reliability. However, during this period most major cities had several rival newspapers, and I have attempted in each case to examine where the reporting was similar and where it was divergent. Furthermore, newspaper reports are a kind of historical "fact" in themselves, not in the sense that they are necessarily accurate about the facts of what happened but in that they are facts in terms of what people at the time were reading as to the murders and the investigations.

By what theory do we link possible or probable cases? If Nelson was embarking on a career as a killer earlier than the conventional 1926 starting date, we might speculate that he did not necessarily suddenly adopt one consistent method of finding his victim and one consistent method of killing, sexually assaulting post-mortem, and stealing. Perhaps, as in most endeavors, there was some period of experimentation. Even when murders are linked by obvious similarities in *modus operandi*, we may wrongly overlook the possibility that the murderer may be inconsistent and seizing other opportunities to satisfy his sexual-sadistic passion for killing. How do we really know that the "dark strangler" was not responsible for some cases where the bodies of various strangled women were found in strange places, floating in the water, dumped in the woods, left on the street? However, if we do include various murders that fall too far outside the rooming house or house for sale circumstance, we are soon into a very unmanageable and almost unlimited terrain.

This book will both revisit the Leonard list to examine each of the 20 American murders, looking for as much information as possible, and examine other unsolved murders that have been considered Nelson possibilities. In addition to the two Winnipeg murders, and the 20 American murders on the "official" list, I have added another nine American murders that would bring the body count to 31, if they indeed were all committed by Nelson.

It is important to note that I am not claiming proof beyond a reasonable doubt that Nelson killed all these women on the list. There are several cases that are only possibilities at best. At the same time there may be murders that Nelson committed that are not on our list at all. There may be both wrongful linkages and failures to link. During the narrative, I will mention a dozen other murders that I have chosen not to include in the book. I have written separate narratives on many of these cases, giving an overview of the murders and the reasons for not finding sufficient evidence to link them with some degree of probability to Earle Nelson. These additional murder narratives are found on my website.[12]

Here now is a list of murders that I have chosen for examination. Names on the conventional "Leonard" list are in bold:

1. August 22, 1925—Elizabeth Jones, 72, San Francisco
2. September 15, 1925—Daisy Anderson, 45, San Francisco
3. October 15, 1925—Olla McCoy, 26, Philadelphia
4. November 6, 1925—Mary Murray, 38, Philadelphia
5. November 10, 1925—Lena Weiner, 33, Philadelphia
6. **February 20, 1926—Clara Newman, 60, San Francisco**
7. **March 2, 1926—Laura Beal, 64, San Jose**
8. **June 10, 1926—Lillian St. Mary, 63, San Francisco**
9. **June 24, 1926—Ollie Russell, 56, Santa Barbara**
10. **August 16, 1926—Mary Nisbet, 52, Oakland**
11. August 17, 1926—Isabelle Gallegos, 75, Stockton
12. September 26–29, 1926—Elma Wells, 35, San Francisco
13. **October 19, 1926—Beata Withers, 36, Portland**
14. **October 20, 1926—Mabel Fluke, 37, Portland**
15. **October 21, 1926—Virginia Grant, 59, Portland**
16. November 11, 1926—Marion Corcoran, 24, Los Angeles
17. **November 18, 1926—Anna Edmonds, 57, San Francisco**
18. **November 23, 1926—Florence Monks, 55, Seattle**
19. **November 29, 1926—Blanche Myers, 49, Portland**
20. **December 23, 1926—Almira Berard, 42, Council Bluffs**
21. **December 27, 1926—Bonnie Pace, 24, Kansas City**
22. **December 28, 1926—Germaine Harpin, 28, Kansas City**
23. **December 28, 1926—Robert Harpin, nine months, Kansas City**
24. **April 27, 1927—Mary McConnell, 53, Philadelphia**
25. **May 30, 1927—Jennie Randolph, 57, Buffalo**
26. **June 1, 1927—Fannie May, 53, Detroit**
27. **June 1, 1927—Maureen Oswald Atorthy, 28, Detroit**
28. **June 2, 1927—Mary Sietsema, 32, Chicago**
29. June 4, 1927—Lena Johannes, 54, Kansas City

30. **June 9, 1927—Lola Cowan, 14, Winnipeg**
31. **June 10, 1927—Emily Patterson, 27, Winnipeg**

Because we are interested in examining the linkages, if any, made to the American murders, we start our narrative at the end of the list of murders, because it was in Canada that Earle Nelson was identified and convicted.

PART I

Background

CHAPTER 1

Two Manitoba Murders
and the Capture, Trial
and Execution of Earle Nelson

30. June 9, 1927—Lola Cowan, 14, Winnipeg
31. June 10, 1927—Emily Patterson, 27, Winnipeg

On Wednesday, June 8, 1927, a young man hitched rides from various motorists and crossed the border from Minnesota into Canada and eventually arrived in Winnipeg, Manitoba.[1] When engaged in a conversation with the wife of one of the motorists, the man claimed to be from Winnipeg and then gave his address as being on a street that did not exist.[2] Arriving with no money, he went to a second-hand store on Main Street and exchanged the nice clothes he was wearing for shabbier ones and received a dollar so that he could make a deposit on a room to rent. At the store he called himself "John Cavanaugh" and again gave an address in Winnipeg that did not exist.[3]

A few blocks from the second-hand store, the man came across a sign outside 133 Smith Street advertising "Rooms to Rent." Now calling himself "Woodcoats," he gave the landlady a dollar deposit for a room upstairs that cost $3 for the week. He had a lengthy conversation with the landlady, Mrs. Hill, and presented himself as a nice, religious man. The elderly landlady and her husband lived on the main floor of the rooming house, and next day, Thursday, June 9, Woodcoats came into their kitchen to tell Mrs. Hill that he still did not have the two dollars that he owed her. The landlady did not see Woodcoats thereafter.[4]

On Thursday evening, Lola Cowan, a few days shy of her 14th birthday, was out selling artificial flowers in the neighborhood where she lived, which included the rooming house where Woodcoats had rented a room. The Cowan family, with six children, was not well to do financially. The father was recently unemployed after having surgery for appendicitis and the mother had taken a temporary job at a hotel on Smith Street.[5] Lola had been selling artificial flowers made by her older sister to help the family financially. Lola Cowan never came home on Thursday night.

It was not until Sunday, June 12, that her body was discovered under the bed in the room that Woodcoats had rented.[6] She was found naked. She had been hit over the head, strangled to death, and sexually assaulted after death. Several days later her clothing was found, stuffed into a drawer in an adjoining room. One of the many

9

mistakes in previous literature includes the information that Lola Cowan's body was mutilated.[7] I have seen the pictures and there were no cuts to her body.[8] Given that her body was nude, with signs of indignity visible in her private parts, I have chosen not to reproduce a picture here. The post-mortem examination revealed various bruises, especially around the neck, and "there were four or five streaks of blood across the front of the left thigh in the middle. On the top of the head there was a haemorrhage of the scalp but there was no wound found inside the scalp…. The skull was not fractured…. The condition of the hymen entering the vagina showed it had been recently torn. Death would be due to asphyxiation due to smothering."[9]

While the murder of Lola Cowan on Thursday night would not be discovered till Sunday, June 12, the second murder in Winnipeg took place on Friday, June 10, but was the first to be discovered. Around noon that day Mrs. Emily Patterson, a 27-year-old housewife, was hit over the head, strangled and sexually assaulted in her home at 100 Riverton Avenue in the Elmwood area of Winnipeg.[10] While Winnipeg police later claimed the house had a "for sale" sign on it,[11] we have some doubts that this was the case.[12] Perhaps the murderer presented himself to Mrs. Patterson as a hobo in need of something to eat or simply entered the home and waited for Mrs. Patterson to return to the house from the garden where she was seen working in the morning. Her husband arrived home from work in the evening and found his wife missing from the house and his two young sons at a neighbor's house. His anxiety increased through the evening, particularly when he noticed that a suitcase containing the family savings of $50 to $70 in crisp ten-dollar bills had been tampered with. When he opened the suitcase, he found that the money was missing and a hammer had been put into the suitcase. Toward midnight he knelt beside the bed to pray to God to help him find his wife, and as he arose, he providentially touched something under the bed. He found it to be the sleeve of his wife's coat, and as he looked under the bed, he discovered the body of his wife.[13]

There was blood on her face, and her clothes were pulled up above her waist and her stockings were rolled down. The post-mortem examination revealed various bruises on the neck and face and on the top of the head, although the skull was not fractured. Evidence also showed that "across the front of the right thigh there was a streak of gelatinous material, which turned out on examination to be human semen."[14] Both the victims in Winnipeg were strangled or smothered by hand rather than with a ligature of some kind.

In the early hours of Saturday, June 11, 1927, while investigating the murder of Mrs. Patterson, it was discovered by the police that the murderer had changed clothes at the scene of the crime. The killer had taken off his shabby working clothes, later traced as the ones he had acquired at the second-hand store on June 8, and had put on an old, worn suit of Mr. Patterson that he found hanging from the bedroom door. The police also discovered that the murderer had taken the wedding ring off the hand of Mrs. Patterson, as well as the money and some other items from the suitcase.

Under the direction of chief detective George Smith, the Winnipeg police on Saturday, June 11, discovered information from a second-hand dealer on Main Street that would be crucial to the eventual capture of the fiend. On Friday after the

Earle Nelson's last victim. The body of Mrs. Emily Patterson, after the bed was removed. Patterson had been strangled and sexually assaulted. Winnipeg police file (courtesy John Burchill).

murder, wearing Mr. Patterson's shabby suit, a man had arrived at the second-hand store of Mr. Waldman and bought a whole new wardrobe: underwear, a top shirt, a necktie, a light gray overcoat, a light gray summer two-piece suit, a fawn sweater with a vee neck, a white scarf, a cream-colored cap with the name "Waldman" on the label, a belt with a blue and white stripe, and brown "bulldog"–style shoes. The man paid Waldman $30 in three crisp ten-dollar bills and changed into the new clothes, leaving the old Patterson suit and other items from the Patterson suitcase on a shelf in the back of Waldman's store.[15]

The newly dressed man then asked Mr. Waldman about where he could get a shave and so Waldman took the man across the street to Nick the barber. Nick later reported that his customer had fresh, bloody scratches on the top of his head and the customer talked about being from San Francisco. He paid Nick with a crisp ten-dollar bill.[16] In addition to the description of the clothing that the suspect had bought at Waldman's, the police now had a good description of the suspect from Waldman and Nick the barber. The man was "considered to be between 26 and 30 years of age, about five foot six or seven inches tall, and weighing about 150 pounds;

large dark eyes, full face, sallow complexion; clean shaven, Jewish, or Italian appearance, but might be any nationality. He speaks good English."[17]

It was later discovered that another item of clothing was then bought at Chevrier's store on Broadway. It was a very fancy, one-of-a-kind hat, and the customer paid for it with a crisp ten-dollar bill. The man insisted on wearing the new hat and so the clerk wrapped up the Waldman hat and put the receipt for the Chevrier hat in the package.[18]

The next link in the evidence was an encounter with a Hutterite couple on the streetcar heading west out of Winnipeg. After various conversations with the Hutterite couple, the man gave them the package with the Waldman cap and the Chevrier receipt. Even though it was not the kind of hat Hutterites could wear, they thought the English schoolteacher in the colony might like it.[19] At some stage, Mr. Hofer, the Hutterite man, contacted the police and handed the cap and receipt to them, and he also noted that the man had talked about going to Regina, Saskatchewan, about 350 miles to the west of Winnipeg.

As the police reconstructed the trail, they soon discovered that indeed on Saturday afternoon, June 11, 1927, a man calling himself "Harry Harcourt" arrived at a rooming house on Lorne Street in Regina and rented a room for $4 for the week. The next day, Sunday, June 12, he had numerous conversations with the landlady, Mrs. Rowe, and at one point took Mrs. Rowe's 10-year-old daughter out for ice cream at a cafe without Mrs. Rowe's permission. He allegedly also asked the child to accompany him to a movie, but the child told him that movies were not shown in Regina on Sundays. Another close encounter involved a young woman at the rooming house who found that Harcourt entered her room as she lay on the bed reading a book. He claimed to have entered the room by accident.[20]

By the time the body of Lola Cowan was found in Winnipeg on Sunday, June 12, the police had already linked the killing of Mrs. Patterson to the American "gorilla man strangler" who had allegedly murdered scores of landladies in the United States from coast to coast but had always eluded capture. The link to the American strangler was aided by the presence of Captain Duncan Matheson of the San Francisco Police Department who was in the city on his way to a police convention in Windsor, Ontario.[21] With the discovery of the body of Lola Cowan the police now also had the description of the suspect from Mrs. Hill and others at the Smith Street rooming house. This description matched that of Waldman and Nick the barber. The strangler was stated to have a "dark and sallow complexion … eyes of a peculiar appearance. The hair is said to be dark brown, thin on top, curly and long and brushed back in pompadour style, newly barbered. The man is said to be fairly well built."[22]

The discovery that two women had been strangled in Winnipeg by the notorious American strangler led to a considerable panic in Winnipeg and an unprecedented amount of publicity was given to the murders in the newspapers in Western Canada.[23] Warnings to landladies were issued throughout the province and a large reward of $1,500 was proclaimed by the province and the city for the capture of the murderer.

On Monday morning, June 13, Harcourt read the local Regina newspaper that reported on the murders in Winnipeg and gave a full description of the suspect and what the "fiend" and "moral degenerate" was now wearing.[24] He promptly went into a jewelry store in Regina and sold Mrs. Patterson's ring for $3.50. He then went to a store and purchased a khaki shirt and blue bib overalls and returned to the Rowe rooming house and changed into these working clothes, leaving most of the fancy clothes that he had purchased in Winnipeg in the room that he rented. He then went out to another second-hand shop to "sell" the fancy hat. When asked, he gave his name to the second-hand dealer as "Willis Wall." The shopkeeper took the fancy hat and gave Wall a dark cloth cap and 50 cents. Willis Wall also wanted to "sell" the bulldog shoes, but he slipped out of the shop when the shopkeeper, seeing the Chevrier label from Winnipeg in the hat, started to ask further questions. Later in the day the shopkeeper contacted the Regina police about the fancy hat he had bought from Wall. The Regina police, in a sweep of rooming houses, soon arrived in the room that Harcourt had rented, and they found the fancy clothes from Waldman that Harcourt had left behind. Mrs. Rowe also informed the police that she had seen Harcourt leave, wearing a khaki shirt and blue bib overalls. Soon the police in Winnipeg were informed that the murderer had undoubtedly been in Regina.[25]

Eventually police in Saskatchewan and Manitoba discovered that on Monday, the man in the khaki shirt and blue bib overalls had hitched various rides heading southeast from Regina.[26] Much later the police discovered that the man was ultimately picked up by Mr. Silverman, a junk dealer from Winnipeg, who offered the man now calling himself "Virgil Wilson" room and board in exchange for helping Silverman pick up various metal materials, mostly lead, from farmers. Silverman would take the scrap to railway sidings to ship to Winnipeg. Virgil Wilson ended up spending Monday night, June 13, with Silverman at a hotel in Arcola, Saskatchewan. Silverman and Wilson then worked together for all of Tuesday, June 14, spending the night together again in a hotel in Deloraine, Manitoba. It was not until Wednesday morning, June 15, that Wilson and Silverman parted ways in Boissevain, Manitoba, with Silverman making his way back to Winnipeg and Wilson walking south toward the American border. Despite a massive manhunt in Manitoba and Saskatchewan the police had lost the trail of the strangler when Wilson had joined up with Silverman.[27]

On Wednesday, June 15, at around suppertime, a man wearing a khaki shirt and blue bib overalls and walking along the railway tracks arrived at the train depot in the little hamlet of Wakopa, Manitoba, which was only about five miles from the United States border. After being told by the depot manager that the mail train was about to arrive, the man said he was hungry, and so the manager directed him to Morgan's General Store. The man bought some cheese, two bottles of Coca-Cola, and a package of cigarettes from Morgan for 70 cents and left the store, heading back to the depot allegedly to jump on the train. While he was not suspicious that the man was the wanted strangler, the train depot manager watched the man's movements, which prevented him from jumping the train. The man walked away in a southerly direction.

Having heard the description of the wanted man from both the newspaper reports and radio broadcasts, Morgan had immediately been suspicious that the strange man in his store was the sought-after strangler. Mr. Dingwall, the elevator agent in the town, who saw the man making his way up the railway tracks, was also immediately of the view that this stranger in town might be the wanted strangler. Dingwall and Morgan confirmed each other's suspicions, and Mr. Morgan phoned Wilton Gray of the Manitoba Provincial Police stationed at Killarney, Manitoba, a "big" town about 15 miles northeast of Wakopa. Gray told Morgan to follow the man while Gray would drive to Bannerman, a town near the railway tracks, to prevent the man from crossing the border.[28]

Morgan had to sort the mail and could not immediately join the chase, but Dingwall and another man, Dickson, started to follow the suspect. They eventually recruited a local farmer, Mr. Merlin, and using his vehicle, they drove up to the man, who refused their offer of a ride and cut into the bush instead. Skipping over the details of the chase, Constable Gray accompanied by Constable Sewell eventually arrested the man three miles from the American border. The man told Gray that he was Virgil Wilson from Vancouver and he was working for a nearby rancher called "George Harrison" and was just out for a little walk. Knowing that nobody by that name lived in the area, Gray confronted Wilson, who admitted that he had lied because he did not want to be arrested as a vagrant. Gray and Sewell took Wilson to Killarney, and after providing him with a nice meal, locked him up in the Killarney town jail in the basement of the town hall at about 11 in the evening. Constable Gray took the boots and socks from the man, thoroughly searched him, placed him in the steel caged cell with a double lock, and after locking him in the cell took the keys to the locks. Gray left the jail to go to his office briefly while the town constable, Mr. Dunn, remained with the prisoner.[29]

Mr. Dunn went out for a few minutes to get matches for his pipe and when he returned the man was gone. Wilson had picked both locks with a sliver of wood and an old nail file that had been left on a ledge outside the cell but were reachable by hand. When Gray was informed that the prisoner had escaped, he immediately rallied the town into action. The fire bell rang. The electric lights remained on. Hundreds of men from the town, carrying every kind of weapon, were organized into search parties. They were soon joined by hundreds more men called in from neighboring towns. The "gorilla man strangler" was loose in Killarney. While the women and children remained safe over the night, the wanted man was not found. It was later revealed that having no shoes on, he had found an old pair of skates in a shed in the yard of the Allen residence, and he ripped off the blades of the skates and put the remaining boots on his feet. He also put on an old green sweater that he found there.

Back in Winnipeg, police officials were informed in the early hours of Thursday, June 16, that the man in custody in Killarney had escaped. Given that the roads were impassable due to heavy rains, the Winnipeg police and the Manitoba Provincial Police organized a special train to go to Killarney. On the train was a score of police officials accompanied by news reporters. The train would arrive in Killarney in the morning.[30]

In the morning of Thursday, June 16, Alfred Wood was mowing the lawn at the Monteith residence near the west end of the town of Killarney when a man walked up and asked him for the makings of a cigarette. Wood gave the man some tobacco. The man told Wood that he had also been out looking for the wanted prisoner and had been in the bush and tore his clothes. Wood noticed that the man had a piece of steel on the heel of one of his boots and was wearing blue overalls, a khaki shirt, and a green sweater. When informed by Wood that a special train was coming from Winnipeg, the man asked for tobacco for another cigarette. The man then sauntered off in the direction of the railway tracks, and Wood, who now thought the man was the suspected escaped prisoner, followed him, as did another fellow from the town. Wood also told the twin boys of Dr. Best, who were on their way to school, to summon the police, which they did in the family car. The Best twins found Constable Renton from the Crystal City detachment who was in town searching for the suspect, and it was Renton who arrested the man in the bush west of town near the railway tracks. Just after the arrest, the special train from Winnipeg arrived, and Renton drove the suspect to the train and Wilson was handcuffed and put on the train and taken to Winnipeg.[31]

The evidence does not support the persistent myth that the strangler was hiding under the railway platform and then jumped on the train to escape, only to find that the train was there to capture him. The man was captured by Renton of the Manitoba Provincial Police before the special train arrived.[32] Various police officers on the special train noted that the scratches on the head of Wilson were still visible. These scratches were presumably made by Mrs. Patterson in her attempt to resist the attack on her.

The case was such a sensation in Winnipeg, fueled by the local press, that thousands of people thronged around various railway depots in Winnipeg hoping to see the "gorilla man strangler" when he arrived in custody on the special train.[33]

≈ ≈ ≈

When taken to police headquarters in Winnipeg on Thursday night, June 16, 1927, the prisoner was interrogated by the chief of detectives, George Smith. Virgil Wilson eventually admitted that his real name was Earle Leonard Nelson, from San Francisco. Nelson also wrote down the names of his dead parents and grandparents, several addresses in San Francisco where he was born and where he subsequently was raised, and the names of various schools he had attended.[34]

Over the next few days, Nelson was placed into various identification lineups, and landlady Mrs. Hill, second-hand dealer Mr. Waldman, Nick the barber, and various drivers who brought him to Winnipeg identified Nelson as the man they had dealt with. Eventually the Regina witnesses also identified Nelson. Even if we doubt that Nelson, with his distinct dark complexion and too-big clothes, had true "look-alike" foils in the lineup, having a lineup at all was an advance in eyewitness identification in 1927.[35] Thus, the police had no doubt that "Cavanaugh," "Woodcoats," "Harcourt," "Wall" and "Wilson" were all Earle Leonard Nelson.[36]

The local press accounts ignored any presumption of innocence, especially as they reported on the various links that were made alleging that there was no doubt that Nelson was guilty of dozens of murders in the United States. This prejudgment was also manifested by Manitoba officials, who placed Nelson in isolation in a death row cell in the Vaughan Street jail before his trial was ever held. They also tried to find a different venue to hang him before he was ever convicted and set an extraordinary trial date to take place on July 26, 1927, during the summer court recess, barely a month after his arrest. The attorney general even announced that the reward could be paid before Nelson was convicted of the murders.[37]

Nelson also had no lawyer when he was charged with the murders of Lola Cowan and Emily Patterson and during the subsequent inquest and the preliminary hearing. The Crown prosecutor was the very accomplished Robert Blackwood Graham.[38] Nelson finally received a court appointed lawyer, James Herbert Stitt,[39] who in a very contentious court proceeding managed to get the trial "postponed" to the normal court session in November 1927. Stitt claimed that there was so much prejudicial media coverage that no jury could be impartial at a trial in July, and furthermore, he did not have adequate time to research and prepare for any trial in July.[40]

The prosecution decided to split the case and Nelson was tried in November 1927 on only the charge of murdering Mrs. Patterson. If he was acquitted, the prosecution could then still try him for the murder of Cowan. The trial was one of the most sensational in the history of Manitoba, with thousands trying to get into the courtroom each day.[41]

Since his arrest Nelson had claimed to the press that he was an innocent man who never traveled to Winnipeg and was framed by the Winnipeg police. However, the circumstantial evidence against him was overwhelming. Despite the known weaknesses in eyewitness testimony, he was consistently identified in numerous lineups. Especially damning were the identifications by those whom he spent much time with like Mrs. Rowe, the landlady from Regina, and Mr. Silverman, the junk dealer from Winnipeg. The clothing evidence also implicated him. For example, Nelson when first arrested near Wakopa was allegedly wearing the exact boots and the belt with the various colored bands

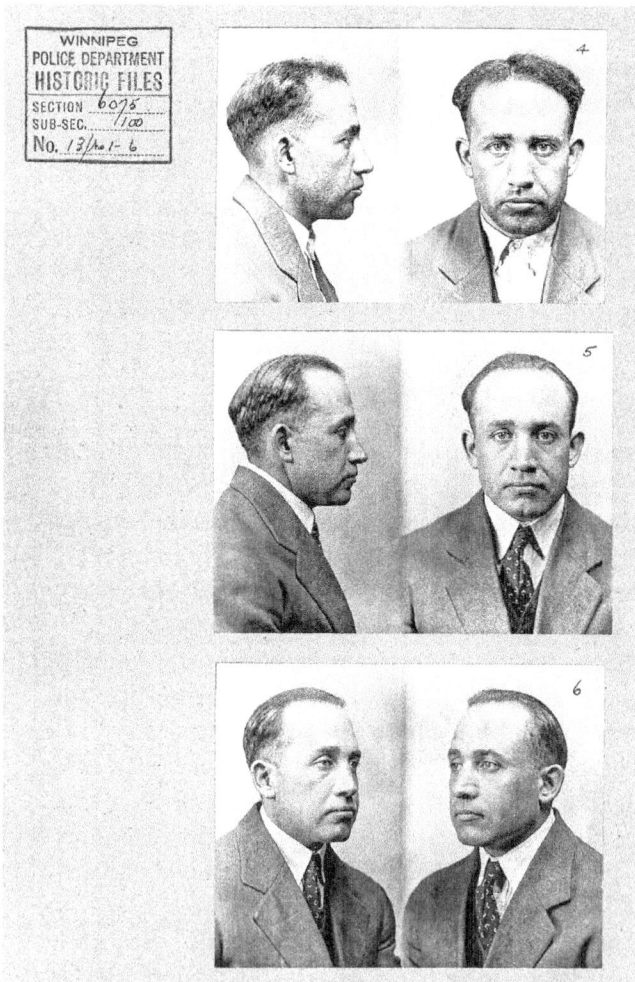

Earle Nelson mug shots in Winnipeg after his capture in Killarney, and within the first days of his confinement in Winnipeg after having a shave. Winnipeg police file (courtesy John Burchill).

that he had bought from Waldman in Winnipeg. The evidence of the ten-dollar money purchases, the sale of Patterson's wedding ring, and the wounds on the head were also incriminating pieces of evidence that led Nelson to the gallows.

The main defense in the case was insanity, but the jury rejected it and Nelson was convicted of murder and sentenced to hang. The defense of insanity at the time only applied to persons who did not know what they were doing or did not know that it was wrong. The insanity test applied to cognitive and moral disability due to a disease of the mind. It did not apply to volitional disability. It did not apply to those who might have an "irresistible impulse" to kill or to psychopaths without additional psychosis at the time of the crime. Stitt was unable to get any psychiatrist to testify against the Crown psychiatrist, Dr. Alvin Mathers, who asserted that Nelson was a psychopath[42] who knew what he was doing when he killed Mrs. Patterson.[43] Stitt had the various medical reports from the Napa Insane Asylum that indicated that Nelson had been diagnosed at various times as being a psychopath with additional psychosis. Mathers asserted that he may have been insane back then, but he was not legally insane at the time of the murder of Mrs. Patterson.

During the many decades in which capital punishment was the only penalty for murder in Canada,[44] those who were convicted of murder would automatically have the penalty reviewed by the federal Department of Justice with a recommendation to the federal cabinet as to whether the penalty should be commuted to life in prison.[45] Sometimes there were various mitigating factors that led to public campaigns and petitions to have a death sentence commuted, but this was not the case with Earle Nelson.[46]

After commutation failed, Nelson was hanged in Winnipeg on January 13, 1928. He was the 13th person to be hanged in the yard at the Vaughan Street jail, and he walked up the 13 steps of the gallows and was hanged on Friday the 13th. Before he was hanged, he was ministered to by Father Joseph Webb and was baptized into the Catholic Church.[47] The hangman was Arthur Ellis (whose real name was Alexander English), who was likely a psychopath himself[48] with a history of abandoning his wife and children in England, multiple subsequent marital indiscretions and assaults on his new wife in Canada, and a history of lying, grandiosity, and alcohol abuse.[49] So in the end one psychopathic serial killer hanged psychopathic serial killer Earle Nelson (albeit on behalf of the government). The body of Earle Nelson was shipped by train to San Francisco and was buried in the Nelson family plots at Cypress Lawn Cemetery.[50]

Obviously today, given the reality of wrongful convictions,[51] we cannot just dismiss Nelson's pleas of innocence, even in the face of what seems to be overwhelming circumstantial evidence of guilt. However, once we look at the character evidence, in addition to the circumstantial evidence, the sliver of doubt goes away. We turn now to the biographical history of Earle Nelson which points precisely to the kind of character that might develop into a serial killer.

CHAPTER 2

Biographical Sketch of Earle Nelson and Possible First Murders

Seventeen-year-old Fannie Nelson married 19-year-old James Carlos Ferrell in Portland in 1895.[1] Earle Leonard Ferrell was born on May 12, 1897, in the home of Fannie Nelson's parents in San Francisco.[2] When Earle was about 10 months old, his mother Fannie died on March 9, 1898, allegedly from the effects of syphilis contracted from her husband.[3] Subsequently, James Carlos Ferrell died in the home of his parents in Portland on October 24, 1898. The obituary for James claimed that he had been employed on a steamer running between San Francisco and San Blas, had been stricken with Panama fever, developed cancer of the brain, and lost the sight of both eyes, and "after suffering intensely, death came to his relief."[4] We have no evidence that Earle subsequently had anything to do with his surviving relatives on his biological father's side. James Ferrell's obituary does not even mention his late wife or surviving child.

When Earle Nelson was later identified as a serial killer and was socially constructed as a "feral" beast of the jungle, it was an easy play on words to point out that he was born Earle Ferrell.[5] However, biologically speaking, his paternal great grandfather was born with the last name Shane but was given the name Ferrell when his mother divorced his father and married Ferdinand Ferrell. Geographically the Shane-Ferrell families lived most of their lives in the Astoria region of Oregon.

While I have provided a more detailed account of his paternal family elsewhere,[6] here is a bare genealogical chart:

1. Great Grandfather: **Carlos Shane** (1817–1901) married 1850 to **Mary Jewett** (1827–1897).
    *   Children: James Shane (1851–1940), **John Carlos Shane** (1854–1920), Warren Shane (1855–1881).
    *   Children change of name to Ferrell when Mary Jewett divorced in 1859 and married Ferdinand Ferrell (1820–1879).
2. Grandfather: **John Carlos (Shane) Ferrell** (1854–1920) married 1875 to **Mary Eberman** (1858–?).
    *   Children: **James Carlos Ferrell** (1876–1898), Elizabeth Ferrell (1878–1967), Fannie Ferrell (1879–1902).
    *   Mary Eberman died, or was divorced, and John married 1880 to Eliza Catherine Butts (Powell) (1857–1927).

- Child of John and Eliza: Katherine Ferrell (1897–1971).

3. Father: **James Carlos Ferrell** (1876–1898) married to **Fannie Nelson** (1878–1898).
   - Child: **Earle Leonard Ferrell** (1897–1928). Name changed to Earle Nelson when brought up in mother's family, but Earle was often also referred to as Earle Ferrell.

Contrary to the myth that he was brought up by his widowed grandmother or within the home of his aunt Lillian,[7] Earle spent his early years in the extended Nelson household which consisted of his grandfather, Lars Nelson, a retired wheelwright blacksmith, born in Denmark in 1836, and his grandmother, Jennie Nelson, born in Maine in 1838.[8] Also living under the same roof were all the Nelson children but for Fannie who had died. The United States Census of 1900 shows that the oldest son, Frank, a tinner, approaching 40 years of age, still lived with his parents. So did the next son, Willis, a butcher, approaching 30 years of age, and the next son, Leonard, a packer, age 27, along with Lillian, age 18, and three-year-old grandson Earle Nelson.[9] The family moved frequently within the same Mission area of San Francisco, but in 1903 when Earle was six years old, they moved to 3525 20th Street, where they stayed for a longer period.[10]

Despite myths that Earle Nelson was brought up within an oppressive religious environment,[11] there is not a shred of evidence that the Nelson family was particularly religious. When Earle was seven years old his grandfather, Lars Nelson, died in December of 1904, at the age of 68.[12] Grandmother Jennie (Mary) Nelson died in June of 1907, also at the age of 68, shortly after Earle had his 10th birthday.[13] Neither of them had a church service associated with their deaths.

Once again Earle Nelson was an orphan. The lack of infant bonding is considered a major factor in the development of psychopathic serial killers.[14] The household dynamics also changed when his uncle Willis got married in 1908 at the age of 36 and took over the household at 3525 20th Street.[15] Willis married Aimee Hobson and they eventually had two daughters, Evelyn and Lyndian. According to the 1910 Census, 12-year-old Earle Nelson was still living with his uncle Willis and aunt Aimee.[16] Willis Nelson had a long career as a salesman for the Western Butcher Supply Company and at one point was vice president of the company. The Willis Nelson family eventually moved to Berkeley.[17] By that time, Earle was already away from "home" and engaged in various misadventures.

While Lillian may have played a special role in Earle's upbringing as the only surviving daughter in the family, Earle Nelson in his youth never lived with his aunt Lillian, who married Luther Clark Fabian in 1906 (before the death of his grandmother Jennie).[18] However, Lillian and Luther lived in the same neighborhood at various addresses close to where Willis lived. The Fabians eventually had two children, Evan and Doris. Luther divorced Lillian in 1915 alleging "habitual intemperance" on her part. However, they subsequently remarried for a short time, until Lillian divorced Luther in 1920 on the grounds of adultery and cruelty.[19] It is noteworthy that Earle's uncle Leonard, unmarried all his life, always lived in the Fabian household after the death of his parents. By 1923, after numerous moves, Earle's aunt

Lillian lived at 3573 20th Street, where she and her children and uncle Len lived for decades. It was only after his uncle Willis moved to Berkeley that Earle Nelson would return from time to time to the home of his aunt Lillian and uncle Leonard.

By way of a summary, this is the genealogical chart of the Nelson family:

Grandparents: **Lars Nelson** (1836–1904) married 1862 to **Mary (Jennie) Roberts** (1838–1907).
- Children: **Frank Nelson** (1861–1942) born out of wedlock. Never married.
- **Willis Nelson** (1871–1949) married 1908 to **Aimee Hobson** (1878–1961).
- Children: **Evelyn Nelson** (1909–1982), **Lyndian Nelson** (1913–2006).
- **Leonard Nelson** (1874–1940) never married.
- **Fannie Nelson** (1878–1898) married 1895 to **James Carlos Ferrell** (1876–1898).
- Child: **Earl Leonard (Ferrell) Nelson** (1897–1928).
- **Lillian Nelson** (1881–1960) married 1906 to **Luther Fabian** (1879–1962).
- Divorced in 1916, remarried, and divorced again in 1920.
- Children: **Evan Fabian** (1908–1954), **Doris Fabian** (1914–1977).

The only reason we know anything about the childhood of Earle Nelson is that his aunt Lillian Fabian came to Winnipeg in November 1927 as a witness for the defense alleging that her nephew was insane. Any narratives not founded on this evidence are simply imaginative fiction. As to the history of feeling abandoned by the death of his parents and grandparents, Lillian testified at trial: "He used to always say, 'I am not good for anything, I never will be good for anything. I will be better off out of this world.' I said you must not feel that way because you are just a young boy and you have got your whole life to live for, and he would say, *Nobody wants me.*'"[20]

Lillian Fabian also testified that when Earle was 10 years old, the year that his grandmother died, he was hit by a streetcar while riding a bike on the street. As a result, he had a "large hole in his temple," was unconscious for six days and was out of school for six weeks, and thereafter had "dreadful headaches and dizziness."[21] Head trauma in childhood, especially to the parts of the brain responsible for emotional processes, is a frequent characteristic of serial killers.[22]

By his own account given in an interview in Winnipeg, Earle Nelson attended various schools until seventh grade but had also been expelled from one school when he was in second grade.[23] Someone who grew up in the same neighborhood with Nelson noted that he was ordered not to play with Nelson who was branded throughout the neighborhood as being "mentally deranged" and had been confined to a reform school and would boast about how easy he could steal.[24]

We have evidence of Nelson's criminality from newspaper reports in July of 1911, when Nelson had just turned 14 years of age. Along with an even younger boy, Nelson was arrested in the process of robbing a grocery store one night. When arrested, the two youths were in possession of numerous weapons and burglary tools, a considerable sum of money, and various items of jewelry. They admitted that they were guilty of dozens of robberies in the Mission and Sunset districts of San Francisco.

They stated that they were planning to steal enough money to leave the city and start holding up trains.[25]

Earle Nelson, when later recounting his juvenile history to Dr. Pritchard at the Napa Insane Asylum, admitted that since puberty he had not only masturbated at least several times a day but had engaged in various sexual activities, homosexual and heterosexual. He had contracted gonorrhea and syphilis, had gone on frequent alcoholic binges, and was unable to ever keep a job for more than a few days or weeks.[26]

Of importance to our linking of Nelson to various murders that we will examine in this book was the trial testimony of his aunt Lillian and his wife, Mary Fuller, as to Nelson's behavior in relationship to clothing and money. They asserted that Nelson from childhood through adulthood loved to dress up in a variety of costumes and was constantly changing his clothing, going out in one outfit and coming back in another. He had a clothing fetish. Furthermore, he never cared for money at all, spending it or giving it away immediately with no thought that he might need some for the next day.[27]

≈ ≈ ≈

In July of 1915, when Nelson was a few months older than 18, he was arrested along with a companion by the name of Newton for robbery in Plumas County, California. The two young men had broken into a remote railway section house where they stole items of jewelry belonging to the section foreman. When a nearby resident came on the scene and attempted to arrest them, Nelson and Newton beat the resident into insensibility and stole the man's wallet which contained a small amount of money. Nelson and Newton were later found down the track and were arrested and taken to Quincy. After a preliminary hearing, they pled guilty and were sentenced to two years in San Quentin.[28]

Nelson learned no useful skills at San Quentin.[29] He was paroled on September 28, 1916, after spending 14 months in jail.

It is possible that Nelson, under some assumed name that we are unaware of, joined the army when he got out of jail. Several years later in the "life story" found in the Napa asylum records we read that "in 1917 he enlisted as a private in the Army and deserted after six weeks because he had to do guard duty in the snow."[30] Subsequently he joined the navy as an apprentice seaman on June 8, 1917, at a navy recruiting station in Salt Lake City, Utah. He was transferred the next day to the naval training station on Goat Island (Yerba Buena) in San Francisco. Not long thereafter he was granted leave that expired at a certain time on July 22, 1917. But he failed to return from his leave on that date, and after 10 days passed, he was declared a deserter.[31] Dr. Pritchard later noted, "In August 1917, he enlisted in the Medical Corps as a private; after six weeks he deserted because two mornings he felt a burning about the anus from 'polypuses' and was bothered by his stricture."[32]

Now a three-time deserter, Nelson also continued his criminal career. He was sentenced to six months in the county jail in Stockton, California, on October 9, 1917, under the alias "Luther Clark" for the petty theft of a bike.[33] As noted, Luther Clark Fabian was the name of his aunt Lillian's husband. After his parole from the

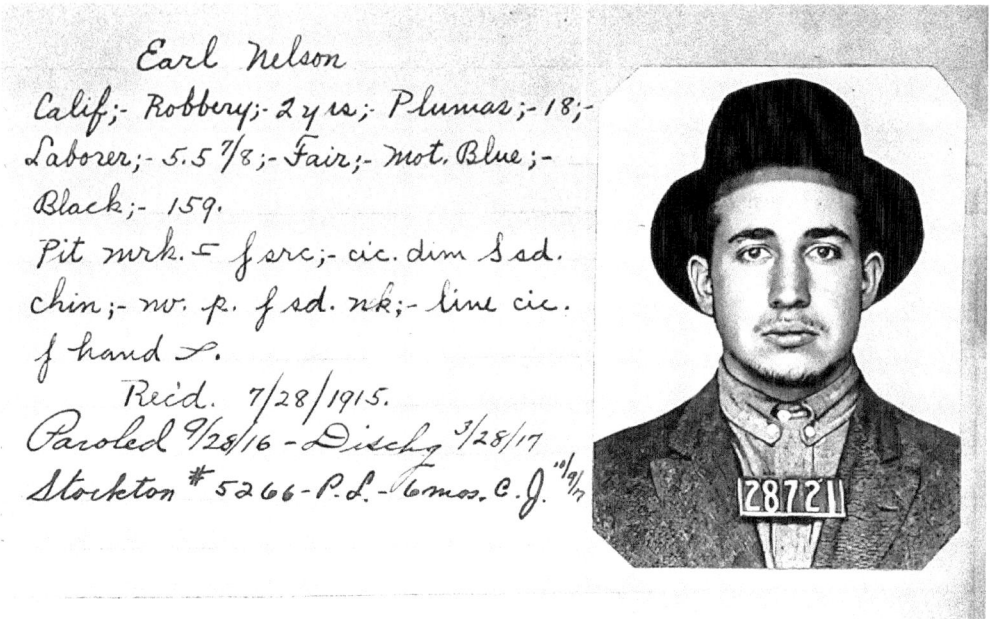

Eighteen-year-old Earle Nelson arrives in San Quentin after being sentenced for robbery (courtesy California State Archives).

jail in Stockton, Nelson suddenly reappeared on December 1, 1917, at the navy training station at Goat Island, wearing his full uniform. He had been away without leave for four months and nine days. On December 21, 1917, Nelson was transferred under guard from the naval training station to the navy yard, Mare Island, for trial by general court martial. The trial took place on January 8, 1918, and "Earle L. Ferrel" was found guilty of desertion and sentenced to two years in the naval prison at the navy yard and thereafter to be dishonorably discharged.[34]

Nelson was confined in the naval prison at Mare Island for about four months but during this time he refused to work for religious reasons and spent his time reading the Bible and staring blankly into space.[35] The naval authorities transferred Nelson to the naval hospital on the same island on April 24, 1918. On May 3, 1918, a naval medical board declared that Earl Ferrel was in a "constitutional psychopathic state" and unfit for service and recommended that he should be transferred to the Napa State Hospital for the Insane at Imola, California.[36]

Nelson later recounted that the treatments he was given at Napa, presumably for syphilis, "were severe, and I didn't like it."[37] Nelson's first commitment to the Napa State Hospital was short lived. He arrived on May 21, 1918, but then escaped from the asylum on June 13, 1918. He returned, or was returned, on June 18, but then he escaped again on August 25, 1918, showing up at his aunt Lillian's house. Fearing for the safety of herself and her children, she gave him some lunch and some money, sent him away, and then contacted the authorities, but Earle was never located.[38]

Several months after the escape from the asylum, we pick up the trail again from the criminal record, this time in Los Angeles. Nelson, dressed in a navy uniform, was arrested and charged with burglary and desertion on October 28, 1918.

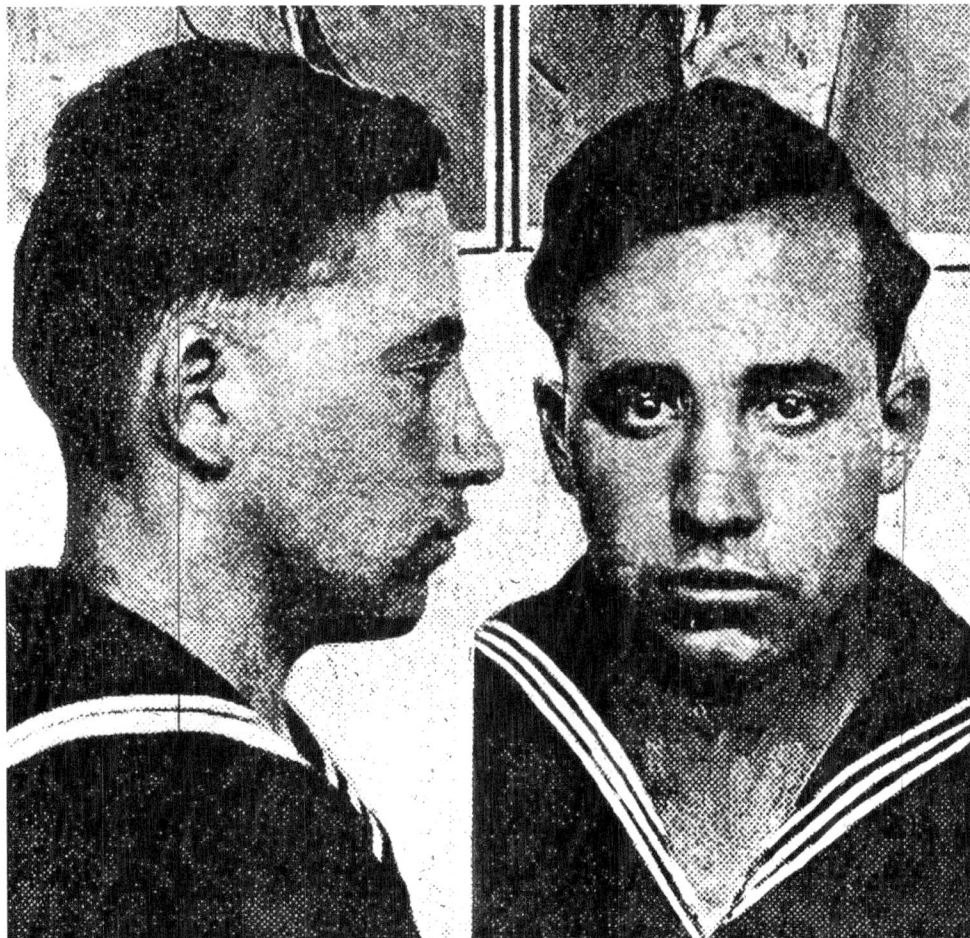

Los Angeles Police Department mug shots of Earle Nelson in 1918 after he was charged with burglary and desertion from the navy (*Oregonian*, June 19, 1927, at 1).

Various newspaper accounts reveal that the arrest was made after a man complained that he had shared an apartment with Nelson who used his birth name "Ferrell." Nelson stole a suitcase, two suits of clothes, an overcoat, a shotgun, a revolver, and other articles from the apartment. The roommate subsequently saw Ferrell in an automobile, and when he gave chase, Ferrell jumped out of the car, leaving the suitcase and clothes behind. A policeman gave chase and tackled Ferrell. It was subsequently noted in the press that Ferrell had already sold the weapons for $15.[39]

Instead of remaining in prison in Los Angeles, Nelson was transferred back to the navy hospital at Mare Island on November 30, 1918. Naval authorities then transferred Nelson back to the Napa State Hospital on December 3, 1918.[40] The next day, December 4, Nelson escaped again. Thus, despite his being committed to Napa on May 21, 1918, Nelson spent less than three months in the asylum in 1918, and he was now on his third escape. Lilian no longer sent him away but rather allowed him to periodically stay with her at her residence. She no longer felt an obligation to notify the authorities.

There is a possibility that Nelson, as a deserter from the army and the navy and the medical corps, enlisted briefly in another service. Subsequent notes from the Napa hospital records state: "In February 1919 he enlisted as a cook in the Coast Guard at the urgent persuasion of the officers who needed a cook but against his own wishes. [He] returned home to get his clothes and never reported for duty again."[41]

$\approx \quad \approx \quad \approx$

While working in the kitchen of a San Francisco hospital in 1919, Nelson, calling himself "Evan Fuller," met a woman who worked in the linen department of the hospital. Her name was Mary Teresa Martin; she was a recent immigrant from Ireland.[42] She was more than twice the age of Fuller, but he pursued her, and she was impressed by his apparent religiosity. Mary Martin and Evan Fuller were married on August 5, 1919, by a Catholic priest in San Francisco. The part of the marriage certificate filled in by Earle Nelson contained a host of lies. He called himself Evan Louis Fuller, age 37, born in Lansing, Michigan, a bookkeeper in the building contracting industry. He listed his father's name as James Fuller from Wisconsin, and his mother's name as Fannie Fuller, of unknown origin, but then Fuller was crossed out and Nelson was written over it, because he realized, or was told, that the mother's maiden name was required. Mary also lied about her age, listing herself as 35, when she was 49 years old, which was 27 years older than the 22-year-old man she was marrying. We know her actual age from her official death record and obituary many years later when she died in 1954.[43]

Eventually, Mary Fuller, the wife of Earle Nelson, came to Winnipeg to testify at Nelson's trial. At the time of the trial in November 1927 she was 57 years old, and while she gave evidence that the marriage had been a disaster and she only lived with the man she called Evan Fuller for six months, she was never divorced from him and continued to see him periodically. She called herself Mrs. Mary Fuller for the rest of her life. Her testimony at the trial was that she only learned after the wedding the real identity of her husband and the fact that he was an escapee from the Napa asylum and a deserter from the army and navy. She learned this when she was first introduced to Lillian. She recounted that she was quickly disillusioned by her husband's religiosity. He never sat through any church services. She recounted many examples of what she called "moral irresponsibility," a term she kept using to describe Nelson's inability to hold a job and support his wife and to describe his nomadic wanderings, his atrocious lack of good hygiene or eating habits, and his frequent changes of clothes. He exhibited bizarre behaviors, including staring off into space when her brother came to visit.[44] She was too embarrassed to testify about sexual matters, but the clinical history of Earle Nelson includes the assertion that sexual intercourse during marriage was unusually "excessive,"[45] and she told lawyer James Stitt that Nelson was a sexual exhibitionist and masturbated frequently while lying in bed with her if she refused sex.[46]

However, the central feature of her testimony was that Nelson was insanely jealous. He would be furious if she smiled at the streetcar conductor when paying her fare or if she even talked to another woman, much less a man. Shortly after their marriage Mrs. Fuller took sick and was admitted to a hospital. While Nelson had donated blood and "saved my life," he was unemployed as usual, and he hung around the hospital to the point of embarrassment. Furthermore, he was very jealous of the doctors who were attending to his wife. Mary testified, "He thought that I was having the doctor there without reason … and seemed to get angry when he was told to leave."[47]

The theme of paranoid jealousy escalated when Evan and Mary Fuller moved to Palo Alto where they both got jobs, as well as room and board, at the Castilleja School. When Mary so much as said "good day" to the night watchman as she was hanging out clothes in the yard, Evan would get insanely angry and threaten her life, accusing her of being flirtatious. Finally, he demanded that they should leave the school, but she refused to leave and Nelson left without her. This would be sometime in early 1920. The decision on her part to refuse to follow her husband also had something to do with what one of the housekeepers at Castilleja told her about her husband, but she was not allowed to testify as to this hearsay.[48]

While never giving dates in her testimony, Mary Fuller stated that Nelson returned to Palo Alto periodically asking her to leave with him, and when she refused, he threatened her life. At some point Mary left the Castilleja School and got a long-term job at Miss Harker's School in Palo Alto. Some of Mary Fuller's testimony related to various events when Evan went to this new place of employment, trying to get her to come back with him or live with him again. On one occasion, as Mrs. Fuller described it, he not only threatened her life but also that of an imaginary suitor that he thought was standing between his wife and him. Another time he came back to the school, and as they sat under a tree, he grabbed her hand and pulled the wedding ring off her finger. Mrs. Fuller recounted another incident when

> he came down and told me that he had come down for me, and of course, I refused to go back to him, and then he threatened my life again. He said he would get me. He threatened my life, and so then Miss Harker sent up for the Chief of Police, and had him arrested, and told him to keep away or she would complain to the authorities herself; take it upon herself and have him sent to the State Hospital for the Insane.[49]

≈ ≈ ≈

It is unfortunate that exact dates were never given at trial as to when these events occurred because there is at least a slim possibility that Nelson may have started murdering women shortly after his wife refused to leave Palo Alto with him in early 1920. Having more specific times for his visits with his estranged wife would help us to identify whether he should be considered a suspect in various murders. Notable in this regard is the murder of 17-year-old Rean Hoxie in New York City on February 2, 1920, while showing rooms for rent in her family apartment. The girl was hit over the head with a blunt instrument and sexually assaulted, likely after death. The case was never solved. Was Nelson already travelling to the East Coast in this period? While it is unlikely that Nelson started murdering at this stage, we are not free of suspicion, and so I have included a detailed account of this case elsewhere.[50]

There was at least one other unsolved case in this early period where the police eventually considered that Nelson might have been the perpetrator, even though this was not a "room for rent" or "house for sale" killing but rather a murder that took place outdoors.[51] Indeed, at some point, Fred Heere, chief of the Piedmont police, alleged that Nelson was responsible for the murder.[52] Ulla Carlson, a 19-year-old domestic servant from Sweden, was murdered in an exclusive area of Piedmont, California, as she was walking back from accompanying a friend to the streetcar line late at night on March 14, 1920.[53] Her body was found in the morning.

This case involved some bizarre circumstances. Several jealous suitors were identified, one of whom was Charlie Nelson, a carpenter. But this Nelson, a widower with a child, was no relation to the subject of our book.[54] There were other mysterious suitors.[55] There was disagreement as to whether Carlson was murdered by strangulation, perhaps after the use of chloroform on a handkerchief to subdue her,[56] or whether she had died of convulsions brought on by a panic attack or some heart condition.[57] All the initial reports stated that she had not been sexually attacked, but then later there were indications that the perpetrator had indeed been a "degenerate," deduced from the stains (presumably semen) found on her coat.[58] There was an attempt by a famous Berkeley criminologist to profile the killer after a minute examination of the evidence of hair and fiber left at the scene.[59] There were numerous letters to the police from "Jack the Strangler" claiming responsibility.[60] There were attempts to pin the crime on another serial killer, "Bluebeard" Watson, confessed murderer of numerous wives and prospective wives.[61] Watson denied that he had anything to do with Carlson's murder.[62] Finally, there was the attempt to link Earle Nelson to the crime, but no follow up reports as to whether anything useful came of this attempt.

The murder does not fit the eventual *modus operandi* of Nelson, killing landladies indoors, usually in the afternoon. However, perhaps Nelson was a more versatile killer. Furthermore, his uncle Willis had moved to Berkeley and lived at 2805 Russell Street which is a short distance north of the Piedmont location where Carlson died. Perhaps Nelson was in the area visiting his aunt and uncle up the railway line? One other little detail that leads to some suspicion was the following report: "A man, who later proved to be a *former soldier and a gardener,* was picked up by the police last night loitering around the scene of the crime…. The man, however, supplied a satisfactory alibi. He explained that his presence at the spot where he was arrested was prompted by idle curiosity."[63]

As noted in the evidence of Nelson's wife, and in the affidavit of Mr. Arnold,[64] Nelson often tried to make a living as a gardener and he was a former soldier. It would be tragic indeed in terms of all the victims to follow if this fellow was Earle Nelson, who talked his way out of incarceration at this stage. As noted, we doubt that Nelson started killing at this point, but we cannot be sure. The Hoxie and the Carlson murders of 1920 illustrate the possibility that Nelson may have killed some women who are not included in our list of 31.

It is also worth considering whether Nelson might have murdered "butterflies" before concentrating on landladies. "Butterflies" was a term used in the jazz age for women who did most of their sleeping in the daytime and had relationships with numerous men and "sugar daddies"[65] at night. For example, Mrs. Ruby Reed, a "gin and jazz" beauty,[66] was found strangled in her apartment in Los Angeles on March 26, 1920.[67] This was less than two weeks after the murder of Carlson in Piedmont.

When the murder was discovered, Reed had been dead for several days; her body was buried under some clothes, and she had been strangled to death with some of her underwear wrapped around her throat and a handkerchief stuffed in her mouth. There were also love letters that had been torn up, and the apartment was in disarray from her struggle with her assailant.[68]

Ruby Reed had many lovers, several of whom were arrested, but the police were unable to prove the guilt of any of them, and the case went into the unsolved file.[69] While Ruby Reed was likely strangled by a jealous lover, it was also reported that she had acted as a decoy for an underworld gang and she may have been murdered in the belief that she had failed in her task.[70] Given the numbers of available suspects, and also the underworld connections of the victim, we doubt that Earle Nelson had anything to do with the murder, but we cannot be sure.

∾ ∾ ∾

We pick up the biographical narrative again just after Nelson's 24th birthday in 1921. He was arrested in San Francisco under the name Earl Ferral on May 19, 1921, and "charged with assault by means and force likely to do great bodily harm, in that he assaulted 12-year-old Mary Somers, 1519 Pacific Avenue, striking her with his clenched fist, violently throwing her to the floor and choking her."[71] The girl was rescued by her brother, who fought with Nelson. The San Francisco police mug shots of Nelson show numerous deep scratches on the face.[72]

Nelson had gained admission to the house by telling 24-year-old Charles Summers (or Somers), the brother of the victim, that he was a plumber sent to fix a leaking gas line. Nelson was allowed to go into the basement of the dwelling where he saw the girl playing with dolls and attacked her. She screamed, thus bringing the brother to her rescue. The brother and Nelson fought each other, and Nelson managed to escape but was later captured by a policeman giving chase on a motorcycle. Ferral had boarded a streetcar upon leaving the house.[73]

After Nelson was arrested and charged, he was transferred from jail by order of the superior court and sent to the detention hospital to be examined as to his sanity. He was put in a straitjacket. When his wife came to visit, "he talked incessantly about seeing faces on the wall," and he stared into space.[74] His aunt said that when she came to visit him in the detention hospital, he had pulled his eyebrows out.[75] Mary Fuller hired lawyer James F. Brennan to have her husband committed to the insane asylum rather than go to jail. This was not a crass attempt to avoid jail by feigning insanity. Rather, from the very moment of his arrest, the newspapers reported him as being insane. *The San Francisco Daily News* reported the story under the headline "Insane Man Is Arrested."[76] *The San Francisco Examiner* headline was "12-Year-Old Girl Attacked by Insane Man."[77] *The Call and Post* stated, "Farrell is plainly unbalanced, mentally, and will be examined by the Lunacy Board."[78]

At a hearing on June 13, 1921, before a judge of the superior court, evidence was submitted to the court by two medical examiners who concluded that Ferral was so far disordered in his mind as to endanger his health and that of other persons. A notation stated: "At Detention Hospital patient apathetic—difficult to elicit information—hears voice of spirits and sees them (auditory and visual

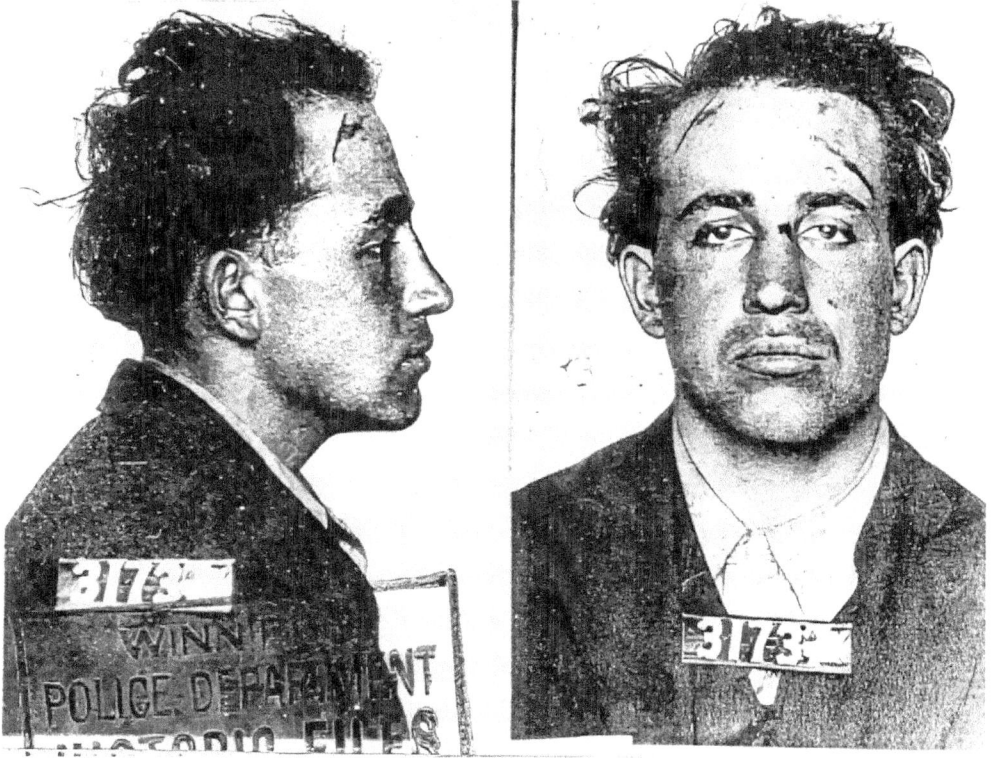

San Francisco Police Department mug shots of Earle Nelson in 1921 after he was charged with assaulting a 12-year-old girl. Numerous scratches can be seen on his face because of a fight with the brother of the girl. Winnipeg police file (courtesy John Burchill).

hallucinations)—threatened to suicide—People about him say that he is crazy—will not associate with him—claims to have lapses of memory."[79]

Mrs. Mary Fuller also gave evidence in the court hearing, but we have no transcript of what she said. In any event, after hearing all the evidence, the judge ordered Earl Ferral to be committed to and confined in the Napa State Hospital.

Thus, on June 14, 1921, Earle Nelson found himself back at the insane asylum from which he had escaped three times in the past. Dr. Pritchard noted that Nelson tested double positive for syphilis, and he diagnosed Nelson as being a "Constitutional Psychopath with outbreaks."[80] The progress notes on Nelson refer to a variety of treatments for syphilis given to him over several years. Nelson's stay at the asylum was much longer this time than it had been in the first committal of 1918. He escaped on July 14, 1921, but was returned the same day. On his return he was admitted by Dr. Rogers who noted that Nelson "threatened to take life of wife, also to suicide ... had auditory and visual hallucinations...."[81] The first six months of his confinement included further attempts to escape, and so the Napa authorities had him in restraints and restricted his movements "to the back yard."[82]

The progress notes took a shift in a more positive direction after the first six months. After November 1921, Nelson was frequently listed as responding well to treatment, behaving himself on the ward, and "feeling much better." Over the next months, Nelson was responding so well to treatment and was so well behaved that restraints in the ward were lifted in February 1922 and restraints in the yard were lifted in April 1922. There was also a note on June 1, 1922, stating, "This is the final note, as patient will have been in hospital one year on June 14th. Patient is well behaved and appears to be cooperating in every way in what is done for him. Physical condition is good."[83] It may be that Nelson believed he would be released after being in the asylum for a year, but for whatever reason, he was not. Nelson thereafter made frequent escape attempts and refused further syphilis treatments.[84] Finally, after a full two years and four months or so in the asylum, Nelson managed to escape on November 2, 1923.

After escaping from the asylum, Nelson apparently continued to periodically visit his wife in Palo Alto, who did not think he was dangerous to other people and did not report him as missing from the Napa asylum.[85] She did not want to "interfere with his freedom," despite that fact that as late as 1926, "he threatened to get someone at school who was keeping me away from him."[86] In addition to working at the Arnold estate in Palo Alto for a time, based on his aunt Lillian's testimony at the trial in Winnipeg, we may assume that after his escape Nelson continued to make periodic visits to the Fabian household in the San Francisco neighborhood where he grew up and perhaps also made visits to Berkeley where his uncle Willis lived.

We have very little information as to Nelson's movements in the years between the escape in late 1923 and the arrest in Winnipeg in June of 1927. We do have a subsequent affidavit of Frank Arnold of Palo Alto, manager of Walter Brunt Press in San Francisco. Nelson was hired by Arnold in 1925 for "about a year and a half" around the Arnold residence on Alma Street in Palo Alto. "Charlie Nelson," as he called himself, worked "on the grounds, keeping the place in order, acting as a gardener, and as a general handy man." Nelson took his meals in the Arnold home but "slept and occupied a small building on the same premises." He was finally dismissed when Mrs. Arnold became "somewhat anxious and fearful of having him around our home and children."[87]

It is unfortunate that the affidavit does not specify the starting and ending dates for this sojourn at the Arnold estate. If indeed the affidavit can be trusted as to the length of time that Nelson was in Palo Alto, we may surmise that Nelson was in the San Francisco region for much of 1925 until he was dismissed from the Arnold household, perhaps as late as August or even September of 1926. We do not know whether Arnold meant that Nelson was continually at his residence during this period or whether at various stages he wandered off the property or took various extended holidays. As we look at the evidence, especially the three murders in Philadelphia in 1925, we suspect that he disappeared from the Arnold household for various periods of time. In any event, aside from the possibility that Nelson was already killing women between the time that he furiously left his wife in early 1920 and the time of his confinement in the asylum on May 19, 1921, the key dates for examination of possible murders committed by Earle Nelson are between his escape from the asylum on November 2, 1923, and his arrest in Winnipeg on June 16, 1927.

≈   ≈   ≈

When did Nelson start killing? This book begins with the murders of landladies in 1925. However, as noted before, in addition to the Hoxie and Carlson cases in 1920, we might speculate whether Nelson murdered "butterflies" before he murdered landladies. Another "butterfly" murder involved Vera Stone who was strangled to death in her apartment in Los Angeles with some of her silk underwear wrapped around her neck on the Friday night of April 4, 1924. Her body was discovered the following night behind a locked bedroom door. While the case does present many suspicious elements that might point to Nelson, as in the previous Ruby Reed case in 1920, there were numerous other suspects in the Stone case. The police were never able to find the murderer of Mrs. Stone. The last entry in the official police record states that two men were arrested on January 23, 1928, but were released several days later because the police were unable to connect them with the murder.[88] Vera Stone had both friends in the police force and many friends who were "underworld denizens."[89] Like Ruby Reed in 1920, Vera Stone in 1924 was probably murdered by a jealous lover, but also like Ruby Reed, having underworld connections, she was very likely not the random victim of a fiend strangler like Nelson but rather more likely murdered by an underworld figure who thought she was an informant of the police.[90] I have given much more detail on the murder and the suspects elsewhere.[91]

Another unsolved "butterfly" case is more difficult to dismiss in terms of a possible linkage to serial killer Earle Nelson. After Nelson was arrested in Winnipeg, the *San Diego Sun* contained an article titled "Canada Strangler Suspect Linked in Local Slaying."[92] It was reported that the San Diego chief of police, Joe Doran, and captain of detectives, Paul Hayes, now believed that Earle Nelson was responsible for the unsolved murder of Mrs. Anna Williams on Friday, October 17, 1924.[93] We have no evidence that Nelson was seen in San Diego at the time. It seems likely that the police were simply trying to close their books on an unsolved murder by pointing to Nelson as the perpetrator. I have also written a detailed account of this case, suggesting that an ex-husband was a better suspect than Nelson, although all doubt cannot be removed.[94]

Finally, we should mention that according to the tabloid the *Daily Mail* (London), the first murder committed by Earle Nelson was on May 31, 1925, in Boston, where he strangled to death Mrs. Mae Price of New York. The article stated: "Mrs. Price was the wardrobe mistress of a theatrical company playing in 'The Brown Derby.' She was known as the 'mother of chorus girls.' Her room was entered during the night by the strangler, her money was taken, and she herself was found dead under the bed next day."[95]

Research into this high-profile case reveals that after a month of police investigations, a Frank Corey, or "Crecorian," was finally arrested on June 23, 1925.[96] Corey was tried for the murder of Price in August 1925.[97] He was acquitted of the murder, but then later in a different jury trial in March 1926, he was convicted of the robbery arising out of the same incident but supposedly based on new evidence.[98] The police authorities never agreed with the jury acquittal in the murder trial, and through an abuse of process bordering on double jeopardy, they got Corey sentenced to life for robbery. The judge argued when affirming the jury verdict that if the "new evidence" had been available in the first trial, Corey would be sentenced to death instead of having a life sentence for robbery.[99] The appeal was argued before the supreme court of Massachusetts on March 5, 1928, and was rendered on June 11, 1928.[100] The court upheld the conviction of Corey, asserting that the indictment for robbery was not the same offense as the indictment for murder and an acquittal for murder did not bar a conviction for robbery. After reviewing the evidence, I would argue that Corey, not Nelson, was indeed the guilty party. I have written a more detailed account of the case elsewhere.[101]

PART II

Five Landladies Murdered in 1925

CHAPTER 3

Elizabeth Jones and Daisy Anderson in San Francisco

1. August 22, 1925—Elizabeth Jones, 72, San Francisco

On Monday, August 24, 1925, the *San Francisco Examiner* contained a front-page story under the heading "Woman Discovered Strangled to Death: Thug Winds Gems Around Victim's Neck."[1] The front page of the *San Francisco Chronicle* had an even larger lead story with a big headline: "Mystery in Aged S.F. Woman's Death."[2]

According to the *Examiner* account, Mrs. Elizabeth Jones, an elderly widow, owned an apartment house at 3565 Market Street and had been trying to rent one of the vacant apartments. On Saturday night, August 22, at around 8:15, some neighbors reportedly saw Mrs. Jones showing the apartment to a young "blond" man wearing a gray tweed coat and white shoes. On Sunday morning, Mr. Daily, who occupied one of the apartments, noticed that the door to Mrs. Jones's own apartment in the house was wide open. A man and a woman then came into the house, attracted by the "For Rent" sign, and wanted to be shown about the place. Mr. Daily took them to see Mrs. Jones, and when they entered her rooms, they noticed that the landlady appeared to be in bed sleeping. Mr. Daily said, "Guess we'd better not wake her now." The visitors left. On Sunday evening, returning to the house with his wife, Mr. Daily noticed that Mrs. Jones's door was still wide open. Now Mr. Daily investigated and discovered that Mrs. Jones was "lying across the bed. She was dead, fully dressed, one arm wound around her as if forced back in a struggle."[3] Mr. Daily made a call to one of the sons of Mrs. Jones. The son eventually called an undertaker, and when the undertaker noticed the cheap pearl necklace wound tightly around the victim's throat, he notified the coroner's office.

According to the *Chronicle*, Mrs. Jones's son, an owner of a candy factory, thought that his mother had died of heart failure, but Deputy Coroner Trabucco noticed that the victim's tongue was protruding, and according to him, "the tongue of a heart failure victim does not protrude."[4] The short account on the front page of the *San Francisco Call and Post* noted that the boarder, Mr. Daily, had said that the "blond" young man wearing a gray tweed suit and a light cap had spent time wandering around the halls of the apartment on the day that Mrs. Jones died.[5] The son finally concluded that his mother was probably murdered and robbery was the motive, although he also thought his mother might have had a heart attack. The son stated that his mother always kept a large sum of money in her purse, but only 70 cents was now discovered in the apartment.

By the time the *San Francisco Daily News* came out on Monday, the autopsy had taken place and the murder theory was already being laid to rest.[6] Dr. Shelby Strange, autopsy surgeon, stated that the woman had been dead for a couple of days before her body was found and that she had died of natural causes, "apparently of pneumonia, super induced by heart trouble."[7] It was also reported that "Lieutenant Charles Dullea of the homicide squad and Dr. Strange satisfied themselves that the marks left on her neck from the string of pearls she was wearing, were the result of the position in which she was lying."[8] In the report from the coroner's office Dr. Strange wrote as the cause of death "acute dilatation of heart due to occlusion of anterior coronary artery."[9] The report also noted that the verdict of an inquest held on September 16, 1925, was that Jones's death was due to natural causes.

So instead of this being a murder case, officials believed that this was just an elderly lady, fully clothed, who came to the end of her life and there were apparently no marks of violence on her body. Case closed. No murder investigation was necessary. Reports that money may have been missing or a suspicious character hanging about were now moot.

As we will note below, after another death of a landlady in 1925 and after four more landladies in San Francisco were strangled in the following year of 1926, the coroner, Dr. Thomas B.W. Leland, who had a great deal of experience in these matters, having been appointed coroner back in 1901,[10] disagreed with Dr. Strange. Leland believed that Mrs. Jones was likely also murdered by the "dark strangler." Subsequently, Mrs. Ethel Spann, one of the daughters of Elizabeth Jones, was interviewed and she stated, "My mother was very old, and at the time of her death it was decided she had died of heart failure, but the undertaker said there were unmistakable marks of fingers on her throat…. We were sure then that she had been murdered but could do nothing. Since then, with the many other deaths, every clue has pointed toward the strangler."[11]

The description of the suspicious "blond" man certainly does not fit the description of the "dark" Earle Nelson, but it is entirely possible that Nelson appeared on the scene at a later point on Saturday night or the description of being "blond" was a mistake by those who described the man. We also note that the Smith rooming house was not far to the west of Earle Nelson's aunt Lillian Fabian's house at 3573 20th Street. The lack of further investigation by the police makes our conclusion entirely speculative, simply based on the *modus operandi* of killing a landlady with a room to rent.

≈ ≈ ≈

What can we say about the victim? The parents of Elizabeth were both born in Wales and immigrated to Ohio.[12] Elizabeth J. Davis married David R. Jones on September 9, 1875, in the county of Gallia in Ohio.[13] The couple eventually had five children, two boys and three girls.[14] By at least 1888 the family had moved to San Francisco, where David was an engineer in a machine shop and Elizabeth ran the boarding house in which she eventually was murdered.[15] We do not have a date of death for husband David Jones, but he died sometime between 1917 and 1920.[16] At the time of her death, the "notice" in the newspapers indicated that Elizabeth was 72 years old, a native of Ohio, and a widow of David R. Jones and that she had two sons and three married daughters.[17] In June of 1926, a legal notice from son David Harry Jones, executor of his mother's estate, listing property for sale, revealed that Elizabeth Jones had owned two more properties in addition to the house on Romain and Market where she was found dead.[18]

≈ ≈ ≈

About a week after the death of Mrs. Jones, a short note in the *Chronicle*, on August 29, 1925, could be easily overlooked in the dense eight columns on the page, with multiple stories in each column. But in light of later developments, the note titled "Woman Beaten by Pretended Tenant" is worth pondering:

> Mrs. Olga McGowan, 24, was beaten on the head by an unidentified assailant yesterday afternoon, when the man, posing as a prospective tenant, asked to be shown some apartments in the premises at 295 Liberty Street, of which Mrs. McGowan's mother, Mrs. Lora Rodden, is the landlady. Mrs. McGowan's screams attracted her neighbors, who came to her assistance, and the attacker fled. At the time of the attack Mrs. McGowan was visiting her mother, who had gone out. At the Mission Emergency Hospital Mrs. McGowan was found to have severe lacerations on the scalp. She was unable to give a clear description of her assailant, other than that he was of medium size and was wearing a dark suit.[19]

2. September 15, 1925—Daisy Anderson, 45, San Francisco

A few weeks later, a front-page headline in the *Examiner* on Wednesday, September 16, 1925, announced, "S.F. Woman Found Strangled to Death: Manager of Apartment Dies Fighting Assailant."[20] Mrs. Daisy Anderson, 45 years of age, was found nude and strangled to death on Tuesday evening, September 15, in a second-floor untenanted apartment at 601-A Fell Street. Her husband had left for work at about 11:30 in the morning. She had been seen by a tenant in the house at around noon on Tuesday making up beds in the apartments.[21] Another tenant reported hearing a "pounding" and sounds of a commotion upstairs in the vacant apartment at around one in the afternoon, but "she believed repair work of some kind was being done and made no investigation."[22]

Mrs. Anderson's eight-year-old son, Theodore, searched for his mother when he returned home from school at two in the afternoon.[23] He searched everywhere and he even opened the door to the vacant room and later stated, "I saw somebody lying on the bed without any clothes on.... I didn't know it was mother, so I went outside to play until she came home."[24] The *Bulletin* suggested that he told the police that he had also seen a man in the room.[25] Then a vacuum cleaner agent arrived at about three in the afternoon and waited in the dining room, saying he had an appointment to see Mrs. Anderson. After waiting some time, he left his card with the boy and said he would return the next morning. He also left a new vacuum cleaner with attachments in the dining room, as discovered by Mr. Anderson when he returned from work that evening.

Mrs. Anderson's body was discovered at six in the evening by another lodger.[26] When the lodger returned from work, he noticed that his bed had not been made and as he searched for Mrs. Anderson he found her dead body in a vacant apartment with the door open.[27] While some reports suggested that "the furniture in the room was thrown about in a manner indicating there had been a terrific struggle,"[28] the *Examiner* account stated:

> Although Mrs. Anderson's body was bruised, indicating that she had made a terrific fight, there was no sign of struggle in the room where the body was found. Everything was in its place, except the clothing, which the murderer had stripped away and tossed at the foot of the bed. The murderer apparently had put things in order and even had used a soaked towel to wash away evidence of the crime.[29]

On the day of the murder, Coroner Leland wrote:

> About 6 p.m. the deceased was found lying naked, dead on her back, lengthwise in center of bed…. Her clothing was on floor in a pile, alongside of bed in the following order: an apron, in pocket of which was the left lens of her glasses, was on top; then a house dress, petticoat dress and [illegible] underwear and corsets on bottom. Shoes and stockings were under bed at foot. Deceased and her husband occupied lower level of 601 Fell and sublet rooms in upper portion as well as rooms on both floors of 601 A Fell, which is entered through a separate entrance. Bed where deceased was found has only a mattress on it, but under body, a bedspread was found. Rectal temperature 90 degrees.[30]

Deputy Coroner Frank Becker reportedly stated that the woman's clothes had been piled at the foot of the bed in a way to indicate someone other than the woman may have placed them there. In other words, they were not arranged in the order of removal.[31] The police believed Anderson was murdered by a man seeking to rent the apartment, because Mrs. Anderson had been showing prospective tenants the room.[32] That the dead woman had been murdered seemed obvious from the *Chronicle* report:

> From marks on her neck and scalp, police reached the conclusion that the woman was beaten on the head severely, and then strangled to death. That she engaged in a struggle with her assailant was evidenced by severe bruises on the body and blood stains on her person…. Mrs. Anderson had blood stains on her face and head, but the face apparently had been washed by the murderer in an attempt to cover up his crime. The washrag used could not be found on the premises, although officers located a blood-stained handkerchief, from which two corners, supposedly bearing laundry marks, had been cut.[33]

The husband, Harry R. Anderson, second engineer at the Granada Hotel, noted that his wife's two diamond rings, a gold necklace, other jewelry, and from $3 to $5 was missing.[34] He also reported that the keys to the apartment were missing.[35] Other reports noted that there was evidence that she was "attacked," which was a frequent code word for sexual assault in this era.[36]

However, as in the Jones case, everything changed when Dr. Shelby Strange concluded that Daisy Anderson had died of acute heart dilation and bronchial pneumonia of the influenza type and had removed her own clothes in a delirium.[37] Dr. Leland initially also suggested that the discoloration plainly visible on the throat might be from strangulation but also might be just "congestion after death."[38] Thus, it was reported that the authorities now thought that "she may herself have inflicted the bruises found on her neck and body."[39] So-called "science" had triumphed over suspicious circumstances.

However, the coroner, Dr. Leland, was not satisfied with this verdict and urged the police to continue to investigate.[40] He stated that even if she had died as Dr. Strange suggested, "this diagnosis did not preclude strangulation as the immediate cause."[41] The husband of Mrs. Anderson also continued to press for a murder investigation. He stated that his wife had been showing the apartment to prospective tenants on the day of her death and that her purse containing a small amount of money was missing, as were the keys to the apartment and her diamond rings. Her eyeglasses were found broken in half, "one section stuffed in a bloody handkerchief in her apron pocket, the other half hanging under the edge of the mattress at the head of the bed. The laundry mark had been torn from the handkerchief, which was a man's handkerchief."[42] He went on to say, "The last thing my wife would do would be to go into a vacant room, leave the door ajar, remove all her clothing and lie down on top of a bed. She was not ill when I left her at 11 o'clock that morning, except for a slight cold."[43]

After the autopsy, Dr. Strange wrote some notes in the official report that I have some difficulty in reading, but here is what I get:

- stomach to chemist
- acute dilation of heart following [hemorrhaging?] congestion of the lungs
- vaginal smears sent to pathologist at S.T. Hospital
- no poisons found[44]

No subsequent mention was made as to the results of the tests, but it is significant that in the Anderson case, unlike the Jones case, Dr. Strange at least ordered a vaginal smear. He announced that he could find no evidence of strangulation.[45] As reported in the press, "no marks were found on the throat … nor wounds on the body."[46] Somewhat more ambiguously, the *Bulletin* noted that Dr. Strange stated Mrs. Anderson had died of acute heart dilation and bronchial pneumonia but that she may also have been choked, though not sufficiently to cause death.[47]

Even in the context of having newspapers warring with each other to increase sales by sensational headlines, it is bizarre to find such a radical gap between the initial press reports of the condition of the body with all sorts of signs of violence indicating murder and the subsequent report of Dr. Strange that this relatively young woman, portrayed by her husband and friends as showing no signs of sickness, was now dead from pneumonia. Despite the misgivings of Dr. Leland, the police investigation was closed the following day.[48]

If the police had known then what they subsequently knew about a year later, namely that the "dark strangler" murdered a host of landladies by posing as a prospective tenant, would this case have been so quickly abandoned? At the inquest into the death of Mrs. Anderson which took place on October 20, 1925, the verdict stated "that said deceased came to her death in a manner unknown to the jury."[49] This implies that while the jury could not say that Mrs. Anderson had been murdered, they were not willing to accept the verdict of science. It seems plausible that the 72-year-old Mrs. Jones may have died of natural causes, and the description of a "blond" prospective boarder certainly does not match the "dark strangler," but the death of Mrs. Anderson, with a host of suspicious circumstances, should have been investigated by the police while the case was still fresh. Mrs. Anderson's death has a stronger relationship to the *modus operandi* of Earle Nelson compared to Mrs. Jones. In the Anderson case the body was nude, and numerous newspapers suggested that there were signs of a sexual attack. Furthermore, unlike the case of Jones where the body was found in the apartment that the landlady occupied, in the Anderson case the body was found in the vacant apartment that was for rent. Furthermore, the theft of jewelry matches a very common characteristic of subsequent Earle Nelson murders.

∾ ∾ ∾

What can we say about the victim? Daisy Emeline Griffin was born on March 9, 1880, in Iowa.[50] She was the seventh of eight children born to Joseph and Elizabeth Griffin.[51] At some stage the family moved to Kansas where, at the age of 18, Daisy Griffin married Joe Pierson in Ottawa in 1899.[52] However, this marriage did not last long because by the time of the Census of 1900, Daisy was back in Melvern, Kansas, living with her parents and listed as single.[53] Ten years later she was still listed as single and living with her aged parents in Melvern.[54] Eventually, Daisy married Harry Roland Anderson in 1912. She would have been about 32 years of age at the time.

Harry Anderson was born in Michigan in December 1871[55] and had been married twice before.[56] He had first been married in 1892 in Ohio and subsequently had two sons with his first wife.[57] In 1904 he married a woman in Kansas, and they ran a grocery store near Lincoln.[58] His second wife had been divorced previously and she brought her son to the marriage. She died suddenly in 1911 of what was said to be a tumor of the stomach.[59] After Harry Anderson married Daisy Griffin in 1912, the couple lived in Daisy's hometown of Ottawa.[60] Harry and Daisy and son moved from Ottawa to San Francisco in 1917.[61] In 1920, Harry Anderson, a machinist in a shop, was living with Daisy at 324 Caselli Avenue in San Francisco.[62] We do not know when the move to Fell Street and the decision to manage an apartment house took place.

Mrs. Anderson's funeral was held on Thursday, the 17th of September, and her body was taken to Williamsburg, Kansas, for interment.[63] She was buried beside her father, Joseph Griffin, who died in Agricola, Kansas, in 1923.[64] Her mother and most of her siblings were alive at the time of her death. Her mother died in 1936 and was also eventually buried beside her.[65]

After the death of his wife, Harry Anderson, an automobile mechanic, eventually lived in San Francisco with one of his sister's families.[66] Harry eventually moved back to his hometown of Litchfield, Michigan, and married for a fourth time in 1939.[67] Harry L. Anderson died in Litchfield at the age of 80 in 1960.[68]

There are so many people named Theodore Anderson that it is difficult to be confident that we have the right person. However, it may be that the eight-year-old boy in our narrative is Theodore Enoch Anderson, born in 1917 in Ottawa, Kansas, who eventually got married in 1937 in Washington State.[69] In 1940 Theodore was a seaman in the coast guard, living with his wife and infant son in Oakland, California.[70] The marriage ended in divorce, and the wife, a devoted Jehovah's Witness, remarried, and the grandson of the murder victim took on the name of his new family.[71] Theodore E. Anderson died at the age of 48 in 1965.[72]

≈ ≈ ≈

These two landlady deaths in 1925 largely disappeared from press reports, even as various landladies in San Francisco were killed by the "dark strangler" in the following year of 1926. Finally, after the fourth strangulation of a landlady in San Francisco in 1926, Dr. Leland presented the cases of Jones and Anderson to an inquest jury examining the death of Mrs. Edmonds. The jury concluded that not only was Mrs. Edmonds another victim of the "dark strangler," but so were the two landladies killed in 1925. As reported:

Anderson and son, Theodore, 8, widower and child of Mrs. Daisy E. Anderson, who died mysteriously in her apartment house.

The husband and distraught eight-year-old son of victim Daisy Anderson (*San Francisco Call and Post*, Sept. 17, 1925, at 17).

> Although police records show that the strangler struck for the first time in San Francisco in February of this year, the jury decided that his activities started in August 1925 with the killing of Mrs. Elizabeth Jones. The second murder heretofore not attributed to the strangler was the case of Mrs. Daisy Anderson, 45, the keeper of a rooming house, who was found dead in her home under unexplained circumstances.[73]

The jury urged the San Francisco board of supervisors to offer a large reward for the capture of the fiend.[74]

CHAPTER 4

Olla McCoy, Mary Murray
and Lena Weiner in Philadelphia

We know that in 1926 and 1927 Earle Nelson was a traveling man, wandering from one end of the country to the other. However, was he already traveling cross-country in 1925? Three strangulation murders of landladies took place in the same northwest Philadelphia neighborhood in the space of about a month in 1925.[1] Mrs. Olla McCoy, a "colored" woman, as the newspapers at the time described her, was killed on October 15, 1925. Miss Mary Murray was murdered on November 6, 1925, and Mrs. Lena Weiner met the same fate on November 10, 1925. While we have reasons to doubt that Nelson was the culprit in these three murders, there are also reasons to suggest that he probably was.

3. October 15, 1925—Olla McCoy, 26, Philadelphia

It was only after the third murder occurred that the *Philadelphia Inquirer* revealed that two previous strangulations had happened in very similar circumstances and noted that on Thursday, October 15, "Olla McCoy, colored, of Montgomery Avenue near Eighteenth Street, was strangled to death in the parlor and carried upstairs to a bed."[2] As we will note, eventually there was considerable press coverage of the search for the strangler as well as public fear of further attacks, but information on this first murder was not supplied. As a Black woman, McCoy was treated as a footnote to the story. The newspapers did not give her age, or the exact address where she lived, or who the members of her family were, or any further details as to the circumstances of her death. Her murder would have faded from history but for the fact that two further strangulations in the same neighborhood subsequently occurred.

The only press coverage I could find at the time of her murder, before the subsequent murders, was a note in the *Harrisburg Telegram*: "Both hands and feet were bound with a rope and a towel was stuffed in her mouth. Marks on the throat caused the police to believe that the murderer strangled her with the towel and then stuffed it in her mouth to make sure she would die. An examination by physicians also revealed that she had been attacked."[3] Even after the other two murders took place, the only details provided in the newswire stories noted that McCoy had likely been surprised in the kitchen of her house, and her head had been shaken violently as indicated by hair combs and pins strewn about, and then she had been taken upstairs to a bedroom where she was bound, gagged, and strangled. She had been tied to a post of her bed.[4]

The best information was provided in the weekly *Philadelphia Tribune*, a paper written by and for the Black community. A picture of the murder victim, "Mrs. Ola McCoy," appeared on the first page of the October 24 edition, and she was described as a very beautiful young woman, although her age was not given.[5]

The *Tribune* reported that she lived at 1815 West Montgomery Avenue, and her body was discovered at about 4:30 in the afternoon on Thursday, October 15, by her mother-in-law, Mrs. Eula McCoy, who lived nearby. At around noon that day, Ola (here spelled with one l) had visited her mother-in-law and then left for home indicating that she was going to "put up some grape jelly."

Who Killed Her?

MRS. OLA McCOY

Murder victim Olla McCoy (*Philadelphia Tribune*, Oct. 24, 1925, at 1).

When Eula went to visit her later in the afternoon, she found Ola's two-month-old baby sitting outside the house, and the doors to the house open. As reported in the *Tribune*:

> Having called several times without receiving an answer, the mother-in-law ascended the stairs and upon entering the bedroom found her daughter-in-law lying on the bed with hands tied and mouth gagged. She immediately sounded an alarm and as soon as the police arrived the body was rushed to the hospital where physicians said she had been dead for at least two hours. It was further discovered that rags had been stuffed into the dead woman's throat and as they were removed some of them were soaked with blood.[6]

The husband came home at five, two roomers in the house were placed under arrest by the police for questioning, and "examination of the body showed no other signs of attack."[7] This report contradicts the story in the *Harrisburg Telegraph* that said she was sexually attacked.[8] The body of Mrs. McCoy was taken home to Virginia for burial. In the *Tribune* the following week, there was a short note that the two roomers were released by the police upon giving a satisfactory account of their activities on the afternoon in question.[9] The mention of roomers in the house raises the distinct possibility that the murderer approached Mrs. McCoy under the pretense of renting a room.

∾ ∾ ∾

The death certificate for Olla McCoy indicated that she was born in Virginia to Oscar Lee and Octavia Bagley and that her husband was Cornell McCoy.[10] Her grave at the Bethlehem Baptist Church Cemetery in Bruington, Virginia, as well as various census documents, indicate that she was born in September 1899 and was therefore about a month past her 26th birthday when she was murdered.[11] She married Cornell McCoy in Philadelphia in 1923, and they had a son, Cornell James McCoy, Jr., on August 5, 1925, a few months before she was murdered.[12] Her husband Cornell McCoy, born in 1889, lived to be a ripe old age and died in 1981.[13] However, the infant at the time of her murder did not fare so well. He fought in the Second World War and eventually joined the Philadelphia police force. He was shot to death at home at the age of 31 by his common law wife in 1957.[14] She was also a member of the police force and acted as a crossing guard.[15]

4. November 6, 1925—Mary Murray, 38, Philadelphia

About three weeks later, on Saturday, November 7, 1925, the body of 37-year-old Miss Mary Murray was found at two in the morning at her home at 1811 North Judson Street, near 23rd Street and Montgomery Avenue.[16] She was likely murdered in the evening of Friday, November 6. Murray was the owner of the boarding house,[17] and according to another source, she was also a downtown restaurant waitress.[18] The body was discovered by a boarder, Thomas Sullivan, 28 years old, who was subsequently detained by the police.[19] The *Philadelphia Bulletin* stated that

> she was found on a bed in a second story front room, her hands tied behind her, ankles bound, and a large blue handkerchief tied over her mouth.... Disarranged furniture, overturned chairs, broken china and a broken talking machine record in the parlor and dining room ... and her false teeth found on the floor of the kitchen, indicated that she had engaged in a furious battle with her assailant before she was strangled.[20]

Given the signs of struggle on the main floor, the murderer had obviously carried the body upstairs to the bedroom.

The boarder, Thomas Sullivan, reported that he had come home at half past midnight, and not seeing Miss Murray on the first floor, and seeing the disarranged furniture, called for her. Not getting an answer, he went to the second floor, opened the door of a bedroom, and found her dead body on the bed. Thomas Sullivan, said to be a cousin of Miss Murray, had lived in the home about a month, having recently arrived from Ireland, and he had been out on Friday night visiting relatives. In his words, when he returned,

> I started playing a phonograph record, a scotch tune, "The Devil in the Kitchen," when I got home.... Then I noticed that bric-a-brac was broken and scattered on the floor and that a

broken record was lying near a chair. I called to my cousin, and she did not answer…. I went to her bedroom and found her bound by a piece of manila rope, and a blue handkerchief stuffed in her mouth. As I did not know what to do, I walked to the police station.[21]

When the police arrived, they discovered marks, presumably a blood trail, where the killer had dragged the body of Miss Murray up the stairs to the bed.

At first the police thought that Thomas Sullivan had killed Murray, especially since the initial medical opinion was that the time of death might have been around the time that Sullivan had reportedly come home, Sullivan was inebriated at the time he made his report to the police,[22] and there was no evidence of forced entry into the home. Searching the cellar, the police found about eight feet of rope partly buried under some coal. The rope was relatively clean, and they surmised that it had not been there long. The rope was of the same kind as had been used on the victim. Furthermore, Lieutenant Pawsner stated, "We found Miss Murray on a bed in Sullivan's room…. She was gagged, but the rope which apparently had bound her hands was loose and merely lay across her arms. There were no marks on her wrists to indicate her hands had been bound tightly."[23] Lieutenant Pawsner's theory was that Sullivan, a heavy drinker, owed rent to Murray and they got into a quarrel that escalated into violence. He stated, "It was evident that the woman had been struck a hard blow in the mouth which knocked out her false teeth. Sullivan has a cut on his hand which might have been inflicted when he struck her teeth with his fist."[24] Sullivan vehemently denied being the murderer and stated, "I got that cut on a tin roof yesterday."[25] Another detective noted that Miss Murray had withdrawn $300 from the bank on Friday, November 6, but at this stage the money had not been found. It was also noted that Miss Murray was only distantly related to Sullivan in that one of his aunts married one of her uncles.

Several days later Sullivan was still in jail, held without bail, because the police asserted that Sullivan failed to account for his actions between 9 and 11 on the Friday night before the alleged discovery of the body at two in the morning on Saturday.[26] The pressure on Sullivan lessened when a third murder took place and the police linked the three strangulations together as the work of one fiend. Obviously, Sullivan could not be that fiend, because he was in jail when the third murder took place.

The *Inquirer* did not mention this murder at all until after the third victim, Mrs. Weiner, was strangled in the same neighborhood, noting that McCoy and Murray were the first and second victims of the same "degenerate" strangler and that McCoy lived within five blocks of the Weiner house, while Murray lived within a mile of the house of the third victim.[27] Sullivan was not released from jail until a week later, police asserting that his alibi had in fact been confirmed.[28]

Mary Murray is such a common name that I have been unable to accurately trace her history. Her death certificate gave her age as 38 but did not give a birthday. She was born in Ireland, but we do not know when she came to the United States. She was listed in the death certificate not as a waitress but rather as a dressmaker.[29] Thomas Sullivan is also such a common name that I cannot accurately trace the boarder's subsequent history.

5. November 10, 1925—Lena Weiner, 33, Philadelphia

A few days after Murray was murdered, 13-year-old Lillian Weiner came home from school on Tuesday, November 10, to find her five-year-old brother, Hyman, sitting on the steps, crying, and saying the door was locked and he could not find their mother.[30] The Weiner family lived at 2421 North Napa Street. Lillian took her brother over to the nearby house of her ailing uncle, since their mother often went there to tend to her own sickly brother. Finding that their mother was not with their uncle, Lillian and Hyman returned home, and Lillian opened a window and pushed her brother through it so that he could unlock the front door. Apparently, this entry was unnecessary since the back door to the house was wide open. The narrative as provided by the *Bulletin* continued:

After Lillian and her brother entered the house they found a side-comb belonging to their mother in the hallway near the dining room door. On the kitchen floor they found a rubber pad which the mother used when scrubbing, and indications were that she had been washing the floor only shortly before. The rear door was open. Sensing something wrong, the girl ran to her mother's room on the second-floor front. No one was there. She then went to her own room, directly in the rear, and then to Britton's room back of it. [Britton was a boarder at the house.] The door was shut. As Lillian opened it, she saw her mother lying on the bed. A silk stocking was drawn taut about her neck and knotted over the windpipe. The other stocking, mate to the one about the neck, had fallen partly from the mother's mouth. Her hands were bound in front with one necktie and the other was drawn about her ankles. Lillian had seen her mother wash the stockings and hang them on a line in the kitchen when she was home for the noon recess from school. "Mamma! Mamma!" the child cried, then in terror dashed to the street.[31]

Murder victim Lena Weiner (*New York Daily News*, Nov. 26, 1925, at 34).

The screaming child now ran to a neighbor, Mrs. Ida Gralnick. According to the *Ledger*, Gralnick stated,

> It was exactly 3:30 o'clock when Lillian Weiner came running to my house and told me something terrible had happened to her mother. I went back to the house with the child and found Mrs. Weiner on the bed in her room. A stocking was thrust deep into her mouth and tied with a cord. Her hands were tied behind her back and her feet were bound. I felt her head and found it was very warm. I untied her and got water to wash her face, but I could not revive her.[32]

The *Inquirer* told the story slightly differently.[33] According to this account, one of the silk stockings with blood on it was found in the kitchen while the other was stuffed in the victim's mouth and a "gaudy red and green necktie was tightly drawn about the throat."[34] The body was fully clothed, and the hands were tied behind the back with some rags. The feet were also tied.

Eventually the husband, Myer Weiner, a frail man of 37, recently employed as a tailor, came home to the grim news. He was in a state of near collapse.[35] A boarder in the house, Samuel Britton, came home and then promptly disappeared, "frightened at the thought that he might be implicated because Mrs. Weiner was found in his room."[36] However, when Britton first arrived from work and found the police in the middle of a murder investigation, he searched the room and told the police that an overcoat, a suit of clothes and a chest of tools were missing.[37] The police were unable to find any fingerprint clues and believed that the man had climbed over the back fence or entered through the back gate and hid in the kitchen when Mrs. Weiner was out scrubbing the front steps. When she had come in, he had attacked her. Various kitchen chairs were found overturned and pots and pans had fallen to the floor.[38]

As news of the murder spread through the neighborhood, hundreds of people gathered around the home, and as the body of the victim was taken from the house, many women "became hysterical and screamed" and about 20 women fainted.[39]

One possible witness came forward to police with the story that he had seen a man "standing about in the vicinity of the Weiner house, and then had seem him walk up the narrow alley in the rear and walk in through the wooden gate, which had been left unlatched."[40] This witness described the man as "about 35 years old; five feet eight inches tall and weighing about 170 pounds. His eyes shone brightly and lustrously. He had a heavy growth of dark hair that covered his face and was dressed in dark clothes with a light cap."[41]

Mrs. Weiner had last been seen scrubbing her steps at about two in the afternoon, while her son, Hyman, played about the street. She then told her neighbors that she was going in to prepare an early supper.[42] Supposedly, one of the immediate neighbor ladies heard Mrs. Weiner pleading for her life as she was being attacked at around three in the afternoon. Mrs. Rachel Silver told police,

> I was hanging clothing in the yard when I heard Mrs. Weiner shout something in Jewish. She seemed to be in the kitchen. I heard her say, "What do you want to do that to me for?" Then there was silence. Then I heard her say, "Please don't kill me," and then, "Oh, my God!" After that there was silence. I listened but heard nothing more and decided maybe I was mistaken in what I heard. I didn't think any more of it until after the murder was discovered.[43]

Another neighbor saw a "heavily built" man run from the rear of the Weiner home holding a suitcase and some clothing under his arm. The police believed the suitcase probably contained the missing tools and the clothing consisting of two suits and an overcoat belonging to the boarder, Samuel Britton, taken from the bedroom where Mrs. Weiner was murdered.[44] The killer had also taken $4.50 from Mrs. Weiner's purse and 40 cents from a child's savings bank.[45] The witness who saw the killer leave also gave a description to the police.

Another neighbor had been approached very shortly before the Weiner murder by a heavy-set man asking about an address. Utilizing the descriptions given by these various witnesses, Lieutenant Sheller, chief of the murder squad, proposed a composite verbal sketch of the suspect as being a man "aged 35, five feet eight inches tall, weighing about 160 pounds and powerfully built. He had black, piercing eyes, dark complexion and wore a dark suit, tweed cap and an army overcoat."[46] Sheller was quoted further as stating, "The man's eyes were piercing black. Some say his complexion was sallow; that his hair was dark and unkempt, but all mention the piercing quality of his eyes. I suppose they were the eyes of a maniac."[47]

Lena Weiner was buried at the Mount Carmel Cemetery in Philadelphia.[48] Her death certificate did not give her date of birth but noted that she was born in Russia and was 33 years old at the time of her death. The certificate does not tell us what her maiden name was but simply states that her father's name was Abraham.[49] Given that the name Weiner in Philadelphia is so common, I have been unable to confidently trace the history of the family after Lena died.

≈　≈　≈

After the Weiner strangulation, the police immediately tied the three recent murders together. All took place in the same part of the city, all three victims were found strangled, bound, and gagged, and all allegedly had been killed in the kitchen and then taken upstairs to a bedroom.[50] Lieutenant Sheller stated, "I'm convinced the same man murdered Mrs. Weiner and the two other women…. The methods used in each case were identical…. The slayer must be powerful, as all of these women were strong. He is a dangerous maniac, without a doubt."[51] The *Ledger* reported Sheller as stating, "This is the work of a degenerate fiend."[52] No mention whatsoever was now made of treating the boarder, Sam Britton, as a suspect as had been done with Sullivan, the boarder in the Murray house.

The label "degenerate" was often code for someone who had committed sexual assault. As the *Ledger* noted, "Dr. William S. Wadsworth, coroner's physician, conducted a post-mortem examination yesterday. It was said that the examination established the fact that Mrs. Weiner had been subjected to the same form of maltreatment as had the women in the two preceding cases."[53] That all three victims were subject to a sexual attack was confirmed in the newswire stories where the murderer was repeatedly referred to as a "fiendish degenerate maniac."[54] One report quoting the results of the post-mortem examination implied that the sexual attack was likely after the death of the victims. The findings were the same in all three of the murders and "in each the fiend assaulted his victim *after* strangling her with his hands."[55]

As reported in the *Inquirer* various suspicious characters had been arrested but essentially the police were "clueless, tipless, and apparently helpless" in making a "determined, but futile effort" to solve the mystery of the three strangulations.[56] However, the *Bulletin*, not sounding as pessimistic, revealed that the police had made an important discovery at a pawn shop at 18th and Federal Street where they had found the stolen clothing that had been taken from the Britton bedroom in the Weiner house. The report suggested that clothes had also been taken at the scene of the second murder, that of Miss Murray, and that these clothes were also found in the same pawn shop.[57] As to the clothes found at the pawn shop, one report stated that they included two suits and an overcoat taken from the Weiner house.[58]

The police investigation got off the rails at this point. The previous witnesses had mentioned that the man's complexion was sallow, but the clerk at the pawn shop reported that the man who had brought in the clothes was a "very light skinned colored man."[59] The police now circulated a flier describing the suspect as a black man but "extremely light skinned, almost white."[60] The police also had another reason to believe that, as they put it, "a maniacal Negro, lately from the South, was responsible for all three killings."[61] This conclusion was based on the idea that the knots that had been used on all three victims were peculiar. The Philadelphia detectives reportedly stated, "They are the kind used on plantations to tie tobacco and cotton bales and are not employed by any other class of workmen who use rope or twine…. To the uninitiated, they appear to be a form of complicated sailor's knot, but investigation showed they were typical of the plantation."[62] The *Inquirer* subsequently also reported that "the knots are of the variety in common with use by Negroes employed in the cotton fields in the south."[63]

Instead of looking for dark-skinned white men like Earle Nelson, the police now focused on light-skinned black men, soon finding their first suspect who fit the description.[64] In rapid succession various black men were arrested and accused of the crimes until they could establish their innocence.[65]

Over the next month numerous foiled or aborted "strangler" attacks were reported, and many powerfully-built black men with lighter skin who had purportedly attacked or simply frightened women were arrested.[66] In some cases they were saved by the police from a mob threatening a lynching. The Black newspaper, the *Tribune*, commented on the discriminatory strangler hysteria, noting, "Every man who stops and looks up at a house is arrested as a suspect." About six suspects were picked up but later released because some white woman or excitable white child said a "light complexioned" Black man looked at her.[67] The following week, the *Tribune* again noted the strangler excitement directed at the black community, citing the example of a Black man who attracted a large crowd of pursuers and was eventually arrested after he had knocked on the door of a house and simply asked for food but was greeted by a scream.[68] Eventually in one tragic case, an eager 19-year-old youth chased and tackled the alleged "strangler" who then pulled a gun and shot the youth in the head between the eyes.[69]

In the following year of 1926 the reports of women having strangler encounters and the arrest of Black suspects in Philadelphia dropped off but did not disappear entirely.[70] After one attack in November, "the police arrested thirty Negroes and subjected them to long grueling cross-examinations."[71] The Philadelphia police came to the conclusion at some point that an important clue was that the three murders in 1925 and various subsequent encounters in that neighborhood all took place on what were called "ash collection days."[72] Given that ash collectors were usually Black men, this was thought to be yet a further indication that the police were on the right trail in seeking a light-skinned Black man.

As late as December of 1926, more than a year after the three strangulations, Philadelphia police came to believe that a Black amateur boxer with unusually light skin by the name of Joseph Wolcott, 25 years of age, might be the long-sought strangler. Wolcott had been arrested in Norristown, allegedly caught in the act of attempting to choke an aged woman in the course of a robbery at her store.[73] Wolcott vehemently denied having anything to do with any Philadelphia murders, but he was brought to Philadelphia so that the pawn shop clerk might have a look at him, as well as several more recent women victims who had foiled "the strangler."[74] Apparently the pawnbroker had "partially identified" him from a picture.[75] Fortunately for Wolcott, when the pawn shop clerk, a Mr. Morris, was brought in to see Wolcott in person, the clerk said that he was positive that Wolcott was not the man who had pawned the clothes from the Wiener house.[76] Despite this, the Philadelphia police kept Wolcott in custody until various women had a chance to confront him.[77] The police then discovered that in fact Wolcott was in jail in Pittsburgh at the time of the Weiner murder. In the meantime, Wolcott went berserk in his cell under this pressure of "being railroaded to the electric chair" and he began tossing his cellmates through the air and apparently descended into delusional mutterings. He was put into a straitjacket and shipped back to Norristown in a state of mental breakdown.[78] He eventually returned to the ring and managed several boxers in Denver. His real name was Carl Shackleford, and he died in 1933.[79]

≈ ≈ ≈

Further "strangler encounters" were reported in Philadelphia in 1927 before Mrs. McConnell of that city was strangled in April.[80] As we will outline in due course, the McConnell murder was eventually placed on the "official" list of Nelson's victims, and there was considerable evidence linking Nelson to the murder. But what of these three earlier strangulation murders in 1925? Unfortunately, original police records and coroner's reports have apparently been destroyed.[81]

Obviously, the timing, location, and circumstances of these three murders tie them together, but can they be tied to Nelson? There are some reasons why we might doubt that Nelson was responsible. The victims of Earle Nelson on the so-called "official list" were often beaten and strangled, but they were not gagged and tied up. But then it is also plausible that Nelson later learned to knock his victims into unconsciousness before strangling them, making further restraints superfluous. Another factor is how the murderer in these three cases met his victim. Nelson's *modus operandi* was the killing of the landlady after renting a room or seeking a room to rent or a house to buy. It is significant that these three cases in 1925 also involved a landlady in each case who had renters in the house, but we have no evidence that there were advertisements for a room to rent in the newspapers or posted at the houses.

It seems more likely, based on the newspaper reports, that the attacks were random or that the killer posed as a beggar or peddler. But again, as to the method of meeting the victims, why should we insist on consistency? Lola Cowan in Winnipeg was not a landlady and was not encountered in the usual way, even if she was killed in a rooming house. Furthermore, as I have noted elsewhere,[82] Mrs. Patterson's house may not have been for sale, as later was asserted by the police so as to firmly link the Winnipeg murder to the "gorilla man" strangler.

It seems to me that at least a plausible case could be made that the circumstances in these three murders point to Earle Nelson. The description of the possible suspect as "sallow or dark" and "strong" is exactly the common description of the suspect in other cases linked to Nelson. The stealing of clothes from the scene in two of the three murders and the immediate pawning of the clothes is a strong circumstantial link. There also is the likelihood that these three women were sexually assaulted after death. In each case, the victim was apparently killed on the main floor of the dwelling and then carried upstairs to a bed. This move does not seem necessary in terms of hiding the body to give extra time for escape. Indeed, fleeing the scene immediately might be preferable in terms of escape. The idea that the killer was motivated, at least in part, by sexual contact with the dead victim seems to be a plausible conclusion.

≈ ≈ ≈

In early June 1927, before Nelson was captured in Canada, one newspaper in Philadelphia reported that the Philadelphia police were convinced that the strangler, commonly called the "Gorilla Man," due to his ferocity and strength, was responsible for the McConnell murder in April 1927 and that this fiend "had killed more women, and over a vastly wider territory than did the notorious 'Jack the Ripper' of the London Whitechapel murders in 1888–89."[83] However, the newspaper went on to report that the police were sure that this fiend was *not* responsible for the three strangulations of women in Philadelphia that had occurred earlier in 1925. As pointed out by the Philadelphia police detectives, "motive, method and every other detail in those cases was different, even to the slayer's manner of gaining access to the house."[84] However, before the end of the month, after Nelson had been captured in Winnipeg, another newspaper reported that the Philadelphia police now *did* believe that the same fiend was also responsible for the earlier murders in 1925.[85] Numerous newspaper reports asserted that Nelson was linked to all four of the Philadelphia murders.[86]

After Nelson was arrested in Winnipeg and his photograph was distributed far and wide, Philadelphia police reported that the photos were shown to Jack Morris, a clerk in a pawn shop at 19th and Federal Street, who declared that the pictures bore a "strong resemblance" to the man who pawned an overcoat stolen from Mrs. Weiner's home.[87] However, Morris was not definite about his identification and was hoping that he could travel to Winnipeg and see the suspect in person.[88] The so-called "partial identification" by Morris illustrates both the problem with such identification and also the honesty of Morris. As reported in the *Inquirer*: "While Morris was not positive, he explained that since the murder, police have brought to his attention hundreds of photographs of suspects and that, as a result, his mind was somewhat befuddled. He asserted, however, that the photograph bore a striking resemblance to the man who pawned the overcoat later identified as one stolen from the Weiner house."[89]

The *Philadelphia Public Ledger* stated that officials in that city were so convinced that Nelson was guilty of all four strangulation murders in Philadelphia, three in 1925 and the murder of McConnell in April 1927, that Captain Wood of the detective squad was planning to confer with District Attorney Fox as to the possibility of issuing a warrant and an extradition proceeding against Nelson, although the article mentions that Nelson would likely hang in Winnipeg in any event.[90]

∽ ∽ ∽

More than three months would pass until another landlady was murdered, this time back in Earle Nelson's hometown of San Francisco. However, if Nelson was responsible for the three murders in Philadelphia, when did he move back across the country? There is at least one murder in the East that is worthy of some examination. While not a rooming house landlady, Emma Kirk, aged 70, was found bound, gagged, and strangled inside her umbrella shop in Washington, D.C., on January 22, 1926. This case was supposedly solved years later when an insane man confessed to strangling the woman, and supposedly his fingerprint matched a fingerprint at the scene. But there was considerable doubt. Because I do not view this case as reaching a sufficient level of possibility as to Nelson being the murderer, I have outlined the case elsewhere.[91]

PART III

1926:
The Dark Strangler

CHAPTER 5

Clara Newman in San Francisco

6. February 20, 1926—Clara Newman, 60, San Francisco

According to the "official list" compiled by Archie Leonard of the Portland police, the string of killings formally attributed to Earle Nelson started in San Francisco on a Saturday afternoon, February 20, 1926. As we have noted, there were probably previous murders, especially in San Francisco and Philadelphia, before this one. However, this murder clearly manifested the basic pattern of the "dark strangler" who would present himself to female landladies or property owners as someone seeking to rent a room or buy or lease a property. When being shown the room or residence he would attack the landlady, strangle her to death, and often also perform sexual violations on or with the dead body. The victim in this case was Miss Clara Newman, a 60-year-old spinster, who owned an apartment house at 2037 Pierce Street.[1]

Back in 1998 I walked up Pierce Street, one of the many sloped streets in the city. I instantly recognized what had once been the Newman house from the police photo. The house, painted pink, no longer had the basement window on the left and the flight of stairs from the sidewalk to the main floor on the right, but rather a double garage had been built into the basement level. The house looked fine. I sometimes wonder whether people who live in old houses, even if renovated, know what events transpired within their dwelling in the past and whether it would bother them if some particularly nasty event happened within their home decades ago. Perhaps not, but the real estate profession would probably not welcome some kind of "geography of crime" map, highlighting the specific locations for past murders, rapes, and other indignities. Of course, in some sensational cases the houses would have to be torn down because no one would want to live in them.

Clara Newman's nationality was listed by coroner Dr. Leland as Canadian.[2] We have confirmation of this in the United States Census of 1900 which listed Clara Newman, then age 35, as born in Canada in March 1865 and now living in Detroit with her widowed mother, Clarinda Newman, age 78. Clarinda was listed as having four surviving children. Living at the same address was Merton Newman, age 21, a grandson of Clarinda.[3] Ten years later in 1910, Clara was still living in Detroit, but this time with her sister and brother-in-law, Fannie and Matthew McAlonan.[4] This sister, along with sister-in-law Laura Eddy Newman, was mentioned in the brief obituary of Clara Newman in a San Francisco paper.[5]

At some stage Clara moved from Detroit to be closer to her nephew's family in

California. By 1920 Merton Newman and his wife were living in an apartment on Sutter Street in San Francisco, and Merton was a mail carrier, while his wife ran the apartment building.[6] Clara lived in an apartment in the same building. At the time of Clara's murder, it was reported that her nephew Merton, about 45 years of age, was also living with his family at the rooming house at 2037 Pierce Street, but Clara was the owner-proprietor of the building, not Merton's wife. Merton was the son of one of Clara's siblings, but Merton had been brought up by Clara's own mother, and thus Clara and Merton were more like brother and sister to each other, although 15 years apart in age.[7] Merton Newman and his wife had a son, Merton Jr., about 20 years old, at the time of the murder. Merton noted that Clara Newman was well to do, owning various properties in addition to the rooming house on Pierce Street where they lived.[8] We have no information that Clara had ever been married.

Clara Newman's body was found in a vacant apartment on the third floor, commonly called the attic floor. Merton Newman and his wife lived on the second floor. We assume Clara lived on the main floor. There was also a Mr. Charles Brown and his wife living in the house in an attic apartment.[9] Merton later told the police:

At about noon, I heard the voice of a man at the door ask her [Clara] if she had a room to rent him. She told him that there were rooms in the attic, if he cared to look at them and he apparently agreed, for then I heard their footsteps go up the stairs. I heard no struggle afterward. There may have been one, but I heard no screams or heavy sounds. A short time after they had passed upstairs, I went downstairs. At about 12:45 a man came down the stairs, passed me in the kitchen and walked out the back door. As he passed, he said in the voice I had heard the stranger at the door use, "Tell the landlady that I'll be back in an hour to take that room." Then he went out. Time passed and I began to wonder why Miss Newman didn't reappear. I called to her but got no answer. Then I ran up the stairs, fearing that something might have happened to her, and there I found her, dead in the attic bathroom.[10]

San Francisco Police Department photograph of the 2037 Pierce Street apartment house where murder victim Clara Newman was found strangled and sexually assaulted. Winnipeg police file (courtesy John Burchill).

The second statement in the same newspaper article gave

a slightly different slant to the event in question. In terms of the crucial meeting between Newman and the killer, Newman was now quoted as saying: "I went down the back stairs to empty some garbage. In Aunt Clara's kitchen I saw a strange man standing there. 'Hello,' I said. 'What are you doing here?' 'Where's the landlady?' he asked. 'What do you want of her?' I asked. 'Well,' he answered, 'just tell her that I'll be back in an hour to take that room.' He walked down the back stairs with me and went away."[11]

After a period of time, Merton and his wife became worried about the disappearance of Clara, and they searched the house. Finding the vacant apartment locked and not being able to find the keys, Merton supposedly kicked in the door and found the body on the kitchen floor.[12] Clara was found in the kitchen, not the bathroom, as first reported.

As the police photograph shows, Clara Newman was found lying flat on her back in the kitchenette with her head pointing to the door and her feet toward the

Murder victim Clara Newman (*San Francisco Examiner*, Feb. 21, 1926, at 1).

wall. She was fully clothed in a thick wool dress and black stockings and leather shoes on her feet. It is hard to see from the photograph, but it may well be that the dress had been elevated somewhat.[13]

From looking at the morgue picture of her neck, with the lines of bruises that look more like cuts, one wonders if the murderer strangled her with something other than his own hands. At least one paper reported that "a thin red line about her neck indicated that she was garroted and strangled by a cord."[14] Another paper stated that she was strangled with a cloth.[15]

The official report of Dr. Leland from the coroner's office reconstructed the murder as follows:

At about 12:45 p.m. the deceased is supposed to have shown an unknown person through her house at 2037 Pierce Street for the purpose of renting a housekeeping apartment. About 2:30 p.m. her nephew, Merton Newman, went looking for her and upon reaching the rear attic apartment found the door locked. Upon forcing it he found the deceased lying on her back

with her legs apart and her clothes raised. Her keys were found on the table. Body was lying on floor of kitchenette adjoining bedrooms.[16]

After the autopsy, Dr. Strange noted the cause of death as "strangulation—apparently by hands around the neck." Reminiscent of the aversion that Dr. Strange seemed to have in concluding that the landladies Jones and Anderson had been strangled in 1925, it was reported that Dr. Strange had initially sent bits of the lungs to the pathologist because he "was not satisfied that death was due to strangulation … rather than fright when assailed."[17] There is also a notation on the official report that a vaginal smear was sent to a laboratory at a hospital for examination and that some other specimens were sent to a pathologist. Unfortunately, the death report does not mention the results of these tests.[18] There is little doubt about this, however, given that Dr. Strange was quoted the next day as saying the victim was "attacked, probably after death."[19] Furthermore, after Nelson's arrest in Winnipeg, acting chief of police W.J. Quinn of San Francisco wrote, "The body was found prone in the small kitchen, the clothing pulled up about the knees. The autopsy showed beyond any question of doubt that she was outraged after death."[20]

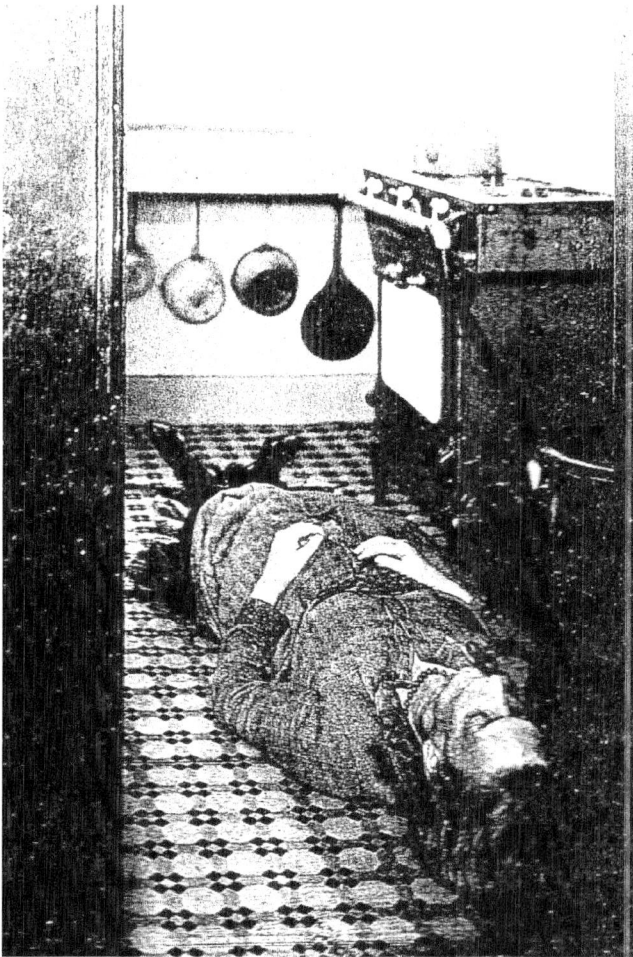

San Francisco Police Department photograph of the body of Clara Newman as found in the kitchenette of the attic apartment. Winnipeg police file (courtesy John Burchill).

Merton Newman, obviously having no warning as to the significance of his fleeting observation of the man walking out of the house, later described the man as wearing a khaki shirt of the army type, a vest (but no coat) and an ordinary hat. Of more significance, Merton described the man as "olive skinned and looking like a foreigner."[21] Apparently, he was about 30 years of age, weighing maybe 170 pounds, with a husky body build, and he was smooth shaven.[22] The dark complexion of the killer ultimately led to the moniker that was often used to describe him, namely the "dark strangler."

Police photographer George Blum took pictures of

fingerprints found on a door to one of the attic rooms.[23] However, the faint traces of fingerprints on the door of the apartment failed to produce plainly enough to provide a clue.[24] Another newspaper stated that when Charles Dullea, head of the murder squad, went back to the scene of the crime the day after it happened, he found several fingerprints on the floor of the kitchen, which he hoped might provide a clue.[25] These fingerprints were to be compared to fingerprints on file at the police department. In the end, nothing was ever heard about fingerprint evidence helping to solve the Newman murder, and when Nelson was arrested, we have no evidence that his prints were compared to any prints found at the scene.

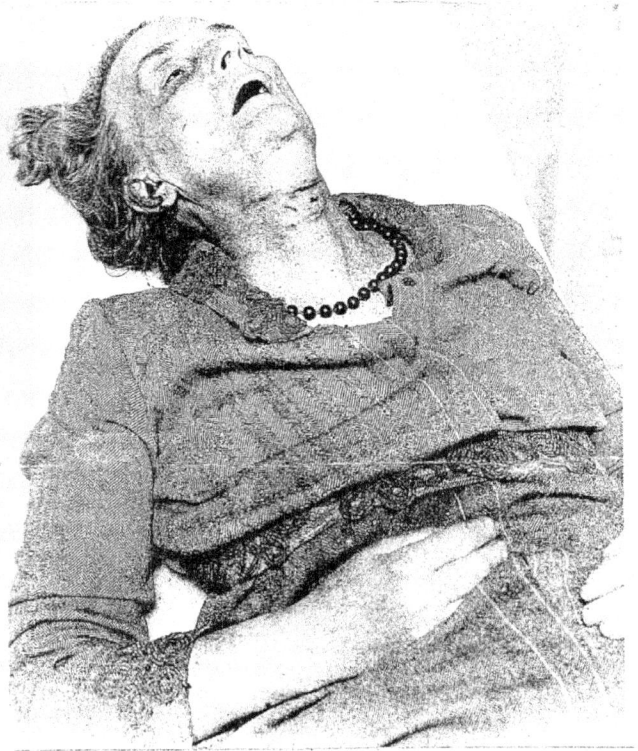

San Francisco Police Department photograph of Clara Newman in the morgue. Winnipeg police file (courtesy John Burchill).

The San Francisco police had the description of the wanted man from Merton Newman and also Coroner Leland's opinion that the marks on the victim's throat indicated that the killer was left handed with a broad thumb and thumbnail.[26] There were also reports made by people in the neighborhood that a man had recently appeared nude at windows of vacant apartments, "grimacing and performing mad dances."[27] The police were also hoping that some men repairing a roof next door had seen the man leave the Newman residence at the time in question.[28]

The inquest was held on February 23, 1926, with a verdict of murder by parties unknown. Apparently, Dr. Strange had told the jury that the fingernail marks on the victim were more than half an inch long.[29] Having given his evidence, Merton Newman was hoping that he could leave town to accompany the body back to Detroit for burial, but Dr. Leland insisted that he stay in San Francisco so he could identify suspects.[30] The *San Francisco Call and Post* linked the Newman murder with that of Mrs. Daisy Anderson in 1925 and suggested that the case was going to end up with the same dead end.[31]

∾ ∾ ∾

After the arrest in Winnipeg, about a year and four months after the Newman murder, Nelson's pictures were sent to San Francisco and it was reported that

Merton Newman, "the only person to meet the strangler face to face," at least in terms of the San Francisco murders, failed to identify the pictures of Nelson as the man who killed his aunt. The report went on to note that Newman declared, "There were similarities of the features, however."[32] Other newspaper reports were more emphatic that Newman did not recognize the picture of Nelson as being the person he recalled at the scene of the crime.[33] The *Chronicle* stated, "Newman saw and spoke to the slayer of Miss Newman, but when shown a picture of Ferrell [Nelson] taken from the police records, declared, 'That is not the man.'"[34] By this time Merton Newman had been shown multiple pictures of suspects and viewed multiple suspects face to face. His memory of the original culprit had been thoroughly compromised and we should not be surprised that he did not recognize Nelson or even if he said that Nelson was not the man.

This was not a problem for Captain Duncan Matheson who firmly believed that Nelson was the "dark strangler" without a doubt. After the arrest of Nelson but before the trial, Matheson reviewed the circumstances that tied Nelson to the murder of Newman in an article for a police magazine. Attached to his own overview of the case was a report from Lieutenant Charles W. Dullea and Detective Sergeant Otto Frederickson, who reported the following about the photo of Nelson sent to San Francisco after Nelson's arrest:

> This photograph was shown to Miss Jule Pottenger, who conducts a rooming house at 2701 Sacramento Street (two doors from where Miss Clara M. Newman was murdered on February 20th, 1926), and she identified him as being the man who called there about an hour before Miss Newman is supposed to have been murdered. This man endeavored to rent a room from her, but Miss Pottenger only showed him one room on the first floor and stood outside near the stairway and the man said something about the room not being suitable and left the place.
>
> The photograph was also shown to Merton Newman, who saw the suspect in the kitchen of his aunt's home at 2037 Pierce Street, as suspect was leaving the house shortly before the body of Miss Newman was found in the attic apartment, and he identifies him as closely resembling the man whom he saw at that time and place.[35]

This report is also found in the Winnipeg police file.[36] It may be that the newspaper reports about Newman's lack of identification dealt with the earlier photo of Nelson when he was arrested in 1921 in San Francisco, which was widely circulated in the press as soon as Nelson's identity was known, compared to his confrontation with the actual photo of what Nelson currently looked like when arrested in Winnipeg in June of 1927. In any case, the movement from "failure to identify," to "similarities of features," to the police report of "closely resembles" just illustrates a very bad identification process, for which Merton Newman cannot be blamed. As noted by this time his memory would have been so compromised by post-event images and memories that it would be difficult to recall accurately what he had originally seen.

Merton Newman and his wife continued to live for several decades in the house at 2037 Pierce Street where Clara was murdered.[37] Merton Newman died at age 71 in 1951.[38]

CHAPTER 6

Laura Beal in San Jose

7. March 2, 1926—Laura Beal, 64, San Jose

The next murder of a landlady took place in the afternoon of Tuesday, March 2, 1926, just 10 days after the last murder. Posing again as a prospective tenant, the strangler entered the Deer Park Apartments at 521 East Santa Clara Street in San Jose and killed the landlady, Mrs. Laura Beal, in the second-floor apartment that she was showing him. The apartment house, with the two life-like statues of deer standing in the garden, was well known in the city.[1] Assuming that Earle Nelson was living in Palo Alto during this period, we note that San Jose is a shorter commute to the south than San Francisco is to the north.

Mrs. Beal, mother of four grown children, was an active Sunday school teacher in the First Methodist Church and a leader in the Women's Temperance Union. Her obituary noted that she was not 65 as earlier reports had indicated but actually a few weeks short of her 64th birthday.[2] Laura Kilgore was born in 1862 in Indiana.[3] She became a schoolteacher and married Harvey Beal in 1883.[4] Harvey and Laura lived most of their lives in Kansas, where they raised their four children (the youngest one was adopted).[5]

Mrs. Beal's body was discovered by her husband, a retired real estate broker, who had been searching all over the neighborhood for her after he found her missing when he came home at six in the evening. The door to their own apartment was open when he arrived, and his wife's reading glasses were right beside her chair with the newspaper open as if she had been interrupted. Thinking that she must have gone to visit some friends, he ate supper alone and then became increasingly worried. He visited various friends who might have seen his wife and started searching the rest of the house and grounds. At around nine in the evening, with growing apprehension and on the suggestion of another roomer, he finally got the key and opened the locked door of the vacant upstairs apartment that was available for rent.[6] The *San Francisco Chronicle* reported:

> She was lying on the bed in a furnished apartment which had been vacant for several days, with a silken cord belt from her own dressing gown tied tightly about her neck. The badly ruffled condition of the bed and two severe bruises on the woman's chin gave evidence of a strenuous struggle with her assailant. According to Coroner Amos Williams, the woman is believed to have been knocked unconscious then strangled with the cord and attacked.[7]

The *San Francisco Examiner* reported, "Wrapped twice around her neck and knotted were the strangling folds of the silken cord, which had been the belt of her dress. Her stockings were torn. Although it has not been definitely established, there were indications that the woman may have been attacked.... Her clothing was in disarray. There were thumb marks on each side of the neck."[8]

The confirmation that Mrs. Beal had indeed been criminally attacked after death was provided by Dr. C.M. Burchfield of San Jose after making lab tests.[9] The local press noted that the silk cord had been wound four times around the throat and tied twice.[10] The time of death was probably between 2:30 in the afternoon, when Mrs. Beal had been on the phone with a friend, and 3:30, when a child living at the apartment house had come home from school and noticed that the door to the Beal apartment was wide open.

The murder of Beal and the murder of Newman were immediately linked together as the work of the "dark strangler." In addition to the obvious similarities in the two cases, there was again an eyewitness to the "leaving of the scene" portion of the crime. Mr. Bailey, who ran a cigar and soft drink store directly across the street from the rooming house, reported seeing a man leave the Beal apartments at three in the afternoon. His description of "an olive-skinned man, of foreign appearance"[11] was said to match that given by Merton Newman.[12] At the request of

Murder victim Laura Beal (*San Jose Mercury Herald*, March 4, 1926, at 1).

J.N. Black, the chief of police in San Jose, the San Francisco police sent Merton Newman to San Jose the day after the Beal murder to consult with the San Jose police.[13]

Duncan Matheson, the captain of detectives of the San Francisco police, now issued an alert throughout the region: "Watch every apartment house with rooms to rent; warn every woman showing rooms to men to look out for herself; get descriptions of every man asking to see rooms, who is at all suspicious."[14] The description of the wanted man, based on the observations of Newman and Bailey, was now given as

evidently a foreigner, thought to be Italian or Greek, about 30 years old, standing about 5 feet 7 inches and weighing about 175 pounds. He speaks with a slight accent, is heavy chested, has wide, square thumbs and is probably left-handed. The man has clear, olive skin which is

Deer Park Apartments in San Jose with an arrow pointing to the second-floor apartment where Laura Beal was murdered, and a cross on the main floor where Mr. and Mrs. Beal lived (*San Jose Mercury Herald*, March 4, 1926, at 1).

smooth shaven, and straight black hair. In San Francisco he wore an olive drab army shirt, but when seen in San Jose he was described as well dressed.[15]

The nature of the murders indicated to the authorities that the man was a "degenerate, dangerous maniac."[16]

Another landlady came forward to San Jose police claiming that a man who met the description of the strangler had tried to rent a room from her several weeks previous to the murders of both Newman and Beal and that she had scared him off just as he put his arms around her by telling him that the car that was just pulling up outside was that of her husband.[17] Another landlady reported that on the very same day as the murder of Beal, earlier in the day at about 12:30, a black-haired, olive-skinned man had called in response to her advertisement of an apartment to rent and tried to lock the door of the apartment after he followed her into it but was prevented by her daughter from doing so.[18] It is not unreasonable to believe that over the course of the dark strangler's career of hunting landladies there were times in which he was turned away at the door or was unsuccessful at achieving his objective when an attempted strangulation failed for various reasons. However, as we will also note in the following chapters, sorting out actual and imagined events became difficult for the police.

A few days after Beal was strangled, it was reported that another woman in San Jose had been rendered unconscious by an intruder in her home who attempted to strangle her with a strip of clothing he tore from her dress, and a second woman claimed to have been attacked by the strangler when she was alone in her father's store.[19] The *Chronicle* stated, "Women are keeping behind locked doors. Children are not being permitted to leave the house alone. Men are secretly arming themselves."[20] As these strangler reports came rolling in and the police were kept busy investigating them, Captain Black in San Jose finally stated, "I am inclined to the opinion their experiences were imaginary, the result of hysteria. It now seems probable that the maniac who murdered Mrs. Laura Beal Tuesday afternoon left the city immediately afterward."[21] Several women responded indignantly to Captain Black that their experiences had been real, and how dare he suggest that they were suffering from hysteria.[22]

The so-called "hysteria" sightings also overwhelmed the San Francisco police. Several women in that city also claimed to have escaped the clutches of the strangler.[23] Some of the encounters involved descriptions that did not match that of the sought-after strangler of Newman and Beal.[24] However, more reports flowed in as to women who claimed to have been attacked and then successfully escaped, this time giving descriptions that matched.[25] The women's stories, accompanied by photos of the women themselves, were printed in the newspapers as gospel truth.[26] The *San Francisco Call and Post* was particularly sensationalist, with huge, two-inch capital-letter headlines announcing every new strangler sighting.[27] Duncan Matheson finally announced that these reports were "hallucinations induced by fear."[28] However, the reports as to encounters with the "dark strangler" continued in various California cities.[29]

As would be the case after every murder, various men were picked up as possible suspects. In San Jose, Joe Kesesek, an Austrian hobo, dressed in an army shirt, was arrested as a promising suspect[30] until he took a bath and then no longer resembled the "dark strangler."[31] Two suspects were picked up in San Francisco and released when Merton Newman emphatically declared that neither was the man he had seen.[32] Merton Newman was subsequently asked to go to Berkeley to see a suspect who had sought to rent a room but was arrested because he fit the description.[33] Merton, upon viewing the man, asserted that he was not the strangler.[34]

As the weeks passed without any clue as to who was responsible for the two murders, but also without any further murders, Duncan Matheson declared that the strangler had fled to Southern California and that while San Francisco landladies should be vigilant, he believed "there will not be any further attacks here from the man guilty of the two murders."[35] Unfortunately, Matheson's prediction turned out to be very wrong, although there was indeed a three-month gap in time before the "dark strangler" killed another landlady in San Francisco.

~ ~ ~

Ten months after the death of his wife, Harvey Beal went back to his hometown in Indiana and married a spinster schoolteacher.[36] However, only seven months into his second marriage, he died suddenly in San Jose at the age of 67 in August of 1927, and his wife moved back to Indiana where she died at the age of 74 in 1936.[37]

≈ ≈ ≈

After Nelson was arrested in Manitoba, we would expect that a picture of Nelson was shown to Bailey who claimed to have seen the man leave the Beal residence. However, we have no evidence of this. Apparently fingerprint evidence was also found on the door of the bedroom where Beal's body was found.[38] We do not know whether the prints on the door were from the killer or someone else or whether the quality of the prints was adequate for comparative purposes. There was one report that chief of police Black thought Nelson's prints "were almost identical" to the prints taken at the Beal apartment and, as we will later discuss, a print taken at a murder scene in Portland.[39] The article mentions that Black intended to call some fingerprint experts to do a closer examination, but nothing further was reported. We may assume that under closer examination the prints from the Beal apartment and from Portland did not match that of Nelson, nor did the print from Portland match the print from San Jose. Given the overwhelming evidence, especially as to the Portland murder, that Nelson was the "dark strangler," we may assume that these prints must have been left by someone else, either before or after the murder.

≈ ≈ ≈

Given the length of the three-month cooling-off period after the Beal murder and before the next murder, there was eventually suspicion that Nelson might have traveled to the East Coast during this time and murdered three women in Newark, just as he had likely killed three women in Philadelphia in 1925. I think this is highly improbable, given the circumstances of the murders.

There were three unsolved murders in Newark in May, July, and August of 1926. If the "dark strangler" was responsible for them, as well as the murders on the West Coast on the conventional list, it would mean that he traveled to Newark to commit the first murder, of Rose Valentino, on May 10, 1926, then returned "home" to California to commit murders on June 10 and June 24, which we will deal with shortly, and then returned to Newark for the murders of Margaret Stanton on July 3 and Lena Tidor on August 9, and then went back to California again in time for a murder on August 16. It seems highly unlikely that Nelson was traveling back and forth across the country in this period not only once but twice. More importantly, there is very little in the circumstances of these three Newark murders that link them together, much less that they should be linked to the "dark strangler."

One may well doubt that Earle Nelson would have been under any suspicion involving the three murders in Newark in 1926 but for the fact that he was undoubtedly in Newark *the following year*. Nelson sent some postcards from Newark on February 8 and 11 of 1927, not 1926. When Nelson was arrested in Winnipeg, there was no report of any activity by Newark police to distribute his photo to potential witnesses in Newark. It was only during Nelson's trial in November that the Newark police apparently were told about the postcards, one of which stated, "I am working steady and have found good church friends."[40] Captain Sebold, chief of the Newark detectives, asked for any of these church friends, whomever they might be, to step forward and talk in confidence to him. Assuming Nelson was telling the truth about having such friends, we have no evidence that any came forward. It was also announced that a detective from Newark would be coming to Winnipeg to interview Nelson.[41]

While Rose Valentino, age 69, was the owner of an apartment building, the murderer came through a window off a fire escape, and Valentino was clubbed over the head in the middle of the night on May 10, 1926, or in the early morning of the next day.[42] The police believed that robbery was the motive, as Valentino was well to do. While there were reports that she was strangled, the autopsy suggested that she had been unconscious after the clubbing and thus she suffocated on the handkerchief that had been stuffed into her mouth as a gag.[43] There was no evidence of sexual assault.

As in the Valentino case, the attacker of Margaret Stanton, age 42, on July 3, 1926, in Newark came through a window in the middle of the night and was said to be hovering around the bed or attempting to attack one of the boys in the household when Mrs. Stanton woke up and fought with the attacker, who shot her with a gun and ran off.[44] Stanton died of a gunshot wound, not by strangulation. While we know Nelson had a gun as a juvenile, and while he pawned a stolen gun in Los Angeles, shooting people does not appear to be part of his *modus operandi* at all. Furthermore, several years later, Peter Kudzinowski, a confessed child killer, became a suspect in the case, with strong circumstantial evidence against him.[45] Kudzinowski was executed at Trenton on December 21, 1929, for the murder of a young boy.[46]

The third Newark murder on August 9, 1926, of Lena Tidor, age 72, again happened in the middle of the night and the attacker was thought to have entered through a window.[47] Mrs. Tidor was strangled with a towel, and while there were initial reports suggesting a sexual element to the offense, these were later denied by the medical examiner.[48] Her husband, 74-year-old Harry Tidor, a recent victim of a stroke and partially paralyzed and deaf, was sleeping in the same room while the attack took place. The elderly couple lived in a small room at the rear of the grocery store they operated on the ground floor of their house, and it is probable that robbery was the motive, but the killer might have been frightened away before accomplishing his purpose.[49] Again, we fail to see how these murders can be linked to the murders attributed to Earle Nelson. While all three of the murders allegedly involved an intruder coming through a window at night, none of them involved a murderer gaining access to the victim by pretending to rent a room from them. None of them involved a sexual assault on the victim. The murder with a gun does not fit any of the other murders attributed to Earle Nelson. I have given more detailed information on the Newark murders elsewhere.[50]

CHAPTER 7

Lillian St. Mary in San Francisco

8. June 10, 1926—Lillian St. Mary, 63, San Francisco

The "dark strangler" did not kill again until the afternoon of Thursday, June 10, 1926, slightly more than three months from the time of the Beal murder in San Jose. The victim this time was 63-year-old Mrs. Lillian St. Mary, who rented out rooms in her own second floor flat at 1073 Dolores Street in San Francisco. Lillian and her son had only moved to the Dolores Street flat about a year before her murder.[1]

The St. Mary flat was on the right-side entrance upstairs. When I walked up to 1073 Dolores on a sunny day in January of 1998, I found the multiple unit house was now painted blue with a red roof. Three very large cedar bushes, growing up from the very narrow blue picket fenced front yard enclosures, separated the house from the sidewalk. Dolores Street had a nice boulevard in the middle of it, with big palm trees, so attractive to a visitor from ice-bound Winnipeg in January.

The body of St. Mary was discovered by a boarder, Mr. Brian,[2] when he returned home after work:

> Walking up the stairs to the second floor flat, Brian went to the kitchen, expecting to find the woman there preparing the evening meal for herself and her son, James St. Maire [he spelled his name differently], who is secretary to a Southern Pacific official. Not finding her, Brian started for his own room but noticed that the door to one of the unoccupied rooms was ajar. Glancing in, he saw the body of Mrs. St. Mary stretched on the bed, her hair disarranged, her hat on the bed beside her and her feet carefully placed on her coat, which had been torn from her shoulders.[3]

Mr. Brian called the police.

Despite initial reports that a pearl necklace had been taken and money was missing from a purse, later investigation indicated that, as in the cases of Newman and Beal, there was no robbery involved.[4] Lillian St. Mary had last been seen by a neighbor lady about noon, when Lillian borrowed a vacuum cleaner from the neighbor.[5] Another neighbor lady living on the main floor directly below the St. Mary flat heard the vacuum cleaner being used shortly after the noon hour.[6] It was believed that Lillian was murdered just before going out for her daily afternoon shopping trip, because she was found in her street clothes. The San Francisco police eventually sent the following report to the Winnipeg police:

> On June 10, 1926, Mrs. Lillian St. Mary … was strangled to death sometime between the hours of 12 noon and 5 p.m. A sign "Rooms to Rent" was displayed in the front window and the strangler entered no doubt for the purpose of interviewing her about renting a room. While

San Francisco Police Department photograph of 1073 Dolores where Lillian St. Mary was murdered. Winnipeg police file (courtesy John Burchill).

doing so, she was seized and strangled in exactly the same manner as Miss Newman and was outraged, and after the outrage was committed, the body was evidently picked up and placed on the bed. The bed was not disarranged, showing conclusively that the assault took place on the floor, where the carpet showed some stains. The clothing in this case was disarranged as in the case of Miss Newman. In this case no living person could be found that saw the strangler either enter or leave the premises and to date no witnesses are available. All the circumstances connected with this case indicate beyond any question of doubt that it was the same party that committed the Newman murder.[7]

The San Francisco police also forwarded pictures to Winnipeg, one of which showed the victim as found on the bed.

As one newspaper reported, she was wearing clothing as if on her way out to do her usual afternoon shopping. She was found still wearing her glasses on her nose, her hat placed beside her, and her coat neatly tucked under her feet.[8]

The handwriting on the death report from the coroner's office noted that she was 63 years of age and divorced and that her death was a strangulation homicide. Another notation stated: "Her earrings were on bed under her, and her clothing disarranged. Wet spot on rug, which had gone through on to the padding, was found in center of the room. She was in the habit of leaving her front door unlocked and displayed a sign on the door, 'room to let.' Rectal temperature—90 degrees."[9]

A notation in the handwriting of Dr. Strange added that the autopsy was performed at 10 in the evening of the day of the murder and the cause of death was "strangulation by compression of the throat and crushing of the chest wall fracturing

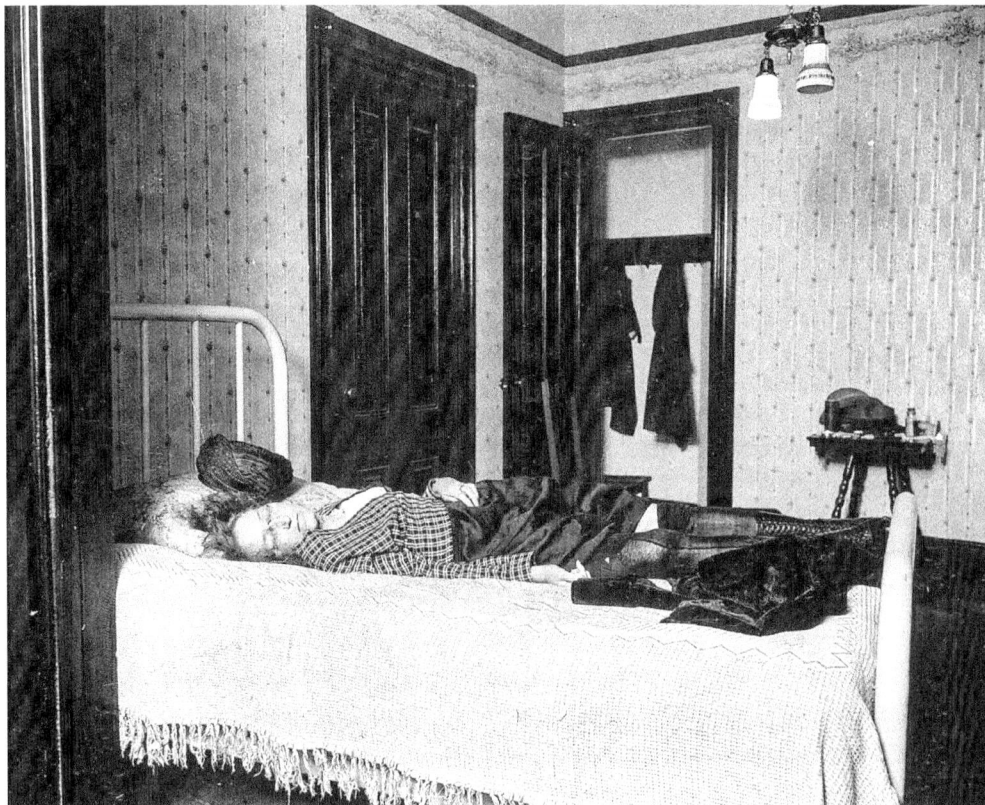

San Francisco Police Department photograph of the body of Lillian St. Mary placed on her bed after she was strangled and sexually assaulted. Winnipeg police file (courtesy John Burchill).

six ribs on right side and three ribs on left side."[10] The press reported that several of the broken ribs had pierced her lungs and one had pierced her heart.[11] Interestingly, this report said nothing about testing for sexual assault, but clearly from other press reports,[12] and from the reports made by the police as noted above, sexual assault must have been obvious. What seems to have been kept from the public was that the sexual assault was post-mortem, because the newspapers regularly suggested that the victim was "ravished" and then strangled, as if it was unimaginable that the fiend could be so perverted as to kill first and then rape the corpse.[13]

It was the crushing of the chest that led to the first use of "gorilla" in relation to the "dark strangler." The local *Bulletin* included the phrase "the *gorilla-like murderer* who yesterday claimed a third woman victim by strangling and crushing to death with seemingly superhuman strength."[14] Several days later the "gorilla" reference appeared in the *Examiner* as well, where a headline read "Maniac Now Described as Man with Strength of Gorilla." The article went on to state, "According to Dr. Shelby Strange, autopsy surgeon, he is in addition a man of terrific strength, and with *gorilla-like hands*. Mrs. St. Mary was literally crushed to death in his arms, the autopsy revealed, and later was lifted from the floor as lightly as a feather and placed on her bed without disturbing the covers."[15]

While no one saw the murderer come to the house or leave the house, there were some tips that were given to the police. The first came from a neighbor lady directly across the street who noted that on Monday (the murder was on Thursday) she was seated at her front window. She noticed "a heavily built stranger, dressed in dark clothes and wearing a coat, tip toe up the front steps of the St. Mary house and peer at the 'for rent' sign in the window, and then tip toe back down the stairs and disappear rapidly down the street."[16] The more sensationalist account asserted that it was Tuesday when the "heavily built, roughly clad man of swarthy complexion and appearing to wear 'soft shoes,' 'sneaked' up the steps … peered at the 'room for rent' sign, hesitated, then leaped from the veranda and disappeared."[17] Whatever the actual observation of the neighbor lady, it was a reasonable assumption that the "dark strangler" might have canvassed the rooming house ahead of time.

A second tip came from a streetcar conductor on the Market line who reported that at about 2:40 in the afternoon of the day of the murder, and about half a block from the St. Mary house, a "heavy-set person of medium height and dark complexion, wearing a blue suit with white pin stripes" boarded the streetcar at 23rd and Dolores and seemed to be very nervous and behaved strangely and got off after only riding for a block.[18] One account noted, "After riding but one block, he leaped to his feet, jumped off the car, and fled along Dolores Street."[19] Another quoted the streetcar conductor as saying the man got off at 22nd and Dolores and "hurried toward Mission Street."[20]

The third tip came from a Mr. Riley who stated that he met a man at 22nd and Guerrero Street. The timing of the encounter was but a few minutes after the man had allegedly left the streetcar two blocks away. The man asked Riley where the Roma rooming house was and where Market Street was, and then he explained that he was from the country.[21] The description of the man by Riley allegedly matched that of the streetcar conductor.

The fourth tip came from a landlady living at 3809 20th Street who said that on Friday afternoon (the day after the murder) a stockily built dark complexioned man knocked on her door and asked to see apartments for rent. "I showed him one on the ground floor…. But with hardly a glance at it he asked me if I had one vacant 'upstairs some place.' I asked him how many apartments he wanted to see, and he said, 'I want to see all of them, especially the upstairs ones.' I became suspicious and excused myself to call the police and when I came back, he left without asking to see any more apartments."[22]

The most interesting tip in hindsight was the profile of the killer provided by the *Daily News* which presented the opinions of four experts.[23] Working only from the premise that the killer had strangled three landladies, Newman, Beal, and St. Mary, and of course not having a clue as to the identity of the killer, these expert opinions were insightful. Dr. Edward Twitchell, the director of the psychiatric ward at San Francisco Hospital, noted that the "brutality of the murders indicates insane frenzy or fury fanned by an obsession to take revenge for some imagined wrong against the particular victim or persons of their type or age, in general." Noting the perversion of natural affection, psychologist Baldwin Vale noted the man was "undoubtedly an absolutely insane maniac." Dr. Joseph Catton, a psychiatrist, noted the killer had a recognized form of insanity, namely psychopathic sadism: "a person who derives pleasure from pain." But, perhaps most interesting, was the opinion of Mr. Chauncy M'Govern, a criminologist, who stated:

> I believe the "crusher" is a man who becomes obsessed with resentment against elderly women at times because of some treatment in boyhood. Probably one who was orphaned at an early age and raised by some elderly woman relative who did not understand his natural desires and impulses. Such types usually live alone, and brood over their imagined resentment against an individual or a class in general.[24]

This almost astonishingly accurate profile was however followed by a much less accurate prediction, namely that the killer was "undoubtedly a man of good education and social standing."[25] The *Examiner* also presented a profile of the killer but only quoted Dr. Catton, who talked about psychopathic sadism and noted, "There is no way in which a sadist may be recognized. He may be a person of mild appearance, a man of intelligence, or, indeed, any exterior that a normal person may assume. The only warning I can give to any of his intended victims is to be suspicious of everybody."[26]

The police combed through the records of various California hospitals for the insane looking for all escaped "madmen."[27] We can only speculate as to whether Earle (Ferrell) Nelson's name came up. Most of the work of the police involved following up on a steady barrage of strangler sightings and encounters that flowed into the police department.[28] While there was not much humor in such a grim topic, at least one of the "encounters" may have caused a few chuckles. As reported:

> Her imagination inflamed by stories, which she had read of the activities of the elusive strangler, she … went to bed last night and had a nightmare. She dreamed the strangler climbed through her window and choked her. She fought with him, desperately, frantically. When it seemed he was about to win, she reached under her pillow, pulled out a revolver and fired full into his face. The bullet struck her left hand and awakened her. At 2 o'clock this morning she called on Dr. John Bennett to have the wound dressed and told how it all happened.[29]

Another report on this incident claimed that "the bullet grazed the head of her two-year-old son, John, sleeping beside her."[30] The *Chronicle* showed a picture of the 30-year-old woman, with her hand bandaged and her left arm in a sling, sitting beside her young son.[31]

In addition to various supposed encounters with the strangler, various suspects were arrested and released. For example, a 63-year-old butcher with olive skin by the name of Otto Krueger was arrested when he got off a boat in Los Angeles. The passengers thought he was acting strangely and looked like the "strangler."[32] He admitted that he had been in San Francisco and San Jose but denied having anything to do with the murders. His age alone made the arrest laughable, and he was soon exonerated when Merton Newman said he was clearly not the wanted fiend.[33] A more likely suspect was an Italian man, Ray Lorenzana, age 30, who was arrested in Santa Cruz after allegedly brutally attacking a woman in that city.[34] While he may have been guilty of the attack, he was not the "strangler" when it was established that he had been in Santa Cruz when the three "dark strangler" murders happened.[35]

Even if the fiend had disappeared without a trace, the San Francisco police, at the risk of creating a degree of hysteria, did a good job of warning people as to the potential for disaster at the hands of the strangler. Landladies were reminded never to take strange men into rooms without a third party present. Chief of police Daniel O'Brien also urged women to scream if they were being molested.[36]

≈　≈　≈

While the circumstances of this murder were squarely within the *modus operandi* of the "dark strangler" and thus attributed to Earle Nelson after he was arrested in Manitoba, we have no evidence that the various persons who gave tips to the police were asked to identify Nelson's picture. Perhaps the tips were dismissed by the police as examples of people getting notoriety by injecting themselves into events. However, one additional circumstance, namely geography, added to the firm belief that Nelson was the murderer of St. Mary. According to the evidence given at the trial in Winnipeg, Earle Nelson sometimes came "home" to the house of his aunt Lillian who used to live on Guerrero but since 1923 lived at 3573 20th Street, not far from 3525 20th Street, which previously had been the Nelson family home of Earle's grandfather and grandmother. After the arrest of Nelson, as reported by San Francisco detectives Dullea and Frederickson,

> we learned from Mrs. Lillian Fabian, 3573–20th St., this city, that at or about this time of the year, the said Earl Nelson (her nephew) was assisting at times in painting the interior of her home. They did not know where he roomed, but he would usually show up around 5 a.m. and often would stop working at uncertain hours during the day and go out and they would not see him again until the next day. This place is near Valencia Street, and only about five blocks from 1073 Dolores Street where Mrs. St. Mary was murdered.[37]

Because the San Francisco police files in these cases have allegedly been destroyed, we are often at a loss as to how fingerprint evidence was handled. For example, months after the St. Mary murder, a landlady was strangled in Stockton. We will deal with this case in due course. A fingerprint on a glass in the Stockton case was apparently sent to San Francisco for comparison to a fingerprint taken from the St. Mary murder scene.[38] As far as I can determine, the press never reported as to the matching or mismatching of these prints, nor do we have any evidence that they were ever compared to Nelson's prints, taken after his arrest in Winnipeg.

≈　≈　≈

According to the death notice in the *Chronicle*,[39] Lillian St. Mary, a native of Iowa, had five surviving sisters, and she was buried in Modesto where she had previously lived and where one of her sisters still lived.[40] Various newspaper reports noted that Lillian had been divorced from her husband for about a dozen years and that her son lived with her.[41] The police eventually interviewed the ex-husband of the victim, who gave a good account of his movements on the day in question.[42]

By researching some of the surviving sisters, we discover that Lillian's maiden name was Hamilton, and while she was born in Iowa, she moved with her large farming family at an early age to Stanislaus County in California, where she grew up.[43] She had six sisters and one brother.[44] Her parents, James and Mary Hamilton, died in 1906.[45] Her oldest sister had died years before, while her only brother died at age 62 a few months before Lillian was murdered.[46]

In 1902, when she was approaching 40 years of age, Lillian married Joseph St. Mary.[47] She had been married previously.[48] Joseph St. Mary had also been married previously to a Dora (Esmah) Montrose and had several children with her. We have no record of the divorce.[49] Lillian and Joseph St. Mary had a son in 1904, and by 1910 they were living in Berkeley where Joseph was a machinist.[50] By 1920, the marriage had ended, and Lillian was listed as divorced and was the manager of a large apartment building on Mission Street in San Francisco, where she lived in one of the apartments with her 16-year-old son.[51] As noted, the move to Dolores Street was fairly recent. Curiously, we have no information as to the son's reaction to his mother's murder, nor of his subsequent life.

An added tragedy in this case occurred not long after Nelson had been hanged. On March 7, 1928, the *Oakland Tribune* carried a story about the identification of a body that had been found in the bay just off Pier 25.[52] There had been a ferryboat disaster in Oakland in which several people had drowned, but it was determined that this body was not from that incident. The body was eventually identified as that of Mr. Joseph St. Mary, the ex-husband of the woman slain by the strangler in June of 1926. Neighbors saw the aged man, coming and going, sleepless and restless, after his ex-wife had been murdered. Apparently, he was so grief-stricken that he finally ended his life by jumping off the pier.

CHAPTER 8

Ollie Russell in Santa Barbara

9. June 24, 1926—Ollie Russell, 56, Santa Barbara

Two weeks after the murder of Lillian St. Mary in San Francisco, another land-lady was murdered, this time in Santa Barbara. On Thursday, June 24, 1926, Mrs. Ollie Russell was strangled to death and then sexually assaulted at 425 Chapala Street in the rooming house that she operated, described as a "small one-story cottage."[1] Her body was discovered by her husband, George Russell, and a roomer, William Franey.

Franey, a Southern Pacific locomotive fireman working the night shift, came home to his room in the boarding house at 7:30 in the morning on the Thursday of the murder. Franey went to sleep. He woke up at about 2:30 in the afternoon to the sounds of a female and a male voice in the adjoining room, followed by various thuds, as if a trunk were being moved. Curious as to whether someone was moving in next door, Franey peered through the keyhole of a door that separated his room from the adjoining room. He saw the central portions of a man "wrestling" on the bed with what he took to be a female, judging by the pink dress material. He could not see their faces. Franey thought that some sexual encounter was taking place. He looked away but then looked again. This time he got a view of the man, who rose up from the bed, brushing back his loose hair hanging over his face. The man then placed the woman's feet down and pulled the blanket over the lower part of the body. He then saw the man wipe his brow with a handkerchief and pick up a gray fedora hat, spit on it, and brush it off as though it had a spot that needed to be removed. Then the man left the room. Franey heard the main door to the room click shut.[2]

William Franey thought that this encounter was none of his business, but never-theless, either out of curiosity or lingering concern about what he had seen, he dressed and left his room and went outside onto a back porch which ran from his room door to the door of the adjoining apartment where he had seen the man. He peered through the blinds of the window of the door for a second and saw the female form on the bed. He went back to his room and finished dressing, but on his way out he went back to the window again and peered through the blinds. This time he looked carefully at the female, who was still motionless, and he thought there was a bloodstain on the bed-spread to the left of the woman. He also thought maybe the woman was the landlady, Mrs. Russell. Had there been an accident? He decided to go around to the front of the building and ring the doorbell to arouse Mrs. Russell, but she did not come to the door. Franey then thought he ought to go and contact Mrs. Russell's husband.[3]

The billiard hall where Mr. Russell worked was only a few blocks away and

Franey started walking up the street, but then he had second thoughts. Was he interfering in some marital issue that was none of his business? He walked back to the house and rang the doorbell again, but Mrs. Russell still did not answer. He went inside and discovered the door to the Russell apartment within the house was wide open, but there was no sign of Mrs. Russell. Finally, he decided to contact George Russell, and this time Franey took his car and drove to the billiard hall.[4]

Understandably, Franey did not tell Russell what he had seen through the keyhole, but rather he suggested that Mrs. Russell seemed to be missing and might be sick. When George Russell returned to the house with Franey, he was surprised to find the door to his own rooms wide open, but the door to the bedroom in question was locked. Russell finally found a key to the door and upon entry George Russell and Franey found Mrs. Russell dead on the bed with a cord tightly wound around her neck. It was later established that the cord, used to wrap a box of billiard balls, had been found by the murderer on the premises.[5]

Chief Lester Desgrandchamp of the Santa Barbara police force immediately linked this landlady strangulation murder with the notorious strangler operating around the San Francisco area.[6] Another landlady had been hit over the head, strangled in an adjoining room, carried to the bedroom, and sexually assaulted after death.[7] It was again likely that the same "dark strangler" had gained entrance to the house by posing as a person seeking a room to rent. Various press reports also linked this case with the previous murdered landladies in San Francisco and San Jose.[8]

Given the bloodstains on the door to the bathroom and a slight fingerprint on the doorknobs of both sides of the bathroom door, the police inferred that the strangler had murdered Mrs. Russell in the bathroom and then dragged her lifeless body to the bed, where the attack witnessed by Franey through the keyhole took place.[9] One of the local newspapers noted that the fingerprints found on the doorknob of the bathroom door probably would be too vague to prove of value, but a greasy handprint on the bedspread might yield fingerprints.[10] The other local newspaper eventually reported that a bloody thumbprint on the door casing between the kitchen and the bedroom might serve as a clue.[11]

Franey stated that the man "was about 35 years old and looked like a foreign laborer. His bushy, sandy hair was his most prominent characteristic. He did not seem to be excited or frightened."[12] The description of hair color does not seem to match Earle Nelson who was usually described as having dark hair. However, when Nelson was arrested in Killarney, Manitoba, a local journalist on the train carrying Nelson to Winnipeg stated that "his hair is dark and looks to be of fine texture…. As light catches it on top, it loses its dark shade, which may have given rise to the story of an occasional red glint."[13]

Since the body was found only about an hour after the murder, the Santa Barbara police immediately dispatched officers to all the rooming houses, hotels, and "hobo hangouts" searching for anyone that might fit the description given by Franey. The police also sent out bulletins to all the surrounding areas. A young man was arrested on the highway near Los Alamos because he fit the description,[14] but when he was lodged in the jail in Santa Barbara, Franey could not identify him.[15] At this point, Franey was also detained in the jail. He was now the prime suspect.

Thus, instead of searching for the "dark strangler," the police suspected that Franey was the culprit. The police had trouble with his story.[16] Franey stated he had looked through the keyhole at 2:30 in the afternoon, while a next-door neighbor lady allegedly asserted that Mrs. Russell had phoned her sometime between 3 and 3:30 and then said, "I have to hang up now; someone is at the front door."[17] Then Captain Kelly of the Santa Barbara police looked through the keyhole and doubted that Franey had told the truth, because, according to Kelly, "it was possible to see only a small portion of the bed, and that under no circumstances could either the face or the feet of any of the occupants be seen."[18] This seems to have ignored Franey's own statement that he only saw the face of the killer when the man got off the bed. The police also looked through the blinds of the window of the bedroom and claimed that Franey could not have seen the blood spot on the bed because the body was between the window and the bed and would have blocked the view of the bloodstain. Further suspicion surrounded Franey because of the greasy handprint on the bloodstained bedspread. Franey, as a person working on the railroads, reportedly had greasy hands.[19]

Franey's clothes and room were examined and Franey underwent several days of intense police grilling. As reported in the local press:

> Slumped wearily in a chair yesterday afternoon, Franey plainly showed signs of the long grilling he had received. "This is an awful affair," he said. "It seems terrible that a fiend who would do a thing like that should happen to pick the room next to mine. But I can't tell them any more than I have. Everything that I have said is true, and I can show them it is. But I'm in a bad way, just the same."[20]

At the request of Clarence Ward, the district attorney, a criminologist by the name of J. Clark Sellers was brought in from Los Angeles to direct the investigation of the crime. Various items were gathered by Sellers to take back to his lab in Los Angeles. Finally, by the time of the inquest, Franey's story was accepted. Mr. Sellers admitted that everything Franey had said was not a product of imagination but was entirely plausible.[21] The police released Franey when the inquest jury determined that Mrs. Russell had been killed by an unknown degenerate, code words for the reality that Mrs. Russell had not only been strangled but also sexually assaulted, probably after death.[22] The chief autopsy surgeon also noted that there were many severe abrasions on the head and some on the left shoulder. Mrs. Russell had furiously fought the strangler before he succeeded in killing her.[23] The thumbprint on the door was sent to the state bureau of identification.[24]

≈ ≈ ≈

Mrs. Ollie Russell was born Ollie Belle Anstine in Galesburg, Knox County, Illinois, in 1870.[25] She was married there in 1892 at the age of 22 to Charles Freeman who was 36. A child named Ruby Marjorie Freeman was born in 1893. We do not know if Charles died or whether Ollie and Charles were divorced, but in November 1897 Ollie Freeman married Harry Minter Trostle in Cook County, Illinois.[26] She was 27 and he was 30. She brought her child, Ruby Marjorie Freeman, to the marriage, while he brought his child, Mary Eva Trostle, to the marriage. Harry Trostle was previously married in Knox County to Anna Norquist in 1889. The Trostles lived for various periods in Illinois, in Tucson, Arizona, and in Los Angeles.[27] In Los Angeles, Ollie Trostle had a series of positions as manager or proprietor of rooming houses and hotels.[28] By 1913, Harry and Ollie were no longer living together at the same address, and we presume they got a divorce or perhaps never bothered. In the census of 1920, Ollie Trostle, age 49, was listed as a "widowed" landlady-proprietor of apartments in Los Angeles and living with her widowed mother, Lucy Anstine, age 67, at 953 Santee Street. Harry Trostle was listed as a "widower" and living in San Diego. He died in San Diego in 1929.[29]

By 1921 Ollie was married for a third time as indicated by a will she made in Los Angeles in February 1921, giving all her property to her married daughter, Ruby Marjorie Miller, but for $1,000 to her new husband, George W. Russell.[30] At some point George and Ollie Russell

Murder victim Ollie (Anstine) Russell (family search.org.)

moved to Santa Barbara where George Russell eventually operated a billiards hall at 622 State Street. They lived at 1327 Anacapa, and Ollie's mother, Lucy Anstine, lived with them.[31] After the death of Lucy in 1925, the residence on Anacapa was turned into a temporary Salvation Army home and the Russells moved a few blocks away to the little rooming house at 425 Chapala Street. It was here that Ollie Russell was murdered on June 24, 1926, precisely a year after her mother had died. Ollie's body was sent back to Knox County, Illinois, to be buried in the Knoxville Cemetery.[32]

≈ ≈ ≈

It was noted in the newspapers about a week after the murder that the search for the killer was now especially focused on Los Angeles,[33] where police chief Desgrandchamp was called to an all-day meeting.[34] Also a more detailed description of the wanted man was circulated in Los Angeles and in Santa Barbara.[35] This description seemed to go well beyond any information that the keyhole witness had provided, yet the source of the information and the reason for the focus on Los Angeles was kept secret from the press. The published description by the Los Angeles police stated:

> Nationality probably Greek, age about 35 years, height 5 feet 7 or 8 inches, medium build, rather high cheek bones, dark skin, rather thin face; long wavy sandy hair; hair not long on

sides, but on top; looks like a laborer; was dressed in a dark gray suit, and rather shabby. Wore a tan colored J.B. Stetson hat, size 7⅛ or 7¼, made for the Maxwell Company, of either Fresno or Stockton; hat bears initial "G.W.R." punched on inside band, and also has a Masonic emblem posted in the crown inside of hat. Hat is probably large for him.[36]

We may infer from this wanted poster that the strangler had taken a hat belonging to Mr. Russell when he left the house and, as we will soon see, had left his own blood-stained hat at the premises. This would be the hat that Franey saw the man try to clean. But what about the other details and the focus on Los Angeles?

While the press at the time did not know the details, after the arrest of Nelson about a year later, the police in Winnipeg were given the story. The Los Angeles police requested a copy of Nelson's picture and fingerprints from Winnipeg.[37] Attached to the letter to Winnipeg was a long narrative that the Los Angeles officers had written and sent to the Portland police in relation to several murders in that city, which we will eventually deal with. The Los Angeles police officials noted that on the morning of June 24, 1926, the day of Mrs. Russell's murder, a Mr. Henry Hyde, operator of the Knickerbocker Hotel in San Francisco, left that city in his Hudson automobile intending to drive to Los Angeles.[38] Just north of Santa Barbara, Hyde was "flagged by a man who was tramping along the highway, and when Hyde stopped, the stranger asked him for a ride."[39] The hitchhiker said he wanted a ride to Los Angeles and Hyde was happy to take him because Hyde had never driven to Los Angeles before and was hoping that this fellow would help him "to keep on the right road."[40]

At about 10 in the morning, Hyde and his passenger stopped for a bite to eat in Santa Barbara, leaving that city about a half hour later. But then about six or seven miles south of Santa Barbara, Hyde had a collision with a truck, which damaged the radiator and headlights of his car. Hyde left the car with the hitchhiker while he hitched his own ride back to Santa Barbara to get a tow truck to pick up the car to get it fixed. When Hyde returned with the tow truck, he suggested that his passenger come back with him to Santa Barbara while the car was being fixed and then they would drive on to Los Angeles.

When they arrived back in Santa Barbara about noon, Hyde and the stranger went to a bank, where Hyde attempted to cash a check. In a somewhat bizarre series of events as later summarized by police,

the attaché of the bank became suspicious and would not cash the same and secretly sent word to the police department. It seems that a few days previous to this someone had defrauded this bank with a bad check, and this caused the bank employee to hold Hyde on suspicion. Hyde and the stranger left the bank and while in that vicinity two plain clothes men of the Santa Barbara department stopped them and questioned them as to their identity and the reason for attempting to cash the check. During this conversation the attention of the two officers was directed to Hyde and they gave the stranger with him but little notice…. Hyde being a businessman and belonging to different organizations had but little difficulty in establishing his identity. The stranger when searched had no money on him and Hyde vouched that he had picked him up on the road north of Santa Barbara and that he was just riding with him to Los Angeles. Due to the fact that the officers paid more attention to Hyde than they did to the stranger, they remembered Hyde's name and address, but forgot the name of the stranger—other than they remembered that it was a peculiar foreign name.[41]

After talking with the police, Hyde and the stranger went to a barber shop where Hyde, wanting a shave and haircut, had to wait a considerable time for other customers to be serviced first. The hitchhiker then stated that he wanted to go to the YMCA, "where they could find a place to sit down and find papers and books to read."[42] Hyde then told the stranger to go there for a time and then meet up with him at the garage where the car was being repaired. After his shave, Hyde made his way back to the repair shop and ran into the hitchhiker walking down Chapala Street. According to Hyde's later recollection, the stranger was now wearing a different hat than he had worn earlier. Hyde and the stranger had been separated from each other for maybe an hour and a half or an hour and 45 minutes, according to Hyde's estimation.[43]

The Los Angeles police now noted that Mrs. Russell on Chapala Street was strangled during this period and furthermore "the fiend responsible for this murder … attempted to wash bloodstains from his hat, but not being successful left the hat and took one of Mr. Russell's."[44] The hat that the murderer left at the scene was later identified as having come from a clothing store in Los Angeles. Los Angeles police officers later "were told by the clerk to whom the hat was shown that they had only a few hats of that style and make, and that he remembered selling the hat about 12 to 18 months before to a dark-skinned man described as being 5'7" or 8" tall." The clerk said he was "a swarthy complexioned man, who appeared to be a foreigner of some sort."[45]

At about 5:30 in the evening the car was finally repaired, and Hyde and his passenger left Santa Barbara for Los Angeles. Hyde reported in retrospect that the hitchhiker now "seemed excited and was perspiring."[46] As they traveled to Los Angeles, the passenger in his conversations presented himself as someone who had worked at various restaurants, both in San Francisco and in Los Angeles. When they arrived in Los Angeles, Hyde put his car into a garage on South Main Street at about 10:30, and then Hyde and his passenger ate at a café, where the stranger said he had worked at one time. When the stranger departed, he agreed that he would meet Hyde the next day at the garage where the car was now parked.

The hitchhiker never showed up the next day. Instead, the police in Santa Barbara remembered Hyde and the stranger from the incident at the bank, and they contacted the Los Angeles police, because that is where the men said they were going. We are not told how the Los Angeles police found Hyde, but evidently, they had no trouble doing so, and Hyde was taken to the Los Angeles police station, where he was kept for several days as police tried to locate the stranger that he had given a ride to. Police in Los Angeles were convinced that it was this hitchhiker who had murdered Mrs. Ollie Russell in Santa Barbara and that the description by the "keyhole" witness and the description of Hyde's passenger matched. There was also the description given by the clerk in Los Angeles who had sold the hat found at the crime scene. As noted by the Los Angeles police:

> We had an order issued in the Daily Bulletin of this Department to canvas every restaurant in this city in search for the suspect. We located many Greeks working in restaurants, but after investigation didn't get the right one. Also, due the fact that we felt morally certain that the murderous maniac was at large in this city, every man available was pressed into service on this detail, as we feared that some woman, under the same circumstances as occurred in San Francisco, San Jose, and Santa Barbara, might be another victim here.[47]

Franey was also brought up to Los Angeles to help in the identification of various suspects that might be found in the so-called Greek district of Los Angeles.[48] The police in Los Angeles believed that the suspect was scared out of town because the local press had published information on the investigation that should not have been published.[49]

≈   ≈   ≈

Over the next several months various suspects were arrested and released.[50] The most promising suspect was arrested in Needles on August 5, 1926, and sentenced to 10 days in the city jail for trespassing.[51] While in jail, Phillip Brown supposedly confessed to being the "dark strangler" who had killed women in a half dozen cities including San Francisco, San Jose, and Santa Barbara and had "attacked" a half dozen more in various places.[52] The sheriff of San Bernardino County transported Brown from Needles to the county jail in San Bernardino, and numerous stories in the press alleged that the strangler had finally been caught.[53] Brown was described as being 31 years old, dark complexioned and five feet, eight inches tall.[54] At the same time that Brown was confessing to being the strangler, another man, Thomas Johnson, an escapee from an insane asylum, was making the same confession in a Seattle police station.[55] As far as the murder of Russell was concerned, the confession of Brown took center stage. Thomas Johnson wanted the credit and was "peeved" at the attention given to Brown.[56]

While Brown's so-called confession was full of incoherent timelines and inconsistent details, the police thought that he knew too much about the Russell murder.[57] While much of Brown's confession was no doubt fed to him by the interviewer, one report suggested that Brown knew more information than could be found in the newspapers.[58] However, the *Los Angeles Times* reported that

> for the most part, he appeared to have a tendency to say what his questioner wished. He responded, as a rule, to leading questions by following the apparent lead. He was shabbily dressed and wore a black felt hat far back on his head. His body is thin and stooped; his fingers long and double-jointed.... In his confession, Brown, in rambling fashion, named himself as the attacker and slayer of a dozen middle-aged women.... Closely questioned as to dates and circumstances of the various stranglings, Brown apparently became befuddled and contradicted himself repeatedly.[59]

Another report stated that police officers believed "that Brown's mentality has reached almost the vanishing point, due to disease and narcotics."[60] In any case, Brown was transported to Santa Barbara to face murder charges for killing Mrs. Russell.

It turned out that Phillip Brown's real name was Paul Cameron and he was a 28-year-old former prison convict who had escaped from an insane asylum in Patton and was a narcotics addict.[61] Brown was brought to San Fernando, where Franey was working at the time, and Franey looked through a keyhole at the prisoner.[62] Franey's identification was "most positive" as reported by San Fernando police officials.[63] One report stated that Franey was "certain" that Brown was indeed the man he saw through the keyhole.[64] However, the local press reported that Franey "was unable to positively identify Cameron as the man he saw in the room with Mrs.

Russell, but that Cameron *resem-bled* the strangler in general build and appearance."[65] Then Merton Newman, the witness from San Francisco, was shown a picture of Brown whom he did not iden-tify,[66] but then Newman was brought to Santa Barbara to see the suspect in person. Newman declared that Brown did not re-semble the man who killed Miss Newman back in February.[67] I assume that Hyde was also asked to identify Brown, but I have no report as to this. I also assume that Hyde would immediately have dismissed Brown as the man who was the hitchhiker.

I think that it would be easy for an eyewitness like Franey look-ing through a keyhole to mistak-enly identify Brown as the man he had seen rather than Earle Nel-son. The prisoner seemed to enjoy all the attention he was receiving and gladly posed for photogra-phers.

Brown changed his tune when taken to Santa Barbara and told he would be charged with the murder of Russell. Now he asserted his innocence, repudiat-ing his confessions and demand-

Suspect "Phillip Brown" who falsely confessed and then was falsely identified as the murderer of Russell (*Santa Cruz Evening News*, Aug. 12, 1926, at 1).

ing a jury trial.[68] Brown reportedly stated, "I did not confess to anything. They told me that I did this and that, that I was here and there. It didn't do me any good to say no, so I said yes."[69] However, the police were not about to charge Mr. Brown until Mr. J. Clark Sellers, the Los Angeles criminologist, examined the prisoner and reviewed the evidence in relation to him.[70] Furthermore, it was obvious to district attorney Ward that Brown would be declared insane in any criminal proceeding.[71]

The innocence of Brown was soon apparent. Another "dark strangler" mur-der took place, this time in Oakland, while Mr. Brown was in custody, obviously vitiating his earlier claim to the title. I will examine this murder in the next chap-ter. Then came the announcement that Brown could not have murdered Russell on June 24 because he was employed at the Salvation Army headquarters in Los Angeles from June 20 through June 26, where he picked up his pay every night when he quit

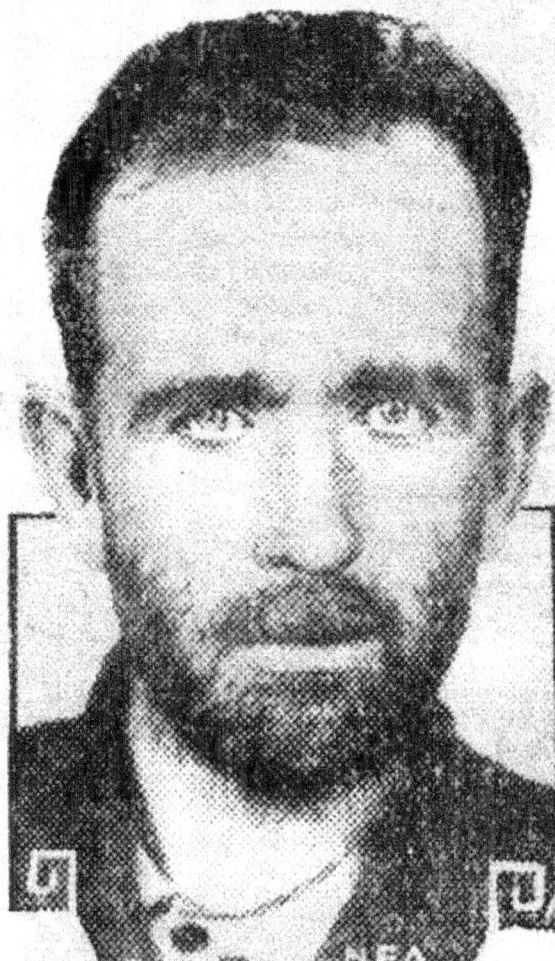

work.[72] Dr. N.H. Brush, a psychiatrist, subsequently reported to district attorney Ward that Brown was mentally incompetent and should be returned to the asylum.[73] So another "dark strangler" suspect was exonerated, despite the positive identification by a witness, and the police were back on the hunt. The process of getting Brown committed took some time, and as late as September 1926, Brown was still locked up in Santa Barbara.[74]

The search for the strangler continued. None of the suspects turned out to be the wanted man.[75] We also have no evidence that Mr. Russell's hat, described in detail, was ever discovered in a second-hand shop somewhere.

≈ ≈ ≈

After Nelson was arrested in Winnipeg, Franey now identified him as the man whom he had seen through the keyhole. The *Los Angeles Times* reported that Nelson had been linked to the murder of Russell "through fingerprints and photographs" including this identification by Franey.[76] However, we do not have any official confirmation of the fingerprint matching, and indeed the local press had described the fingerprints as indistinct.[77] The most important link was that Henry Hyde in San Francisco positively identified Nelson as the hitchhiker, based on the pictures of Nelson sent to the Los Angeles police. The eventual news as to this did not come from Los Angeles but rather from Chief D.J. O'Brien of the San Francisco police, given that Hyde lived in San Francisco. Chief O'Brien stated that the pictures of Nelson were shown to Hyde and "he stated that these photographs are of the man whom he picked up on the highway and brought to Santa Barbara…. Hyde further states that the appearance of the man at that time was identical with the first photograph forwarded to us from Winnipeg, which shows the prisoner before he was shaven."[78] The chief of police in Santa Barbara confirmed the positive identification of Nelson by Hyde.[79]

Whatever difficulties we have with eyewitness testimony, especially when the witness is presented with photos of only the suspect, rather than including the suspect's picture within an array of photos of similar-looking people, this identification of Nelson as Hyde's hitchhiker provides a very strong link between Nelson and the Russell murder, if we assume that the hitchhiker in fact was the strangler of Mrs. Russell, which seems like a reasonable assumption given the circumstances. Unlike Merton Newman, who had a fleeting glance of and conversation with the strangler, or Franey, who saw someone at a distance through a keyhole, Hyde spent a whole day with the man—talking to him, eating several meals with him, and having a variety of experiences in different settings with him.

Before the trial of Nelson in Winnipeg, the police in Santa Barbara stated that they wanted to bring Nelson to Santa Barbara to face a murder charge, given the identification of Nelson by Henry Hyde.[80] However, district attorney Clarence Ward asserted that Nelson should be tried first in Winnipeg, and "it would be foolish to make such a request since he [Nelson] has a better chance to hang in Canada than he has in California where insanity defenses often free degenerates of this kind."[81]

CHAPTER 9

Mary Nisbet in Oakland

10. August 16, 1926—Mary Nisbet, 52, Oakland

The fifth murder ultimately attributed to Nelson on the so-called official list took place in Oakland on the Monday afternoon of August 16, 1926, when Mrs. Mary C. Nisbet, 52 years old, was strangled in a vacant apartment at 525 27th Street. She was the manager of the apartment house.[1]

Mary's husband, Stephen Nisbet, a janitor at a school, arrived home at about six in the evening and found the door to the apartment that he shared with his wife wide open. Some food was on the stove ready to be cooked for supper, but there was no sign of his wife. Time passed, and Mr. Nisbet grew more apprehensive. He searched the apartment and finally went around to the neighbors. According to them his wife was last seen at 11 in the morning going out to shop. Later, other witnesses had seen her making her way back to the house, groceries in hand, at about two in the afternoon.[2] Mr. Nisbet went to the police station around 8 p.m. to report his wife missing and then returned home.[3] He finally decided to search the vacant apartment. According to the *Oakland Tribune*, "he entered the rear door, which was unlocked, but found the door leading into the living-room and front part of the house firmly fastened. He got the keys and entered by the front door. Opening the bathroom door in the dimly lit place, he struck an object with his feet. Switching on the light, he discovered Mrs. Nisbet's body, with clothes torn and a towel around her neck."[4] He screamed out an alarm, and a man visiting a neighboring tenant lady came over and they carried the body of Mrs. Nisbet to the dining room of the Nisbet apartment. Mr. Nisbet did not even initially notice the towel around his wife's neck until it was pointed out to him by the man helping to move the body.

Mr. Nisbet may well have initially considered that his wife had collapsed. Unlike the local *Tribune* story that the men had moved the body all the way to the Nisbet apartment, the rival *Post-Enquirer* reported that the body was moved from the bathroom floor and into the main room of the vacant apartment.[5] In any event, the first person summoned to the scene was a medical doctor as opposed to the police, again supporting the view that Nisbet probably initially thought that his wife had collapsed.

After the doctor pronounced her dead and the police arrived, the officials discovered that the woman's clothing had been torn but her body showed only four small bruises on the right arm and two slight scratches on the cheek, and Mrs. Nisbet was still wearing her glasses, with a rough towel tightly knotted about her throat.[6] The ordinarily staid *San Francisco Chronicle* presented the scene as having a great deal more violence associated with it:

> Mrs. Nisbet had apparently put up a terrific struggle for her life when the strangler garroted her from behind. Her clothing was torn, her hair disheveled and there were large bruises on the body—showing the violence used by the strangler in choking his victim. The towel had been knotted from behind and the dead woman's face was blue and bruised, as the strangler apparently had beaten her face and head against the floor in his attack on her.[7]

Several women tenants vacated the apartment house after the discovery of the body, "refusing to spend the night in the building."[8]

The first reports made no mention of a sexual attack, but several days later Dr. O.D. Hamlin indicated that Mrs. Nisbet had been sexually assaulted.[9] The vacant apartment had no linen in it. The most plausible explanation for the towel found around the victim's neck was that Mrs. Nisbet was preparing food for supper and had the towel in her hands or slung over her shoulder as she was interrupted by the man seeking to look at a vacant apartment.

Mr. Nisbet reportedly stated that he could not find his wife's purse.[10] The next day the purse was still not found.[11] The introduction of robbery as a secondary motive in relation to Earle Nelson makes sense. Assuming that Nelson had been working and living at the Arnold estate as a gardener, arguably he would not need to support himself by robbery in the local California murders until now, unlike the murders that he may have committed in 1925. As we will see, many of the subsequent strangler murders involved theft of jewelry and money, as did the murder of Mrs. Patterson in Winnipeg. It seems plausible that Nelson lost his room and board with the Arnold family at about this time in August of 1926. As we have noted previously, it is unfortunate that the Arnold affidavit does not make it clear just when Nelson was dismissed.[12]

The two most promising clues came from two eyewitnesses who claimed they saw the "dark strangler" near the scene of the crime. One was a mailman, David Atwood, who saw a man hanging about the

Murder victim Mary Nisbet (*Oakland Tribune*, Aug. 17, 1926, at 1).

premises at the bottom of the stairs before Mrs. Nisbet was murdered. The man allegedly watched the mailman and did not enter the Nisbet house until the mailman proceeded on his route. He was described by the mailman as dark, broad shouldered, and foreign looking with a "peculiar, ghastly smile that sent shivers up and down my spine."[13] The mailman stated,

> I had [previously] noticed a man loitering around the neighborhood. Yesterday about 2:30 or 3 o'clock I left mail at the Nisbet home. As I proceeded down the steps, I noticed this man standing at one side at the foot of the steps. I spoke to him, but at the time the thought ran through my head that he might be a mail thief, as something about him struck me as being mysterious. I scanned the face closely and I was struck forcibly by the peculiar gleam of his eye and something strange in his smile.[14]

The Nisbet apartment house at 525 27th Street, Oakland (*Oakland Post-Enquirer*, Aug. 17, 1926, at 1).

An eyewitness, of course, is subject to having their original memories contaminated by the information they subsequently receive. The mailman had gone to the police after reading about the case in the newspapers.[15]

Whether independently or by post-event information, a similar reference to a "strange man with a strange smile" was made by a female tenant, Miss Charlotte Jaffey, living in another apartment in the house who claimed she also saw the man in question.[16] According to the *Chronicle*, "Miss Jaffey said she left her apartment about 2:30 on Monday afternoon and that she noticed a man on the steps. He smiled at her and half spoke, she said, but she continued down the street and paid no further attention to him."[17] The man had "tipped his hat to her" as she passed him.[18] A different report was that Miss Jaffey saw the man leave the premises when she passed him in the hallway inside the house when she returned at about three in the afternoon.[19]

Apparently, Stephen Nisbet was held in jail while the authorities investigated his story.[20] He was cooperative with the police, who claimed he was held not as a suspect but because he was so distraught that the police thought he might harm himself.[21] The police turned their attention to trying to match the description given by the mailman to someone on the local "moron's list" of degenerates known to have attacked women or children.[22] Fingerprints were lifted from the bathroom and living room, and the police claimed they would make an arrest in 24 hours.[23] How wrong they were.

≈   ≈   ≈

Mrs. Mary Nisbet was born Mary Cardoza in 1874 in Alameda County, California. Her father and mother were immigrants from the Azores Islands of Portugal.[24] In 1892 she married John C. Vargas, a Portuguese man 10 years her senior, who had been born in the Azores.[25] John and Mary farmed for several decades near San Leandro, California, and had four children, two daughters and two sons.[26] By the time of the United States Census of 1920, John and Mary were separated or divorced. John Vargas was listed as widowed, which, as we have previously noted with Mrs. Ollie Russell, seems to have been a designation used to avoid the stigma of divorce. John Vargas continued to operate the farm for several decades and died in 1944.[27] Meanwhile, Mary Cardoza Vargas became Mrs. Nisbet in 1921, when at the age of 46 she married Stephen W. Nisbet.[28] Stephen was born in Canada in 1875, immigrated to the United States in 1892, and was listed in the 1920 Census as divorced.[29]

Mary and Stephen had only been married for five years when she was murdered. Many newspapers reported that they were a very happy couple. "My how I love you," were the last words Stephen Nisbet heard from his wife when he left for work on that fateful day.[30] Mary Nisbet's elderly parents, Mr. and Mrs. Cardoza, were still alive, living in San Leandro, but the news of the death of their daughter "put them in critical condition."[31] Mary Nisbet was buried at Holy Sepulchre Cemetery in Hayward, a community just south of Oakland.[32] Stephen Nisbet, who died in 1953, is buried with her.[33]

≈   ≈   ≈

The strangulation and sexual assault of this landlady in Oakland by a man posing as a prospective tenant was obviously immediately linked to the previous landlady killings in California in 1926. After Nelson was arrested in Manitoba, it was reported that the Oakland police were convinced that Nelson was the murderer of Mrs. Nisbet.[34] When the photos of Nelson were circulated, the Oakland police were also provided with Nelson's handwriting. Oakland police officers checked all the rooming house registers in the city. In one rooming house they found that "Earl Wilson" had registered on August 26, 1926. This would be 10 days after the murder of Mrs. Nisbet. "Virgil Wilson" was one of the numerous aliases Nelson had used in Canada and was the name he had used when signing a hotel register in Arcola, Saskatchewan. According to the initial assessment by the police, the handwriting on the Oakland register was "strikingly" similar to the handwriting of Nelson sent by Winnipeg police. When they showed the pictures of Nelson to the landlady, she said the pictures "strongly resembled" the man who had rented a room at her establishment, the location of which the police chose not to divulge to the press.[35] Furthermore, this "Earl Wilson" had asked for a room away from the street where little noise would come through the window. When he took the room, he apparently asked the landlady to bring him a towel. She was afraid to do so and sent her husband with the towel. "Wilson" took the towel, laid it on the bed, and very shortly left the establishment without returning even though he had paid several days in advance.[36]

We presume that Nelson's picture was shown to the mailman and to the lady boarder, but we have no reports as to their identification, one way or the other.

CHAPTER 10

Isabelle Gallegos in Stockton

11. August 17, 1926—Isabelle Gallegos, 75, Stockton

Another landlady, 75-year-old Isabelle Gallegos, with a "rooms to let" sign in her window, was strangled in Stockton at 1230 East Channel Street on Tuesday, August 17, one day after the murder of Mrs. Nisbet in Oakland. The Gallegos residence was described as "old fashioned and situated about two blocks from the railroad in a cheap residential section."[1]

Mrs. Gallegos was alone at the house because she had no roomers but was looking for one. The victim's body was found on Wednesday, August 18, the day after the murder, when a former roomer, Mr. C.C. Parlett, came by at about three in the afternoon to see if there was some mail for him. He found the front door locked and went in through an unlocked back door. According to the narrative in the *San Francisco Call and Post*:

> In opposite corners of the kitchen lay Mrs. Gallegos' shoes. The furniture was slightly disarranged. Parlett investigated. In the middle bedroom he came upon a tumbled bed. Beside it on the floor, a pair of woman's stockings. In the front bedroom, lying half-clothed in a kimono across the bed, with her feet dangling on the floor, he found Mrs. Gallegos, dead by strangulation. Her clothing was torn and disarranged. A bureau scarf had been knotted tightly around her throat. The room itself had been thoroughly searched, drawers pulled out, contents tumbled about. But a money belt [hidden in her clothing] containing $130 in currency and a $20 check were undisturbed. Horrified, Parlett ran for assistance…. Investigation in the house where the crime was committed shows a number of cigarette stubs of hand rolled cigarettes. [The victim only smoked the ready-made variety.] They were found in the kitchen where the woman was first attacked. The evidence indicated that she had a caller late Tuesday night to whom she sat and talked for some time. Some time during this visit or shortly afterward the murder took place, detectives say….[2]

The subsequent police investigation revealed that "the twisted scarf had not been the cause of death, the aged woman having been throttled by her murderer and the scarf tied on afterward."[3] Because the time of death was likely in the evening, unlike the "dark strangler" afternoon appointments, "it is the theory of the Stockton authorities that the strangling of Mrs. Gallegos is the work of a local murderer who staged certain effects for sensationalism, and that a degenerate motive and not robbery was the actuating impulse behind the crime."[4]

As is common when we compare newspapers, the details of the crime scene varied. It was a pillow slip that was wound around her neck, and the attack started in the rear bedroom, said one newswire story.[5] It was a handkerchief around her neck, stated another report.[6] There were also conflicting stories as to the extent of the killer's supposed search for something in the drawers, with one report noting a few drawers had been opened,[7] while another stated that "the whole house had been ransacked, bureau drawers emptied, and the contents of closets scattered about the floor in the three bedrooms the house contained."[8]

A neighbor had seen Mrs. Gallegos watering her garden at about 7:30 on Tuesday evening and another lady had heard a scream at about 8:00 in the evening but thought it came from children playing. Some fingerprints were found on a water pitcher and on a glass.[9]

The vast majority of initial newspaper reports, including in the local press,[10] concluded that this was another murder of the "dark strangler," obvious by the existence of the "rooms to let" sign, the strangulation murder, and the presumption that the victim was also sexually assaulted.[11] Captain J.A. Norris of the Stockton police stated, "There was no doubt Mrs. Gallegos was choked to death by the strangler."[12] Coroner Oscar Pape also asserted that he had no doubt the murderer was the "dark strangler" because "all the evidence in this case corresponds exactly with that in the murders about the bay."[13] The *San Francisco Examiner* also implied that this was another murder involving sexual assault, "the condition of the clothing telling mutely of the unspeakable atrocity that had taken place."[14] As this murder was linked to the previous cases, so-called experts were called upon to comment on the nature of this "degenerate monster" and the puzzle that he was killing landladies past middle age.[15]

Murder victim Isabelle Gallegos (*Oakland Tribune*, Aug. 19, 1926, at 1).

However, instead of linking this murder to the "dark strangler," some of the Stockton police believed a local copycat might be to blame.[16] The most important initial reason for the copycat theory was the finding that the scarf or pillow case was tied loosely around the victim's throat after she had already been throttled to death by the killer's own hands, and this was supposedly different from the previous murders.[17] But was the winding of the scarf around the neck really an attempt by a copycat to make it look like another "dark strangler" case? One wonders if the authorities ever asked Mr. Parlett whether he loosened the cloth when he found the body, which is precisely what happened in the previous case of

The Gallegos house at 1230 East Channel Street, Stockton (*Oakland Tribune*, Aug. 19, 1926, at 1).

Mrs. Nisbet. Famed criminologist E.O. Heinrich commented on how the removal of the towel in the Nisbet case had destroyed the valuable clue in terms of how the towel was knotted.[18] Furthermore, by all accounts Mrs. Gallegos was a small, old, and frail woman and might easily have died in the hands of the killer who might only have realized that she was already dead as he was tying the fabric around her neck. In any case, the police now believed a local degenerate copycat was responsible and the emptying of drawers was just a ruse to make it look like robbery was a motive.

On Thursday, the day after the body was discovered, the delinking of the murder from previous "dark strangler" cases gained even more ground as the autopsy performed by Drs. Lynch and Sanderson indicated that Mrs. Gallegos had not been criminally assaulted,[19] and, as noted, "the 'dark strangler' invariably has feloniously attacked his victims."[20] Attempting to get confirmation that Mrs. Gallegos was not in fact sexually assaulted, I received the original coroner's record from the sheriff-coroner of San Joaquin County.[21] The report was even less revealing than the reports received from the San Francisco Medical Examiner's office. Nothing was said about performing any tests or sending tests to the lab. The cause of death was listed as "asphyxiation from strangulation at the hands of party or parties unknown.... Murder for evident purpose of robbery."

In the case of Mrs. Nisbet, most first reports on the case noted the absence of evidence of sexual assault, and then came confirmation of an assault after lab tests were done. In the case of Mrs. Gallegos, the opposite occurred. The first reports, based on both the lack of clothing and the position of the remaining clothing, assumed a sexual assault, and then purportedly the autopsy results revealed that no assault had taken place. Should we really make much of this difference? The "dark strangler" may have been satiated at times in the very act of killing, without the need for post-mortem rape. If a sexual dimension was required, perhaps the fiend masturbated without "violating" the body. Perhaps this victim, older still than most of the elderly landladies killed so far, elicited some reaction in the strangler that suppressed a desire for post-mortem sexual activity.

The police now moved from the position that evidence of a robbery motive was a ruse, to the theory that robbery, although unsuccessful, was the real motive for the murder. One of the daughters of Mrs. Gallegos told the police that people wrongly thought her mother was wealthy.[22] This morphed into a theory that robbery was the only motive, and Mrs. Gallegos was not murdered by the sought-after strangler. As reported in the local press:

> Police Chief C.W. Potter is now working on the supposition that the crime was committed by someone who was familiar with the habits of the murdered woman in her early life. It was well known that during the years that she had large amounts of money, she would not entrust it to the banks but would place it in tin cans and bury it in the back yard.... Chief Potter now believes that ... the only motive was that of robbery. Chief Potter said, "It must have been someone who knew of her early life and recent habits ... that there were no roomers then in place, and there would be no possibility of interruption. After gaining entrance and threatening her, he must have begun to beat and mistreat her in an effort to make her disclose the location of the money. It is possible that she died of fright and not of strangulation. The pillow sham was only a ruse."[23]

The delinking of the Gallegos murder by Potter continued even as no local culprit was ever charged with the murder. When Nelson was hanged in Winnipeg the local press reported that police in Stockton still believed he was not responsible for the murder of Gallegos, due to the supposedly different circumstances in this case.[24]

However, just as we have noted with the untied cloth around the throat, and the apparent lack of penetrative sexual assault, the robbery motive, if indeed it was present in this case, was not inconsistent with the theory that this was another Earle Nelson murder. As noted in the last chapter, it is plausible that Nelson did not rob victims initially because he did not need to while working as a gardener or being supported by his relatives, but as will be very apparent in subsequent cases, robbery was a frequent secondary motive when he was away from his home base or unemployed.

≈ ≈ ≈

While we believe that Mrs. Gallegos was more likely murdered by Earle Nelson than by some local person, we need to examine the history of the victim to see what other suspects emerged. Isabelle Gallegos was born in Mexico in 1850.[25] Her last name was Rivas.[26] On various census documents the date of her immigration to California varies from 1857 to 1860 to as late as 1866.[27] Isabelle gave birth to two daughters in San Francisco: Laura in 1872 and Sophia (Sophie) in 1875. Who was the father? Subsequent records relating to Laura and Sophia indicate that their maiden names were Drolet (sometimes Drollet).[28] Numerous genealogy family trees suggest the father was John E. Drolet (1863–1899), a notorious criminal, but it is impossible that he fathered a child in 1872 at the age of nine with 22-year-old Isabelle Rivas.[29] In fact, the father was John A. Drolet (1835–1906), the father of John E. Drolet.

John A. Drolet was originally from Chile and operated a grocery store in San Francisco.[30] In 1872 when Isabelle first gave birth, he was a 37-year-old married man with seven children. We have no indication that he divorced his wife to marry his mistress, Isabelle, who after the birth of her daughters eventually moved to Stockton. Back in San Francisco, John A. Drolet and his wife had three more children,[31] and then in 1888 at the age of 55, he divorced his wife and married a girl who was a few days over 15 years old who shortly after the marriage took rat poison and committed suicide.[32] He had persuaded the girl's poor family that he was a rich man with ownership of gold stock and other property, a claim that turned out to be untrue.

More scandal followed him in 1889 when he was charged with incest involving his own 13-year-old daughter named Sophie.[33] A list of his children by his marriage includes no Sophie as a child, so obviously the child was one of Isabelle's daughters. After reviewing the history of Drolet, the Chilean grocer who had divorced his wife and married a child who committed suicide, the *San Francisco Chronicle* reported:

> Many years ago, Drollet [Drolet] who was married at the time took Isabella Reavis [Revis] as his mistress and she had two children by him, one of whom is the girl Sophie…. For some time, Drollet has had his elder daughter by Isabella living with him, but he sent her back to Stockton about a fortnight ago, and ten days ago Sophie came down to the city. Her arrival was noted by the neighbors, who saw certain suspicious actions and informed the police…. Sophie finally acknowledged (to the police) that on the night of her arrival in the city her father forced her to submit to his unnatural desires, and that he had continued his beastly conduct ever since. Drollet denies the entire story and says that it is trumped up by enemies.[34]

Another newspaper suggested that John A. Drolet's "treatment of his four other (unmarried) daughters is said to have been their initial step in the life they are leading at present."[35] Several days later it was reported that Sophie was examined by Dr. Enright and found "in a most pitiable condition."[36] However, after two trials in which the jury could not agree on a verdict, the charges were dropped.[37]

When chief of police Potter fastened on the copycat theory, he turned to Mrs. Gallegos's so-called first husband as a possible suspect. As reported in the local press, however inaccurately, "the first husband was tried and convicted on a felony charge on his wife's testimony." At the time of his conviction, he was heard to say that "some day I will get you for this."[38] Of course the police soon learned that John A. Drolet had died in 1906, long before the murder of his ex-mistress.

After leaving San Francisco for Stockton, taking her two daughters with her, Isabelle, at age 29, married Blas Gallegos, a poor Mexican laborer, who was only 19 years old. She subsequently gave birth to three sons, in 1880, 1882, and 1887.[39] The marriage ended, though we do not have evidence of divorce. In numerous documents, Isabelle Gallegos listed herself as a widow.[40] As the children grew old enough to work, their main employment was in the Stockton woolen mill.[41]

At some point the "widowed" Belle Gallegos, as she called herself, owned and operated a Mexican restaurant. From local advertisements, we note that she operated The Spanish Restaurant at 105 South El Dorado Street in 1895 and then in 1896 opened the O.K. Tamale House on California Street, which continued till at least 1900.[42] In 1902 she opened Tamales Parlor. Presumably the references to hiding money in tin cans refer to this period when she was a successful businesswoman.

Isabella's oldest child, Laura Drolet, was married in Stockton in 1895,[43] and her second child, Sophia Drolet, was married in 1902.[44] The oldest son, George Gallegos, died tragically in 1906 when he was a brakeman on a train which derailed and a carload of dynamite exploded.[45] The youngest two children, Peter and Louis, were able to escape the poverty of their youth. Peter Gallegos was the foreman at a steel casting plant in Oakland when his mother died.[46] The third son, Louis Gallegos, was a successful businessman, manager of the Sunset Lumber Company in Stockton for many years and then president of the American Lumber Company in Modesto where he also was president of the Chamber of Commerce.[47]

Isabelle's young husband, Blas Gallegos, turned out to be a drug addict who acquired a lengthy criminal record. In 1881 he was charged with shooting at his "hoodlum" friend during a drunken argument while emerging out of a brothel.[48] In 1885 he caused a major disturbance while drunk in a bar, thrusting his knife into the bar when told to leave and cutting his hand in the process. He subsequently resisted arrest.[49] He was charged in 1887 with attempting to murder an ex-policeman who had once arrested him.[50] By that time he was already "notorious" within the Stockton police department as a narcotics offender.[51] After spending five months in jail, he pled guilty to a lesser charge of assault.[52] He was charged with burglary in 1892 but was not convicted because of the lack of sufficient evidence.[53] In 1911 he was arrested and confined in a hospital "after thirty years of drug use."[54] By 1920 he was in a Federal prison in McNeil Island, convicted of narcotic possession and trafficking.[55] After serving his sentence, he was arrested and jailed again briefly for cocaine possession in 1922.[56] The following year he was arrested several times again and sentenced to jail.[57]

At the time of the murder of Mrs. Gallegos in 1926, he was evidently not incarcerated. The local press reporting on the funeral of Mrs. Gallegos stated, "Just as the services were about to begin, an aged Spaniard entered the parlors to join in the last tribute. He was the estranged second husband who for years had never had more than a casual word with his wife and who many times passed her on the street as if they were absolute strangers."[58] Obviously Blas Gallegos was a suspect and was interviewed by Chief Potter both before and after the funeral. Another account noted that "he was questioned by the police but was not detained."[59] We can only conclude that he had a good alibi. Blas Gallegos was sentenced to prison again on narcotics charges in 1928[60] and was confined in the State Narcotic Hospital in San Jose in 1930.[61] He died in 1932.

≈ ≈ ≈

Over the next few days after the Nisbet and Gallegos murders, there were many reports from various women claiming to have encountered the strangler.[62] There were also various suspects arrested,[63] but the most press coverage was given to 42-year-old John Slivkoff, arrested in Sacramento.[64] Various witnesses in Oakland and San Francisco eventually viewed Slivkoff, and they all said, "No, he's not the man."[65] When the police decided that they had nothing on Slivkoff stronger than a vagrancy charge, they released him.[66]

CHAPTER 11

Elma Wells in San Francisco

12. September 26–29, 1926—Elma Wells, 35, San Francisco

More than a month passed before another divorced landlady was murdered in San Francisco in late September 1926. The body of Elma Wells was not found until Friday, October 1. All the press reports stated that she was 32 years old, but as we will note from the official records, she was 35, and the name Wells was likely an adopted one.

On the evening of the finding of the body, the coroner, Dr. Leland, wrote the following:

> The deceased was found dead in a closet of a furnished flat at 628A Guerrero Street this p.m. at about 6 o'clock by Dewey Blair, a friend of the deceased. The body was nude, and her clothes were piled on top of the body. A strong odor came from the deceased, evidently dead since [Monday] the 27th, 1926. The deceased resided at 3516 23rd St, and Dewey Blair at #404 Vicksburg St. The deceased had been associated with him in furnishing the said flat for sale at 628A Guerrero St. The deceased was last seen alive on Sept. 27, 1926. Blair stated he called at the flat, forced open a window and gained entrance, searching through the house. He found the door of the bedroom open, the closet in said room was locked. He got a key from rear door, unlocked closet door, lifting coat, found the deceased as stated above. He then notified Police officer P.J. Griffin. Blair is held by the Police.[1]

While Dr. Leland initially fixed the date of death as Monday, September 27, as we will note below, it may have been earlier on Sunday night or as late as Wednesday, September 29.

Despite numerous first reports that this was likely another strangulation murder of a landlady by the "dark strangler,"[2] the police developed the theory that Mrs. Wells (as she called herself) was murdered by an unknown jealous suitor. To test the plausibility of this, we need to find out more about the victim.

The divorced Mrs. Wells had a married brother, Edmund Willette, living in Oakland, and a sister, Mrs. Clara (Claire) Hopkins, the estranged wife of chiropractor Dr. Hopkins living in Seattle.[3] Elma Wells was listed in the official death records as born in 1891 in Elma, Washington, and her parents were Frank and Emerance (Valad) Willette, both originally from "French" Canada.[4] The mother, Emerance, was previously married and had three children before she married Frank Willette and then had three more children: Edmund in 1884, Clara in 1887 and Emma (Elma) in 1891.[5] Now calling herself Elma, perhaps in honor of her hometown, rather than Emma, she was listed in the 1910 census as a roomer in Seattle, age 19, working as a cashier in a department store.[6] In 1911 Elma Willette married George Hagen in Seattle.[7] Interestingly, given that we believe she later adopted the name of Wells, George's mother's maiden name was Wells, and this may have been the source for Elma's adoption of the name. If she married someone called Wells after her marriage to Hagen, we can find no record of it. We also have no record of when Elma and George Hagen divorced or whether George Hagen died, but in 1922, under the name Elma Wells, she married J.D. Taylor in Sacramento, California.[8] Back in Seattle, a daughter was born to her in 1924, named Claire Lorraine Taylor.[9] However, the baby died four months later. The death certificate for the child listed the father as "Lawrence" Taylor, and the mother as Elma Willette. We do not know why husband James D. Taylor was listed as "Lawrence" Taylor in the death certificate. The child died because of injuries she received in utero because of an attempted abortion during the second month of pregnancy compounded by having congenital syphilis.[10]

When the police searched Elma Wells' apartment after her murder, they found a will that gave all her property to her sister Clara (Claire) Hopkins and stated that she wanted to be cremated and her ashes put in the same urn as that of her baby.[11] There was also a note that indicated that she perhaps feared for her safety. The note stated, "My name is Elma Wells. In case of accident notify Dr. F.A. Hopkins.... Seattle."[12] After the murder of Wells, police allegedly searched for a Lawrence Wells as the ex-husband of Elma. As noted, this was probably false information, and they should have been searching for a J.D. "Lawrence" Taylor. The name Taylor is so common that we have not been able to identify the records that might be applicable.

According to press reports Elma Wells at some point after the death of her child moved to Oakland where she became the manager of or agent for apartment buildings. It was here that she met Dewey Blair, whose sister lived in one of the apartments that she was the agent for.[13] Wells and Blair eventually moved to San Francisco and went into business together, buying or leasing empty apartments, furnishing them, and then subletting or selling them when renovated and furnished. According to her sister-in-law in Oakland, the main profit was in the buying of old furniture and repainting or reupholstering the furniture and then selling it. The sister-in-law noted that Elma's career was as a milliner.[14]

Dewey Blair was only 22 years old while Elma Wells was 35, but he fell in love with her, although he claimed their relationship was not yet intimate.[15] The picture of Elma Wells' swollen body found in the San Francisco police photograph album is gruesome, given the decomposition of the body before it was found,[16] but the newspapers reported that in life she was a very "attractive" woman,[17] and the *Chronicle* added that she was "unusually attractive and always stylishly garbed."[18]

The police investigation focused on Dewey Blair, business partner and suitor, who frequently visited Wells at her apartment and even pretended to be her husband, even though he was more than 10 years her junior. Blair admitted that "several times when I went to see her at her rooming house, 3516 23rd Street, she asked me to leave because she had an appointment with another man.... I was jealous of her. There was another man. But I guess he never was a great bar between us, for I am positive that we would have been married soon if we could have sold the furniture here."[19] Another report noted that a "mystery man" had met Elma Wells only two weeks previously on Market Street and then had taken her to the theater and later escorted her to her apartment on 23rd Street.[20] "Elma was secretive about this man," said Blair. "I don't know who he was. He was violently in love and jealous."[21]

Blair and Wells had apparently rented the Guerrero apartment six weeks previous, furnished it, and renovated it for lease. Blair had put in $300, and Mrs. Wells contributed $80.[22] A different report stated Blair had put in $347 and Wells $83, and they were worried because the option on the apartment was running out and they had not been able as yet to sell the furniture or lease.[23] The advertisement that appeared in the local San Francisco papers on Thursday, September 23, 1926, about one week before the body of Elma Wells was found by Dewey Blair, stated:

> BEAUTIFULLY furnished sunny 5-rm. Flat, only $525; cheap rent; terms, Call bet. 12–3. 628 Guerrero St.[24]

There was also a sign in the window of the apartment or at the main entrance advertising the flat for rent.[25]

The folks who lived in the apartment on 23rd Street where Mrs. Wells lived claimed they had not seen her since Thursday, the day that the advertisement came out.[26] Captain of Detectives Matheson at first fixed on this date as the probable date of death, even though Dr. Leland, as noted, suggested that Wells had been last seen on Monday, the 27th. We do not have any information as to this alleged sighting. However, Dewey Blair stated that he had last seen Wells on the Saturday night of September 25 in her apartment. Thus, it is likely that Mrs. Wells was murdered on Sunday, September 26. However, it might have been later in the week as she might have stayed at Guerrero rather than returning to her own apartment. Later, when the inquest was held, it was reported that

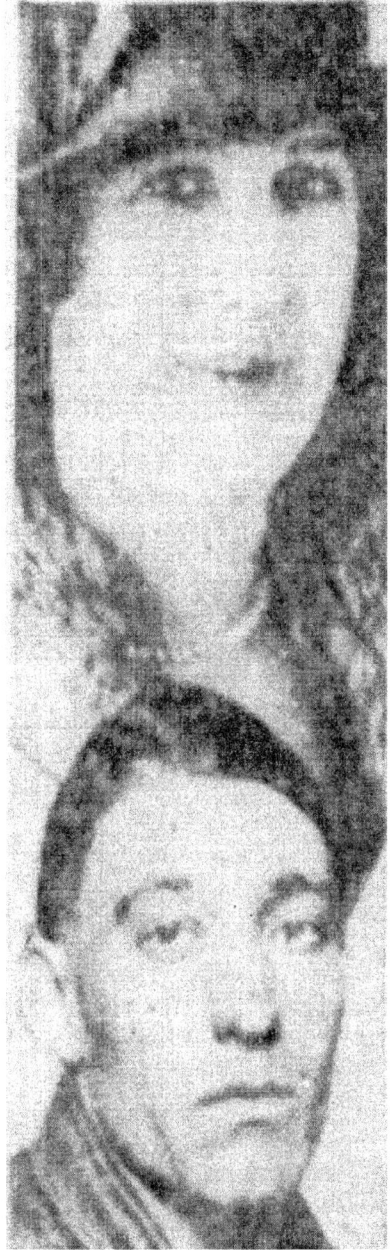

Murder victim Elma Wells and her lover, Dewey Blair (*San Francisco Examiner*, Oct. 2, 1926, at 1).

Dullea (detective) announced … that he had learned that Mrs. Wells had a large number of suitors, and that she had taken many of them to the vacant apartment in the absence of Blair. That was supported by Egan (lawyer for Blair) who said he had questioned three persons, whose names he would not disclose, who said they saw three different men go to the Guerrero Street apartment on the Sunday night [September 26] before the body was found.[27]

The implication was that these encounters were not related to showing the apartment to potential purchasers or renters.

Dewey Blair became increasingly anxious as to the disappearance of his business partner, whom he had not seen since Saturday night. He checked at her apartment every day.[28] On Thursday night, September 30, Blair returned to the apartment on 23rd Street, and when she once again did not answer the door, another neighbor, Mrs. Finn, let him into the apartment, but he could not find Mrs. Wells. The next day he decided to go to the flat on Guerrero to look for her. His story, as presented as an amalgam from various news reports, was as follows:

> "When she was missing so long, I became worried. I searched for her everywhere, including in a number of apartments that we leased. I finally came here, but the apartment was locked, so I climbed the stairs to a third-story window, and then swung outside and managed to grasp the sill of another window on the next floor. I swung myself in. I noticed a peculiar odor when passing the closet door. The door was locked. I opened it with a key from the kitchen door. There, to my horror, I found the gruesome sight," he added, pointing to the body of Mrs. Wells, which lay huddled on the floor of the closet, her clothing piled on top of her … a nude limb protruding from under the pile…. "What did I do? I dashed out and found Officer Griffin and notified him. That is all!"[29]

Blair was greatly excited when he ran out of the apartment and stopped Patrolman J. Griffin at 19th and Mission Street. The *Bulletin* also reported the scene confronting the policeman when he went with Blair to the apartment. "In a clothes closet lay the crumpled body of Mrs. Wells." She was nude, with the exception of her stockings and lingerie, which had been torn to shreds. Her throat was swollen as from strangulation. She had apparently been subjected to an assault.[30]

Dewey Blair insisted that he had nothing to do with the murder of Mrs. Wells and that the "dark strangler" was probably responsible. "I never hurt anyone in my life," he said plaintively. "And above all I would never hurt Mrs. Wells. She was a fine woman, and I thought a great deal of her."[31] Aside from the key that the owner of the building had, the only other key to the apartment was found in the coat of Mrs. Wells at the scene of her death.[32] Thus Blair, not having a key, performed his formidable acrobatics to get in. Given that the police did not believe Blair, he had to reenact the feat a second time later in the week for their satisfaction.[33]

The police investigation of the scene of the crime revealed bloody fingerprints in the closet which later proved not to be those of Blair.[34] Also as reported, "The place probably was used by Mrs. Wells and someone else as a rendezvous, for neighbors told of having heard talking there at night, although there was no light in the place. The gas and electricity had not been turned on and the detectives found a partly burned candle."[35]

Returning again to the issue of just when the murder took place, Mrs. Allison, who lived in the building, claimed that she heard noises from the apartment on Sunday "as if someone was dropping a pair of shoes, one shoe after another."[36] But then she also claimed that she saw a man answering Blair's description "sneak" out of the basement of the apartment building at four in the morning on Wednesday (September 29).[37] Mrs. Allison also claimed that sometime on Wednesday she went down to the rear basement door and tied it shut with a rope. Then she claimed that on Thursday or Friday morning she noticed that the rope had been cut, and the police said portions of the rope were found in the flat near the closet where the victim was found.[38] Mr. and Mrs. McDermott, who lived across the hall from the flat in which the body was found, reported that they were awakened in the early hours of Wednesday by the sounds of voices and a "desperate struggle" coming from the flat next door.

These reports led to the theory that the murderer had revisited the scene of the crime. Indeed, it was suggested that both the noises on Wednesday morning and the cut rope on the Thursday constituted two separate visits to the scenes of the crime, given the belief that Mrs. Wells had been murdered on Sunday or Monday. Chief Matheson now believed the murder took place on Sunday night (September 26),[39] and he "also believed the murderer visited the woman's apartment at least twice after the slaying and viewed the body."[40] It may be that the police were wrong in their theory that Wells was murdered on Sunday night or early Monday. Perhaps it was late Tuesday or the early hours of Wednesday. This still does not account for the alleged later

Illustration of Dewey Blair leaping from the staircase window in the middle section of the apartment building and up to the window of the locked flat on the right side of the building where he discovered Elma Wells' body (*San Francisco Bulletin*, Oct. 2, 1926, at 2).

story of a cut rope to the basement door and the supposed finding of the rope at the scene of the crime.

After Dr. Strange performed an autopsy, he declared he could find no evidence of strangulation and the wounds on the head of the victim might not even have been sufficient to cause death.[41] The autopsy certificate of October 2 by Dr. Strange stated, "shock from blows on head, and suffocation from confinement in small closet. Cause of death unable to be verified by autopsy due to decomposition of body." He also noted that the stomach contents were sent to a chemist and no poison was found and that some smears were sent to the hospital for examination. Results were not noted.[42] Coroner Leland expressed the theory that Wells may have been beaten into unconsciousness and then sexually attacked and then thrown into the closet where she suffocated to death.[43] Police still discounted Blair's own theory that the "dark strangler" was responsible, because Dr. Strange had determined that Mrs. Wells was not strangled, thus the "strangler" could not possibly be responsible.[44] The *Call and Post* reported that the "dark strangler" was not involved because Dr. Strange announced that "there were no marks that would indicate that she had been strangled, as first thought. He said that she had been dealt a heavy blow on the right side of the head and that there were lacerations on the left side."[45] Other reports were more ambiguous, noting that Dr. Strange could find no evidence of strangulation or sexual assault *due to the condition of the body*.[46] Was Dr. Selby Strange correct in his view that the victim was not strangled?

Dewey Blair was finally released late Wednesday, October 6, after the inquest jury found that Mrs. Wells was murdered by blows to the head by parties unknown.[47] At the inquest Detective Dullea stated that Blair had accounted for all of his time during the week previous to the discovery of the body.[48] Probably the treatment by police of Dewey Blair in keeping him in custody, holding him incommunicado, and subjecting him to the "third degree" for six days was partly driven by racism as he was half Native.[49]

Several years later, Dewey Blair married Evelyn Huntington in 1930, but they were divorced in 1938.[50] Blair spent his life as a sheet metal worker.[51] He remained single until 1955 when he married Nellie Carey.[52] He died at age 58 in 1963.

≈ ≈ ≈

While this case was not on the official list of murders of Earle Nelson eventually compiled by Archie Leonard of Portland, the Wells case was frequently listed in the press as a murder of the "dark strangler," especially after the murder of Mrs. Edmunds in San Francisco in November.[53] Some newspapers also included the Wells case on the list when Nelson was arrested in Winnipeg.[54] After the release of Blair there were no further newspaper reports as to the murder investigation of Elma Wells and the murder remained unsolved. After the arrest of Earle Nelson, the San Francisco police sent photographs and written memos to Winnipeg as to the San Francisco murders of the "dark strangler." The Wells murder was not included. We have no evidence that the San Francisco police attempted to link this case to Nelson as they did with other landlady strangulation cases. For example, were his fingerprints ever compared to the bloody prints that were allegedly compared with Blair's fingerprints?

However, Dr. Leland did not agree with chief of detectives Matheson. As we will eventually note, Leland believed that Earle Nelson was responsible for the murder of Elma Wells. We believe that Leland was probably correct. It is noteworthy that the apartment for rent or sale at 628 Guerrero was only two blocks from where Earle Nelson frequently visited with his aunt Lillian after he lost his gardening position in Palo Alto. Indeed, the site of the murder was even closer to the Nelson "home" compared to the murder of Mrs. St. Mary in the same Mission district that took place three months earlier and was officially attributed to Nelson. Even if this murder might be classified as another "butterfly" murder like that of Reed, Stone, and Williams that we have noted previously, here we have the "butterfly" as a landlady in a vacant apartment for sale or rent and therefore squarely within the *modus operandi* of Earle Nelson. Perhaps the so-called "mystery man," rival to Blair, was Earle Nelson himself who may have been courting Elma Wells before he killed her. It is also not improbable that Earle Nelson, as a necrophiliac, might have revisited a dead body for sexual purposes, if he felt it safe to do so. The nude condition of the body seems to point to a sexual attack of some kind. While the murders attributed to Nelson rarely involved completely nude corpses, it should be recalled that Lola Cowan was found completely nude in Winnipeg, as was Mrs. Anderson in 1925.

The whole case went off the rails, as it were, because Dr. Strange had concluded that Mrs. Wells had been murdered by some method other than strangulation. If we can trust that judgment, would it matter? If we place this case in context with the murders to follow in Portland, where bodies were now hidden in a trunk, behind a furnace, and in a crawl space in an attic, the hiding of the body in a locked closet seems to be consistent with Earle Nelson murders. In Portland we also see the conclusion of the medical examiner in several of the cases that there did not seem to be any signs of violence on the bodies indicating strangulation. Yet these cases ended up on the "official list" while the murder of Mrs. Wells did not.

CHAPTER 12

Beata Withers in Portland

Three mysterious deaths occurred in Portland, Oregon, on three successive days from October 19 to 21, 1926. All three women met their deaths while advertising their homes for rent. However, Portland police and medical experts initially concluded that these were not murders but were suicides in two cases and a natural death from a weak heart in the third. It was only after a fourth landlady in Portland was murdered more than a month later that these three deaths were added to the list of "dark strangler" murders.

13. October 19, 1926—Beata Withers, 36, Portland

Mrs. Beata Withers, a slender woman of 31 years of age, was last seen alive on Tuesday morning, October 19, 1926, at her home at 815 East Lincoln Street. She had placed an advertisement in the local newspapers: "Widow will share modern home with couple, or ladies; close in; very reasonable."[1] The idea that Mrs. Withers, who was divorced, would state that she was a widow perhaps indicates both the social disapproval of being divorced at this time and her own personal unease with her situation. Given the subsequent renumbering of Portland streets and avenues, the house at 815 East Lincoln is now 2525 S.E. Lincoln.[2]

On Tuesday afternoon Beata's 15-year-old son, Charles, came home from the Benson Polytechnic School to an empty house. The initial narrative in the *Oregonian* stated that Charles, with the help of a Mr. Bob Frentzel, described as being a friend of the family, eventually made various phone calls to family, friends and hospitals.[3] Not finding his mother, Charles slept alone in the house on Tuesday night. The next day Charles and Mr. Frentzel searched the house. Eventually looking for missing items of clothing, especially a coat and hat that could not be found, they went up into the unfinished attic and opened a trunk. Removing the tray of the trunk and various clothes inside the trunk, they discovered the body of Mrs. Withers packed into the trunk.

The *Oregonian* stated, "The body had been wedged in with such force that one hand caught between the two legs had been pressed so hard that it retained its natural color, despite a discoloration of the rest of the body."[4] The same paper later stated that despite being seen fully dressed earlier in the day, she was found with only "a thin house dress wrapped around her neck and arm pits."[5] The *Portland News* added, "A pair of stockings covered the lower limbs. A house dress was pulled up under the arms. The head reclined on the right arm and faced the hinged side of the trunk. The knees were drawn up, with the left arm extending between them."[6]

The *Portland Telegram* provided a much more detailed account as to what Bob Frentzel told the police about the finding of the body.[7] On Monday night, October 18, Bob and Beata had visited Bob's mother, who was in a hospital. They returned to the house after the visit and Bob left at around 11 in the evening. Mr. Frentzel noted that Beata "wore a dark, heavy, fancy dress and a dark brown coat, trimmed with dark fox fur around the neck and down the front and on the bottom edge in places. She also wore a lighter brown felt hat, recently purchased." The coat and hat, and another hat, were now missing from the house. Frentzel noted that Mrs. Withers was in a good mood that evening, speaking about finishing the cleaning of the house to rent it again and that she had renewed the advertising for the house in the papers.

The next day, Tuesday, the day of her death, Beata had phoned Bob at 10 in the morning. Bob said he had some work for her to do at his business and she agreed to meet him at two in the afternoon. She did not show up. At five in the evening, he called the house and Charles told him that he did not know where his mother was. Bob phoned again at around seven. Getting the same reply from Charles, he fulfilled a business appointment starting at eight and then phoned again at around 11 in the evening. On being informed that Mrs. Withers still was not home, Bob Frentzel came over to the house shortly before midnight with a view to calling various hospitals in case Beata might have had an accident and calling some friends. With no success in locating Beata, Bob left for his own home at about one in the morning.

On Wednesday morning, October 20, upon arriving at "his factory," Bob had a message to call Charles, who informed him that Mrs. Withers had not come home. Bob advised Charles to give him the names of every friend of his mother that he could think of and told Charles to go to school. After making numerous calls, Bob left his work and went to the Withers house at around 11 in the morning, with a view to looking for Beata's coat and making an inventory of other clothing, which might indicate that she had gone out or even decided to run away, taking clothing with her, and provide a description for a possible police report for a missing person. Finding the house locked, he went over to the neighbors, Mr. and Mrs. Cook, and called the school to have Charles sent home. When Charles arrived and unlocked the door, the first search of the house was made. Charles went to the basement, and Mr. Cook and Mr. Frentzel went to the attic.

Mr. Frentzel at first told the police he was unsure whether the door to the attic was locked,[8] but then several days later he swore that the attic door was indeed locked with the key stuck in the hole on the outside of the door. This was confirmed by Mr. Cook, who noted the key was in the lock when they arrived at the door leading up the stairs to the attic. Cook and Frentzel looked around the attic, and even opened the trunk in which the body would be subsequently found, but seeing nothing unusual, they returned to the main floor. Mr. Cook went home, and Mr. Frentzel and Charles Withers made another round of calling hospitals and friends. Charles suggested another search, and it was on this second foray to the attic that the trunk was explored. Bob Frentzel stated, "Charles reached it before I did, he having raised the lid. I assisted him in making it stay back. While I was doing this, he picked out the tray and dropped it on the floor upside down. Then we saw a lot of Charles's clothing seeming disarranged. I thereupon picked up his trousers baring the naked knee of Mrs. Withers."[9]

As to the mystery of the locked attic door, the *News* reported that apparently the police confirmed that the attic door, unless it was locked, slid open.[10] This would reinforce Frentzel's eventual recollection that the door was locked, which obviously indicated that Mrs. Withers was placed in the trunk by a third party. Charles Withers insisted that he had not locked the door in any earlier movements around the house in search of his mother.[11] However, the police notebook of detectives Moloney and Schulpius states that Frentzel was unsure as to whether the door was locked or not when first questioned on October 20 and also when questioned again on October 22.[12] I assume that if the police had been sure of the locked door the suicide theory that arose would have been discounted.

When the police were called, Detective Tackabery quickly concluded that Mrs. Withers had committed suicide by way of suffocating herself to death in the trunk, probably also taking poison before she placed herself there. She had supposedly buried herself under the clothes in the trunk and had still been able to put the tray in place and then close the lid. Supposedly, there were no marks of violence on the body or signs of any attack or resistance to attack. This suicide theory was either constructed or reinforced by a framed motto that Tackabery found hanging on the wall of Mrs. Wither's bedroom. The *Oregonian* included a picture of the "poem" titled "Then Laugh," which read:

> Build yourself a strong box/ Fashion each part with care/ When its as strong as your hand can make it/ Put all your troubles there/ Hide there all thought of your failures/ And each bitter cup that you quaff/ Lock all your heartaches within it/ Then sit on the lid and laugh!/ Tell no one else its contents/ Never its secrets share/ When you've dropped in your care and worry/ Keep them forever there/ Hide them from sight so completely/ That the world will never dream half/ Fasten the strong box securely/ Then sit on the lid and laugh![13]

"Mrs. Withers read that motto and took it too seriously," said Detective Tackabery. Supporting the suicide theory was deputy coroner Gulbrandson, who supposedly demonstrated to a reporter how any violence, even a trivial struggle, would show some bruising on a body after death. He then stated, "I have examined Mrs. Withers' body, not once but a hundred times. There is not the slightest mark to indicate that she was lifted, or pulled, or struck by anyone."[14]

As to why Beata would commit suicide, Frentzel told the police that Mrs. Withers had health issues that prevented her from keeping a job for long, that she had financial issues, and according to the *News*, Frentzel added that "her son was a great worry. His disobedience aggravated her. He takes after his father for bad temper and grows more like him as he grows older. Mrs. Withers was behind in her payments. She owed on her furniture, and inability to meet the installments was only one of the worries she had. Her mother, Mrs. Duhrkoop, who is well-to-do, refused to help her in any way. Her brother, Carl Duhrkoop, refused to aid. Her husband's family was even worse."[15] During the first day of the investigation Frentzel never mentioned his own role in why Mrs. Withers might commit suicide.

Various neighbors admitted they did not know Mrs. Withers very well, but they nevertheless gave the opinion that she was "exceptionally devoted" to her son, that she was a "frail and sensitive" person who had lost her position as a stenographer, that she had been hospitalized for three months in the winter, that she had been away all summer at the beach while the house was sublet, and that she must have been having financial problems, given that she was buying the house on the installment plan and when the neighbors entered the house on the day of the tragedy "they found no signs of anything to eat."[16]

While the police had never heard of a case of "suicide by trunk," they staged a demonstration of how one might be smothered to death by getting into the trunk. It is interesting in hindsight that not only was there a police detective in Portland named Earl Nelson and another detective named William Nelson, the demonstration of how a person could get into the trunk and close the lid over themselves was performed by yet another Nelson, namely R.L. Nelson, the driver for the coroner.[17]

While the pawn shops of Portland were being searched unsuccessfully for the missing coat, the police basically continued to investigate motives for suicide and discounted motives for murder. The suicide theory was reinforced on the second day of the investigation by the finding of a diary and the finding of a half empty bottle of mercury in the attic. The contents of the diary were disclosed to the world through the newspapers. The diary contained an account of Mrs. Withers falling in love with Mr. Frentzel, and then after a considerable period of being in a relationship with him, discovering that he was in fact a married man, unable to marry her and unwilling to get a divorce. The diary, addressed to her son, not to be read until after her death, was written about two years after she met Bob, and the last diary entries were well over a year before her death. Beata noted in the diary that she had been invited by Bob to attend a New Year's party:

> Well, Bob and I had a wonderful time and he put me in a taxi and took me home after the show. I remember it was bitter cold out, and on the way home he took me on his lap and made love to me…. Me, who had never let any man make love to me before except your father, Charles, and then not until I had known him over three years. Yes, I had fallen desperately in love that it seemed the perfectly right thing for me to let him "love me." When we got home, I made some hot chocolate and we sat over the cups a while and talked, wholly absorbed in one another. Bob told me he was divorced and had a little girl. Even told me where he got his divorce, which I believe he said, was either in Hailey, Idaho, or in Caldwell, Idaho. I had never been as happy in anyone's company before in my life. I was so wonderfully at peace with the world. I had always been lonely, looking for the person who would understand me as well as I thought he did. Poor little me. How happy one can be "when ignorance is bliss." This was the beginning of almost constant companionship between Bob and I. He was idle most of the day … making love to me. I believe it was five days after I first went out with him that we pledged our troth. I swear it, Charles, before the sight of God, we were married, and it was only because Bob told me that he had lost everything and that as soon as he made good in Silverile [his business] we would legally be married.[18]

The *Journal* gave more details from the "pathetic diary," as the paper called it. The account now turned to the discovery that Bob had lied to her about being divorced and in fact he was married and living with his wife in Portland:

> She tells of the shock when she learned that Frentzel was married and when his wife came to Portland, and also tells of the financial assistance she had given him when his business was

failing, often going without proper food and clothing to help him. "Dear God, how I have repented only too late for ever having helped him, as he has been my ruin," she says in one place. She gave up all her friends because he urged her to, she says…. On one occasion when he failed to keep an engagement with her, she wrote that he was always making excuses and that it was terrible to have to be "fairly killed by this slow process."[19]

After hearing about the diary, Bob Frentzel admitted that Beata had disliked him several years ago and had even threatened suicide, but "he said that he was positive Mrs. Withers, at the time of her death, loved him more than ever before."[20] In the culture of the 1920s the phrase "made love to me" does not necessarily mean what it implies today but could simply mean kissing and other acts of affection. The reference to being married in the sight of God, however, implies that Bob and Beata were probably fully engaged in a sexual relationship, even though he was a married man, living with his wife and child, and apparently making no immediate move to get divorced and marry Beata.

If these reports are accurate, Mr. Frentzel seems to have been quite a piece of work, not only winning Mrs. Wither's love through deception but also maligning her son and family. Frentzel, after reading the diary, stated, "That was the only happy time in my life…. I have never known true happiness and I shall never know it again. The light went out of my life when the little woman went out of the picture."[21] At the time of the inquest into Wither's death, Mr. Frentzel reportedly testified that he and Beata had plans to marry, "after we had performed our obligations to the children."[22] In the Withers' family archives are several promissory notes showing that Beata had loaned money to Mr. Frentzel in January of 1924. One note was for $180 and another note was for $450.[23] These were not insignificant sums for that era.

≈ ≈ ≈

Wallmuth (Walter) Robert (Bob) Frentzel was born in 1887 in Chicago of German immigrant parents.[24] In 1909 in Chicago he married Elsie Weyforth.[25] In 1910 they were living in Hillsboro, Oregon, just west of Portland, and they had an infant daughter, Catherine (Kathryn). Walter was a merchant in the lumber business.[26] Shortly thereafter they moved to Portland.[27] By 1920 they had moved to Boise, Idaho, where he was as a teacher[28] and Elsie ran the Knit-Wear and Bonnet Shop.[29] At some stage they moved back to Portland. In 1926, before the murder of Mrs. Withers, Frentzel was listed as the president of his company, Rafter Mitre Manufacturing Co.[30]

While it is hard to believe that their marriage would survive the massive publicity given to Frentzel's affair with Mrs. Withers, we find that Bob and Elsie continued thereafter living together in Portland. The 1930 Census listed Bob Frentzel, commercial traveler, living in Portland with Elsie and daughter Kathryn, now 20 years of age.[31] Not surprisingly, given the publicity in Portland, they eventually moved to Seattle.[32] In 1931, Frentzel was sued by an investor for allegedly misrepresenting stock in a mining company that turned out to be worthless.[33] Daughter Kathryn Frentzel was married in Seattle in 1936.[34] In 1940, W.R. Frentzel and wife, Elsie, were listed as living in Seattle where he was the president of Flexible-Forms, Inc., while Elsie was the secretary treasurer of the business.[35] Frentzel was hoping to manufacture and market a machine that he invented that supposedly restored women's dresses to their original form, either making them larger when they had shrunk or making them smaller when they had been stretched.[36] The machine probably only worked for a few kinds of fabrics and we suspect the venture did not succeed. Another reason to question Frentzel's business practices occurred when he was accused in criminal court of collecting nearly $50,000 in a fraudulent scheme of misrepresenting the manufacture and sale of crab pots to investors.[37] We do not know the outcome of the trial. During the decade of the 1950s he was often described as a building contractor.[38] He died in 1961.[39] His wife, Elsie Frentzel, died in Seattle in 1972.[40]

≈ ≈ ≈

Returning to the death of Mrs. Withers in 1926, on the second day of newspaper coverage, the *Oregonian* noted that the suicide theory was not accepted by everyone.[41] Mr. Charles Withers, the ex-husband living in Seattle, could not believe that Beata would do such a thing as commit suicide, nor did Mr. Frentzel, even if he had given police reasons for why she might do so. Furthermore, Frentzel was now quite positive that when he first came to the door leading to the attic, the key to the door was in the lock facing him in the hall and the door was locked. That meant obviously that someone had put Mrs. Withers in the trunk and locked the door when they left. Further hints of murder included the fact that the body was dressed in only a thin house dress which had been pulled up underneath the victim's armpits. Also "blood spots were found on the pillows and underneath the mattress of Mrs. Withers' bed in her room downstairs. The blood was mixed with saliva, however, and the spots might have been caused by some throat trouble."[42] Various items of clothing, including a coat, which had been highly prized by Mrs. Withers, were missing from the house. Her purse was empty.

There also were reports from neighbors that a mysterious automobile had been seen parked for some time near the Withers house on the Tuesday afternoon when she had died. Another neighbor lady had talked to Mrs. Withers just before noon on that day, and she recalled, "Mrs. Withers was working out in the yard in her dahlias…. She appeared unusually happy; she talked about plans for her garden this winter and next spring. Why, it seems impossible that a few hours later she could have crawled into the trunk and committed suicide."[43] Another neighbor stated, "She was singing and washing the windows the last time I saw her and it seems impossible that she could have taken her own life."[44] In a rather sad commentary on the condition of females of the era, the *News* had earlier noted on the list against suicide that "she was the beloved creature of at least one man, and possibly others, and could have found escape from financial difficulties through marriage."[45] Mr. Frentzel expressed the theory that the missing fur coat was used by the fiend to smother her "and then was carried away by the murderer because it was stained with blood and froth."[46]

On the murder side of the argument, it was also reported that on Monday, October 25, Carl Duhrkoop, a brother to Mrs. Withers, went to the house to find clothing to take to the funeral parlor with which to clothe his dead sister for her funeral. What he discovered was the complete absence of any underwear or stockings. He reported this to the police, as well as noting that a leather handbag and some shoes were also missing from the house.[47]

The theory that Mrs. Withers was murdered gained some precedence over the suicide theory when two other women advertising houses for rent were found dead under mysterious circumstances over the following days. On the same day that the *Sunday Oregonian* gave extensive coverage to the death of Mrs. Fluke, to be dealt with in the next chapter, the paper asserted that there was a rumor that the autopsy report would indicate that Mrs. Withers had a broken neck.[48] In fact this rumor turned out to be false, but the article also mentioned that Dr. Smith, the county coroner, believed that Mrs. Withers had been murdered, because in his opinion the condition of the body was inconsistent with the scientific evidence of suffocation, where the body at some stage involuntarily moves about violently. She had been killed and then dumped in the trunk, he concluded.[49] The eager detective who had made so much of the poem now also asserted that all three women were murdered.[50] Furthermore, for the first time in Portland, the *Oregonian* noted the similarities to the "dark strangler" murders in San Francisco.[51]

However, like a see-saw, the opinion on suicide versus strangulation by a fiend eventually swung in the suicide direction again.[52] All of the circumstantial evidence of a locked door, hidden body, theft of clothing, including undergarments, and two other deaths of landladies within the next two days in the same general area of the city were less important than the "professional" opinion of the medical examiners that it was improbable that Mrs. Withers had been murdered.[53] Even after the deaths of two more landladies, the coroner's jury consisting of two women and four men could not agree as to whether Mrs. Withers was murdered or had committed suicide. Dr. Benson reported that no poison had been found, and this was confirmed by Dr. Harold Myers. Cause of death was determined to be by suffocation, but the jury split three to three as to whether the suffocation was suicidal or homicidal. Thus, the death of Mrs. Withers was officially recorded as undetermined.[54] With some difficulties I was able to obtain and examine the autopsy report myself.[55] As to the coroner's report for Mrs. Withers we note that when the autopsy was first done on the day that she was brought to the morgue, *Dr. Benson wrote that the cause of death was strangulation.* Only later was the inquest jury verdict of October 27, 1926, that she had died of suffocation, inserted into the report.[56] There is no evidence in the report of tests done to see if there was a sexual assault.

∽ ∽ ∽

While in Portland in 2006, I visited the Portland Police Museum and met the executive director, who at that time was Lori Shea Kuechler. She put me in touch with Mrs. Nancy Salmon, granddaughter of Mrs. Withers and the oldest daughter of Charles Withers, Jr., the young teenager who had found his mother dead in the trunk back in 1926. Before the day was out, I was invited to the home of Mr. and Mrs. Salmon who kindly spent some time with me.[57] As a consequence of meeting Nancy Salmon, I have more information about Beata Withers than I do for any other victim in this book. Mrs. Salmon also gave me copies of many letters, pictures, and other documents from the family archives. The information on Mrs. Beata Withers and her husband Charles Withers and their family history is interesting but goes far beyond what readers of this book would probably want to know. We will highlight only a few biographical details.

Beata Duhrkoop, born on February 17, 1890, was married to Charles H. Withers on November 25, 1909.[58] About a year later, Charles Henry Withers III was born in Portland. Beata's husband at this point appears to have been quite successful in his architectural career. For example, he was doing architectural work for the State of Oregon designing and building the mental hospital in Salem. Charles and Beata moved to a rented farm in Stayton for a two-year period while he was supervising the building in Salem. In 1914 the family moved to Astoria where Charles designed several homes and a school. In 1916 Charles moved to Detroit and took a job with an architectural firm in that city. Eventually he was joined in Detroit by Beata and their son, Charles. Nancy Salmon recalls that she was told that Beata was an excellent seamstress and for periods of time during her marriage worked as a dressmaker out of her home.

Beata Withers and her son Charles Jr. some years before her murder in 1926 (*Oregonian*, Oct. 23, 1926, at 6).

With the entry of the United States into World War I, Charles shifted to tool design for auto manufacturers. At some point the marriage ended, and Beata took Charles Junior and moved to San Diego to live with one of her sisters, Ann, who was also divorced. In 1919 Beata moved back to Portland, moving in with her mother, Johanna Duhrkoop. According to Nancy Salmon, Charles Junior later stated that it was his mother who obtained the divorce in 1919 from Charles Senior, and in his view, "his parents were both strong willed and even though they loved each other they couldn't seem to be able to get along." For several years Beata and her son lived in the Chancellor Apartments at 3rd and Montgomery before buying the house on 30th and Lincoln.

On September 21, 1926, which is about a month before her death, Beata wrote to her sister Vera who had been or was ill. She told Vera, "I am quitting my job Saturday, as I can't stand the work. It is too much for me. I have to think of my health first, for if I get sick, there is no one who will help me…. This time of the year there are lots of jobs, but not many where they pay anything. The girls here work for next to nothing."[59] Just weeks before her death, Beata Withers spent some time (several weeks or even months) at the beach at Gearhart, Oregon, swimming, clam digging, lying in the sun and resting. There is a surviving letter that she wrote to her son dated October 4, 1926, in which Beata stated that she was having a great time and that she wished Charles could be with her.[60]

As to Beata's ex-husband, Charles Withers, after the murder he moved to Portland to look after his son. He was introduced to a woman named Viola Day sometime in 1929. They dated secretly for many years and then got married in August of 1933. Charles and Viola had a baby girl in 1934. While we have a lot more information about his career thereafter, sufficient for our purposes is that he died of leukemia at age 79 on September 10, 1966. Nancy Salmon recalled her grandfather as "a very strong, hard-working man and a wonderful storyteller."[61] His wife, Viola, lived to be almost 106 years old.

After the death of his mother, Charles Junior lived with his paternal grandmother Withers in Portland and an aunt on the Withers side, still living at home. His father lived there as well when he returned from Seattle. Charles eventually studied at Oregon State College. In 1935 he married Florence Davis, whom he had met at college while taking a secretarial training course for court reporting. They were married for 60 years and had three children, two girls and a boy. Nancy was the oldest. As she notes, "her parents were devoted to each other and joined at the hip."

Charles got a position with the Immigration Department in Seattle in 1938. This was the beginning of a long and distinguished career in which Charles climbed the ladder to high administrative positions. He moved to Tacoma in 1947, to Helena, Montana, in 1956, to Albany, New York, in 1958 and finally to Los Angeles in 1962, where he retired in 1975 and remained a resident for the rest of his life. Nancy says that in Los Angeles he was a case officer in charge of "celebrity-show business" immigration affairs and thus would get to know various celebrities. As I recall, Nancy mentioned Julie Andrews as an example. Nancy remarked that her father was very family oriented. He maintained good relations with both the Duhrkoop and Withers sides of the family and, of course, with his own children and grandchildren. He was an active Methodist and sang in church choirs and maintained an interest in classical music. He also was supportive of and involved with the Boy Scouts. Charles died in 2001, and his wife Florence died in 2003.

Presumably we all have various tragedies in and "dark sides" to our lives, but this biography of a man, living to be 90 years old, with a long and distinguished career, and devoted to wife and family, certainly seems a happy outcome for a person who could have been seriously traumatized by the circumstances of finding his mother dead in a trunk in the attic and facing the stigma in that era of the official view that his mother had probably committed suicide. As we will eventually conclude after dealing with the other murders in Portland, Mrs. Withers did not commit suicide but was very likely another murder victim of Earle Nelson.

CHAPTER 13

Mabel Fluke in Portland

14. *October 20, 1926—Mabel McDonald Fluke, 37, Portland*

Mrs. Withers died on Tuesday, October 19, 1926. The next day, Wednesday, October 20, Mrs. Mabel Fluke died, and again officials eventually struggled with whether she died of suicide or homicide. Her body was not discovered until after the third victim in a row, Mrs. Virginia Grant, was discovered on Thursday, October 21. In the case of Grant, as we will see in the next chapter, the counter narrative to homicide was a heart attack. Chronologically in terms of time of death, we will deal first with Mabel Fluke, even though she was the third body to be discovered.

Mabel Fluke was born in Helena, Montana, in 1889, one of four children of William and Annie Macdonald. In 1913 Mabel married Frank Fluke of Independence, Oregon.[1] He was a 36-year-old carpenter and Mabel was a 24-year-old housekeeper. They lived on a small ranch south of Independence for a dozen years and they may have resided briefly in the Molalla area.[2] Eventually, Mrs. Fluke and her husband traded their small ranch in the country for a house in the Westmoreland-Sellwood district of Portland across from the golf course. (After the Portland renumbering, the Fluke house at 1521 East 21st Street is now 7765 S.E. 21st Avenue). The move was made necessary by the bad health of Mr. Fluke. Indeed, on May 31, 1926, Mr. Fluke died at the age of 49 of cancer.[3]

After becoming a widow, Mabel Fluke decided to live with her parents residing at 409 Roberts Avenue in the St. Johns district of Portland. Next door to her parents lived her brother and sister-in-law. The house in Sellwood was fully paid for and Mabel had several thousand dollars in her bank account. She planned to take stenography courses when she could be admitted to the training college. In the meanwhile, she rented her fully furnished home. After the previous renters had departed, Mabel Fluke had some workmen over to the house putting in a concrete floor in the basement and installing a sewer connection. She also advertised her house for rent as follows:

> Furnished house: Five room bungalow, completely furnished, electric range, one-half block not paved, garage on paved street; reasonable to responsible party. 1521 E. 21st St. There Wednesday, 10 a.m. to 5 p.m.[4]

On that fateful Wednesday, October 20, 1926, Mabel, a tiny 37-year-old woman, only five feet, four inches tall and weighing less than a hundred pounds, bid farewell to her parents and happily made her way to her house to clean it and meet prospective tenants. When she arrived at the house she spoke cheerfully to Mrs. Schultz, the next-door neighbor, mentioning her plan to make a visit to Independence after renting her home. Mrs. Schultz subsequently saw Mabel scrubbing the front porch. Mabel Fluke visited the office of her attorney, Mr. James Stapleton, at about noon that day. He reported that Mabel Fluke was in excellent spirits when he talked to her.[5] Another neighbor, Mrs. Newton, saw Mabel work around the house and saw various parties come to the house in response to the advertisement. Mrs. Newton last saw Mabel at about one in the afternoon. At three in the afternoon a family drove up and no one answered the doorbell, so they drove away.

When Mabel did not come home on Wednesday night, her parents, Mr. and Mrs. Macdonald, assumed that Mabel had not been able to find a renter that day and had decided to simply sleep over in her fully furnished house. When she did not come home the next day, they assumed that she had gone to Independence as she had planned. However, several days later, on Friday, Mr. Macdonald received a communication from some people from Independence asking why Mabel had not kept an appointment to see them. Now the worry started. Mabel's brother, William Macdonald, went to the house on Friday night and found it locked. He climbed through an open basement window, searched the house, and found nothing amiss. However, on Saturday, October 23, the very worried father decided to search the house himself and he took Patrolman Maxwell with him.

Using a skeleton key, Maxwell entered the house with Mr. Macdonald. As reported in the *Oregonian*, "The house was found in a tidy condition throughout. There was no indication that any drawers had been ransacked. On the kitchen table was found a little package of tea, a sack with four eggs and the woman's keys. In a drawer in the buffet was found her pocketbook. There was no change in it."[6] Upstairs was a pitch-black attic crawl space under a sloping roof accessible only through a removable panel. After describing the attic and the entrance to it, the *Oregonian* continued:

> Officer Maxwell opened this entrance into the attic [thrust his flashlight within] and found the body about three feet from the entrance, lying along the wall, with the feet toward the entrance. There was a crate of extra table leaves between the feet and the panel. Only a narrow portion of the attic is floored, and the body was lying nearby. A dresser scarf was tied tightly around her neck, with a single knot in front…. The body was lying on its back, one knee slightly upraised, and both arms by its side. The woman was clad in a light house dress, which showed no evidence of any struggle having preceded the victim's death. Except for the hat, which had fallen off, and one slipper, which also was lying beside the body, the clothing was not disarranged. The woman was fully dressed.[7]

The police at first believed that "the manner in which the scarf was tied, and the fact that two knots were tightly pulled in the cloth made it difficult to believe the woman had tied it herself."[8] Other newspapers implied elements of sexual violence missing from the *Oregonian* account. According to the *Telegram*:

> About her neck was tied, tightly, a dresser scarf. It had been tied in a single knot at the front, then looped about her neck and tied in a loose double knot beneath the left ear. Her left shoe appeared to have been pulled forcibly from her foot, and it lay there, feet away, close to the panel door. Her dress was pulled up upon her chest. A brown sweater she wore was forced down off her shoulders and held her upper arms securely pinioned to her sides. Over her abdomen was spread, smoothly, a rubber apron.[9]

Similarly, the *Journal* stated:

> One of Mrs. Fluke's slippers lay about four feet from her left foot, while her hat was on the floor near her head. Around her neck was the cloth. Her light house dress and petticoat were up around her waist and the lower part of her body was clothed only in underwear. Thrown over her knees and lap was a rubber apron.[10]

In the surviving police notebooks, we find confirmation from detectives Hyde and Leonard as to the actual state of Mrs. Fluke's clothing. They wrote, "her dress was up around her waist, and she had long underwear drawers on ... one shoe was on and the other off about two feet away ... her hat was off near her head."[11] The police notebook of detectives Williams and Jewell added, "We ... noticed the electric water heater turned on, so shut it off. We noticed a stain on the bed spread near the pillow in East bedroom upstairs, and some dirt on the foot of bed spread. We noticed a good many burnt matches in a cigar tray, but no evidence of smoking."[12]

In addition to the implications of murder and sexual assault given by the location and condition of the

Murder victim Mable Fluke (*Oregonian*, Oct. 24, 1926, at 14).

body and clothing, there were obvious signs that robbery was involved. While the house was not ransacked in any way, Mrs. Fluke's pocketbook found in the buffet contained no money, and the reddish coat with black fur that she had been wearing was gone, as were the two rings that she had been wearing. That robbery was involved was subsequently confirmed by detectives Williams and Jewell who went to the Peninsula Security Company with Mr. Macdonald and opened the safety deposit box of Mrs. Fluke. Not finding the rings, they searched the Macdonald house on Roberts Avenue. Mrs. Macdonald, mother, and Mrs. Macdonald, sister-in-law, both noted that Mabel had worn the rings and coat on the day she went missing and that she was "in very good spirits."[13]

Incredibly, despite all the indications of homicide, the official story was that Mrs. Fluke had crawled into the attic and strangled herself to death! Initially, as reported in the *Oregonian*:

One end of the scarf had been drawn almost completely around her neck again and was fastened on the side with two knots. The second loop around the neck, however, was not drawn tight, and Deputy Coroner Gulbrandsen regards this as significant and bearing out his theory that the woman had not met with foul play. Bruises were found on both elbows, and a slight abrasion on the body and on one side of the face. The deputy coroner thought these might have been incurred in efforts to draw knots tight, one arm having struck the side wall of the attic, and the other the floor.[14]

The *Journal* noted:

> Dr. Menne said in the case of Mrs. Fluke he did not believe it would have been possible for an assailant to tie the cloth about her neck in the careful way it was tied without struggling with her and he found no evidence of a fight. The cloth was bound tightly around the neck and tied into a careful knot. She had no bruises on the face, neck or body, and there was no brain haemorrhage. "If the knot were tied by another person it was done with exceeding and exceptional cunning, consequently it appears to be a case of suicide," he said.[15]

The *Telegram* also reported that after the autopsy, Dr. Frank Menne concluded that Mrs. Fluke died of strangulation, but it was likely that she strangled herself.[16] If a fiend had done it, there would be more marks of violence. Furthermore, there was no evidence of sexual assault on the woman's body.[17] As confirmed by detectives Williams and Jewell in their notebook, "Doctor Minnie took slides and found she had not been ravished. He also stated she came to her death by strangulation. Postmortem will not be completed for several days."[18] The subsequent official autopsy report that I obtained for Mrs. Fluke simply noted that she died of strangulation and gave the jury verdict of November 3, 1926, that it was self-inflicted.[19] Her death certificate stated that she died of strangulation, and then there was a handwritten notation, "suicide."[20]

On must wonder whether Coroner Gulbrandson and Dr. Menne had biases that viewed women as suicidal. As noted, when a coroner's jury eventually met to deal with the death of Mrs. Fluke, the verdict was that she had committed suicide.[21] The verdict for Mrs. Withers had at least been split between suicide and murder, and here in the case of Fluke, the verdict was suicide. Does this make sense? If the case of Fluke had occurred in San Francisco, I think the police would have immediately classified it as another "dark strangler" murder, given the house for rent or sale advertisement, the hiding of the body, the strangulation, the robbery, and the probable sexual activity, even without penetration.

CHAPTER 14

Virginia Grant in Portland

15. October 21, 1926—Virginia Grant, 59, Portland

The second body to be discovered, but the third death chronologically in the same neighborhood of Portland, was that of Mrs. Virginia Grant, 59, who was found dead on Thursday, October 21, behind the furnace in the basement of her vacant house that she was attempting to rent at 604 East 22nd Street.[1] The *Oregonian* reported that Mrs. Grant had owned the house for many years and was renting it because she was moving to Seattle to be with her husband, who had a job as a chef in that city.[2] The paper noted that she had advertised the house in the papers for several days.[3] Mrs. Grant lived at 700 Ladd Avenue while the house was being remodeled with a view to being rented.

Her death was attributed to heart disease, but nevertheless, when her family noted that her two very valuable diamond rings and one of her diamond earrings were missing, the police opened an investigation. If it had not been for the missing rings, the death of Mrs. Grant would have been treated as a heart attack case without any police investigation.[4]

Given that the newspapers were focused on the sensational trunk case mystery, to be followed by the sensational attic case mystery, the press provided very little information on the Grant case, even when it was eventually linked to the investigation of the other two mysterious deaths. The *Oregon Journal* provided at least a bare bones narrative, albeit on the 11th page.[5]

On Thursday, October 21, Mrs. Grant was supervising the remodeling and she was last seen at the house with her daughter and son-in-law, Mrs. and Mr. Myers, that afternoon. In the evening, Mr. Myers, her son-in-law, a chef at the Elks Club, came to pick up his mother-in-law to take her for dinner. The *Journal* narrative continued:

> After finding the body, Myers called H.S. Fries [*sic*] ... another son-in-law. Together they carried the body to the first floor. As they laid it on the couch a diamond earring fell into Myers' hand. Examination revealed that the other earring was gone, and that two diamond rings were also missing.... Doctor and undertaker were called. Hearing of the circumstances, they notified the coroner. When he learned the facts, he ordered everyone to stay in the house and called for police detectives. Inspectors Thomas, Rockwell and W. Nelson responded.[6]

The *Journal* also stated that deputy coroner Ross declared that Mrs. Grant had died from a heart attack. Subsequently the autopsy revealed that Mrs. Grant was suffering from a heart condition and "she was in such bad physical shape, postmortem

113

examination showed, that if she had suddenly been seized by a man she would have succumbed from the sudden fright."[7]

Mrs. Grant always wore the jewelry that was now missing from her body. Detectives Hyde and Leonard searched everywhere for the jewelry and could not find it. The jewelry was said to be very valuable; the diamond rings were worth $800, and the missing earring was worth $65.[8]

Two bruises were found on Mrs. Grant's head.[9] The *Telegram* reported that these were "slight bruises, such as might have been caused by a sandbag, according to Dr. Menne, but the brain showed no haemorrhage or damage to the brain tissues as a sandbag would probably have caused. The bruises were probably caused by falling, he said."[10] So again, the medical opinion discounted murder and concluded that Mrs. Grant had died of natural causes, namely heart failure. The autopsy report by Dr. Frank Menne stated: "Acute dilatation of the heart. Fatty degeneration of heart. Chronic senile arteriole sclerosis of coronary arteries."[11] The inquest jury report of November 3, 1926, was recorded as "death by natural causes." Her death certificate stated that she died of a heart attack.[12]

Not all police officials agreed with the medical opinion, nor did the newspapers. For example, the *Oregonian* reported that a suspicious man had been seen lurking around Mrs. Grant's home on the day of her murder. Some carpenters working on the roof of a nearby house had seen the man described from a distance "as between the ages of 40 and 50 years, medium height, heavy build and stoop shoulders. He was wearing a gray cap and a heavy mackinaw coat with a sheepskin collar."[13] The article also noted that while Mrs. Grant had died from a heart attack, it might have been induced by the shock of being the victim of a robbery or even attempted strangulation or suffocation. Furthermore, there was clearly evidence of robbery, in that money was missing from Mrs. Grant's purse, in addition to the original discoveries of the missing jewelry. Mrs. Grant apparently owned three houses and the detectives Hyde and Leonard searched all three for the missing diamond rings.[14] Detectives Thomas and Rockwell interviewed one of the men who had seen a suspicious character in the back yard of the Grant home.[15]

≈ ≈ ≈

Once again, we find that the victim had been divorced. Mrs. Grant was born Virginia Ada Gray in 1867 in Pennsylvania. The Gray family moved to Blair, Nebraska, where Virginia, at the age of 18, married George F. Chittenden in 1885.[16] The couple subsequently had two daughters, Eva May Chittenden, who would become Mrs. Myers (1888–1966), and Norma Vivian Chittenden, who would become Mrs. Ries (1890–1949).[17] For some time George and Virginia lived in Sioux City, Iowa, but by 1900 they were living in Omaha, Nebraska, with their daughters.[18] The divorce was finalized in Denver in 1902.[19] George Chittenden, a shopkeeper, got married again in 1907.[20] He died at age 64 on February 1, 1926.[21] Thus, Eva Myers and Norma Ries lost both of their birth parents within the same year.

After the divorce, Virginia (Gray) Chittenden married James Charles Grant in 1903.[22] She would have been 36 years of age, with two teenage daughters, while James Charles Grant was 33 years of age. It was the second marriage for both. The city directories of Portland as early as 1907 listed Mr. Grant as a chef at various hotels or restaurants through the years and living at 604 E. 22nd Street.[23]

When Virginia Grant was buried in the Rose City Cemetery, her tombstone was carved with the other half blank, leaving space for her husband James Charles Grant to be buried beside her. The blank second half of the tombstone remains to this day.[24] Mr. Grant, who was now living in Seattle, married Anna Jensen, a decade younger than him, and lived with her until he died in 1953. His wife, Anna, died in 1955 and they are buried together in Idaho.[25]

≈ ≈ ≈

After the third body (Fluke) was discovered, and before the autopsy reports were completed, the theory of murder took precedence for a brief period. How could it not? Three women who advertised their homes for rent had died on three successive days in the same general area of the city. The bodies of all three had been hidden: in a trunk, behind a furnace, and in an attic. Property of all three of the victims had been stolen. All the deaths occurred in the early afternoon. While the medical examiner had found no evidence of sexual assault, the *Journal* made a good point about how two of the bodies were not only hidden but also found with exposed body parts that had been covered:

> Mrs. Withers' body, lying in the trunk with a house dress pulled above the waist, was covered over the middle with a pair of her son's trousers … the police could not understand why, if she crept into the trunk of her own volition, she could not simply have pulled her dress down. Mrs. Fluke's body, hidden in a dark corner of the attic, the dress pulled up just below the arms and a rubber kitchen apron thrown over the exposed part of her body.… Why should two women, contemplating suicide, perform such unusual dying gestures?[26]

As to the lack of evidence of sexual assault, the *Oregonian* stated that the "police have given little thought to this angle." Varieties of perverts are numerous, and it is not uncommon in police annals to find one that kills solely for the thrill of killing.[27]

The *Oregonian* noted, "in all three cases strangulation is a possible cause of death," and Captain John T. Moore issued a warning that women should not be showing their rooms or houses to men unless accompanied by someone else for protection.[28] Detective Tackabery now also agreed that all three women were probably murdered.[29] However, even after a week had gone by, the *Telegram* never once mentioned any link to the "dark strangler" in San Francisco. It was as if Portland was in a different country, cut off from any developments in California. The *News* and the *Journal* finally noted the possible connection to the California strangler in stories on Monday, October 25.[30] This was done after the *Oregonian* had added a little note on the "dark strangler" of California on October 24.[31]

However, after the autopsy reports came out, there was another swing away from the homicide theory. As we have noted, Dr. Menne concluded that Mrs. Fluke died of strangulation, probably self-inflicted, and Mrs. Grant died a natural death from heart failure. He concluded that a murderer would have left more marks beyond those found on the body. He stated that "there were no marks on Mrs. Fluke's body to speak of … even under the scarf that was bound around her throat." Mrs. Grant's head showed slight bruises, but the brain showed no hemorrhage or damage to its tissues. The bruises were probably caused by falling, he said.[32] The *Journal* reported that one "high police officer" noted the lack of any evidence that even a struggle had taken place in any of the cases: "This included a microscopic search for lint from other clothing. It included an examination of the fingernails. No particles of skin or hair were found under them. There were no hairs of any sort except those which belonged to the possessors. He did not believe it possible that a slayer could so handle his victims that plain bruises would not indicate the manner of their death."[33]

However, some police officials, including Detective Tackabery, continued to support the murder theory, as did Captain Jenkins, who to his credit continued the investigation of all three cases as possible murders. In the absence of any eyewitnesses or promising suspects, the focus was on searching for the missing items. After a futile search at pawn shops, a bulletin from the police eventually listed the missing property as follows:

> Mrs. Beata Withers: 1 imitation leather hand bag; 1 pair of black galoshes, size six; 1 lady's purse, very light tan color, ten inches long, with partitions; 1 lady's coat, dark brown goods with dark brown fur collar and cuffs, 1 large black button in front, bought at Liebes, Portland; 1 lady's hat, orange or reddish brown felt material; some new lady's silk underclothing of good material; 1 pair of lady's slippers, and some lady's hose.
>
> Mrs. Virginia Grant: 1. screw earring with ¼-karat white diamond, Tiffany setting…; 1 lady's blue diamond ring, Tiffany setting, size 1 karat, 16 and 32; 1 gentleman's ring, yellow gold set with bluish white diamond, about 2 karats, with flaw, heavy claw setting; $6 or $8 in money was missing from her purse.
>
> Mrs. Mabel Fluke: 1. home-tanned coon skin used for a rug…; 1 lady's coat, reddish maroon or henna color…; 1 lady's wedding ring, small and narrow with round edge, yellow gold; 1 lady's yellow gold ring, set with ¾ karat diamond, white stone, Tiffany setting, with prongs which look like silver or platinum, and a few dollars missing from her purse.[34]

Murder victim Virginia Grant (*Oregonian*, Oct. 24, 1926, at 16).

Police chief Jenkins conferred with Mayor Baker on the possibility of having the city make an emergency appropriation of $1000 to bring a nationally known criminologist into the case.[35] Mayor Baker agreed that the money was secondary if further deaths could be prevented by catching the killer. To this end a conference was held on Tuesday, October 26, involving the mayor, chief of police, a host of detectives, the head coroner (Dr. Smith), and several other physicians who had conducted autopsies or tests.[36] A picture of the 26 men at this meeting (and there were only men) was printed in the *Oregonian*.[37] This distinguished body of men could not agree one way or another whether these women had been murdered. The idea of bringing in an outside criminologist was also discounted. Earlier a report had noted that bringing in an outsider would be seen as showing a lack of faith by the police chief in his own detective force.[38] Perhaps that lack of faith was based on good grounds. An editorial in the *Capital Journal* eventually noted the ineptitude of the Portland police, stating, "If they ever solved a mystery or caught a master criminal—it is not of record."[39]

The police continued to search for clues as to homicide or suicide, but after a month of investigation, nothing came to light. A final report by six police detectives was submitted to John Moore, chief of detectives, reviewing the entire month-long investigation and concluding that unless the missing items came to light, there were no clues to work with.[40] Further strangulations in California brought no response from Portland. More than a month would go by before a landlady was strangled in Seattle. At that point, Detective Archie Leonard noted that this strangulation had features in common with the Portland mysteries, and he traveled to Seattle to consult with police there.[41] While he was in Seattle, the "dark strangler" came back to Portland and murdered a fourth landlady. It was not until this fourth murder, which we will eventually look at, that the Portland police accepted the theory that all four of these deaths were the unfortunate work of the "dark strangler." However, in the annual report of the Portland police for 1926, we find 11 murders listed for the year, one of which was Mrs. Myers. The deaths of Withers, Grant and Fluke were not listed at all.[42]

≈   ≈   ≈

As we will review in detail later, the prime link between Earle Nelson and the four Portland landlady murders was made around the circumstances and subsequent identification of Nelson in relation to the Myers murder, the fourth and last murder by the "dark strangler" in Portland. However, there was another important link. Earle Nelson's picture was identified by a Mrs. Lewis.[43] She said the man in the picture had come to her house, which was for sale, on October 20, the same day that Mabel Fluke died. Mrs. Lewis lived only two blocks away from the Fluke house. She had told her story to the police back in October during the events in question, describing the man as "5.6, 140, dark complexion, small black sharp eyes, looked badly dressed in a grey coat long and loose fitting, and gray hat pulled down front and back."[44] Now about eight months later, she provided the same narrative to the *Journal*, replete with post-event coloration:

> The man drove up in a ramshackle small automobile she said. She answered the door in response to the bell and was greeted by the surly stranger with the words, "house for sale?" Mrs. Lewis answered in the affirmative and the man entered. The supposed house hunter had an evil appearance, did not remove his hat, and never allowed his eyes to meet hers,

Mrs. Lewis recalled. Once in the house, he proceeded to the attic trunk room, similar to the place in which Mrs. Fluke's body was found. "Come up and see what's the matter with this door," the stranger called from above. Mrs. Lewis replied that the door would be repaired but remained on the lower floor. The man then went into the basement, calling for the woman to follow and "see what's the matter with this furnace." Again Mrs. Lewis replied evasively and stood her ground. The stranger then went back to the first floor of the house only to find Mrs. Lewis, somewhat frightened, hastening through the back door of her home. "Come and see my pretty flowers," the woman called, pointing to her garden. "To hell with your flowers," the man replied angrily, according to Mrs. Lewis' story. He thereupon left hurriedly, jumping into his car and driving in the direction of the Fluke home, Mrs. Lewis said. Police Inspectors Leonard and Hyde exhibited six pictures before the woman. "That is the man. I'll never forget him," Mrs. Lewis said selecting the photograph sent from Winnipeg.[45]

The same story appeared in the *Oregonian*.[46]

Despite the post-event coloration, the basic story matches what she first told police.[47] Given what we now know about the frailty of eyewitness testimony, the police were ahead of their time when they presented to Mrs. Lewis not just Nelson's picture alone but Nelson's picture with others like a lineup.[48] This makes Mrs. Lewis's identification of Nelson particularly important in terms of linkage to the Portland murders.

Chapter 15

Marion Corcoran in Los Angeles

16. November 11, 1926—Marion Corcoran, 24, Los Angeles

Another case that was dismissed as suicide but might well have been a homicide occurred in Los Angeles about three weeks after the triple deaths in Portland. The body of Mrs. Marion Corcoran, 24 years of age, was found by her husband after he came home from work on Thursday, November 11, 1926.[1] One report stated that Mr. Corcoran was a vacuum cleaner salesman,[2] while several others said he was the proprietor of an electrical supply shop.[3] The young couple lived at 6850 Camrose Drive in the Hollywood district of Los Angeles, occupying one half of a side-by-side bungalow.[4] The house was for sale, listed with several realty firms, and there was a "For Sale" sign on the outside of the house.[5]

David Corcoran noted that his wife Marion had been in a good mood when he left her in the morning. When he came home from work at about six in the evening, he found the front door of the house standing open, and "inside the house his wife's feet were protruding from a closet. Her body was partially covered by clothing which had been pulled from hooks and thrown over her."[6] David found her with an apron string fastened in a noose around her neck.[7] He called a local doctor who declared that Mrs. Corcoran had bruises about the neck and scratches on her left cheek and had been strangled.[8] While the Los Angeles Times stated that nothing in the house was disturbed or missing, another account mentioned that furniture was strewn about the house, indicating that a struggle had taken place.[9]

When the police arrived, they immediately treated the case as a brutal murder. Mrs. Corcoran, partially clad, had been strangled to death with the strings of her apron, declared Dr. Webb, autopsy surgeon, and police detectives said she had been "brutally attacked,"[10] code words used at the time for being sexually assaulted. All the newspaper reports treated the case as a murder.[11] Los Angeles officers found some fingerprints on several pieces of furniture, and what appeared to be fresh shoe prints in the soft earth around the house, and they took pictures of these.[12] Despite the belief by the police that the strangler had met the victim by posing as a prospective purchaser of the house, no connection to the "dark strangler" was mentioned, as if the murders in San Francisco and Portland were unknown in Los Angeles, despite the Los Angeles connection in the Russell case that we have examined previously.

The Times reported that a friend of the family, Dr. Joseph Rock, had knocked on the door at three in the afternoon. Not receiving an answer, he had left. Perhaps this scared the fiend away?[13] Dr. Rock apparently went to Mr. Corcoran's place of business at 2210 West Eleventh Street and informed Mr. Corcoran that he had received no answer at the house when he called. If Dr. Rock had been there at three and the door was closed, and Mr. Corcoran came at six and the door was open, perhaps the killer was at the house when Dr. Rock was knocking on the door? It was reported by neighbors that they had heard Mrs. Corcoran singing about the house during the day and making a long phone call to someone in the afternoon, but they had not heard any sounds of a struggle.[14]

According to a rival paper, the *Los Angeles Record*, Marion's sister, Mrs. Lohman, had come for a visit at three and then departed, following which Dr. Rock arrived at four and found the door open but no one came to the door.[15] These reports are obviously inconsistent. What time did Rock show up, and was the door open or closed?

The following day the whole picture of the Corcoran case changed radically. Now the police asserted that Corcoran, "a delicate woman in ill health," had likely killed herself.[16] The long phone call had apparently been made to one of her brothers-in-law, R.B. Johnson, living in Los Angeles. Shortly after the call, she had probably executed herself by fashioning her apron strings into a noose and hanging herself from a hook in the clothes closet, even though the police could not explain why she was not found hanging, but rather in a heap on the floor of the closet with clothes thrown over her! There was no explanation of who had cut Marion down if she had hanged herself from the bars of the closet. The apron strings were cut cleanly, not torn as if she had fallen down on her own after hanging herself.[17] Nevertheless, to give credence to the theory that she had every reason to be suicidal, it was reported that

> Coroner Nance yesterday stated that Corcoran [husband], a vacuum cleaner salesman, had called his office during the morning and indicated that he believed his wife had taken her own life and was not the victim of a phantom garrotter, as was first supposed…. The husband also told Coroner Nance that his wife, though apparently happy and even joyous during the last six months, was still subject to black moods and fits of sinister depression, a reminder of the tragedies which had come to her with the deaths successively of their three small children…. The fits of melancholy became more frequent…. The fact that nothing in the home was disturbed and that an autopsy disclosed that the woman was not attacked discredited the theory of murder.[18]

Another reason for the suicide theory was that if she had been attacked, surely the next-door duplex neighbor, Mrs. Crone, would have heard something. "The slightest sound penetrates through the divisional wall," declared Captain Bean.[19]

On Monday, November 15, the case was closed when Coroner Nance issued a certificate of suicide.[20] The funeral was held the next day with interment at Des Moines, Iowa.[21] Today the Los Angeles police have no record of this case on their historical homicide investigation ledger.[22]

≈   ≈   ≈

Marion's life was touched by numerous tragedies that might well have affected her mental health. Her maiden name was Cravens. She was born in Spirit Lake, Iowa, in 1902. Her father, John W. Cravens, at the age of 28 had married her mother,

Mary Colby, age 17, in 1890.[23] They subsequently had five children, Marion being the youngest. John Cravens was a wealthy man, owner of the First National Bank of Spirit Lake, and he also had investments in several other banks in Iowa and Minnesota. When Marion was only a few years old, her parents divorced in 1904.[24] John Cravens continued to live in Spirit Lake while Mary took the children and moved to Des Moines, Iowa. Apparently the five Craven children were shuttled from time to time between their father in Spirit Lake and their mother in Des Moines.[25]

After the divorce, John Cravens, at age 46, married a recently widowed woman, Mrs. Anna Copley, in Spirit Lake in 1907.[26] In August of 1909, when Marion was only seven years old, her father died tragically. John and his new

Strangler's Victim

Mrs. Marion A. Corcoran, whose husband found her strangled to death in a closet in their home. The picture also shows their baby, who died some months ago.

Murder victim Marion Corcoran (*Los Angeles Evening Record***, Nov. 12, 1926, at 1).**

wife were traveling in their automobile, and they both died when the car was hit by a commuter train about a mile north of Alexandria, Indiana. There was a corn field that blocked the view from both the car and the train. The collision was horrific, as reports noted that Mr. and Mrs. Cravens were thrown from the car and John's head was nearly severed from his body, while his wife's body was also horribly mangled. The press noted that they had expensive diamonds and lots of cash on their persons when rescuers came to the scene.[27]

In 1914 Marion lost her other parent. Her mother died at age 42 from colon cancer.[28] The head of the family, after the loss of the parents, appears to have been taken by the eldest child, Margaret. The local society pages in Des Moines made frequent references over the years to the attendance at events or achievements of Marion's older siblings, Margaret, Minnie, John, and Jane. Additionally, there were references every summer as to the comings and goings of the family members to a cottage they owned at Okoboji Lake called Craven's Nest. While oldest sibling Margaret apparently did not marry, the marriages of her siblings were covered in the society pages in the Des Moines press.[29]

Marion A. Cravens married David Michael Corcoran in Des Moines in September 1920.[30] Nine months later Marion gave birth to a son, John David Corcoran.[31] Marion and David moved to Los Angeles where David Corcoran ran an electric appliance shop, mainly selling vacuum cleaners. While at the Craven's Nest cottage at Okoboji Lake in July of 1922, Marion's 14-month-old son died after being poisoned when he swallowed a bottle of pills.[32] The death certificate states, "Asphyxia from convulsions due to poisoning."[33] Marion became pregnant again, this time with twins. Then tragedy struck once more. In April of 1925, the twins were born prematurely at six months. The girl was born alive, but died after a few days, while the boy was stillborn.[34]

≈　≈　≈

Despite all the tragic personal history that we have noted above, the hasty judgment that Corcoran committed suicide seems highly suspicious, especially when it seems to have been primarily driven by information from the victim's husband. That Mrs. Corcoran may have had ample reason to be despondent and that she may well have been suffering from depressive mental illness does not mean she in fact committed suicide. Earle Nelson, searching for houses for sale or rooms to rent, might have simply ended up by coincidence with a depressed victim. Because both the police and the press accepted the theory of suicide, the case was never investigated further. We have no investigation of the possible link to the "dark strangler" in terms of questioning other landladies in the neighborhood who might have been approached by a prospective purchaser or renter on the day in question. We have no investigation as to what the conversations were with her sister, Mrs. Lohman, or with her brother-in-law, Mr. Johnson, or what Dr. Rock's visit was about. While there was apparently no robbery or sexual assault, Nelson might have been scared away before fully accomplishing his mission. On the other hand, the coincidence could go the other way. A landlady might have strangled herself and this had nothing to do with the "for sale" sign on her house. I doubt it. As far as I know, the murder of Marion Corcoran was never linked as a possible murder of Earle Nelson. I believe it should have been.

≈　≈　≈

After the supposed suicide of his wife, David Corcoran remarried in April 1928.[35] He declared bankruptcy in June of that year.[36] The 1930 Census indicates that he continued to be a sales manager for vacuum cleaners and was living with his wife and a daughter in Los Angeles. By 1940 he was still a vacuum cleaner salesman and the Corcorans had two daughters at that point. He died in Kern, California, in 1957.[37]

CHAPTER 16

Attempted Murders of Landladies?

Over the many months that the "dark strangler" terrorized women in the San Francisco area, there were numerous press reports about women who claimed to have been confronted by the strangler or attacked by him and escaped.[1] Some of these reports may have been true; others may have involved attacks by men who were not the wanted fiend; and some may have been fabricated to cover up the real story behind some awkward situation. Some may even have been false due to a psychological phenomenon involving people who want to thrust themselves into the headlines of the day to achieve their five minutes of fame. In any case, these strangler encounters must always be taken with a grain of salt.

However, in some cases the victims later identified a picture of Nelson as the person they encountered, as Mrs. Lewis did in Portland. For example, on November 4, 1926, Mrs. Annie Maly, 45, almost died after being hit on the head with a hatchet in the basement of her house in San Francisco. The house was for sale.[2] The narrative changed from homicide to accident when Captain Duncan Matheson declared that the woman had fallen down the stairs. He stated, "She probably fell down the stairs and hit her head on the table. We found blood and hair on the edge of the table, which indicated that she struck her head there. As far as I know there was no robbery, or any motive for an assault."[3] However, Mr. Maly believed that his wife had been attacked and asserted that his wife carried cash around with her and not a cent was found on her person.[4] Several weeks later it was reported that the police were re-examining the case, given that the house had been for sale. At this point, with Mrs. Maly still in the hospital, the *Examiner* noted, "Unable to recall the events that led up to her injury, she was wavering in her stories to the police between the theory that she was attacked by a man who had posed as a prospective purchaser of her home and the theory that she had fallen while doing housework."[5]

About eight months later, after Earle Nelson was arrested in Winnipeg, Mrs. Maly supposedly identified Nelson as the man who attacked her. According to detectives Dullea and Frederickson:

Mrs. Annie Maly identified the photograph as that of the man who called at her home, 2445 Ocean Ave on November 4th, 1926 (which place she had for sale with a "For Sale" sign in the front of the premises) and, when he got her into the basement of the house, the man grabbed her, but she put up a game battle, but was finally struck on the head with the hatchet which was lying nearby and rendered unconscious. Mrs. Maly had a severe fracture of the skull and was at St. Luke's Hospital for a long time before she was able to tell anything about the assault.[6]

One may well wonder why she was not strangled to death if indeed she had been attacked by Earle Nelson.

That Earle Nelson was hunting for victims at this point was reinforced by Dullea and Fredrickson who reported another identification made from an encounter that took place a few days after Mrs. Maly was allegedly attacked. The detectives continued:

> Mrs. Annie Eaton, 1357 Plymouth Avenue, states that [Nelson's] photograph is of the man who came to her home at about 5:45 p.m., Nov. 6, 1926, and enquired about the house being for sale as there was a "For Sale" sign in front of the premises. Mrs. Eaton admitted this man to the house, and he asked her if he could look through the house. Mrs. Eaton then called for her daughter, who came in from an adjoining room, and they went through the house, but the man only took a casual glance at the rooms and said that he would bring his wife over from Berkeley on the following day. Miss Allison Eaton, employed by the Mercantile Trust Company, positively identifies the photograph as that of the man who was at her mother's home at time above stated.[7]

Presumably Nelson was not interested because the landlady was not alone in the house. It is noteworthy that the home of Mrs. Eaton on Plymouth Avenue was quite close to the home of Mrs. Maly on Ocean Avenue.

While we must take all these reports with a grain of skepticism, it is equally unrealistic to expect that the strangler succeeded in murdering every landlady that he hoped to murder. This account of Mrs. Eaton and her daughter seems quite plausible, but all the identifications suffer from post-event information problems as the witnesses may have seen pictures of Nelson in the newspapers. Then we have the added problem that these witnesses were likely asked to look at a single picture brought to them by the police instead of looking at a package of pictures as was done with Mrs. Lewis in Portland.

~ ~ ~

There is one case of an attempted murder that needs to be highlighted. A week after Marion Corcoran died in Los Angeles, and one day before another landlady would be murdered in San Francisco, there was a report of a failed attempt which was given far more publicity compared to the earlier cases like that of Mrs. Maly with the skull fracture. The police and press took this most recent encounter very seriously in terms of the credibility of the report and the accuracy of the description of the "dark strangler."

Mrs. H.C. Murray, living at 1114 Grove Avenue in Burlingame near the railway tracks, was 28 years old and eight months pregnant.[8] There was a "for sale" sign on the house. Burlingame is just south of San Francisco. On Wednesday, November 17, a man pretending to be a prospective purchaser visited her. Given the length of time she spent with the alleged strangler, and that she lived to tell the tale, her story in the *San Francisco Chronicle*, as given from her hospital bed several days later, is worthy of consideration:

> The man first asked the price of the place and then said he would like to look at it…. I let him in, and he examined the rooms in much detail. He is evidently very familiar with building and construction work for he uses expressions relating to such things that I did not

understand myself. During the course of the conversation, he mentioned the fact that he was to be married in three days. "This will be my third marriage," he said. "The first time my wife nagged me to death. The second one I took to dances and would find sitting on the laps of other men. I couldn't stand that." I left the front door open when he came in and I took care to keep six or eight feet away from him during the whole interview. He sat down every chance he got, and he examined the closets and ceilings very carefully, as well as the locks on all the doors. I realized afterward that he was trying to get me to look up toward the ceiling so that he could get behind me and grab my throat or get me where he could lock me up in a closet or one of the rooms. The shades were up and I lighted the lights when he entered. Several times he went to the shades and examined them and once remarked, "Whoever designed this house sure put the windows in places to give plenty of light." Foolishly, in the course of the interview, I let him know that my husband was working in town, and he would not return until 6 o'clock. He immediately took out his watch and said: "I wonder if I have the right time?" It was then about 5:30. We went through the house thoroughly and finally inspected the sleeping room porch in the rear. He seemed particularly interested in this and several times called attention to the ceiling. I kept my distance, however, though I never once dreamed he was the strangler. After exhausting every pretext for lingering, he started out. When he reached the front door, he suddenly turned and said: "There's something about that sleeping porch I'd like to see again." I returned there with him. As we stepped on to the porch, which is screened in, he suddenly pointed to the garage outside. "What sort of a roof is that on the garage?" he asked. For the first time, I turned my back on him, and in that instant, I felt his hands closing about my neck from the rear. And for the first time I realized that I was dealing with the strangler himself. I screamed for help before his grip tightened and tore at his hands with my nails. Fear must have given me strength, for I succeeded in breaking that terrible grip. I almost threw myself through the door, and nearly fell down the steps leading from the porch. The strangler turned and ran out the front door.[9]

Mrs. Murray apparently started a hue and cry, going so far as jumping on the running board of a passing automobile and shouting to the occupants, "Stop that man! Stop that man!" The strangler escaped and the shock of the whole encounter was so great that Mrs. Murray was taken to the hospital. Given the late stage of her pregnancy, the newspapers at first reported her to be in a potentially fatal condition.[10]

That this encounter was taken seriously by the police was evidenced by the fact that swarms of police and volunteers formed a posse, throwing a cordon around the Burlingame and San Mateo area, searching streetcars and automobiles, watching all the roads, and sending 15 men with shotguns to the nearby marshes in search of the fiend.[11]

Her description of the man dispelled the image that the strangler was some easily recognizable "foreign" monster or that he had the "features of an ape or gorilla, or that he was uncouth in speech or manner."[12] Rather he was ordinary and pleasant enough not to raise suspicion. Her original description as given to the *Chronicle* was

> dark complexioned, black hair, recently clipped, black eyebrows and green eyes. He is 32 to 35 years old; weighs 145 to 155 pounds; has an unusually good set of teeth. He has a high forehead. He is 5 feet, 7 or 8 inches tall. His hands are not unusually large or strong. He is not a foreigner, but an American. He uses fairly good English.[13]

Mrs. Murray said that because the man had told her that he was to be married, she accorded him a closer inspection, "to see what kind of man the woman was getting."[14] The police searched for a man matching this description, with scratches on his face and hands.

≈ ≈ ≈

About seven months later Mrs. Murray was presented with Nelson's picture from Winnipeg and she allegedly said, "That is the man!"[15] This identification was apparently made in the evening of June 17, 1927.[16] The problem again is that several local papers had already printed the pictures of Earle Nelson taken back in 1921 when he was arrested in San Francisco.[17] Some reports suggested that Mrs. Murray saw Nelson's old picture in the newspaper and then phoned police saying that she could identify him as being the man who had attempted to attack her.[18] In the Winnipeg police files we have a letter from W.J. Quinn, acting chief of police in San Francisco in early July of 1927. This letter states, "Mrs. Murray is an exceedingly keen woman who gave a very correct description of him; in fact, the best description that this department was able to obtain, and she instantly identified the photograph."[19] Quinn also attached a letter from John J. Harper, chief of police of Burlingame, who stated that the photograph of Nelson sent from Winnipeg was viewed by Mrs. Murray. Immediately she stated, "That is the man, and started pointing out the features she formerly gave when reporting his description."[20]

The link to Nelson was not only made by Mrs. Murray but also by a second woman in Burlingame. A man had arrived at her home which was for sale about an hour and a half before the attempted strangulation of Murray. Her story as to what he said, and how he presented himself, allegedly matched that of Murray, and as he inspected her house, the man noticed her son studying in the dining room at a table. The man then completely lost interest and could not wait to leave. After Nelson was arrested in Winnipeg, his picture was presented to this woman, who also identified Nelson as being the man who had inspected her home in Burlingame.[21]

CHAPTER 17

Anna Edmonds in San Francisco

17. November 18, 1926—Anna Edmonds, 57, San Francisco

On Thursday, November 18, one day after the attempt to strangle Mrs. Murray in Burlingame, another landlady was found murdered in San Francisco. Mrs. Anna Edmonds, one day shy of 57 years of age, was strangled to death in her spacious San Francisco home at 3524 Fulton Street, facing Golden Gate Park. The house had a "For Sale" sign posted in the front.

Mrs. Edmonds' maiden name was Ragsdale, and she was born in Mississippi in 1869.[1] In 1888 at the age of 18 she married James Edmonds, age 27, in Arkansas.[2] For many years they lived in Little Rock, Arkansas, where James was a salesman. Later in their marriage they had a child, Raul Edmonds, born in 1900.[3] After being ill for several years, James Edmonds died in Little Rock in 1917 at the age of 56. The notice in the local paper stated that he had been engaged in the retail cigar business and for many years was connected with the Gleason Hotel.[4] After her husband died, Anna lived in Los Angeles where her mother and sisters lived.[5] She was the proprietor of a rooming house on Soto Street. Son Raul went on to graduate from Stanford University and then secured an engineering job with Pacific Telephones in San Francisco.[6] We presume that Anna Edmonds moved to San Francisco to be near her son, but we do not know why she was selling her house.

In the official documents subsequently sent to Winnipeg, San Francisco detectives Dullea and Frederickson noted that Mrs. Edmonds "was frail and in ill health and at that time had a broken collar bone and her right arm and shoulder were bandaged and strapped."[7] Acting chief of police W.J. Quinn provided the following narrative:

> At about 7 p.m. of that day [November 18] her body was discovered in a small room where she had a radio and the door was found locked with the key missing and on entering the room her body was found, clothing being disarranged as in the other cases, with two marks ... visible on the neck. The autopsy proved beyond any question of doubt that she was outraged after death. In this case, there are witnesses who saw the suspect and the description tallies exactly with that of Earl[e] Nelson. In this case considerable jewelry was stolen as per circular forwarded to your department, and in case defendant should talk, would you kindly question him about this jewelry.[8]

The San Francisco police sent several pictures to Winnipeg of Mrs. Edmonds on the floor of the radio room, taken from different angles. The upper part of her body appears to be lying flat on her back, while the lower part is twisted to her right with her legs slightly folded and bent. She is fully clothed, with shoes, stockings, heavy housecoat or robe and long apron, and her right arm is in a sling tied around her neck. One of the photos shows that the many layers of clothes were hiked well up over the knees and the stockings appear to have some runs and breaks in them. Curiously, she is lying on top of open newspapers strewn about the floor, and the open newspapers appear also to be covering the top of what appears to be a table or shelf that may have radio equipment on it. Perhaps in the struggle various sheets of newspaper fell on the floor from this shelf before Mrs. Edmonds was thrown on the floor.

The report from the medical examiner's office stated:

> About four weeks ago she fell on inside stairway and fractured her left [should be right] shoulder. About 6 p.m. today her son Raul went to the house as was his custom to see how she was. Not finding her in any of the rooms, he found the door to the radio room locked, but no key in the hole. He took all the keys from other doors and found one that opened the door. Deceased was found lying on her back on floor, with her clothing raised under her. Dr. Connolly was called and pronounced her dead. Three purses, two diamond earrings and several rings could not be found. Rear door to house was standing open. Had sign in window advertising home for sale and is known to have been showing the place to an unknown man between 11:30 a.m. and 12:45 p.m.. Rectal temperature 86.[9]

There was also a notation from Dr. Strange that vaginal and rectal smears were sent to the laboratory for "microscopical examination" and the cause of death was "strangulation by compression of larynx."[10]

The *San Francisco Chronicle* account noted that Raul Edmonds came to his mother's house at about six in the evening. He had come to make plans for his mother's birthday.[11] Not getting a response to his ring, he went around to the back and was surprised by the open door. His mother always had it locked. On the other hand, the fact that the radio room in the upstairs level of the house was locked raised his alarm even further because it was never locked. After finding the body of his mother, Raul rushed to the next-door neighbor, Mrs. Bloc.

Eventually, Mrs. Bloc and another neighbor, Mrs. Patch, told police about seeing a man

San Francisco Police Department photograph of the 3524 Fulton Street home of Anna Edmonds with a "For Sale" sign on the lawn in the front of the house, and in front window. Winnipeg police file (courtesy John Burchill).

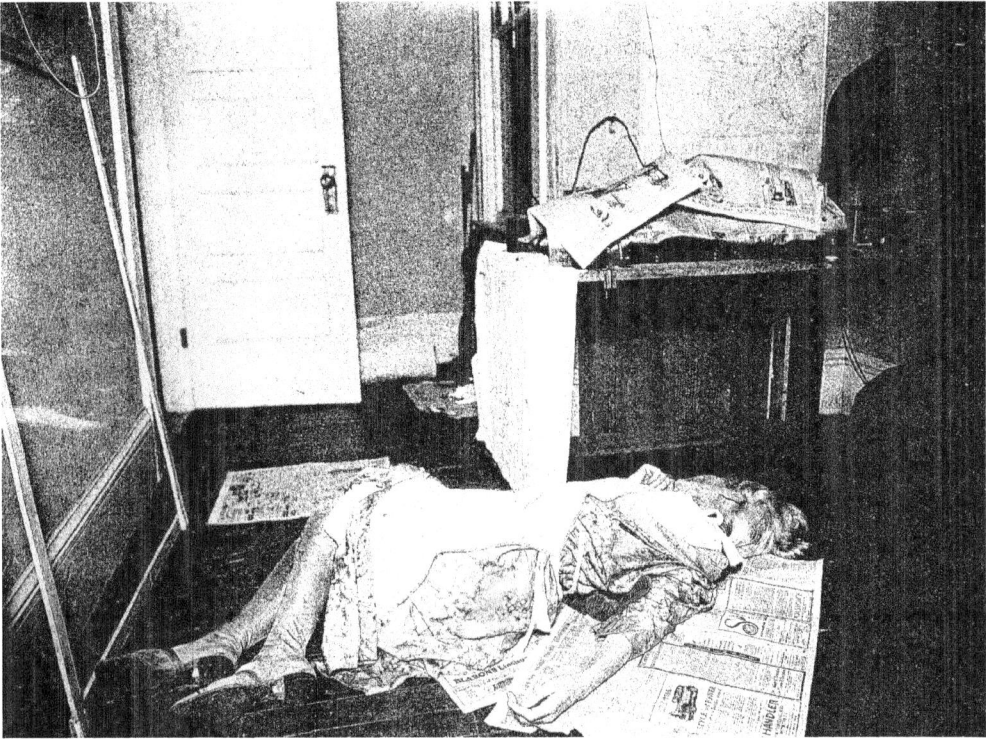

San Francisco Police Department photograph of body of Anna Edmonds as found in the radio room. Winnipeg police file (courtesy John Burchill).

at the house, presumably inspecting it for possible purchase. The initial report of who saw what and when was quite confusing. However, next day the *Chronicle* narrative stated:

> According to Mrs. Patch's story it was about 1:30 in the afternoon that she let herself into the widow's home and went to the lower front sitting room to find Mrs. Edmonds talking to a strange man. She quickly excused herself for intruding saying that she was just leaving on a brief shopping trip and wanted to know whether or not Mrs. Edmonds wished to accompany her on a ride afterward. Mrs. Edmonds, whose house has been advertised for sale … responded that she was engaged with a business deal and would not be able to get away. As she remembers him, he looked like a well-dressed working man, was smooth shaven, about 35 or 40 years old and appeared to be a man who was employed out-of-doors most of the time.… She does not recall the hue of his complexion.[12]

As to the other neighbor lady, Mrs. Bloc, she claimed that about 15 minutes later she saw Mrs. Edmonds sitting in her living room. She waved to her neighbor and Mrs. Edmonds waved back.

The first story in the rival *San Francisco Examiner* noted that if it were not for the locked door and the missing jewelry stripped from the body of the victim, the case would not have been treated as a homicide. Dr. Connolly who first arrived at the scene pronounced that death was from natural causes, likely heart problems. There were no obvious marks on the body.[13] The *San Francisco Bulletin* suggested that the two neighbor ladies saw a man with a "tanned face."[14] In addition to Mrs. Patch who walked into the room and saw the man speaking to Mrs. Edmonds, the neighbor on the other side of the house, described as Mrs. Block, claimed that as she was washing windows in her house she saw the man talking to Mrs. Edmonds. Her windows looked directly into the living room windows of her neighbor, separated by a narrow corridor. The man in this narrative was smoking a cigar.

Illustrative of journalistic license when the facts are missing, the *Oakland Post-Enquirer* noted that Raul Edmonds, finding the door of the radio room locked, battered it down to find the body of his mother.[15] In this account, Mrs. Bloc (*Chronicle*) / Mrs. Block (*Bulletin*) became Mrs. Black, who stated that "late yesterday she saw a swarthy, heavy-set man call at the house. He was wearing a dark overcoat and well-tailored clothes."[16] It was also reported that a man was seen "hurriedly leaving the place."

The murder of Mrs. Edmonds was obviously linked by the police and the press with the previous murders in the San Francisco area. However, press accounts about which cases were linked together varied. While the attack on Murray in Burlingame, and now the murder of Edmonds, were linked with the cases of Newman, Beal, St. Mary, Russell, and Nisbet, the *Bulletin* added Anderson and Gallegos.[17] The *Call and Post* and *Oakland Tribune* also added Gallegos but not Wells, Anderson and Jones.[18] Several days later the *Chronicle* included Wells but not Gallegos.[19] Ignoring the Portland murders, there were also references as to the Edmonds case being the first in which robbery was also a motive[20] and also the first case in which the strangulation was done with the hands rather than with some cord or rope.[21] While the police claimed that up to this point no fingerprints were found, pieces of the neck of Mrs. Edmonds were sent to famous criminologist Dr. Heinrich for examination.[22] Eventually the police linked the cases in California with at least two of the cases in Portland.[23]

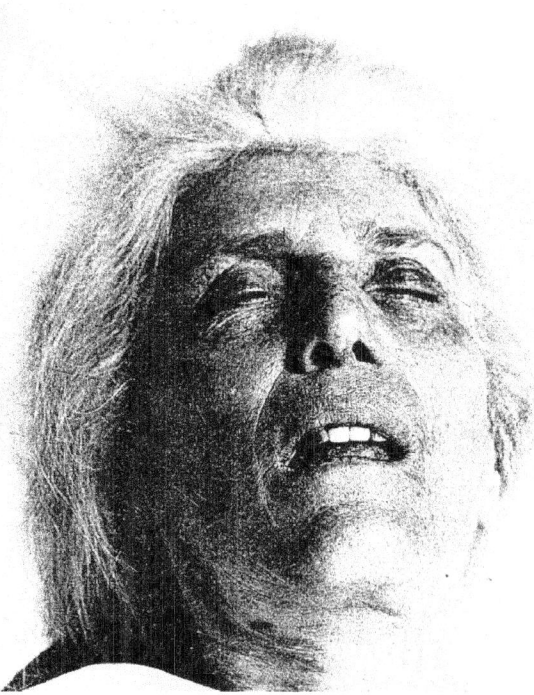

San Francisco Police Department photograph of face and neck of Anna Edmonds upon her body's arrival at the morgue. Winnipeg police file (courtesy John Burchill).

As to the question of linking cases together, the most important development was the verdict of the jury at the inquest held into Mrs. Edmonds' death on December 3, 1926. Driven by the opinion of Coroner Leland that there were seven cases of murder by the "dark strangler" within San Francisco proper, the jury verdict now linked them all. The verdict as recorded stated:

That said deceased was murdered by a person unknown to the jury and from evidence presented it would appear to have been committed by the same person concerned in a series of six similar crimes occurring in San Francisco, the first, August 1925, the last Nov. 18, 1926. We the jury recommend that extraordinary measures be used by the Chief of Police and Captain of Detectives to apprehend the fiend and that the Board of Supervisors or other qualified authority authorizes the offering of a large reward for his capture.[24]

Thus, the inquest jury verdict into Edmonds announced the opinion that Jones, Anderson, Newman, St. Mary, Wells, and Edmonds were all San Francisco victims of the same strangler. Notice that Beal in San Jose, Russell in Santa Barbara, Nisbet in Oakland and Gallegos in Stockton are not listed simply because they were outside San Francisco proper. We presume the cases in Philadelphia in 1925 and the case of Corcoran in Los Angeles were not even known to the police in San Francisco at this point.

≈ ≈ ≈

The San Francisco police again warned all women to use extreme caution in showing rooms or houses to men. Captain of Detectives Duncan Matheson, utilizing the information from the attempted strangulation of Mrs. Murray and the observation of Mrs. Patch in the Edmonds case, stated:

The man is not of a repulsive appearance and appears to be able through his suave manner to gain an amicable footing with elderly women. It is a mistake to believe that he has the features of an ape or gorilla or that he is uncouth in speech or manner. Presumably, he attacks elderly women because they lack strength to offer effective resistance and are so shocked by the realization of their helplessness as to be rendered easy prey. Mrs. Murray was a much younger woman than he was accustomed to attempt to strangle and was able to break away from him…. The strangler seems now to have switched his operations from rented rooms to houses for sale.[25] The strangler is an itinerant drifter. He moves from spot to spot, living outdoors most of the time. He picks up rides with passing motorists. He goes from one end of the coast to the other, attacking and strangling women and drifting out of town. He is the hardest type in the world to catch.[26]

Chief O'Brien of the San Francisco police now circulated a new description of the elusive strangler in 2500 circulars sent "the length and breadth of the Coast."[27] The poster included:

Apparent age, 30 to 40 years, about five feet six to 7 inches tall; Weight about 160 pounds, broad shoulders, rather heavy build, smooth olive skin, clean-shaven, dark complexion, dark eyes, black hair, very good white even teeth, speaks good English, usually talks in monosyllables, has the appearance of leading an outdoor life…. From his conversations he is evidently familiar with building construction. He is evidently of an ingratiating nature….[28]

The police circulated the poster to police departments nationwide.[29] The police in San Francisco expressed optimism that with such wide warnings and publicity, the wanted man "would fall into their hands soon."[30] Ironically, or as a consequence, just as the search for the strangler intensified as never before in San Francisco and up and down the California coast, Earle Nelson left the area and apparently never returned to California.

≈ ≈ ≈

Alleged strangler encounters over the next few months in San Francisco continued, but the circumstances of these reports were highly questionable in terms of any link to the "dark strangler."[31] As to suspects, San Francisco police thought they might have their man when Clifford Pacey, a former inmate of the Patton asylum with a long criminal record, was arrested in January of 1927.[32] He was caught in broad daylight choking a landlady on her steps, after she had allegedly refused him admittance to a rooming house because she was suspicious of him.[33] Police found twisted strands of rope in a room that Pacey occupied at 205 3rd Street, and the arrested man apparently admitted that he had "once choked another woman."[34] Once again Merton Newman was called upon to view another suspect who looked like the "dark strangler" in that he had "dark skin, high cheek bones, and large hands."[35] Once again, however, Newman asserted that this was not the man who had killed his aunt.[36] Captain Duncan Matheson asserted that a study of the movements of Pacey in no way matched the trail left by the "dark strangler."[37] Another suspect, Steve Kelmas, 51, was arrested in Santa Barbara when it was discovered among other things that he kept a newspaper clipping describing the "dark strangler's exploits" under his pillow.[38] Police subsequently agreed that Kelmas was not the "dark strangler."[39]

∾ ∾ ∾

As we have noted previously, after the arrest of Nelson in Winnipeg in June 1927, identification efforts were made by detectives Charles Dullea and Otto Frederickson to link the San Francisco murders to Earle Nelson. Their report was sent to Winnipeg[40] and was published as an attachment to a brief article by Duncan Matheson in the *Police Journal*.[41] In regard to the Edmonds murder, Dullea and Frederickson wrote:

> Mrs. G.H. Patch, 3526 Fulton St., states that the photograph is that of the man she saw in the living room of Mrs. W.A. Edmond's home at 3524 Fulton St. at about 1:30 p.m. on November 18th, 1926, when she came into Mrs. Edmond's house to ask Mrs. Edmonds if she wanted to take an automobile ride.....
>
> Mrs. Irving L. Kaufman, 1464 Francisco St., was shown the photograph and she states that he is the man who called at her bungalow at 449–39th Avenue on the afternoon of Nov. 17, 1926 (the day before Mrs. Edmonds was killed). The place was advertised (TO LET-FURNISHED ROOMS). While the man was being shown through the house another prospective client called and Mrs. Kaufman asked the man to go and get his wife and come back, but when she got through showing the latest applicant around the house, she looked in the front room and this man was sitting there. He wanted her to show him the cellar, but she was much alarmed, and, after he went to the cellar himself, he returned and made another inspection of the closets and commented on their depth. She finally got him out and shut the door.[42]

Again, it is significant that the Kaufman house and the Edmonds house were in the same general Richmond area of the city, not that far from each other. Mrs. Kaufman's story seems entirely credible. We suspect that both Patch and Kaufman were presented with just the picture of Nelson rather than an array of pictures, which diminished the value of their identification. However, Kaufman spent considerable time with the prospective renter, and her identification of Earle Nelson is another important link.

CHAPTER 18

Florence Monks in Seattle

18. November 23, 1926—Florence Monks, 55, Seattle

It was only five days after the murder of Mrs. Edmunds in San Francisco when the next landlady was strangled to death, this time in Seattle. Mrs. Florence Fithian Monks was a wealthy widow who apparently carefully guarded her actual age from her friends. It was widely reported that she was 45 or 48 years old.[1] The formal death notice in the *Seattle Times* listed her age as 48.[2] However, her actual age was 55.[3] She was born Florence Mabel Swift in 1871 in New York.[4] She had been married three times.[5] In 1890 she was married to John Bruen who died in 1905. In 1909, at the age of 38, she married an elderly widower, Richard Fithian, who then died a few years later in 1912 at the age of 65.[6] She then married John Monks, age 52, in 1919.[7] They moved to the Seattle area, where John died in 1922.[8]

While her age may have been a carefully guarded secret, apparently her wealth, inherited from her husbands, was not. According to her friends, she was worth at least $500,000 (about $8.5 million today), and she displayed her wealthy status by the jewelry she wore.[9] She habitually had four or five diamond rings on her fingers and a diamond cluster bar pin on her chest, along with "the jeweled pins of the Eastern Star, the White Shrine, the Daughters of the Nile and the Order of Amaranth."[10] Her friends had warned her that her conspicuous display of jewelry put her at risk of robbery, especially when she was trying to sell or rent her home and staying there alone at night. Mrs. Monks had laughed at their concerns and stated, "I'm not afraid. Anyhow, I hope I'll sell the place soon."[11] After her murder, chief detective Charles Tennant came close to blaming the victim for her own demise because of her open display of costly jewelry, inviting thugs to "come and take them."[12]

Mrs. Monks' main social connections related to Masonic activities. She was the treasurer of the Seattle chapter of the Eastern Star for several years, royal matron of Evergreen Lodge, Order of Amaranth, and good friend to Mr. Charles McMinimee, royal patron of Evergreen Court, and his wife, Agnes, who was the beneficiary of Mrs. Monks' diamond sunburst pin according to her will. Mrs. Monks reportedly did not trust lawyers and based on her own legal studies had drawn up her own will,[13] although she was a friend to the lawyer, Mr. Walter F. Meier, grand master of Masonic lodges in the State of Washington.[14]

Mrs. Monks owned a large house in Seattle at 723 12th Avenue North (now East) in the Capital Hill District and an even grander "country home" at Echo Lake Park, north of Seattle. She decided to sell or rent her house in Seattle and move to the country home. Most of the furniture and possessions in the Seattle house had already been moved but for one bedroom where Mrs. Monks occasionally slept when staying over for the night in Seattle. Her pattern during this transitional move was to drive in her own car to the Seattle home during the day to show the house to prospective purchasers or renters and then return to Cedar Lodge, her estate at Echo Lake Park, which was looked after by a full-time caretaker, Mr. T.J. Raymond.[15] The *Times* stated that Mrs. Monks had a "To Let" sign in the window of the house at 723 12th Avenue as well as advertisements in the newspapers.[16] Her last advertisement on the Monday before her death invited prospective buyers to call between the hours of 11 and 3 and gave her phone number.[17]

On Tuesday, November 23, Mrs. Monks was at her Seattle home and had conversed on the phone with several women in the morning about her plans for Thanksgiving dinner and various upcoming lodge events. At about one in the afternoon, Mr. and Mrs. Carpenter, who lived only walking distance away, came over to view the house of Mrs. Monks. They had an appointment to do so at that time. As they were being shown through the place the doorbell rang and Mrs. Monks admitted a tall blond man "with sandy hair and ruddy face."[18] He sat in a little room off the hall until Mr. and Mrs. Carpenter left. However, the tall blond man was quickly identified when he came to the police of his own accord. He was a radio repairman who had come to the house to repair a radio. After Mr. and Mrs. Carpenter left, he worked on the radio for a while but could not finish the job before he had to leave for another appointment. He told Mrs. Monks that he would return the next day. He returned on Wednesday morning, and not receiving an answer to his ring, he left a card under the door. The police did not view him as a suspect.[19]

Murder victim Florence Monks (*Seattle Star*, Nov. 26, 1926, at 8).

Later investigations revealed that Mrs. Monks had made a long phone call to Mr. Otto Kirchbach of the Art Bake Shop at about 2:30 in the afternoon, dealing with the turkey she wanted for a Thanksgiving dinner at her house as well as a big dinner planned at the Masonic temple on December 4. According to Kirchbach, "they must have talked fifteen or twenty minutes, for his arm ached from holding up the receiver." The conversation was broken off when Mrs. Monks said, "I've got to go now, Otto, there's someone at the door."[20] The "someone at the door" just before three in the afternoon may well have been her murderer.

At about eight in the evening, Mr. Coy, a friend of Mrs. Monks, arrived at the house to keep an appointment with her. When he arrived at the house Coy rang the doorbell and got no response. "The house was dark," he declared. "I thought that very strange since the date had been so definite. I went to a nearby drug store to call her and received no reply. So, I came back at 8:15, only to find the house still apparently deserted."

The next day, Wednesday, November 24, not knowing why Mrs. Monks was absent, the next-door neighbors, Mr. and Mrs. McDonald, who had a key to the house, took various prospective purchasers through the Monks house, and even into the basement, without a clue that Mrs. Monks lay dead behind the furnace.[21] At some stage on Wednesday evening Mr. McDonald started to seriously worry about the missing lady next door. As quoted in the *Times*:

> "I went over to the garage behind Mrs. Monks' house to see if her automobile was there.... When I saw it was, I decided something must have happened to Mrs. Monks. Only last week she told my wife and me that she had been having dizzy spells. So, I went next door to Mr. Gordon's and told him that something was wrong. I asked him to go with me to search the Monks' house and he did. We started from the attic and searched the place to the cellar. We couldn't find the electric light switch in the dark when we got down in the cellar, so we burned matches and peered through the shadows. The furnace hid the body from us."[22]

Not long after this, Mr. Raymond, the caretaker of the country estate, showed up at the Seattle house. He was worried because Mrs. Monks had failed to answer the phone calls he had been making to her all day. He was the one who found the body of Mrs. Monks behind the furnace of the house. As described in the *Times*, "When she failed to answer his ring, he entered the house. Upstairs he noticed evidence of burglary and descended to the cellar and noticed marks where some object had been dragged over the floor. Following the marks, he discovered the body of his employer. He immediately notified police."[23]

Because Coroner Willis Corson was out of town, the police left the body of Mrs. Monks lying on the basement floor all Wednesday night while they guarded the house and waited the arrival of Corson on Thursday morning.[24] Various neighbor ladies gathered around on the main floor and wept.[25] S.B. Groff, a *Seattle Star* reporter, evidently gained entrance to the house and wrote:

> In the basement the position of every article had been carefully charted on the concrete floor with chalk, and a coal shovel, which at first was believed to be the weapon with which Mrs. Monks was killed, was later said to be free of blood stains and fingerprints. Where the woman had fallen there was a mark on the dusty floor. Her glasses lay nearby ... also a pair of canvas gloves. From here, there was a wide mark, where she had been dragged around the furnace into the shadow. Her clothes showed that she had been systematically searched for valuables

and her diamonds had been torn loose. There was an open safety pin at her throat where the sunburst had been carried. The house upstairs was scantily furnished. Mrs. Monks had taken most of her home furnishing away. In the dining room she had a writing desk. This had been broken open, and her private letters, stationery and keepsakes had been thrown around in confusion as the murderer searched for valuables. A sealskin coat valued at approximately $1000 had been left hanging against the wall. The living room contained only a few chairs and a small table. The fireplace had been piled full of letters and papers and these were all carefully saved for examination. Detective Bradley meanwhile developed three fingerprints on a little handbag…. He also found the lace handkerchief which she had used to carry her jewelry. The handkerchief was lying in the living room upstairs and was identified by her neighbors and other friends.[26]

Another paper noted that there was only one fingerprint on the bag or purse, not three.[27] The police were not confident that the fingerprint was necessarily that of the murderer.[28]

Mrs. Monks had apparently been aware of the danger of wearing her jewelry while showing the house, because at the time of her death she had much of her jewelry wrapped in a handkerchief and pinned to her undergarments. When her body was discovered, the pin holding the jewelry bag was found on the floor and it was believed the little bag of jewels had been torn from her clothing by the fiend.[29] The reports dealing with what jewels she was wearing and what were hidden varied from newspaper to newspaper.[30]

On Thursday morning the autopsy was performed by Dr. W.H. Corson. As reported in the *Times*:

> Mrs. Monks had been choked. Finger marks were found on her throat. A heavy layer of dust and dirt on her dress, one for evening wear, gave plain evidence that she had been dragged to the place where her body was found. There was also a bruise on her head, but there had been no skull fracture. Whether the woman died from being choked, or from fright which induced a heart attack, the coroner could not say. She was known to have a weak heart.[31]

Nothing was mentioned as to whether Mrs. Monks had been sexually assaulted or whether the coroner had even considered this possibility. It was the *Star* that eventually noted the opinion of Dr. William J. Jones, the deputy coroner, that Mrs. Monks "had not been attacked."[32]

The murder of Monks in Seattle was obviously similar to the so-called "mysterious" deaths of three landladies in Portland, and Detective Archie Leonard of Portland traveled to Seattle to discover as much as he could about the murder of Monks and aid the Seattle police in their investigation.[33] Despite the apparent absence of evidence of sexual assault in the Portland cases and in the Seattle case, as well as the prominence of the robbery motive, various press reports also linked the Seattle and Portland cases to the "dark strangler" of California and the latest murder of Edmonds.[34]

Over the next days while Leonard was in Seattle, chief detective Charles Tennant came to the firm conclusion that the "dark strangler" had murdered Monks. However, he was vigorously opposed by Dr. Corson and some police officers, who believed that Monks was murdered by an acquaintance for her jewelry and that the case should not be linked to the "dark strangler." Dr. Corson believed that Mrs. Monks had been murdered for greed and not for lust, given that a microscopic examination, made in the laboratory of Dr. P.C. West, had failed to disclose the slightest evidence that the woman had been subjected to any indignity beyond the beating and choking which resulted in her death. "Taking this in conjunction with the outward condition of the body," Dr. Corson said, "it seems to me the conclusion that robbery was the *only* motive for the crime admits of scarcely any doubt. Moreover, it is my opinion that the murderer was one who had intimate knowledge of Mrs. Monks' habits. I say this because of the fact that he evidently knew just where she kept her diamonds and wasted no time in getting them. According to her friends, she used to keep the jewels wrapped up in a handkerchief which she pinned to her underclothing beneath the left shoulder and was in the habit of opening her waist and reaching in with her right hand when she wanted to get them out. The murderer got at them in precisely the same way. He undid the single snap on the waist and then jerked the jewels free, without bothering to unfasten them, as evidenced by the broken safety pin which was found nearby."[35]

Despite Tennant's opinion as to the link with the "dark strangler," it was not until Saturday night, a full three days after the discovery of the body, that chief of police William Searing sounded a warning to local landladies. The notice was buried in the eighth page of the next day's *Times*.[36] However, Chief Searing, in giving his warning, added, "The [Monks] case is in no way similar to the strangler cases in California."[37]

Finally, on Monday, November 29, when the Seattle police received the most recent circular from the San Francisco police dealing with the murder of Edmonds and the description given by Mrs. Murray, the *Times* noted that Seattle officers were now of the opinion that the Portland and Seattle murders were indeed connected with those in San Francisco.[38] By Monday, after the strangler had killed another woman in Portland, the details of which we will turn to in the next chapter, Chief Searing had changed his mind and now agreed that Mrs. Monks was murdered by the "dark strangler" of San Francisco and Portland.[39] Chief of detectives Tennant added, "In none of these cases was murder necessary. There was no necessity of killing Mrs. Monks. There was none in any of the Portland cases. It is simply that the killer took delight in his work. He killed for the satisfaction it gave him."[40]

However, the alternative theory that Monks was murdered by an acquaintance who knew where she secreted her jewels persisted and various detectives continued to investigate this angle and even had someone in mind.[41] Even after another landlady was murdered in Portland, some detectives in Seattle continued to defy the opinion of their superiors and persisted in gathering evidence against a specific "friend" of Mrs. Monks.[42] Coroner Corson and coroner-elect Dr. Jones supported the rebel detectives. Dr. Corson was still of the view that robbery was the sole motive and that someone who knew Monks killed her.[43] As we will eventually show, the "acquaintance" theory was finally put to rest and the "dark strangler" theory was accepted when some jewelry belonging to Mrs. Monks was subsequently discovered in Portland.

In addition to the fingerprint clue, the Seattle police investigated all the persons who were acquainted with Mrs. Monks. They also tried to find out if the jewels could be located in pawn shops. However, detectives had some difficulties finding the bank where Mrs. Monks kept her safety deposit box which might provide a clue as to just what jewelry had been stolen.[44] It was eventually discovered that in October she had discontinued using her safety box at the Seattle National Bank. So where was the safety deposit box she had used subsequently? A slender safety deposit box key, bearing the number 307, was found in her home, but the police checked every bank in the business district of Seattle looking for an account with Mrs. Monks and found none. Had she hidden her jewelry, silver plate, and securities in her houses? Finally, the new box was discovered at the Marine National Bank, and an exact inventory of what was missing and what was not could be attempted.[45] There was some jewelry in the box, including the large sunburst of diamonds that initially was thought to be missing. After the inventory, the police released a long list of the stolen jewelry.[46] According to the *Times*, this tidy loot was estimated by captain of detectives W.B. Kent to be worth between $4,000 and $5,000.[47] The *Post-Intelligencer*, however, suggested that the missing jewelry was worth at least $5,000 and could be worth up to $20,000, depending on the quality of the diamonds.[48] The jewelry list was circulated immediately to all the pawn shops and police departments along the Pacific Coast.[49]

More than 400 people attended the funeral for Mrs. Monks on Saturday, December 4, in the Masonic temple followed by interment at the Lake View Cemetery beside her late husband, John Monks.[50]

≈ ≈ ≈

The Monks murder received relatively little press attention compared to two sensational murders in Seattle in 1926 which received voluminous coverage. On June 16, 1926, the body of Sylvia Gaines, 22, was found in a grove of trees at Green Lake. She had been strangled the night before while out walking around the lake, hit over the head with a rock when she resisted, and her clothes were partly removed, suggesting sexual assault. After a dramatic trial in August 1926, her father was convicted of murder. Considerable evidence was introduced that her alcoholic father was in an incestuous relationship with Sylvia and that he had killed her in a drunken rage after she had complained about his drinking and was threatening to leave. He was convicted and eventually after a series of appeals was hanged in August of 1928.[51] Was she killed by her father or by a fiend like Earle Nelson? I find it hard to believe that a father would kill his own daughter, but after reviewing the trial evidence, it seems the case against the father was compelling.

The same cannot be said for the second murder, that of 14-year-old Letitia Whitehall who was abducted while walking home from a dental appointment on the evening of October 30, 1926. Her body was found several weeks later in the Sammamish River. She had likely been thrown off the Kenwood Bridge after being strangled and raped. At the time of the Monks murder the local press was full of stories as to the investigation of a host of suspects. Eventually in April of 1927, the dentist, Dr. Chester Dobbs, was put on trial for the murder of his patient. The sensational trial turned into a farce, with the prosecution lacking any evidence, and Dobbs was declared to be innocent. Dr. Dobbs had nothing to do with the murder of Letitia Whitehall which remains unsolved to this day.[52] Interestingly, the same fiend versus father issue eventually also arose in the Whitehall case.[53]

The Whitehall murder did not involve a landlady and we presume the killer had a vehicle to pick up the girl while she was walking home and to drive to the bridge where she was thrown into the river. We usually think of Nelson as a hitchhiker, not an owner of a vehicle, although there were reports of a suspicious vehicle in the first Portland murders in October, including the encounter with Mrs. Lewis.[54] I doubt that this murder, outside Nelson's usual *modus operandi*, was committed by him, but I cannot dismiss all suspicion.

CHAPTER 19

Blanche Myers in Portland

19. November 29, 1926—Blanche Myers, 49, Portland

Mrs. Myers was born Mary Blanche Lawrence in Indiana in 1877.[1] While the newspapers referred to her as being 48 when she died, she was in fact a month or so past 49 years of age.[2] She married Christian David Myers in 1899 in Columbia City, Indiana.[3] Christian Myers was a veteran of the Spanish–American War of 1898 and worked in Fort Wayne as a bookkeeper.[4] Their first son, Robert, was born in 1903 in Fort Wayne. Due to the fragile health of Christian, the family moved to Redlands, California, in 1905, where son David Lawrence Myers was born in 1908.[5] Blanche was well known in Redlands as a soloist for several churches. She also was involved in various women's civic groups.[6] Christian Myers died of "tubercular trouble" at the age of 41 in Redlands.[7] After the early death of her husband, Blanche moved to Portland, where her brother, Robert Lawrence, a shoe merchant, lived.[8]

Blanche Myers did not share the social prominence and affluence of Florence Monks in Seattle. She had been living on a meager army pension, supplemented by modest fees earned by playing the organ or singing at funerals, by teaching music to children, and by renting rooms in her house at 449 10th Street in Portland.[9] Mrs. Myers did not even own the modest house, but rather she rented from a Mr. Muir living on Stark Street. At the time of her death, her 23-year-old son, Robert, was at college in Walla Walla, Washington, and her second son, David Lawrence, 18 years old, was a high school student at Lincoln High.[10] However, after 10 years as a widow, Mrs. Myers had recently been engaged to be married to a Mr. Laurence Stangl, a Portland real estate agent.[11]

A lengthy typed memo on the murder of Mrs. Myers is found in the police notebook of detectives Rockwell and Thomas.[12] The newspaper reports on the case accurately follow, for the most part, the official police narrative. On Monday, November 29, Mrs. Myers called the landlord, Mr. Alexander Muir, to come over and fix a leak in the roof. Myers had rented the house from him for the past seven years. He arrived at about 11, fixed the roof, and then went into the house, washed his hands in the sink, and asked Mrs. Myers if he could stay for lunch. She agreed but told him that he would need to go to the store for some bread. Muir went to the store and picked up some bread and some donuts.[13] When he returned, Lawrence, son of Mrs. Myers, had already finished lunch and was on his way back to school.

Mr. Muir and Mrs. Myers were sitting at the kitchen table when the doorbell rang at about 1 in the afternoon. There was a "Room to Rent" sign in the window of the house.[14] Mrs. Myers answered the door. Mr. Muir, described as a "man advanced in years," remained sitting at the kitchen table and never saw the young man who came in and went upstairs with Mrs. Myers.[15] He could only describe the conversation that he had with Mrs. Myers after she came back downstairs, removed the sign from the window, and rejoined him at the table. Mr. Muir provided the following narrative to the police and the press:

> I could not see the person to whom she was talking. They then went upstairs with Mrs. Myers staying up there twelve or fifteen minutes, which seemed to me to be an unusually long time, as I finished my lunch and partly smoked a cigar before she came downstairs, leaving the stranger upstairs. When she came down, I remarked, "Well, you have rented a room," and she said, "I have," and showed me $3.50 in 50-cent pieces, which she put on the table beside her wristwatch, which she had taken off while doing the wash. Mrs. Myers also had 5 dollars in currency in her left hand. I asked whom she rented the room to, and Mrs. Myers said, "To a young man who looks to me to be a logger." I replied, "It is unusual for a logger to come up this far." Mrs. Myers answered, "I don't like his looks very much, so I asked him if he drank, and he said not very much, but once in a while he did." She said that when she left the room the man said he was tired and was going to lie down. She also said that this man had come to the house two or three days before, but at that time she was unable to rent it to him because he thought the price too high.[16]

Murder victim Blanche Myers (*Oregonian*, Dec. 1, 1926, at 8).

Muir says that he left the home shortly after 1 o'clock.[17] Many months later a report stated that the young man had called himself "Abner Vogel."[18]

At about 2:10 in the afternoon, a man came to deliver two tons of coal briquettes as had been ordered by Mrs. Myers. He rang the doorbell but received no answer. Going around to the back of the house, he found the cellar door open and so he called his two helpers from the truck, and they delivered the briquettes and left the bill under the front door. The man from the coal company told the police that the house was "absolutely quiet" when they delivered the coal.[19]

Lawrence Myers came home from school at about 3:45 in the afternoon of that Monday and found the house empty, and, according to the *Oregonian*, both front and back doors of the house stood open.[20] However, the police report states that he entered the front door which was closed but unlocked.[21] Not finding his mother at home, he was not at first worried, thinking she had gone out and would return soon. He practiced music on his banjo for a while.[22] However, he eventually became very worried about the absence of his mother, and he cooked two eggs for supper, and after waiting on the porch, he left the house at about seven, leaving a note that he would be home early. When he arrived back at the house at 10:30 in the evening and still found no sign of his mother, he started the process of making inquiries of his uncle and friends, and he finally called the police at around midnight.[23] This is also the account provided in the *Telegram*, which noted that Lawrence became increasingly worried about his mother's absence because she would usually leave a note if she was out of the house. "Then he laughed at his fears. She had probably gone somewhere with her fiancé, Lawrence Stangl, or over to his uncle's place, J.A. Lawrence, manager of the shoe department at Meier and Frank…. So, he went to a show."[24]

The police arrived at the house after midnight. Patrolman Chase was first on the scene and, using his flashlight, he found the body of Mrs. Myers under the bed in the center upstairs bedroom, which was the room that had been for rent.[25] Police lieutenant Thatcher and detectives Rockwell, Thomas, Westcott, Fleming, Eichenberger, and the detective with the interesting name, Earl Nelson, soon arrived, with deputy coroner Gulbrandson and fingerprint expert Payne in tow.[26] The *Journal* presented the scene:

> She was lying not quite all the way under the bed, her right-side protruding slightly, but the white bedspread had been pulled down almost to the floor so that, to the casual observer, she was concealed…. The body was lying under the bed, on its back, with the feet crossed. The right arm was straight down at the side, but the left arm was slightly bent at the elbow, the hand extending outward. Her head was turned slightly to her left shoulder. The body was clothed fully, and the clothes were not torn. That Mrs. Myers had been dragged to the position she was found was indicated by the fact that her hair was straight down in the back and her skirt was just above her knees. The body had been so placed that it was necessary to shift the bed to remove it. A pink apron had been tied around her neck; a square knot drawn tightly after the first turn. The apron was wrapped around four more times and tied with square knots until all the apron and strings were used up by the murderer.[27]

Portland Police Department photograph of the Myers house at 449 10th Street. Winnipeg police file (courtesy John Burchill).

The *Oregonian* noted that the pink tea apron knotting was recalled by the police as being like the method used in the Fluke case.[28]

The *Telegram* emphasized the violence, so apparent compared to the earlier Portland cases of Withers and Grant and even Fluke. "Blood streamed from an ear…. Her arms were bruised. Her face was bruised. The tightly drawn apron had cut deep into her throat."[29] The police also noticed various blood stains on the floor:

> They were not discovered until a small rug spread before the bed was removed. These stains were smeared and covered an area about the length of the bed, which is a light single bed. Detectives came to the conclusion the murderer, either during a scuffle with Mrs. Myers or while dragging her body, had scuffed the rug out of place with his feet, and that after he had placed the body under the bed, he discovered the stains and smeared the underside of the rug and put the rug back in place.[30]

In the now-familiar pattern of "dark strangler" cases, various items had been stolen. Lawrence Myers noticed that his mother's yellow gold wristwatch was missing, her diamond engagement ring had been taken off her finger, and a brownish coat and about $8.50 in cash was also gone. The empty purse was on the kitchen table.[31] It was later reported that the killer had chain-smoked two cigarettes, as police discovered two stubs and a match on the windowsill.[32]

The original group of officials and detectives stayed at the house all night, and then at 6:30 on Tuesday morning a whole new crew arrived, including chief of detectives Moore and detectives Goltz, Collins, Tackabery, Phillips, Hyde and Leonard.[33] That Mrs. Myers had fought for her life became evident after the autopsy report was released:

> Mrs. Myers, according to … Dr. Benson, suffered haemorrhages at the larynx, eyes and ears. Two ribs were broken: Nos. 1 and 3 on the right side in front, as though from being struck by a fist or an instrument. Around the shoulders were marks that might have come from a severe struggle. The fingernails were bent back, as though from scratching. No blood was on them, however. They might have been bent back from scratching her assailants clothing.[34]

No mention was made in the *Journal* or *Telegram* as to whether Mrs. Meyers had been sexually assaulted. The *Oregonian* denied that there was a sexual assault, stating, "The slayer did not attack the woman, at least no visible sign of such an attack could be found by the coroner. The clothes were not disarranged, except that the skirt was slightly above the knees, as if the body had been dragged by the feet."[35] However, the more sensational *Portland News*, without reporting any other details of the autopsy, said that Coroner Smith told the jury that she had been "brutally attacked either before or after death."[36] However, unlike the other murders in Portland, we have some confirmation that Mrs. Meyers was probably sexually assaulted. After subsequent murders in Kansas City occurred in late December, J.T. Moore, acting chief of police in Portland, wrote a letter to Kansas City in which he specifically stated that Mrs. Myers had been strangled and her body had been "violated."[37] Unlike the other reports of the coroner, the official report on Mrs. Myers states unambiguously that she was murdered by strangulation. However, nothing is said about testing for sexual assault.[38]

The most important clue in this case, according to the police, was the presence of fingerprints. The investigative notebook of Thomas and Rockwell stated, "The upper parts of both head and foot of bedstead bore many prints of bloody or grimy fingers, as though the bed had been grasped and pulled about the room. We did not move the bed clothing, leaving it just as we found it. The bed itself was rolled away so

that the body could be removed. As far as we know no one else had touched the bedstead where the fingerprints are."[39] The *Journal* added that the prints "were distinct
and due to the white enamel background, excellent photographs were made of them.
There were at least a dozen capable of being used for identification."[40] As we will note
in the next chapter, the fingerprint evidence in this case was widely overstated in the
press and was eventually reduced to one useable print.

≈ ≈ ≈

After the fourth landlady murder in Portland, the previous talk about suicide
and natural deaths pretty much vanished. Now all four murders were declared to be
the work of the "dark strangler" who had killed women in the San Francisco area
and in Seattle, even if the sexual assault element was apparently missing in the Portland and Seattle cases.[41] The police nevertheless believed that the killing itself was
what motivated the fiend, with robbery a secondary motivation.[42] There were even
links made to earlier cases. For example, the *Oregonian* noted that detectives were
considering whether the strangler might have started his gruesome string of killings
on the Atlantic Coast. "In Philadelphia, they learned, three middle-aged women

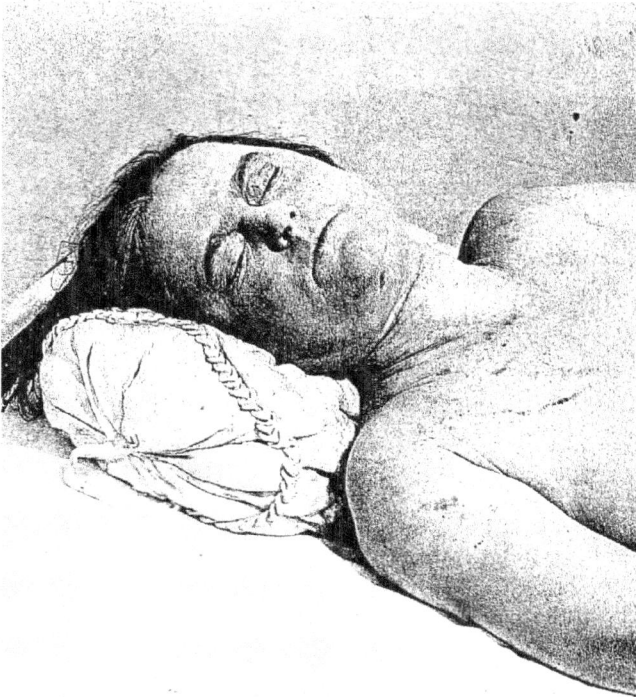

were murdered under similar
circumstances on October 15,
November 7, and November 10
of 1925. All were strangled; all
had their houses for rent or for
sale, and in each case jewelry
and other small articles were
said to have been missing.
Philadelphia police were asked
to send complete details of
their investigation to the Portland detectives."[43]

Captain of inspectors
John Moore stated that the
police were now working in
emergency mode, and the
mayor of Portland, Mr. Baker,
personally donated $100 for a
reward for the capture of the
fiend and asked the city council to authorize a further $500
for a reward. Instead, the Portland city council authorized a
reward of $1000.[44] The Amer-
ican Legion added $100, as did
Mr. Macdonald, the father of
Mrs. Fluke, and with other
contributions the reward soon

Portland Police Department photograph of the body
of Blanche Myers at the morgue. Notice the numerous
scratches and bruises on the shoulder and neck as well as
the deep mark across the throat left by the tightly bound
apron strings. We have edited out the naked breasts
and therefore also the numerous scratches on her arms.
Winnipeg police file (courtesy John Burchill).

was $1500 for the capture of the "dark strangler."[45] Various Portland detectives raised $100 of their own money to put into the pot.[46] The brother of Mrs. Myers put in $100 as well.[47] Eventually, the city council raised the reward by another $1000, bringing the total to $2500.[48]

As to any descriptions of what the fiend looked like, the police in Portland were basically following the descriptions given by the San Francisco police after the attempted strangulation of Mrs. Murray a few weeks previously in Burlingame, followed by the brief descriptions given by Mrs. Patch who walked into a conversation between the strangler and Mrs. Edmunds. They also looked for loggers, given the statements made by Mrs. Myers to Mr. Muir. But then the Portland police hit a goldmine of information when two women contacted them. Their story provided the police with a major breakthrough in the description and ultimate identification of the "dark strangler."

CHAPTER 20

The Link Between the Murders
of Monks and Myers, and
"Adrian Harris" as the Dark Strangler

American Thanksgiving falls on the Thursday of the fourth week of November. On Wednesday, November 24, 1926, the day before the big celebration, and the day after the murder of Mrs. Monks in Seattle, a man calling himself "Adrian Harris" showed up at a shabby rooming house at 426 Third Street in Portland.[1] At the rooming house were three elderly women, Mrs. Cayfort, Mrs. Yates, and a third lady who "had practically nothing to do with the man."[2] The notebook of detectives Tackabery and Phillips gives the name of the third lady as Mrs. Stats.[3] Carrying what appeared to be an almost new suitcase, Harris paid Mrs. Cayfort $2 in advance to rent a room for a week.

At some point on the day of his arrival, Adrian Harris went out and bought $14 worth of groceries so that the ladies in the house could all have a lovely Thanksgiving dinner with him. Presumably the women did all the cooking. At the feast the next day, as the women would later relate:

> They talked of this, that, and everything … with religion being the principal subject. Harris could talk fluently on all kinds of religion. In fact, they said, he seemed to be a religious fanatic…. He told them he was born in Denmark and had come to this country when five years old and that he was a carpenter and had been building bunkhouses and such things in logging camps. In Portland, however, he said he expected to build small houses and accordingly he had placed $1200 in a bank here.[4]

The third lady left after the meal ended, but Harris continued to talk at length with Cayfort and Yates, and before the night was out, he got Mrs. Yates to agree to make him breakfast every morning, which she did during his stay at the house. It was reported that "during his stay in the rooming house he was slightly ill with influenza. The two women gave him some attention and one day permitted him to sit in front of the fire in one of their rooms. The women said he talked like a 'gentleman.'"[5] Harris rarely left the house during the day, but "he went out each night and purchased copies of afternoon papers, reading them with avidity. This, despite the 'bad cold' he told them he had."[6]

The day after the Thanksgiving feast, Friday, November 26, Harris met with Mrs. Cayfort and with Mrs. Yates separately and gave each of them jewelry, without telling the other what he had done.[7] The *Oregonian* described the jewelry received by each of them, noting that "Harris" said, "You do not have a great deal, and I don't need this stuff," adding that jewelry would do them "more good than me." In addition, he offered Mrs. Yates a watch, which had the diamonds pried out of the back of its old case, but Mrs. Yates did not accept it. She gave as an explanation that he had given her too many things already.[8] Perhaps Adrian Harris had a particular shine for Mrs. Yates?

In any event, for several days Cayfort and Yates were unaware that the other had also been given a gift of jewelry, but on Monday morning, Harris woke up to hear the two women arguing. They had discovered each other's gifts, and the argument had apparently involved the fact that Mrs. Yates had clearly been given more valuable amounts of jewelry. As reported, "Harris came to the room himself." He had heard them quarrelling. "I'm going to beat it out of here," he was quoted as saying, "you folks will have the police up here." And with that he went to his room, obtained his suitcase and left, saying he was going to Vancouver, Washington. "His room rent was paid for two more days."[9] An alternative narrative found in the *Journal* stated:

> His reason for leaving, the police learned, was because the women in the house disagreed in their attitude toward him. There is a third woman who lives at the house who took exception to his being treated in too much of a friendly way, the police believe. This morning Mrs. Cayfort denied that there had been any disagreement over the distribution of his loot and said that she and Mrs. Yates both knew he had given articles of jewelry to the other and had not had any argument over that at all.[10]

Whatever the cause of the argument, after leaving the rooming house on that Monday morning, Adrian Harris did not go to Vancouver, Washington, but instead he went to the rooming house of Mrs. Myers. This assumption became a logical conclusion when the jewelry that Harris had given to the women turned out without a doubt to be some of the gems that had been owned by Mrs. Monks. Harris had murdered Monks and the logical inference was that his leaving the rooming house of Cayfort and Yates led almost immediately to the murder of Myers.

When the ladies at the boarding house on Third Street read about the Myers murder and the description of the "dark strangler," they immediately contacted the police and handed over the jewels that Harris had given them. There was a picture in the *Journal* and in the *Oregonian* of Inspector Westcott holding the jewelry.[11] Harris had given the women the least expensive items in his jewelry stash taken from Mrs. Monks. As noted in the Seattle press, "The total value of the pearls, 'diamond' necklace and bracelet, gold pens and fountain pens, sent here by the Portland authorities, probably does not exceed $15 or $20, it was said. The pins which contained real stones are still missing."[12] Before these jewels were even sent to Seattle, friends of Mrs. Monks identified them as having been hers based on seeing newspaper pictures sent to Seattle, but their identification was confirmed when the jewels themselves were sent to Seattle.[13]

Oregon detectives on pawn shop duty soon discovered that four separate Portland pawnbrokers had received visits "no longer ago than Tuesday," the day after the murder of Mrs. Myers, from a man "attempting to dispose of a gold Shrine pin with a diamond setting, identical with that taken from Mrs. Monks."[14] The pawnbrokers did not accept the pin because they believed it was stolen and their descriptions of the man conformed pretty closely to the San Francisco descriptions of the "dark strangler," except his age was given as around 40. The pawn shop owners were probably less concerned about possession of stolen goods and had instead offered a price for the pin that was too low, and the man had refused to relinquish it for so low a price.[15]

Obviously, the ladies on Third Street, having spent so much time with Adrian Harris, could also give a detailed description of him, which matched in significant ways the description given by Mrs. Murray in San Francisco. They described the man "as being about 24 or 26, 5 feet 7 inches in height, with a dark complexion, dark eyes and brown hair. He was dressed fairly well and said he was a Dane."[16] "When he talked, he bulged his lips slightly and he had a slight accent. He wore a brown cap and a brown overcoat."[17] Subsequently it was reported that the "slight accent" had been misinformation and that the women meant "slight lisp."[18] The women also mentioned that Harris claimed to have been married and divorced; claimed to have attended Aimee Semple McPherson services in Los Angeles several months ago; and was an inveterate cigarette smoker.[19] The *Seattle Post* stated that the man "has large dark eyes which he rolls and blinks when addressing women."[20] Much was made of the so-called "religious fanatic" connection, and as reported in the *Seattle Star*, "he gave not the slightest indication of his insane tendencies and talked rationally on every subject except religion…. He spoke also of belonging to the Holy Rollers and mentioned numerous religious missions."[21]

Two grocery men, Mr. Gordon and Mr. Holliway, who had sold the $14 worth of food to Adrian Harris and had dealt with him several other times while he had been at the Third Street rooming house, also came forward with a description of Harris.[22] As reported in the *Oregonian*, "The strangler suspect, according to the grocery men, is pleasant in his appearance and gives no intimation of possessing any talents for crimes such as the police believe him guilty of. He is quiet, well mannered, and one of the grocery men expressed his impressions, 'I never spoke to a nicer mannered fellow.'"[23] According to the *Journal*, "He spent nearly half an hour in the store the day before Thanksgiving, it was said, and after leaving with numerous purchases for the holiday feast both grocers had occasion to call at Mrs. Cayfort's home, and while there, talked to the man." Both said he was about five feet, seven inches tall, weighed about 150 pounds, and had piercing eyes of undetermined color and dark, wiry hair.[24] The curious reference to the grocers going to the Cayfort home was later explained:

> A $10 gold piece was misplaced in the store and the grocery man thought that it might possibly have been dropped among the things which had been purchased by his customer. He went to the house where the strangler was rooming, and together they went through the packages. Later the coin was found at the store, after further search. During the hunt, the grocery man held a conversation with the man, and when he next appeared at the store, they had become quite friendly.[25]

Rolling up these eyewitness accounts from the ladies and grocers, the police in Portland now issued a new description of the fiend:

> Age, 26 to 30 years; height, 5 feet 6 or 7 inches; weight 140 to 150 pounds. Build, broad shoulders, muscular and generally well built. Complexion of Spanish, Mexican or Italian type, but

might resemble a Dane. Hair, dark brown; face, smooth shaven; eyes, large, piercing and dark, given to rolling or blinking when talking. Speech without foreign accent, given to lisping at times when talking, showing upper and lower teeth.... Carried mahogany colored suitcase, nearly new; posed as bunkhouse carpenter in logging camp, as jewelry peddler, spoke frequently of religious meetings and of having attended Holy Roller and Aimee Semple McPherson meetings. An inveterate cigarette smoker posed as having been divorced. Believed to have an old model Ford coupe with dull finish.[26]

The *Times* noted that the rooming house ladies also mentioned that he dressed rather shabbily, and when last seen, he was wearing a coat that seemed too long for him and a gray felt hat.[27]

The *Journal* described the clothes as being a "blue grey hat with mixed colored hat band, a gray suit at times, also light-colored corduroy trousers with yellow sweater having a two-inch dark red border."[28]

Based on the fact that Adrian Harris had the jewels from Mrs. Monks, and that he generally fit the description of the "dark strangler" wanted in San Francisco, and that Mrs. Myers had been killed within hours after Harris had left the Cayfort house, both Seattle and Portland police were convinced that the same man had killed Monks and Myers and probably was the wanted fiend who had strangled a host of women to this point in time. The elderly ladies Cayfort and Yates not only gave up their cheap gems in the public spirit of catching the dangerous killer but they also gave up their privacy. According to one account they subsequently moved away from the rooming house because of the publicity generated by the case, and the police did not know where they had moved to.[29]

~ ~ ~

The description of the strangler as well as the offer of a reward were printed and sent out to every police office on the Pacific Coast and throughout the United States. It was also broadcast on the radio and placed in every rooming house, hotel, and public place within the city.[30] Men with a stocky build who looked like loggers had no chance of obtaining rooms in Portland. If they were carrying a suitcase, they were particularly vulnerable to arrest.

Over the next week, the police dealt with more than one thousand reports from citizens as to suspicious characters and suspects.[31] As usual, various women claimed that they had encountered the strangler seeking a room or acting suspiciously.[32] Various suspects were arrested and ultimately released.[33] For example, Morris Yoffe, who had no recollection of his behavior for the last 10 days, was held in Eugene, and the fingerprint from Portland was sent up to Eugene.[34] Yoffe had apparently been using the name Harris at various rooming houses, had a suitcase, and was acting suspiciously. That Yoffe was missing a dozen teeth and wore thick glasses and was 37 years of age should have been enough to exonerate him. His fingerprint did not match the Portland print and that circumstance was treated as conclusive.[35] Another suspect, George Hutchinson, a logger from Portland and a "half-breed Cherokee," was arrested in San Francisco as a "strangler" suspect[36] and then released after several days when he accounted for his movements and when his fingerprint did not match the print from Portland. He was reportedly looking for a lawyer for a possible false imprisonment case.[37]

One wonders about the veracity of such a late report in the context of post-event information, but on Friday, December 3, a woman informed the police that she had actually seen a man carrying a leather suitcase enter the home of Mrs. Myers between 12 and 1 o'clock on the fateful Monday in question.[38] The woman claimed she had been passing the house at that time and saw the man with the suitcase go up the steps, but she did not come forward with the information sooner "because she was afraid of becoming involved in the publicity of this sensational case."[39] According to the *Oregonian*:

> The detectives … declared that the woman's word was unquestionable and that she had been within a few feet of the man when he entered the residence of Mrs. Myers. The woman said specifically that she had been close enough to the man to see his eyes, which were said to have been "dark and piercing." He was under 30, five feet and seven inches tall, with dark complexion and dark brown hair. He weighed about 150 pounds.[40]

After a week of intense effort, the Portland police admitted that they had nothing as to the whereabouts of Adrian Harris. Detective James M. Tackabery predicted that the "Dr. Jekyll and Mr. Hyde" fiend would be caught some day and pay for his crimes. He added that the strangler "will go down in criminal annals as the master killer of the age."[41]

≈ ≈ ≈

The narrative around the fingerprints changed over time. As noted previously, the Seattle police were not confident that the print on the handbag in the Monks house was that of the murderer.[42] However, the Portland police treated their fingerprints in the Myers case as authoritative. As reported in the *Journal*, "the police have made a careful check against prints of every person who visited the house after the murder in order to make sure they had not been left there carelessly by investigators."[43] Eventually one of the Portland prints, thought to be the middle finger of the right hand, was blown up to a large size and attached to the wanted poster sent to police departments around the country, including Winnipeg.[44]

This so-called "authoritative" print from Portland was sent to Seattle to compare with the print taken from the bag in the Monks house. It was widely reported subsequently that Seattle police found that the prints matched.[45] However, it was noted that the Seattle print would be sent to Harold Anderson, Portland police expert, to make a more definitive comparison.[46] One might read between the lines that the Seattle expert was not confident in his own conclusions. After the Seattle print was sent to Anderson in Portland, there was complete silence in the press on the issue of matching prints. We believe that the prints did not in fact match, because if they did, the Portland police would have issued a report, given the importance of such a definitive linking of the Monks and Myers cases.

When Nelson was arrested in Winnipeg, but before any identification in the United States was attempted, the *Journal* presented a different perspective on the famous fingerprints in the Myers case. Previously the press had suggested that there were a host of usable bloody prints left on the bars of the bed. Now the story was that "the lone print on the bedstead was the only [usable] one found." Furthermore, previously it had been asserted that there was a print in Seattle that matched the print

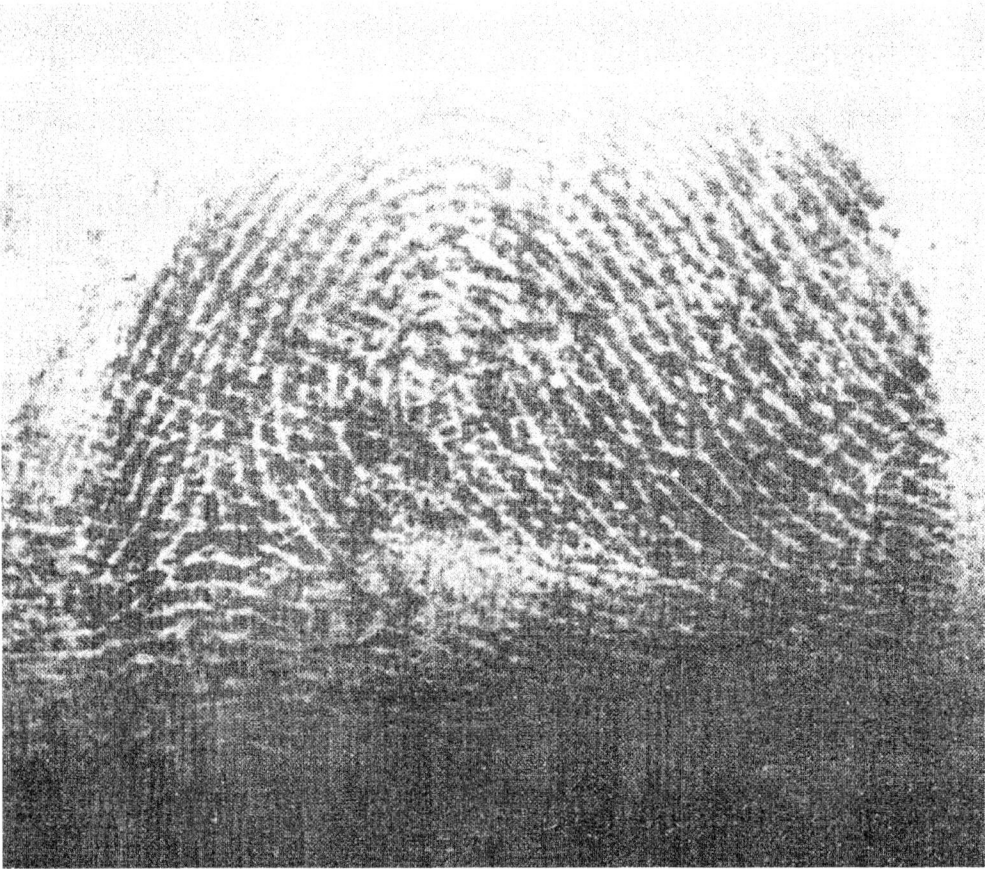

Portland Police Department fingerprint taken from the Myers murder scene which did not match Earle Nelson's print. Winnipeg police file (courtesy John Burchill).

in Portland. Now the story was that the Portland police were the only force to have secured a fingerprint of Harris.[47] It was widely reported that Portland police were jubilant when they received a telegram from Winnipeg that Earle Nelson was "Harris without a doubt."[48] But the identification of Harris was not based on matching fingerprints with the Portland print. The description and mannerisms of Harris perfectly matched Nelson, but *the fingerprint did not*. The next day the *Journal* reported that Winnipeg chief detective George Smith admitted that the Portland print did not match the fingerprint of Earle Nelson, but nevertheless, without a shadow of a doubt, Smith asserted that Nelson was Harris.[49] In retrospect, if Earle Nelson would have been picked up in Portland shortly after the murder of Myers, he might have actually been released given that his fingerprint did not match the fingerprint on the bed of the victim. I have independently verified with the more modern fingerprint experts at the Winnipeg police that the Portland print is in fact not the fingerprint of Earle Nelson.[50] We do not have a copy of the Seattle print.

Despite all the previous arguments that the police had been vigilant in controlling the crime scene, now the argument from Lieutenant Fred Graves, acting chief of inspectors in Portland, was that the Portland circular had stated that the print was "believed" to be that of the strangler, indicating that "there was the possibility that someone handled the bed from which the bloody print was obtained other than the murderer."[51] The same story appeared in the *Oregonian*.[52] The *Journal* also stated, "At that time [of the Myers murder] efforts were made to eliminate all persons who had been in the room, and even though a thorough scrutiny was made, it was impossible to find out definitely how many persons had been in the room between the time the body was found and the prints taken from the white enameled bedstead."[53]

≈ ≈ ≈

Before ever receiving an up-to-date picture of Nelson in June 1927, Portland police found that they had in their own files a card on Earle Leonard Ferrel, arrested in Los Angeles on October 28, 1918, on a burglary charge and as being a Navy deserter. As stated earlier, the police did not know where Cayfort and Yates had moved, but even though the picture of Nelson on the card was nine years old, the police detectives in Portland, now under the direction of Frank Graves, decided to at least present the picture to one of the grocery clerks, instead of waiting for a proper picture to arrive from Winnipeg. "That certainly is a close resemblance, but isn't it an old photograph?" inquired the clerk. He then was told that it was taken nine years earlier. "The clerk, whose name is withheld by police, noted the peculiarities, and although he would not positively put himself on record that it was 'Harris' he was emphatic in declaring there was a decided resemblance."[54] To further muddy future identifications, the *Journal* and the *Oregonian* published the old photos.[55] Several days later, after the mug shots of Nelson from Winnipeg arrived in Portland, the paper also published the new pictures together with the old pictures to prove that indeed the deserter of 1918 was the Earle Nelson under guard in Winnipeg.[56]

Portland police finally discovered that Mrs. Yates was now living near Salem. Police inspectors Goltz, Tackabery and Phillips added the photo of Nelson from Winnipeg to eight random photos taken from files at the police station and then showed the pictures to Mrs. Yates in Salem and to Mr. Gordon, the clerk at the grocery store.[57] We know that Gordon had probably already been shown the old photo of Nelson, and we may well suspect that Yates had seen pictures in the newspapers, but nevertheless, it should be remembered that these individuals, especially Yates, had spent considerable time with Harris. This was not a momentary glimpse at the man, as had been the case with Merton Newman in San Francisco.

Inspector Goltz phoned back from Salem that Mrs. Sophie Yates had positively identified the picture of Nelson as the man who had given her jewelry and spent five days with her at the Third Street rooming house.[58] Russell Gordon, the grocer, also apparently said without hesitancy, "That's the man I sold the groceries to last Thanksgiving eve. When he was in the store, however, he was shaved and cleaned up a bit, and was far from having the slovenly appearance which he evidently had when this Winnipeg snapshot was taken. But that's the man just the same."[59]

The *Oregonian* also noted that another woman, with rooms to rent in the area where Mrs. Myers was murdered, recognized Nelson's picture as the man who had inspected rooms at about noon on the same day that Mrs. Myers was murdered. The paper also identified the woman who had claimed to see the man with the suitcase enter the home of Mrs. Myers. Her name was Mrs. Martha Hayes, 451 Tenth Street, and the report stated, "Police Inspector Goltz said Mrs. Hayes readily picked Nelson's photograph from a group of pictures and declared she was positive that he was the man she had seen carrying the suitcase into the Myers home."[60] A few other women who claimed to have encountered the strangler in Portland also gave positive identifications when shown the picture of Nelson,[61] but one of the most important witnesses, Mrs. Cayfort, was apparently never heard from. Nevertheless, Portland authorities were convinced, on the bases of the positive identifications, that Earle Nelson was Adrian Harris and was the murderer of Mrs. Myers and presumably the other three landladies in Portland, Mrs. Monks in Seattle, and whatever other murders in California and elsewhere were attributed to the "dark strangler."

Inspector Collins from Portland, who was in Detroit on vacation, was instructed by Chief Jenkins to pass by Winnipeg on his way home to see if he could learn anything from the Winnipeg prisoner or authorities in that city.[62] When Collins returned from Winnipeg, he reported that after Nelson was transferred from the hands of the police into the hands of the Crown for prosecution, no one was allowed to interview Nelson but for his own lawyers, at least until after his trial. However, Collins did speak to the Winnipeg police, and despite the report that Nelson had denied ever being in any of the cities where the murders attributed to him took place, including Winnipeg, Collins was quite convinced Nelson was in fact the wanted fiend and would hang in Winnipeg.[63]

Chapter 21

Almira Berard in Council Bluffs

Given the intense police search for the "dark strangler" and the amount of publicity given to his description, Earle Nelson fled from the West Coast. The death of Mrs. Myers at the end of November 1926 in Portland was the last murder attributed to him on the Pacific Coast. Before the year was over, however, there would be another four victims, but the hunting grounds had shifted east, to Iowa and Missouri.

20. December 23, 1926—Almira Clements Berard, 42, Council Bluffs, Iowa

Almira Clements was born on December 28, 1884, at Havensville, Kansas, but moved with her family to Hennessey, Oklahoma, at age seven. She graduated from Central State Teacher's College at Edmond and taught school in Kingfisher for a number of years.[1] She married John E. Berard, a railway station agent, in 1907.[2] The couple moved to Cromwell, Iowa, near Creston, where two daughters, Evelyn and Corene, were born.[3] As a station agent, John was moved to various towns in Iowa, but eventually in 1922, the family moved from Emerson to Council Bluffs.[4] Almira was a faithful Sunday school teacher, the president of various missionary societies, and an active worker in the Broadway Methodist Church.

Council Bluffs, Iowa, is just across the Missouri River from Omaha, Nebraska. When viewing a map of Council Bluffs, one immediately notices several railroads that converge in the town and a very large area devoted to railway yards. Back in 1926, the little city of Council Bluffs had six railway depots.[5] John Berard worked as a Burlington Railroad passenger agent and telegraph operator.[6] Also living in the Berard house at 351 Willow Avenue was a boarder by the name of Robert Moore, 34, who had roomed at the Berard home for more than a year and who worked as a fireman on the Milwaukee railroad line.[7] Allegedly there was a card in the window of the Berard house advertising a room for rent.[8]

Shortly before three in the afternoon on Thursday, December 23, Robert Moore came home to change his clothes in preparation for work. He noticed that Mrs. Berard was sitting in the living room with a stranger. Mrs. Berard introduced the man as "Mr. Williams." Mr. Moore shook his hand and left the house to go to work. Moore later stated, "When Mrs. Berard introduced him to me, I thought nothing of it and did not stop to talk…. I thought he probably was some worker in the Seventh Day

Adventist Church of which Mrs. Berard was an active member."[9] Mr. Moore paid so little attention to the man that he doubted he would be able to identify him.[10] All he could recall was that the man was dark and heavy-set and poorly dressed.[11] After questioning him at length, the police believed Moore was entirely trustworthy and had nothing to do with the death of his landlady.[12]

Shortly after Moore left for work, daughter Corene Berard, a 16-year-old high school student, accomplished musician, and president of the glee club, was driven home from school by a male friend. They were in the house for just 15 minutes, and not finding her mother at home, Corene's friend drove Corene to the Burlington station, where she could go on a planned Christmas shopping trip with her father.[13] After arriving home from the shopping trip, Mr. Berard found the body of his wife.

Murder victim Almira Berard (*Dubuque Telegraph Herald*, Dec. 27, 1926, at 1).

His disjointed narrative was reported as follows:

Corene came home from shopping about half an hour earlier. She said she called for her mother but got no answer. The house was chilly. I went downstairs to fire the furnace. The door [to the cellar] was open. The fire was low. I looked around. There was a dent in the furnace casing I had never seen before. I reached to the floor and picked up a tuft of my wife's hair. It was obvious there had been a struggle. I looked further and found the body of my wife crammed behind the furnace. It was jammed so that the knees touched the face. One of my shirts was twisted around her neck. The body was partly covered by other clothing [which] I grabbed away. Her head and face were bruised. I suppose I went crazy for a while. My wife was beaten unconscious and then strangled by a man trying to attack her. Of that, I am sure. She was a beautiful woman. Whoever tried to attack her knew she would call me, so he killed her. A few months ago, my wife was in a weak and nervous state. She was in the hospital for a time. She said she wished she were dead then, but the Bible kept her from killing herself. But lately she has been very happy, and she had no thought of destroying herself. Besides, she couldn't have killed herself in the way she was found.[14]

Corene heard her father's cry of alarm from the basement, and upon receiving his "half-choked explanation of what he had discovered," Corene rushed to the neighbor lady, Mrs. Frandsen.[15]

When first contacted, the county coroner was told that a lady had committed

suicide.[16] Upon investigation, he soon realized that the case was one of murder and contacted the police. They found Mrs. Berard wedged behind the "dented" furnace and a basement wall, with a "soiled" shirt twisted about her neck.[17] The shirt had been knotted twice in front and once behind.[18] The autopsy that was performed later that night indicated that Mrs. Berard had died of strangulation, but there was no evidence of a sexual assault.[19] While an Associated Press story[20] and a nearby Omaha report[21] noted that "there were no bruises on the body," the local press reported a different story: "Her face was badly swollen and there were bruises and abrasions about her head and body. Blood and hair on the floor near the furnace and overturned furnace utensils indicated that the woman had put up a terrific struggle. Bloodmarks on the furnace door, which stood open, indicated, investigators said, that the murderer may have attempted to ram the body into the fire."[22] The local press subsequently reported that the body was badly burned on one hip while being wedged up against a hot furnace pipe.[23] In what looked like a further attempt to hide the body, the killer had also taken some old clothes, an overcoat, and other wraps from a rack in the basement and thrown them over the dead body.[24]

Mr. Berard was initially unable to find his wife's pocketbook.[25] The missing brown purse was found next day on a closet shelf, but the little money in it had been stolen.[26]

The county attorney was not completely sure that Mrs. Berard had been murdered and advanced the alternative theory of suicide.[27] Mrs. Berard suffered from severe nervous disorders and had been an "inmate" in St. Bernard's Hospital, and she was supposedly frail and sickly at the time of her death.[28] However, the police pointed out that the position of the body made it humanly impossible for her to have committed suicide. The chief deputy sheriff stated, "Between the furnace and wall, where the body lay, the distance is less than a foot…. It appeared to me as if the body had been wedged in there, in a manner not possible in a fall. The overcoat, and other wraps, taken from a rack in the basement, appeared to have been thrown over the body."[29] It was also pointed out that Mrs. Berard was an extremely religious person, and even if she had wished death, she had a firm religious belief that suicides "cannot be admitted to heaven."[30]

Understandably, the Berard family was devastated by this random murder. Evelyn, a nurse in training at Methodist Hospital, had been called to come home on the night of the murder to be with her grief-stricken father and sister. Corene wept continually the day after the murder, saying, "How could my pretty mother be murdered? She was so good to everyone. Only Wednesday morning she made up a list of presents which she intended to give to poor people. No more religious and God-fearing woman ever lived."[31] Instead of celebrating Christmas together, the family accompanied the body by train to Hennessey, Oklahoma, where Mrs. Berard had grown up and where her mother and several sisters and brothers still lived. The day of her death, December 23, 1926, was obviously just a few days before Christmas, but it was also just a few days before Mrs. Berard's 42nd birthday on December 28.

The day after Mr. Berard and his two daughters came home from the funeral in Hennessey, Mr. Berard was acting so irrationally that the daughters tried to take him for medical attention and called for help from Mrs. Frandsen. The daughters stated that their father had the delusion that someone else in the house was about to be murdered, so he chased them out and locked himself in the house. The women sat outside on the porch in the cold without hats or coats for half an hour. When the sheriffs arrived, they had to break into the house, put the hysterical Berard in a straitjacket, and haul him off to the psychiatric ward.[32] He was released after several days.

Obviously, the meager description of "Mr. Williams" by the roomer Moore was an important clue as the identity of the killer. However, the link to the "dark strangler" was strengthened when another woman, Mrs. Brown, came forward. Only half an hour or so before Moore saw Williams talking to Mrs. Berard, a man calling himself "Williams," and representing himself as a switchman on the Northwestern line and wanting to move from Omaha to Council Bluffs to be closer to work,[33] appeared at Mrs. Brown's house on 10th Street that had a "for sale" sign on the property. The Brown house was only six blocks from the Berard house.[34] The description of this man from the landlady matched the "meager" description given by Moore.[35]

Mrs. O.H. Brown let Williams inspect her home for sale. The man examined all the rooms in the house and then apparently made three trips to the basement, trying to lure Mrs. Brown to accompany him.[36] "I was afraid of him, though," Mrs. Brown said, "his eyes were so black and piercing with an odd glint in them that I became afraid and hurried him to the door, asking him to call the store and talk to my husband."[37] A more detailed account perhaps shows the effect of post-event information on recall:

> His mannerisms and "staring" eyes aroused her suspicions, she said, when he had asked twice to be shown the basement of her home. The first time, Mrs. Brown had followed him to the basement, but the second inspection he made alone. During his visit he failed to remove his hat, and kept his hands in his pockets, she said. "He frightened me by the expression in his eyes," Mrs. Brown related. "Every time I turned around, he seemed to be staring at me. He ignored my reluctance to have him in the house and looked through all the closets. I finally ushered him out and told him to see my husband."[38]

Presumably, if Mrs. Brown had followed Williams to the basement a second time, she would have been the victim that day instead of Mrs. Berard. Northwestern Railroad officials noted that there was no Williams employed as a switchman at the company.

A third potential witness said a man matching the description of Mr. Williams had come to her house a few hours before the body of Mrs. Berard was found. The man asked for a sandwich, and Mrs. Herman Meyerson consented to make one, "but she kept the door on the latch when he seemed to desire entrance."[39]

Based on the various descriptions from Moore, Brown, and Meyerson, the police issued the following description of the wanted man: height 5'8", weight 180 pounds, complexion dark, eyes black and piercing, with a shifting maniacal light in them. "He wears overshoes and is poorly, but not shabbily dressed."[40]

The local press immediately linked the murder of Berard with the murders on the Pacific Coast,[41] not only the murders that ultimately were on the conventional list but also Jones, Anderson, Gallegos, and Wells.[42] Other press reports also linked the murder of Berard to the murders by the "dark strangler" from the Pacific

Coast.[43] Police in Council Bluffs confirmed that the description of Williams generally matched the description of the wanted man in San Francisco.[44] The Portland police also contacted the Council Bluffs authorities upon hearing of the murder of Mrs. Berard.[45] The link to the wanted strangler was reinforced not only by looking backwards to the Pacific Coast murders but also forward to the next murders that took place in Kansas City shortly after the Berard murder. These murders, which we will examine in the next chapter, were immediately linked to the Berard murder.[46]

As usually happened when the strangler had already left town, various vagrant men who appeared at doors became subject to suspicion and were arrested and then released.[47] A suspect in Creston received a lot of attention until it was determined that he had not been in Council Bluffs during the Berard murder.[48] Frustrated at not solving the murder, the police revived the theory that Mrs. Berard had committed suicide.[49] Supposedly the police in Council Bluffs discounted the murder theory because there was a lack of motive for murder![50] Several months later the police reopened the murder investigation on the basis of "new evidence."[51]

~ ~ ~

After Nelson was arrested in Winnipeg, the local Council Bluffs police apparently did not bother to communicate with Winnipeg authorities.[52] There is nothing in the Winnipeg police file, except for newspaper clippings sent by a brother of Mrs. Berard. The current Council Bluffs police department claims to have no existing records on the murder of Mrs. Berard.[53] It was the local newspaper that submitted a photo of Earle Nelson to the Council Bluffs witnesses. The results of the identification process were mixed. Mrs. Brown stated that the picture of Earle Nelson matched the features of Williams who had inspected her house, except Williams had worn a hat and was clean shaven, while the photo of Nelson, taken shortly after his arrest, showed him without a hat and without having shaved for some time.[54] The newspaper discovered that Mr. Moore had moved to Savannah, Illinois. When it sent the photo of Nelson to him, Moore now stated, despite his brief encounter with Williams, that Nelson was not Williams.[55] Given the statement he made many months before that he would be unlikely to identify the man, his positive rejection of Nelson's picture as Williams is questionable. Other accounts simply stated that he failed to identify him, which is more logical.[56]

However, despite the immediate links that had been made in the press, and the immediate similarities in descriptions as to the murderer in other cases, and the subsequent placing of the Berard murder case on the conventional list of murders by Earle Nelson, the local Council Bluffs police seemed to believe Moore over Mrs. Brown and they asserted that Nelson did not murder Berard because "he does not answer to the description of the man sought in the local case."[57] Chief of police Ed Catterlin stated, "I believe the Berard strangling is purely a local case…. We believe we are weaving a good case about a local man under suspicion."[58] Of course, the local case never materialized.

Despite the apparent lack of a sexual assault, the circumstances of the murder of Mrs. Berard points logically to Earle Nelson as the killer. The descriptions of Williams given by Mr. Moore and Mrs. Brown and Mrs. Meyerson fall within the parameters of other descriptions of the "dark strangler." We also have other evidence that Nelson was in the neighborhood. Nelson wrote a letter from Salt Lake City to his aunt Lillian Fabian in San Francisco a week before the murder of Mrs. Berard and stated that he was going to Omaha.[59]

~ ~ ~

After his brief "nervous breakdown" John Berard continued to work as a station agent. By 1930 he was living with his daughters in Glenwood, Iowa.[60] Corene, the talented musician who went on to study at Drake University and study voice in Paris, ironically eventually married a man named Roger Williams in Des Moines in 1933.[61] Evelyn, a talented violinist, eventually married John Houghton and moved to San Diego. The tragedy of Almira Berard is that she never lived to see, play with, and care for her grandchildren. John Berard died in 1961 at the age of 80. His obituary noted that "he was a station agent and telegrapher for the Creston division of the Burlington Railroad for 43 years."[62] Robert Moore was so upset at the murder of his friend and landlady that he quit his job and "dedicated his life to find the slayer."[63] This was short lived, however, because in 1956 the local press announced that Robert Moore, who never married, had worked on the railway since 1910 and had been awarded a lifetime pass on the Milwaukee line. He was still working at the date of the article.[64] Earle Nelson passed through Council Bluffs again, a few blocks from the scene of the murder. This time he was a dead body. After his hanging in Winnipeg, he was transported back to California on the Great Western train No. 15 on his way to be buried in the Nelson family plot in Cypress Lawn near San Francisco.[65]

Chapter 22

Bonnie Pace and Germaine Harpin (and Infant Harpin) in Kansas City

Within a few days after murdering Mrs. Berard in Council Bluffs, the "dark strangler" finished off 1926 with the murder of two landladies and an infant boy in Kansas City within the space of a day.

21. December 27, 1926—Bonnie Pace, 24, Kansas City, Missouri

The first victim, Bonnie Copenhaver, was born in 1902 in Oyer, Roscoe Township, Missouri.[1] At the age of 18 in 1920 she married Raymond Pace in Osceola, Missouri.[2] A son, Victor, was born in January 1921.[3] We do not know when the Pace family moved to Kansas City, but the home in which she was murdered was at 3920 Hammond Place, an address which no longer exists. Ben Simmons, a Kansas City crime scene technician, noted that "it was located southeast of the old Sears building at Truman and Cleveland. The street extended between Cleveland and Myrtle and between 18th Street and 19th Street. The area is now occupied by a housing development built in the early 1980s near Bernard Powell and Cleveland."[4]

At the time of the murder, the Pace family was reportedly in trouble. The son, Victor, almost six years old, was sick and confined to a bed on the main floor of the house. Mrs. Pace had been employed in a dress factory, but about two weeks before her murder she left her position to care for the child.[5] Additionally, Bonnie and Raymond were allegedly having marital difficulties. They had separated in early November and Mr. Pace had been away until a few days before Christmas. Mr. Pace was jealous of his wife's attention to actual or imagined rivals and upset with her for giving financial assistance to her family back in Oyer.[6] The *Kansas City Times* added that "Mr. Pace has a silver plate in his skull, the result of an injury when a child and neighbors say he was given to 'fits of passion.'"[7] However, Mr. Pace denied being separated from his wife, saying that he had simply been husking corn in Iowa.[8]

On Monday, December 27, 1926, there was a "room for rent" sign in the window of the house.[9] Some of the upstairs rooms were rented to a married couple who had gone to work in the morning.[10] Raymond Pace left the house at about seven in the morning and worked digging a ditch for a bricklayer contractor.[11] Raymond returned to his home at about two in the afternoon. Not finding Bonnie at home, he had first

160

gone to the basement when told by his "practically invalid" son that "mother had fallen down the stairs." He then subsequently went upstairs and found the body in the unoccupied bedroom that was for rent. The screams of Mr. Pace upon finding the body attracted the neighbors, who summoned police and an ambulance.

The body was still warm when found. Mr. Pace was so distraught that he was placed in a hospital for the night, as was his invalid son.[12] The police report subsequently stated:

> She was dressed, laying across the floor in about the middle of the room, marks on her neck indicated that she had been choked to death as a man's finger and thumb prints showed very plainly on both sides of her neck and throat, her right limb was bruised. There was no evidence of robbery in the house, nothing had been disturbed.... A Post-mortem found that she had been criminally assaulted.... Mr. Pace was hysterical, and we sent him to the General Hospital with a hold order.... He was released after we questioned him.[13]

Murder victim Bonnie Pace with husband and son (*Kansas City Times*, Dec. 28, 1926, at 2).

The police report also suggested that a neighbor, Mr. Buck, had seen a man drive up and ring the bell at about 9:40 in the morning but Buck could not give an accurate description of the man.[14] Buck said the man "rushed to the door ... rang the doorbell insistently and finally was admitted to the house."[15] This person was likely not the killer as the deputy coroner believed the victim was strangled around noon.[16]

Subsequently, however, the obvious link to the "dark strangler" was reinforced when a Mr. W.D. Potts, living on Hammond Place, a block from where Mrs. Pace had been strangled, told Kansas City detectives that a man had arrived at his house looking for a room a half hour before Mrs. Pace was murdered:

> "The man," Potts said, "was about 5 feet 6 inches tall, with dark hair and complexion and staring eyes. He spoke nervously and seemed ill at ease." He said the man who appeared at his door asked about a room but insisted on one on the first floor.... Detectives assigned to the case, point out the strangler, finding a man in the house, easily may have used this as an excuse to leave without causing suspicion.[17]

As to the sick boy, Victor Pace, described as "anemic and inarticulate,"[18] we may assume that the killer probably did not see the boy in the house and did not know of his existence, as the lad later told the police he assumed a man who was a frequent visitor to the house had called on his mother. The boy had heard a commotion and assumed his mother had fallen because she did not come downstairs after he heard the man leave. This man, a truck driver, was of course immediately a suspect, until he provided an alibi.[19] As to the boy, the *Times* reported that "physicians from the General hospital ordered Victor taken to the institution when it was discovered he was suffering from a tubercular spine. The child was in a dangerous condition and the disease had made incapable the only witness who was in the house at the time of the murder."[20]

While suspicion that he had killed his wife disappeared when another landlady was murdered in Kansas City the next day, the grieving Mr. Pace soon faced another tragedy. Several weeks later his son died in the hospital. The boy had been ill from birth.[21] Victor Pace was five years, 11 months, and 26 days old when he died on January 18, 1927. The cause of death appears to have been malignant endocarditis, but the secondary cause was pneumonia.[22] While speculative, we might argue that the murder of his mother hastened his death and that Victor Pace was another secondary murder victim of Earle Nelson. Accounts of the boy's death noted that, "deprived of the care of his mother, he failed rapidly from the day of her tragic end."[23]

After the murder of his wife and death of his son, Raymond Pace eventually got married to a Louise Martin.[24] She died in El Dorado Springs, Missouri, in 1962 of a heart attack.[25] In 1963, Raymond married a much younger widow, Lovell Motley, whose husband had died of a heart attack in 1961.[26] They lived in Montrose, Missouri, where Raymond was the town marshal. In 1964 at the age of 69, Raymond Pace died in a fatal car accident near Montrose.[27] His third wife, Lovell, survived the crash and died in 1979.[28]

≈ ≈ ≈

22. and 23. December 28, 1926—Germaine Harpin, 28, and Robert Harpin, nine months, Kansas City, Missouri

The next day, Tuesday, December 28, 1926, the strangler not only killed Mrs. Germaine Harpin, 28 years old, but also her nine-month-old baby, Robert Harpin. Marius Harpin and Germaine Troquet, both born and raised in France, were married in Paris in 1921 and sailed for America three days later. Mr. Harpin was a veteran of the world war, "taking part in the battles of Verdun, Argonne and many others, receiving the Croix de Guerre for bravery."[29] Upon arriving in Kansas City, Mr. Harpin worked for a year for the Union Pacific Railway and then for the last four years for the Kansas City Structural Steel Company. The couple had only recently moved to 2330 Mercier Street after the birth of their son, Robert.[30] Previously they had lived in the Kansas side of the city before moving to the Missouri side.

Unlike the Pace residence in a middle-class neighborhood, the Harpin house was in the poor "Mexican colony" part of the city.[31] The upper floor of the residence had previously been rented furnished, but when the last tenants vacated it, Harpin had been unable to rent it again and he sold the furniture. However, a sign was still in the front of the house.[32] The sign announced, "For Sale—Rooms and Board."[33] Like the street on which the Pace house once was, the portion of Mercier Street on which the Harpin house once stood is now gone.[34]

On the fateful Tuesday morning, Mr. Harpin, 32, went to work at about 6:30. Later investigations revealed that a grocer had been called to take an order for groceries at about 7:30 in the morning. The grocer, John Magerl, made rounds in the neighborhood taking orders from various people, including Mrs. Harpin.[35] Mrs. Harpin also asked the grocer to cut a ham that her husband had received for Christmas because she did not have a proper knife for the task.[36] At about 10 in the morning, Steve Magerl, the 14-year-old brother of the grocer, delivered the groceries and picked up the ham and returned with it about a half hour later whereupon Mrs. Harpin ordered some onions. Steve told her the store had no onions, but he would bring her some later in the morning. There was also evidence that a postman came to the Harpin house at about 10:45 in the morning and called for Mrs. Harpin. When she did not come to the door, he left the mail in the box. He did not see anyone around the property.[37] According to the *Times* narrative:

> Steve Magerl returned at 11:45 with the onions and knocked on the back door. Getting no response he turned the knob, he said, intending to leave the onions on the kitchen table. The door was locked. The front door was also locked, he said, and he left the onions between the door and the screen…. Steve Magerl said at his first visit with the ham the baby was crying. When he returned with the onions, he said, there was no sound.[38]

If the grocery boy found Mrs. Harpin alive at about 10:30 when he took her supplemental order for onions and she did not come to the door for the postman at 10:45, we may surmise that the strangler must have arrived very shortly after the grocery boy left. A friend of the Harpin family came by the house at about two in the afternoon and nobody answered the door.[39]

Mr. Harpin got home from work about 5:30 in the evening and was immediately alarmed upon finding two bottles of milk on the porch. The milk would normally be delivered at around 10 in the morning. Interestingly, the youthful grocer had claimed that both doors had been locked when he came with the onions before noon, but now, in the evening, Mr. Harpin found both doors to the house were closed but not locked.[40] When Harpin entered the house, he called for his wife and got no answer. What he saw in the kitchen was hardly reassuring:

> On the floor of the kitchen were several pools of blood and in a corner lay a mop, the handle of which appeared to be freshly broken…. He noticed the mop handle and picked it up…. Sitting on the kitchen table were a baby's nursing bottle, half full of sour milk, and a carving block on which lay bread and cheese which had been used in preparing a lunch for Mr. Harpin to take to work. The breakfast dishes, unwashed, were in the kitchen sink.[41]

Harpin also noticed an order of groceries still on the kitchen table, so after searching through the neighborhood, he went to the grocery story on 23rd and Mercier and told the grocer about his missing wife, the groceries on the table and the broken mop. The grocer phoned the police and Harpin and the police returned to the house. The *Journal* narrative continued:

H.A. Vincent, patrolman, and J.F. Weaver, chauffer, went to the Harpin home, and with Mr. Harpin searched the house. Finding the door of the unoccupied bedroom locked and the key missing, they opened it with a key to another door. Mrs. Harpin's body, the face and arms bloody and bruised lay on the floor. Close beside it was the body of her baby.... Mrs. Harpin's clothing was badly disarranged, her hair tangled, and her face and arms scratched and bruised. The baby's body was marked only by the rag drawn closely around its neck.... Both mother and child had been strangled with rags tightly knotted around their necks.[42]

With the trail of blood from the kitchen to the upstairs bedroom, the police believed that Mrs. Harpin was probably beaten with the mop handle and choked and then dragged or carried to the upstairs bedroom.

As to the condition of the bodies, the detectives at the scene noted that the mother was lying on her back, while the infant was on the floor on his stomach. Both had been strangled with a cloth. As far as I can reconstruct the largely unreadable copy, detectives Shumway and Bendure wrote something about the garments of Mrs. Harpin being raised, exposing the lower limbs, but "the undergarments were not molested." Furthermore, the detectives stated that Dr. Nelson's examination of the body of Mrs. Harpin "revealed that she had *not* been assaulted." The nose and mouth of Mrs. Harpin were bloody and there was a bruise or (unreadable writing) on the forehead.[43]

As to investigative details, the detectives noted that the broken mop handle found in the kitchen had blood smeared on it. Furthermore, "a bath towel was hanging upon a chair in the kitchen and there were small blood spots upon it." While all the press reports claimed that Mrs. Harpin had been beaten over the head in the kitchen and then carried upstairs, the detectives thought that the murderer himself might have been injured during Mrs. Harpin's furious defense of herself. Perhaps it was even the strangler who had been hit with the mop and he had subsequently washed himself in the kitchen sink, leaving some blood behind in drying himself with the towel.[44]

While Ben Simmons has written that both Mrs. Pace and Mrs. Harpin were sexually assaulted after death, the evidence we have suggests that Mrs. Harpin was not. It is plausible that Nelson was still in the house when the postman called and the baby boy was killed to stop the distressed sounds that he may have been making. Harpin told the police that his wife, given the neighborhood they lived in, had expressed a fear that someone might take their baby boy.[45] Perhaps Mrs. Harpin had grabbed the baby from the crib and tried to protect the baby, misunderstanding the nature of the fiend's attack on her? Thus, perhaps the baby was present during the attack in some way that also led the murderer to kill him? Nelson may have also been scared away by the arrival of the postman and thus did not complete the usual sexual assault on the victim. Chief detective Toyne later stated that Mrs. Pace was strangled manually and sexually assaulted and there was no sign of robbery, and Mrs. Harpin was strangled with a cloth and there was no sign of robbery, but Toyne did not mention anything about Mrs. Harpin being sexually assaulted.[46]

The official surviving death certificate indicates that Mrs. Germaine Harpin was 28 years, nine months, and 13 days old, the daughter of Aristide Troquet. Her mother's name was listed as unknown. Cause of death was strangulation by a towel.[47]

The infant lived to be nine months and 14 days old and the cause of death was homicide-strangulation by a towel.[48] At some stage, answering another inquiry from the Los Angeles police asking for crime scene photos and pictures of the houses, chief of detectives Toyne in Kansas City stated that the Kansas City police took no pictures of the crime scenes or the houses in the Pace and Harpin murders.[49] Nothing was ever said in the press about fingerprints being sought or taken in the Kansas City murders.

After the discovery of the murders, detectives immediately utilized bloodhounds in an attempt to follow the trail of the fiend from the house. However, it would appear that the smell taken from the mop led the hounds to follow the route taken by Mr. Harpin in search of his wife, rather than the route taken by the strangler leaving the scene.[50] The *Star* reported that detectives found a cigarette in the bathroom of the house but were not sure if it had been left by the killer or by someone else.[51] There was some money found undisturbed in the icebox, and there was no sign of robbery. There were a couple of suspects who were picked up and investigated.[52] However, they apparently had alibis sufficient to eliminate the suspicion surrounding them.

Obviously, given the circumstances, the murders of Pace and Harpin were linked immediately to the multiple murders of the Pacific Coast Strangler[53] as well as the most recent murder in Council Bluffs.[54] The description of Adrian Harris from Portland was printed in the newspapers,[55] and Chief Toyne warned rooming house ladies to take down "for rent" signs from their buildings.[56]

Murder victims Germaine Harpin and infant son (*Kansas City Times*, Dec. 29, 1926, at 1).

~ ~ ~

After Nelson was captured and placed in jail in Winnipeg, the Kansas City police asked Winnipeg authorities to send fingerprints and photos of the prisoner.[57] However, we have no evidence that the Kansas City police presented Nelson's pictures to any witnesses, particularly Mr. Potts on Hammond Street who claimed that a man had come looking for a room shortly before the murder of Mrs. Pace.

The French war hero, full of hopes for the future in America, and working as a laborer for 40 cents an hour, now faced a shattered life.[58]

We have little information as to what happened to Marius Harpin. He was still in the United States four years later, living at St. Anne, Illinois, where he was a barber, and he was naturalized there in 1937.[59] At some point Marius Harpin returned to France where he died in 1974.[60]

PART IV

1927:
The Gorilla Man Strangler

CHAPTER 23

The Gorilla Sleeps?

As 1926 came to an end and the new year of 1927 rolled around, the newspaper coverage of the search for the "dark strangler" sometimes shifted to calling him the "gorilla man strangler." By the time the suspect was in Canada, he was consistently called the "gorilla man."[1] The idea of calling a criminal by this moniker was not new. Given the atavist idea that "degenerate" killers were a throwback on the evolutionary chain, the moniker evoked a kind of ferocious animal monstrosity that made the suspect less than human. Often the moniker was attached to criminals who also appeared to have certain physical features like powerful muscles, long arms, big hands, dark complexions, and sloping foreheads. When Nelson was arrested in Manitoba, the explorer Herbert F. Fenn expressed the idea that to call Nelson a "gorilla man" was to defame and libel gorillas, who were strict vegetarians, shy, and only aggressive when attacked or intruded upon.[2]

In addition to various prize fighters who were called "gorilla man," and gorillas (or orangutans) who "acted" in movies or were dressed in clothes at circuses and called "gorilla man," various alleged criminals were also called "gorilla man." For example, Jacob Oppenheimer, sentenced to hang in San Quentin, was called a "gorilla man."[3] Various suspects who were said to look like gorillas were arrested for various offenses from time to time and labeled "gorilla man."[4] A man described as a ferocious "gorilla man" serving a life sentence for murder apparently became a docile reformed prisoner after he had an operation to remove an old bullet from his brain that had been there unknown to him for 25 years.[5] A different prisoner labeled "gorilla man," given his ferocious nature, was allegedly murdered by a prison guard who was sought for the killing.[6] However, the "gorilla man" who was given the most press coverage across the nation was Frank Benner, who confessed to the murder of a young lady in a rooming house in New York in 1923.[7] There was speculation at the time that Benner might have been the killer of Rean Hoxie and other female victims.[8] However, he pled guilty to only one murder after the prosecution reduced the charge to second-degree murder to avoid the death penalty, given Benner's mental instability.[9] Famous German serial killer Fritz Haarmann was called the "the butcher/vampire of Hanover" or "the wolfman," but he was also called the "gorilla man" in some press reports when he was tried and sentenced to death in 1924.[10]

As the first four months of 1927 rolled by, American police forces had completely lost the trail of Adrian Harris, the murderer of landladies from one coast to the other. There were no further landlady murders that seemed to match the work of the fiend. Where was he and why did the orgy of slaughter stop? Was the strangler successfully following a new year's resolution? Were his circumstances adequate to prevent the frustration that might trigger his mania?

Suspects continued to be arrested.[11] A rooming house lady in Helena, Montana, complained that a man, self-confessing that he was the strangler, tried to entice her into his room. While he did not match the description of Adrian Harris, the police thought they might have their man, until it was established that the suspect was delusional and he was sent to the asylum.[12] Clifford Pacey, a former inmate of an insane asylum, attempted to strangle a rooming house lady in broad daylight in front of her home in San Francisco.[13] However, it was soon established that his movements over the previous months did not tally with the locations of the "dark strangler" murders.[14]

As we have noted previously, the first reference to "gorilla man" in relation to the murders later attributed to Earle Nelson was back in June of 1926 when murder victim Lillian St. Mary in San Francisco was found to have broken ribs. Some press reports called the suspect a "gorilla man."[15] However, the moniker did not overtake the "dark strangler" until a suspect was arrested near Petersburg, Indiana, in January 1927, and the sheriff was convinced that the man matched the description of Adrian Harris. Newspapers all across America proclaimed that the "gorilla man" murderer of landladies had been caught.[16] The suspect was Peter Ojers, described as "about 38 or 40 years old, apparently of Italian or Greek stock, 5 feet 8 inches tall, stockily built, thick-chested, noticeably stooped shoulders, short-heavy hands, black hair, dark complexion, and beady-black eyes with a tendency to squint … weighing about 175 pounds."[17] Ojers was arrested because he had frightened some women when he entered their homes demanding to be fed. Apparently he could not speak English, although police thought he was faking, and he was sentenced to 45 days for vagrancy, so as to allow police time to investigate him as to the landlady murders. The story quickly disappeared as it became evident that Ojers was not the "gorilla man" strangler of landladies. Duncan Matheson in San Francisco immediately responded that "our man is shorter and speaks good English."[18]

Over the course of the first four months of 1927 there were numerous other instances of the police picking up vagrants or rooming house occupants who might be the sought-after strangler based on their descriptions or behavior.[19] One falsely accused man in Ohio reportedly stated from behind the bars of prison, "Look at me…. Do I look like a Gorilla? Gorillas have long arms and walk on all fours, don't they? Gorilla. Blah!"[20]

≈   ≈   ≈

What we do know without a doubt is that Earle Nelson was in the Eastern United States in the first months of 1927. The existing police files in Winnipeg include five postal cards and one letter envelope sent by Earle Nelson and received by Mrs. Lillian Fabian, Nelson's aunt in San Francisco, and mostly addressed to her 17-year-old son, Evan Fabian, cousin of Nelson. From these cards we can see from the postal stamp that Nelson was in Wheeling, West Virginia, on January 25, 1927; in West Alexander, Pennsylvania, on January 26; in Philadelphia on February 3; and in Newark, New Jersey, on February 8 and 11 of 1927.[21] We do not believe that Earle Nelson went back to the West Coast during this period. Nelson's wife, Mary Fuller, claimed that the last time she saw Earle was in October 1926.[22] Lillian Fabian testified at the trial in Winnipeg in early November 1927 that it had been more than a year previously that Earle had last come to her home.[23] What was Nelson doing in the East for the first four months of 1927?

There was another unsolved case during this period where Nelson at some point was mentioned as a possible suspect. This was the "bathtub murder" in Chicago that had some parallels to the "butterfly" murders we mentioned previously. On February 28, 1927, Mrs. Mabel Wood, 18, was strangled and her nude body was dumped in a bathtub of water in a shared bathroom that was across the hall and 30 feet from the room in the Chicago apartment hotel where she lived with her husband.[24] Her body was discovered by her husband when he came home from work as a chef at a nearby hotel at around 8 p.m., and finding the door to their room locked, he had gone into the bathroom down the hall and discovered his young wife in the tub. There were no clothes or towels in the bathroom. Furthermore, the clothing Mabel had been wearing when she came back to the hotel just after 7 p.m. from her job as a cashier at the Lemon Fluff restaurant was also missing from her own room. As we know by now, taking clothing from the scene of the crime was a well-known circumstantial factor in attributing murders to Earle Nelson. So was the locking of the door of the bedroom or house in which the murder occurred.

The theory developed that Mabel Wood had been attacked and while resisting the attack had been struck on the head and strangled and then carried to the bathroom and her body fully submerged in the water in the tub to make it look like an accidental drowning.[25] When the apartment was opened, it was said to be in disarray, and blood spots were found in the hall between the apartment and the bathroom, the room key was found on the dresser, and a match box, not belonging to the Wood couple, was later found on the floor.[26] The match box had the insignia of a leading jewelry company.[27] This would be another circumstance pointing to the possibility that Earle Nelson was involved. The killer may have been scared off before finishing the deed, because, despite being strangled, Mabel was not dead when found shortly after 8 p.m., but died shortly thereafter, despite attempts at reviving her.[28] There was no, or little, water in the lungs, and the coroner stated that she had been strangled, given the severe contusions found on her throat and neck.[29] There were also bruises on the head and upper part of the body.[30]

As in the Williams case in San Diego in 1924, when a number of suspects appeared to have alibis, the police suggested that the murder might be the work of the "gorilla man strangler."[31] However, like the "butterfly" murders of Reed, Allen, Stone, and Williams, the case of Mabel Wood involved multiple suspects without the need to throw "the gorilla man" into the mix. After considerable research into the various suspects, I have decided not to include this case on the list of Earle Nelson's probable or possible murders. You can visit my website for a full account of the case and my conclusion that Delbert Prevo, a friend of Mabel's, was a better suspect than Earle Nelson, even though the case remains unsolved to this day.[32]

CHAPTER 24

Mary McConnell in Philadelphia

24. April 27, 1927—Mary McConnell, 53, Philadelphia

The circumstances or resolutions that had prevented the triggering of a new round of killings for most of the first four months of 1927 came to an end. The "sleeping gorilla" woke up and the murders started again. In an earlier chapter we outlined the three strangulation murders in Philadelphia in 1925. Two years later another murder, this one on the "official" list, took place in Philadelphia on Wednesday, April 27, 1927. The site of the murder was the McConnell house at 1942 South 60th Street which had a "For Sale" sign on it.

This residence was in the southwest area of the city, not the same northwest neighborhood as the previous three murders in 1925.

Mary (Klingbeil) McConnell was born on May 19, 1874.[1] Thus, she was a few weeks shy of her 53rd birthday when she was murdered. She was married to William McConnell in Philadelphia in 1892.[2] While we are not certain, Mary and William may have had a son, Frederick Wakefield McConnell, in 1894.[3] The son must have died, as he was not listed with them subsequently.[4] A daughter, Alice, was born in October 1904.[5] William was a coffee salesman, and the family lived for many years on Carpenter Street.[6] Daughter Alice, a public school teacher, married John Donovan, a bank clerk, in 1926.[7] The newly married couple lived with William and Mary McConnell at 1942 South 60th Street at the time of the tragedy. The strangled body of Mrs. Mary McConnell was found under the bed in a second-floor bedroom by her married daughter, Alice, and her son-in-law, John Donovan, upon their returning home from work.[8]

The narrative as found in the *Philadelphia Evening Bulletin* stated that "a heavy woolen cloth she had been using to dust furniture was knotted tightly around her throat, so tightly that her daughter had to cut it off with scissors. A black cotton stocking had been draped over her neck, as though to hide the knotted rag."[9] The paper quoted Mr. Donovan:

> I got home shortly after 4 o'clock. When I got in, I couldn't hear Mrs. McConnell and I shouted, "Mother!" Not getting any reply, I walked through the rooms on the first floor and then went upstairs. I didn't notice anything peculiar until I went into the bathroom, where there was some water on the floor. That surprised me, as Mrs. McConnell was a very careful housekeeper, but I didn't think it very strange, as she had been doing her spring housecleaning and I thought she might have spilled some water accidentally. After looking through the three bedrooms, I went to the basement and looked around. Then I concluded Mrs. McConnell had been called to a hospital, where her father is seriously ill, or that her husband,

William, had become ill and had sent for her.... Finally, I went out and sat down on the sun porch and waited until my wife came home. She arrived shortly before 5 o'clock. We thought it was peculiar Mrs. McConnell would leave the house without leaving us a note, but finally my wife suggested we prepare dinner. On her suggestion I went out and asked several of the neighbors if they had seen her. None of them had and when I returned to the house, we decided to make another search. The second time we went over the house we found one of Mrs. McConnell's slippers in the first-floor hall. We went to the second floor again and searched the bedrooms. We noticed that the bed in the room my wife and I occupy was slightly out of place. A moment later my wife saw Mrs. McConnell's foot, protruding slightly under the side of the bed. We pushed the bed away and found her body, with the cloth knotted tightly around the throat. We cut the cloth, hoping she might still be alive. Then we called the police.[10]

The McConnell house at 1942 South 60th Street, Philadelphia, with a circle around the "For Sale" sign and an arrow pointing to the bedroom where the victim was found (*Philadelphia Evening Bulletin*, April 28, 1927, at 1, and courtesy Special Collections Record Center at Temple University).

Notice how vastly different the story becomes when journalists are more interested in writing dramatic fiction than interviewing sources. The *Philadelphia Public Ledger* narrated the story as follows:

> As he entered the house, Donovan came upon evidence of a terrific struggle. Furniture had been upset, a vase of flowers had been hurled across a room and a rug was ripped from the floor. Donovan called "mother" several times and received no answer. Then he saw a torn fragment of a garment on the stairs leading to the second floor. As he mounted them, his wife, Alice, a schoolteacher, also returned home. They entered their mother's bed chamber together and in this room there were also marks of a struggle. A dressing table had been ransacked, and three diamond rings and a platinum watch set with diamonds were gone. Stooping to pick a splinter of a broken eyeglass lens from the floor, Mrs. Donovan saw her mother's body under the bed. The couple drew the body to the center of the room and with a pair of scissors the daughter cut the stocking from Mrs. McConnell's neck. The throat bore the bruises of fingers where the strangler's hands had been, Donovan told the police. A handkerchief was crammed into her mouth.[11]

The *Ledger* suggested that the strangler had a terrific struggle with his victim on the main floor of the house, not only in the living room with the overturned furniture, misplaced rug, and broken vase with flowers strewn on the floor, but also in the dining room where the table was tipped on its side.

However, the *Bulletin* and the *Philadelphia Inquirer*[12] stated that there were no signs of struggle in the house.[13] This seems the more logical narrative, given that Alice and John would have immediately gone to the authorities had the scene been as the *Ledger* painted it. Both of the rival papers to the *Ledger* also noted that for whatever reason the body had been wrongly removed to the morgue before the police had completed their investigation.[14] More than a month later at the coroner's inquest it was revealed that John Donavan had not gone to the police first, but rather to a doctor who had come to the scene, and without knowing about the rags that had been cut from the victim's throat, the doctor thought initially that Mrs. McConnell had died of a stroke. It was the doctor who called police when he was told that the victim was found under the bed with rags tightly tied at the throat.[15] The police discovered that several rings and a watch had been taken from various jewelry boxes in two bedrooms of the house, although other jewelry had apparently been left untouched.

Mr. William McConnell, husband of the victim, was a traveling salesman who was on the road at the time of the murder. Police issued a bulletin read over radio stations asking him to come home. Mr. McConnell went to bed at a hotel in Wilkes-Barre on Wednesday night not having heard the radio bulletin, and then in the morning he read the horrible news in a newspaper while having breakfast.[16] Mr. McConnell came home "in a pitiable condition of grief and shock"[17] and eventually reported to police that more jewels and coins and mementos were missing from the house, as compared to the items noticed missing right away. A long list of these jewelry items and coins, including Canadian coins, was published in the newspapers and circulated to pawnshops.[18] The immediately known missing items were also published in a police circular dated April 29, the day after the murder.[19] Some of these items obviously belonged to daughter Alice, as they had the initials "A.N.McC." on their backs.

Despite the apparent lack of any sexual assault, the Philadelphia police immediately linked this murder to the "Pacific Coast" strangler, most obviously because the murderer here had evidently gained entrance to the McConnell home by posing as a prospective purchaser.[20] Portland detectives Leonard and Hyde asserted that there was no doubt that the West Coast strangler murdered McConnell.[21] So did Captain of Detectives Duncan Matheson in San Francisco.[22] The press also linked the case to the earlier murders in Philadelphia in 1925.[23]

As well as issuing a general warning to landladies and providing a description of the wanted strangler, the police swept through the pawnshops of Philadelphia looking for the missing jewelry.[24] The police did indeed find a pawn clerk who stated that a swarthy man had tried to sell some jewelry that matched the description of some of the rings taken at the murder scene, but "the man, evidently frightened by the pawnbroker's persistent questioning, took up his stuff and fled."[25] About a week after the murder, the watch, with its distinctive initials and numbers, was found in a New York pawnshop. It had been pledged on April 28, the day after the murder.[26] As we will note, the pawnshop owner, several months later, identified the picture of Earle Nelson as the man who pawned the watch.

A neighbor lady, described as an invalid, living almost directly across the street from the McConnell house, stated that as she was sitting and looking out her window, she saw a man "sauntering" up the steps to the McConnell house and leave about a half hour later.[27] Given that the neighbor gave no significance to the man at the time, thinking simply that someone was inspecting the house, she could not give much of a description and doubted that she would recognize the man again. Nevertheless, "she described him as about five feet, seven inches tall, weighing about 135 pounds, with a sharp face, and wearing a light gray felt hat with a black band and a dark gray coat. She said there was a white streak on the back of the coat."[28] This last point about the white streak was significant because indeed there were rooms in the McConnell house that were being repapered, and "pieces of paper and plastering were hanging from the wall in places and whitewash had been smudged on some sections of the wall."[29] Presumably the neighbor lady was describing the white streak on the man after he left the house, rather than upon his arrival. The neighbor lady also stated that "he had the appearance of a native of Southern Europe."[30]

The police bulletin broadcast over the radio, based on the description of the witness, sought a "dark complexioned white man, of possible Serbian, Greek or Italian origin, about 35 or 40 years old, 5 feet 8 inches in height, smooth-faced and of chunky build, wearing a gray soft hat and shabby gray overcoat; somewhat too long for him."[31] Given that the newspapers had already linked this crime to the "dark strangler" of the Pacific Coast, one wonders how accurate these reports were as to what the neighbor lady really saw and described. Other witnesses included two landladies on Allman Street who had both allegedly been visited by the strangler a few hours before the murder of Mrs. McConnell.[32]

In the next few weeks a veritable rash of women, each supposedly living in a house that was for sale, reported to police that a strange man had inspected their house either before the murder of McConnell or after, and these women now suspected that their prospective customer had been the wanted strangler.[33] As had occurred in 1925, Philadelphia was involved in a kind of "strangler hysteria" for some time to come. All sorts of stories were reported from women, some of whom had been severely beaten and who had claimed to have escaped the strangler.[34] There were many accounts over the next two weeks, especially in the southwestern portion of West Philadelphia, from women who claimed to have met the strangler.[35] The strangler hysteria no doubt labeled many suspicious but innocent characters with the strangler moniker.[36] The police finally had to cool things down by insisting that the strangler had left town, and they pointed out how the strangler hysteria had actually been used in some cases in a self-serving way. For example, "one woman had lost or misused a sum of money for which she had to account to her husband." She concocted a "strangler" attack and robbery to account for the loss. "Another had been caught entertaining a man friend in her home during the day and her hastily devised strangler story helped deceive her husband."[37]

In a front-page story in the *Inquirer*, accompanied by various illustrative pictures, Mr. Beam, a physical training instructor, gave information as to how women should defend themselves. He stated that "by placing one arm between the arms of 'the strangler' as the latter grasps the throat, and then giving the shoulder a sudden twist, the most deadly strangle-hold can be broken instantly." During the recoil from the movement, a stinging blow may be administered to the face of the attacker which will confuse him.[38] The pictures of Mr. Beam and a young woman illustrating the defensive moves were rather stupid, because Beam and the woman were facing each other, while the real strangler likely attacked from behind. Mr. Beam went on to suggest that women should smash a window and scream as a way of summoning help.[39]

Various suspects were arrested and released.[40] A coroner's inquest dealing with the death of Mrs. McConnell was finally held on May 31, 1927, and the jury concluded that the victim had been strangled at the hands of a person or persons unknown.[41] But was Mrs. McConnell sexually assaulted after death? Nothing was said about this in the press. However, while linking the murder to other murders by the "dark strangler," the *Inquirer* seemed to suggest that sexual assault was absent in the Philadelphia case, reporting that "no assault other than the cruel garroting of the victim after her desperate struggle against the inhuman invader of her home was apparently attempted."[42]

≈   ≈   ≈

As soon as Nelson was arrested in Manitoba, the Philadelphia police were anxious to possibly link the McConnell murder, as well as the three earlier strangulation murders in 1925, to the "Gorilla Man."[43] The head of the Philadelphia detective squad, William Belshaw, wrote to the Winnipeg police authorities asking for pictures, fingerprints, and measurements of Nelson.[44] When the arrest photos of Earle Nelson arrived in Philadelphia, the police took the mug shots to show various witnesses. One witness was Mrs. Marie Kuhn. While earlier newspaper reports after the murder said nothing about her, it was now alleged that a man had walked into her bake shop on South 61st Street in the afternoon immediately after Mrs. McConnell had been murdered. The strange man offered to sell a watch to Mrs. Kuhn.[45] The watch was ultimately found in a pawnshop in Brooklyn, New York. This story sounds a little suspicious, since, if indeed Nelson was the fiend, he was quite capable of distinguishing a pawnshop from a bake shop, although we might surmise that he was so desperate for money that he offered a watch for sale to someone right after the murder. In any event, Mrs. Kuhn was now presented with a picture of Earle Nelson. Kuhn made a positive identification linking Nelson to the crime. As dramatically reported in the *Inquirer*:

> As Detective Choplinski of the "murder squad" showed the photograph to Mrs. Kuhn, she drew back in seeming terror. Recovering quickly, she said: "That is the man who came into my bakery at four o'clock that day and offered me a watch for sale. That positively is the man. The only difference between the picture and the man who stood at the counter here is that the man you show me is unshaven and his hair is mussed. The man who came into my store was smooth shaven and his hair was neatly combed. I know the man by his eyes. I'll never forget those eyes. They were terrible, haunting eyes."[46]

Adding to the supposed reliability of the identification, the *Ledger* stated, "Mrs. Kuhn's identification of the 'gorilla man' as the killer of Mrs. McConnell was strengthened by her description of the man as walking 'flat-footed and with a limp as though he had corns on his feet.'"[47] This description comes from post-event information concerning the suspect sent to Philadelphia by the Winnipeg police.[48]

Three other women also positively identified the Nelson photos as portraying the man who tried to inspect their homes on the very day that Mrs. McConnell was killed.[49] Furthermore, the manager of an apartment house in West Philadelphia positively identified the Nelson pictures as portraying the man who had taken a room there the day before the McConnell murder and had left early on the day of the murder and had not returned.[50] For all we know, these identifications of Nelson as the strangler might well be correct, but the process of identification was, of course, seriously flawed. There is no evidence that the police used a photo line-up, where they put Nelson's picture into a pack of other pictures of similar-looking men.

As to the McConnell murder, arguably a more important witness than Mrs. Kuhn or other Philadelphians was the pawnshop clerk in New York where it was established without doubt that a watch, with the distinct initials on the back case, had been pawned. Much later, writing to the Winnipeg police after the conviction of Nelson, William Lahey of the New York police department stated that a pawnbroker in Brooklyn had indeed identified Nelson from the Winnipeg photos as the person who had pledged the McConnell watch on April 28, 1927, which would be the day after the murder in Philadelphia.[51] That the pawnbroker had positively identified the picture of Nelson was also reported in the press.[52]

Whether Nelson might also have been the strangler of the three Philadelphia women who were killed in 1925 was also something that the Philadelphia police explored. Perhaps the most important witness was the clerk in the Philadelphia pawnshop where some of the clothes from the Weiner house (and the Murray house, if press reports were accurate) were found. As noted earlier, the clerk in the pawnshop said that Nelson "bore a strong resemblance" to the man who had pawned the clothes.[53]

Whatever the weaknesses of eyewitness identification, it would appear that the police in Philadelphia, while not absolutely convinced that the evidence was strong enough against Nelson for the three 1925 murders, were certainly convinced that Nelson had murdered Mrs. McConnell, and they were willing to seek a warrant for Nelson's arrest on a murder indictment, just in case he was released after the trial in Winnipeg.[54] Philadelphia justice officials later decided to delay moving in this direction and would only seek such a warrant and extradition if Nelson's trial in Winnipeg had a different outcome than expected.[55] However, later reports indicated that a warrant had been issued in Philadelphia.[56] There were attempts to send Mrs. Kuhn and the Brooklyn pawnbroker to Winnipeg to see Earle Nelson face to face.[57] However, the Winnipeg authorities were not allowing any interchange with the prisoner until after the trial in November.

The Philadelphia narrative is not complete without mentioning that Mr. McConnell went all the way to Winnipeg in January of 1928 to meet Earle Nelson, the alleged killer of his wife. He first requested and then received letters from the Philadelphia district attorney and from the chief of detectives giving him credentials and asking that the Winnipeg authorities grant him access to Nelson.[58] The authorities in Winnipeg allowed Mr. McConnell to visit Nelson for two hours just a few days before he was to be executed, but with the condition that McConnell not reveal to the press his conversations with Nelson.[59] After Nelson was hanged, the *Bulletin* reported:

Disclosing for the first time the result of his interview with Nelson, McConnell declared the "dark strangler" repeated over and over: "I did not do it. I did not do it…. I have no confession to make." But the evidence against Nelson was so strong, McConnell added, that his denial was incredible. "I have no malice whatever against him, though," the Philadelphian said, "I think he was insane. I hope he is at peace with God."[60]

The *Public Ledger* also interviewed Mr. McConnell, who stated: "When he told me he had never been in Philadelphia in his life, I produced from my pocket a wristwatch of my daughter which had been stolen from my home at the time my wife was murdered…. He denied ever having seen it."[61] Mr. McConnell was a persistent man. He had spent two hours with Nelson on Wednesday, January 11, 1928, trying to get a confession from him without luck. Now he returned for another hour on the day before the execution, Thursday, without success again.[62] He had shaken hands with Nelson on Wednesday, but on the second visit on Thursday, "Nelson's peculiar staring eyes so unnerved him that he was afraid of him."[63]

≈   ≈   ≈

The Philadelphia police claim that no files from this period have survived, at least within the records of the police department.[64] Additional information from the Philadelphia City Archives indicates that these murders are not included in the few detective division case files that have survived.[65]

The coffee salesman, William McConnell, subsequently lived with his daughter Alice and son-in-law John Donovan. For a few years they lived in Philadelphia but then moved to Yeadon, a town to the west of Philadelphia.[66] It was here that William died at the age of 65 in 1938.[67] Bank clerk John Donovan died in the same house in Yeadon in 1969, and schoolteacher Alice died in 1990.[68] Mary McConnell had no grandchildren.

CHAPTER 25

Jennie Randolph in Buffalo

25. May 30, 1927—Jennie Randolph, 57, Buffalo

About a month later, in the early hours of Monday, May 30, 1927, Mrs. Jennie Randolph, 57 years of age, was hit over the head, strangled to death and sexually assaulted and then hidden under a bed in her rooming house at 175 Plymouth Avenue in Buffalo. Unlike most of the murders we have been dealing with where the police files have been destroyed or are unavailable, we have the complete police file on this case.[1] The file allows us to reconstruct a more accurate narrative without relying on newspaper reports.

At around 11 in the morning on Saturday, May 28, a man calling himself "Charles Harrison" and claiming to be a painting contractor arrived at the house and rang the doorbell, after seeing the "ROOMERS" sign in the window.[2] Henry Gillett opened the door and later recalled:

> "He asked if I had any rooms. I told him we had no small room, but we had two larger rooms, one on the first and one on the second floor. I was talking to this man in the front hallway when my sister, Jennie Randolph, came down the stairs. She gave him the price of the rooms. He said it was more than he wanted to pay, and he went away and said he might return if he did not find what he wanted. About 4 p.m. on Saturday he returned and had five one-dollar bills in his hand which he handed to me and said, 'I don't see why I should look any further for a more home-like place than this.' He took the room and left his suitcase. Later he went out to buy a hat."[3]

The Buffalo police later confirmed that a man meeting the description of Harrison purchased a Panama straw hat at a store at 598 Main Street at about 4:30 in the afternoon of May 28.[4] Mr. Gillett reported that at some stage Harrison mentioned that "he was well acquainted with New York City and he talked freely about it, and he also said that he had been in Albany, New York."[5] It was also reported that Harrison seemed quite uninterested in the rooming house till he saw Mrs. Randolph come into the picture.[6]

Perhaps in this case Earle Nelson did not initially intend to murder the landlady or, alternatively, he was becoming very bold in regard to his ability to escape capture. Posing as Harrison, he did not hide away in his upstairs room waiting for the right moment to kill the landlady, but rather he fully risked later identification. For example, after spending Saturday night in his room, he went to the Normal Restaurant on Connecticut Street for breakfast on Sunday morning with another roomer, Mr. Fred Merritt, a 22-year-old night watchman. Merritt stated, "While we were eating breakfast, he started a conversation about Mrs. Randolph and her brother, Gideon

Gillett. He asked me if they were nice people to live with and I told them they were, and told him that I had been there for nearly three years myself…. When Harrison was talking to me, he asked if they had money. I said they did not."[7] Evidently Harrison must have appeared to Fred Merritt as a comfortable person to be around and converse with, because at about three on that Sunday afternoon, after having his day-sleep, Merritt went to the new boarder's room and conversed with him for about 15 minutes. Harrison then suggested they go out for supper, which they did at the Florian Restaurant on Connecticut Street. After returning from the meal, they conversed with each other on the front veranda.

Later that Sunday evening, Harrison got into a lively discussion about religion with Merritt and with Mrs. Randolph and her brother. When Mrs. Randolph invited Harrison to attend her evening church service at the Plymouth Methodist Episcopal Church he declined. However, he continued his conversation with Merritt until the night watchman went to work, and then, when Mrs. Randolph returned from church, he continued to converse with her on religious subjects into the night, as confirmed by the brother, Mr. Gillett, who later said that Harrison and Mrs. Randolph were still talking at midnight.[8]

We might speculate that some killers, with at least a shred of conscience, might be less likely to kill victims who are no longer anonymous. But Harrison seemed to have no qualms about killing a woman who must have become quite well known to him after spending so many hours in conversation with her.

On Monday morning, May 30, 1927, Fred Merritt returned home from working the night shift and found the elderly Henry Gillett sleeping downstairs on the couch. Mr. Gillett had got up at three in the morning and set out the milk bottles, and instead of returning to his bedroom, he lay down on the couch in the dining room, covered himself with his overcoat, and fell back asleep.[9] Upon noticing that Mrs. Randolph was not making breakfast, Merritt woke Gillett and asked where Mrs. Randolph was. Both men subsequently called out to Mrs. Randolph. There was no reply. They went upstairs to Mrs. Randolph's bedroom and found it locked. While Gillett phoned the YWCA to inquire as to whether his sister was already at work, Merritt climbed up onto the balcony roof and entered the second-floor bedroom, only to find it undisturbed.[10]

The two men started getting more worried when they saw bloodstains on the floor of the kitchen and then in the dining room and then on the stairs leading to the bedrooms. They went to the room rented by Harrison and found it locked as well. Merritt peered through the keyhole and noticed that the roomer's traveling bag was not on the chair. Merritt went back downstairs, got a key to the bedroom, and then when Merritt and Gillett entered the room, they noticed that the bed was made up.[11] Mr. Gillett, in a worried state, left the room and went downstairs. Merritt then looked under the bed and to his horror found the body of his landlady. As described in the press report the following day, "The clothes from the lower part of her body and one stocking had been torn off…. Both eyes were blackened, her nose discolored and the side of her face badly scratched. A wound on the side of the head had been caused by a blow from a hammer or some blunt instrument."[12] Mrs. Randolph had been strangled with a towel found near the body.[13]

At least two newspapers noted that Mrs. Randolph's body had been "maltreated after death."[14] The medical examiner confirmed that "there had been an attempt made to criminally assault Jennie Randolph."[15] The coroner's report on Mrs. Randolph included the following:

> Face markedly cyanotic, haematoma about left eye, marked haemorrhage in cornea, ecchyonasis at inner angle of right eye, haemorrhage in cornea. Bleeding from nose, tongue between teeth, discoloration of neck, semi-circular mark exact size of thumbnail over trachea, evidence of traumatism to neck. Inner sides of thighs bloodstained, posterior walls of vagina lacerated, also dilated; extensive haemorrhage under scalp on left side extending from temporal to occipital region.... Cause of death: Strangulation, traumatism of head.[16]

The report confirms that the sexual assault was not just an attempt but that the victim had been raped, presumably after she was dead.

The police believed Randolph had been attacked in the kitchen. The killer had then dragged the body through the dining room and up the stairs to the bedroom. Before being crammed under the bed, the body had been on the bed as indicated by the fact that when the bed was unmade, a considerable amount of blood was discovered on the sheets.[17] That Mrs. Randolph was sexually assaulted was again confirmed in a letter to Kansas City police in which James Higgins, chief of the Buffalo police, wrote that she had been strangled and then "raped."[18] Amazingly, not only did Gillett not wake up to any disturbing noises as the killer attacked his sister in the kitchen and dragged her body upstairs, but neither did two other roomers in the house.[19]

The Buffalo police immediately associated the murder of Randolph with the fiend from the West known as Adrian Harris.[20] The description of Harrison given to the police by Gillett and Merritt and the other roomers matched the description of Adrian Harris sent to the Buffalo police by the Portland and Seattle police. While the immediate link was made to the Seattle and Portland cases, over the next days after the murder, the links were also made to the California cases and to Philadelphia but, curiously, not to Kansas City or Council Bluffs, as far as I know.

Police officials in Buffalo stated that Adrian Harris was "the most brutal murderer of whom they ever have heard."[21] The Buffalo police immediately requested all police departments within 500 miles of the city to send out warnings to landladies that the fiend might be in the area.[22] The circular, distributed on the same day as the murder, partly based on previous descriptions of Harris, stated:

> Gave name as Charles Harrison, 33 years old, 5 ft. 7, 155 to 160 pounds, stocky build, very full face, dark complexion, black coarse hair combed back, blue eyes with white spots on blue surface of eyes, very peculiar, speaks with a Scottish accent, wore blue striped shirt with white silk blocks, soft white collar, dark tan suit, grey felt hat or Panama straw hat with light brown silk band, no bow pleats all around band, carried a new tan cream colored traveling bag, wore oxfords, grey overcoat, had yellow color paint about his fingernails. Said he was a painter contractor.[23]

The day after the murder, a railway detective noticed a man fitting the description of the wanted murderer jumping on a freight train in Depew, just east of Buffalo, heading for New York City. Detective chief Roche ordered the train to be stopped and searched at Batavia. When the train was stopped and a search made, it was discovered that the man had jumped off the train when it slowed down around Wende.[24] We do not know whether this man was Earle Nelson, but if he was, he came close to being captured, which would have prevented the murder of the subsequent victims. As we will note, however, it is likely that Nelson headed west rather than east, because in a few days after the murder in Buffalo, he killed two women in Detroit.

There is no indication that Nelson stole anything less important than a life in the Plymouth Avenue premises. However, as the Buffalo police searched the pawnshops of the city, they discovered that a man matching the description of the wanted killer showed up at a pawnshop at 186 Seneca Street on Monday morning, May 30, at 7:30. The man gave his name as Frank Walters living at 108 Ferry Street and proceeded to pawn his suitcase full of clothing, while the pawnshop proprietor faithfully recorded the transaction on little cards.[25] The police were certain "Walters" was "Harrison" given that the items pawned consisted of a large brown traveling bag, an old pair of blue painter's overalls, a brown knit topcoat, one black round hat, one gray soft hat, one Panama straw hat, a tremolo concert harp, and other items of clothing that were not separately recorded by the pawnshop owner. It appears from the pawn records that Walters received $12 for these items. Other reports said Walters only received $4 for the clothes.[26] In any event, the newspapers noted that he must have been low on funds.[27] The police also discovered a charm inside the pockets of the clothing or perhaps in the traveling bag.[28] The police thought the charm might have come from the person or house of Mrs. Randolph.[29]

Various items of clothing from the pawnshop and chips of wood from the stairs of the Randolph house were now sent to the city chemist. Tests indicated that there were fresh blood stains on the top of the crown of the hat and a blood stain on the underside of the right side of the brim. Both the left and right shoe had various blood stains, and there were slight blood stains on the right shoulder of the shirt. Seven wood chips taken from the stairs contained fresh blood stains.[30]

The discovery of the pawned clothing led to another clue. The label on the straw hat was local, and, as previously noted, the police were soon at the door of H.B. Moore at 598 Main Street, where a clerk recounted that a dark-complexioned man had bought the Panama hat on Saturday, May 28, at around 4:30 p.m.[31] This discovery confirmed what G. Henry Gillett had earlier told the police as to Harrison's activities on Saturday.

Now having some of the clothing that the murderer had worn, the Buffalo police revised their initial circular and added some new information as to the possible sizes of clothing that might be found on the wanted man:

> Shoes size 8, shirt size 15, collar size 15¼, gloves 8½, hat 7⅛. When working wore blue overalls and athletic shoes, otherwise a very flashy dresser. Wore gray topcoat marked J.P. Carey Grand Central Terminal, New York City, knit tex size 40.[32]

One might not make too much of the actual sizing of clothes, assuming we are dealing with Nelson, given his by now well-known proclivity for wearing whatever was handy.

Despite a glowing report published shortly after the murder about how Buffalo police used fingerprints to catch 55 crooks over the past year,[33] there was no mention in the file or in the newspapers of taking fingerprints at the scene of this murder, which one would think could have been done, given the amount of time that Harrison had been in the house.

The main police activity in the first week after the murder consisted of tracking down every painting contractor or business employing painters. A host of police officers in every precinct reported their findings in writing to John Marnon, deputy chief of police.[34] The only information yielded by this search was the discovery that there was an actual Charles Harrison who worked as a painter.[35] This person was eventually located and hauled into police headquarters. Fred Merritt was then brought in to view the real Charles Harrison, and when Merritt confirmed that he was not the killer, the real Harrison was released.[36] The police file and newspapers contain information on other suspects who were eventually cleared.[37]

~ ~ ~

After the arrest of Nelson in Manitoba, detectives in Buffalo at first thought Nelson did not match the description of the Buffalo slayer,[38] but at the request of the Buffalo police,[39] Winnipeg police authorities sent some pictures of Nelson as well as fingerprints and details of his alleged Winnipeg murders.[40] However dangerous eyewitness evidence might be based on a photo recognition test, especially when presented to the witness as a single photograph, we might still consider the reality that in this case "Harrison" spent considerable time with both Merritt and Gillett a few weeks before the picture of Nelson was shown to them, just as "Harris" had spent a lot of time with the women, Cayfort and Yates, in Portland in late November 1926. A confident identification by these persons that Nelson was "Harris" and "Harrison" is probably the most important evidence we have as to Nelson being the sought-after fiend.

On June 20, the picture of Nelson was shown to Fred Merritt at Buffalo police headquarters, and he said immediately, "This is the man!"[41] According to one report, Mr. Merritt said, "That's the man; I'm positive he's the man I was introduced to at Mrs. Randolph's home two days before the murder. I talked to him on several occasions and had several meals with him. I remember his face very distinctly."[42] Then Detective Carroll took the picture to 175 Plymouth and showed it to Mr. Gillett, and he also positively identified Nelson as Harrison.[43] The positive identification was duly reported in the press.[44]

The pawnshop owner, who admittedly spent much less time with Harrison, was unable to identify the picture of Nelson as being the man who pawned the suitcase and clothes, although he had earlier confirmed that the man fit the general description of Adrian Harris.[45] Quite properly the clerk at the pawnshop admitted that he paid no particular attention to the man who had pawned the clothes, not knowing at the time that he was a wanted killer.[46] He told Detective Carroll that "he did not take a good look at the man's face and cannot say this picture is the man or not."[47] Similarly, the employees of the restaurant where Merritt and the killer had eaten meals were unable to make an identification based on the photographs.[48] The identification of Merritt and Gillette of Nelson as the killer of Randolph was duly relayed to the

Winnipeg police, who no doubt were reinforced in their view that they had the long sought after "gorilla man" in their custody.[49]

On June 15, Detective Madigan presented the Randolph murder to the grand jury and subsequently obtained a "John Doe" felony warrant against Nelson on June 23.[50] The link between Nelson and the Buffalo murder was so strong that justice officials got a grand jury first- degree murder indictment against Nelson, which would prevent his release from custody just in case the Winnipeg charges were dismissed.[51] Unlike many other American newspapers, even in cities where murders attributed to Nelson took place, the leading Buffalo newspapers carried regular, if short, updates of the trial of Nelson in Winnipeg, culminating in front-page headlines when he was convicted.[52]

The circumstantial and identification evidence linking Nelson to the Buffalo murder of Mrs. Randolph is overwhelming. The strangulation murder of a rooming house proprietor, the sexual assault after death, the hiding of the body under the bed, and the pawning of clothes all point to the work of Earle Nelson. Additionally, Nelson used the name Harrison, and when first confronted in Wakopa, Manitoba, Nelson said he worked for a rancher named Harrison. We also have here the identification from people who spent considerable time with Nelson shortly before being asked to identify him.

∿ ∿ ∿

In reporting the crime, the press consistently referred to Mrs. Randolph as a widow of 55 years of age. However, our own investigation shows that she was 57 (almost 58), and she was likely not a widow but rather divorced. Jennie Gillett was born in August 1869 to Gideon and Lucy Gillett in Ceres, Pennsylvania. For the era, the family was very small. Jennie had only one sibling, an older brother, G. Henry Gillett, born in March 1862.[53] Gideon Gillett was involved in the lumber business in Pennsylvania, but the family eventually moved across the border to the nearby town of Olean in New York State.[54] Gideon and Lucy also established a boarding house in Olean. Son Henry, or Gideon Jr., as he was sometimes called, established a printing shop in Olean and was married to Elizabeth Weston in 1894. They had a son named Weston in 1896. The family lived with the elder Gilletts at the boarding house, as did daughter Jennie.

At the age of 25 in January of 1895, Jennie married a younger man, Daniel F. Randolph, who was only 18 years old.[55] They were married in the Gillett house in Olean. Jennie gave birth to a son, Orville Randolph, in 1897.[56] While Jennie and her child lived with her parents back in Olean, her husband Daniel Randolph joined the navy as a yeoman in 1898 and served as a clerk to the captain on the battleship *Iowa*.[57] He returned to Olean at the end of May 1899[58] but then allegedly abandoned his wife and son. Jennie Randolph eventually tracked him down in November of 1900. Her husband, who was only 24 at the time, was working as a stenographer in a law office in New York and living with another woman. Daniel Randolph was arrested on a civil warrant taken out by his wife in Olean on a charge of abandonment of wife and child.[59] When taken to court, Daniel presented himself to the judge as a navy veteran, which was true, but then claimed as well that he was a "graduate of Franklin College in Pittsburgh and a teacher at a seminary in Pittsburgh."[60] We believe this information was false, but it impressed the judge, who released him on his own recognizance. Randolph did not appear again for his scheduled hearing, and a warrant was issued for his arrest. However, unless there was reconciliation between Jennie and Daniel, he disappeared again for several years.

In 1901 the extended Gillett family moved from Olean to Buffalo and Jennie at some stage discovered that her husband was in the city. Jennie Randolph applied in court for support pending a separation and the order was granted.[61] She then learned that Daniel was leaving the state, so she secured a warrant and Daniel was arrested, this time in the lobby of the Iroquois Hotel in Buffalo in November of 1902, and held under a bond of $1,000.[62] We have no information as to the subsequent proceedings, but we presume that Jennie and Daniel were divorced. Daniel Randolph subsequently had several marriages and divorces and died in Los Angeles in 1951.[63] Thus, we believe Mrs. Jennie Randolph was not a widow at the time of her murder, even though she said she was.[64] As we have noted in other cases, it was a common practice for divorced or separated women, during an era when divorce was socially unacceptable, especially within religious communities, to claim that they were widows.

Jennie Randolph's father, Gideon Gillett, died in Buffalo in 1903,[65] and Jennie and her son continued to live with her mother Lucy and with her brother's family at the rooming house they ran on Porter Avenue. In 1905, along with the various family members, there were a dozen roomers at the house.[66] At some stage the family moved to a smaller house at 175 Plymouth Avenue, with a much smaller number of boarders.[67] It was here that Jennie would be murdered.

Aside from her disastrous marriage, Mrs. Jennie Randolph faced tragedy again when her 16-year-old son and only child, Orville, died after undergoing an operation in 1913 for a ruptured appendix.[68] He had just graduated from high school and was about to attend college to enter

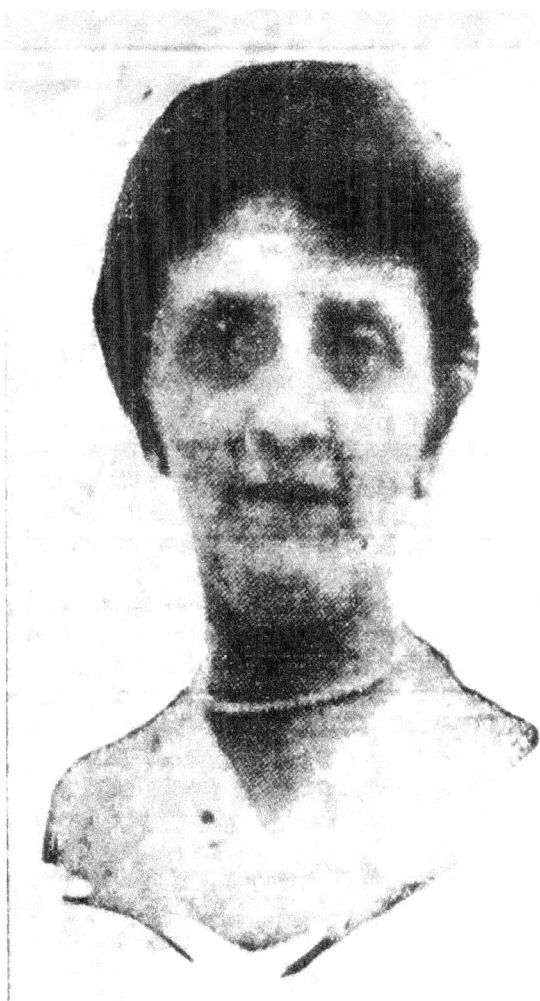

Murder victim Jennie Randolph (*Buffalo Times*, May 31, 1927, at 17).

the printing trade which was the occupation of his uncle G. Henry Gillett.[69] Jennie Randolph, a woman acquainted with grief, was a hard-working person, running her own rooming house, holding down a job as a waitress at the YWCA, and working as a leader in her church.[70] As part of the church's cradle roll, Mrs. Randolph paid weekly visits to the slums of the city, "searching out the needy mothers and their young babies, seeing that clothing was provided for the newborns, and welcoming the mothers to visit the church."[71] Jennie's mother Lucy died in 1924, and Jennie continued to live with her brother and his wife at the house on Plymouth.[72]

≈   ≈   ≈

After the murder of his sister, Gideon Henry Gillett and his wife Elizabeth moved to Charleroi, Pennsylvania, where their son, Weston, was a chemist in a glass factory.[73] Henry died of a heart attack at age 76 in Charleroi.[74] Elizabeth died at age 93 in 1959.[75] Curiously, nothing was said in the press about Elizabeth being present in the Plymouth Avenue house when her sister-in-law died. We assume she was out of town during these events.

CHAPTER 26

Fannie May
and Maureen Oswald Atorthy
in Detroit

26. and 27. June 1, 1927—Fannie May, 53,
and Maureen Oswald Atorthy, 28

Several days after the murder in Buffalo, chief of detectives Roche stated, "The mad killer, who appears outwardly calm and collected and a perfect gentleman while his crazed brain is hatching vicious crimes, will not go into hiding, but will seek the society of rooming house proprietresses in large cities just as he has in the past."[1] Roche was correct. On Wednesday, June 1, while a distraught G. Henry Gilett in Buffalo was hosting the funeral reception for his sister and speaking about her life "in a voice broken with sobs,"[2] Nelson was killing two women in Detroit.

Mr. Sink was the owner of an apartment house in Detroit located at 640 and 644 West Philadelphia Avenue. The building was divided into two separate dwellings. The upper floor (644) had been rented by a widow, Mrs. Fannie May, who was trying to rent out rooms in her portion of the building to supplement her meager income from selling her artwork, consisting of paintings and decorative lamp shades.[3] The one person who was currently renting a room from Mrs. May was Mrs. Maureen Oswald Atorthy, a young, divorced woman who had only moved in a few weeks earlier.

On Wednesday, June 1, Leonard Sink, the owner's son, went to the flat of Mrs. May to pick up the rent, but he got no response at the door. Over the next few days, he came back, noticing that the mail was not being picked up and the newspapers were accumulating on the porch.[4] The milkman's deliveries were also sitting untouched.[5] On Sunday, June 5, Mr. Sink was told by the neighbors that a light in the bathroom of the flat was burning continuously. He then went to the local police station and informed the authorities that he thought the occupants of the flat must be in some sort of difficulty. At about seven on that Sunday evening, using a pass key provided by Mr. Sink, several police officers entered the flat. They found two decomposing bodies.

It was eventually determined that the women had been killed on the Wednesday afternoon of June 1. Mrs. Hopkins who lived on the first floor flat initially told the police:

Shortly after noon…. I noticed a man of medium build and dark complexion and wearing a dark coat go to the front door…. He rang the bell, and someone spoke to him. An instant later he was admitted and shortly after that the young woman left the house. She was using a toothpick and I thought she had just finished having her lunch. That is the last I saw of anyone from the upper flat and it was later that I heard the sounds of something being moved around.[6]

Subsequently, when the police revisited Mrs. Hopkins, she stated, "He was tall and of dark complexion and well dressed."[7] If this report is accurate, we might note that Nelson could hardly be called tall. Another report was that she saw a man "of slight build, and dark-skinned."[8] Slight build does not fit Nelson either, although we must remember that eyewitness descriptions, particularly of very short events that have no significance at the time they are witnessed, can be notoriously unreliable.

We found the most important information on the murders in Detroit in the Kansas City police files. Writing on June 17, 1927, chief of detectives Edward Fox of Detroit wrote to Kansas City and Philadelphia asking for information as to murders in those cities[9] and attaching a report on the Detroit murders written by Fred Frahm on June 13.[10] The Frahm memo is worthy of extensive quotation, although I have sometimes changed the order of the paragraphs to follow a more chronological order:

On Sunday, June 5, 1927, at 6:35 p.m., Fannie C. May and Maureen Oswald were found strangled to death in their home at 644 Philadelphia Ave. West. It has been determined that this murder occurred between noon and 2 p.m. Wednesday, June 1, 1927. The place of occurrence is the upper of a two-family flat dwelling, occupied by Mrs. Fannie May, a widow, who earned her livelihood by doing art painting at her home. Miss Oswald was the only boarder at this house and at the time of the murder was unemployed. She was the divorced wife of a Hindu physician….

Mrs. May had inserted an advertisement in one of the local newspapers for board and room, giving both the street address and telephone number. She also displayed a sign reading "Board and Room" on the street door at the foot of the stair. The street door was controlled by an electric button from the second floor.

Early in the morning [June 1], Mrs. May informed her downstairs neighbors that she was busy papering the backroom of the flat…. At about 10:30 a.m., while Mrs. May was home alone, a man [described as medium build, wearing a black suit which was well pressed] came to the door and was admitted by Mrs. May. The downstairs neighbors could plainly hear the footsteps of the man and Mrs. May through the whole house, at least twice, as though inspecting the premises.

At about 11:30 a.m. Miss Oswald came home and was admitted to the upper flat. After some time, Miss Oswald left the house, fully dressed, and was picking her teeth as though she had just finished lunch. It is not known what time Miss Oswald returned, but she did visit a neighborhood grocery store and purchased several articles of groceries…. There was no tea in the house. A package of tea was found in the paper bag that Miss Oswald purchased at the grocery store and carried home with her when she returned to the house.

At about 12:10 p.m. the downstairs neighbor, a Mrs. Hopkins, heard a noise such as the moving of furniture would make in the upper flat but thought nothing of it because of Mrs. May's statement about papering. After this, all was quiet, and no one was seen to enter or leave the flat. Mrs. Oswald, however, must have returned later as she was out of the flat at this time.

Mrs. May was found [June 5] in the toilet [room] with her head between the stool and the wall. She had been struck three times in the head with a blunt instrument and strangled to death. She had a towel and an electric cord knotted tightly around her neck. The condition of the blood on the floor and on the two rugs indicated that she was killed where she was found and not dragged into the toilet. The electric cord used to strangle Mrs. May was cut from the table lamp on the buffet in the dining room. A cord was also cut off the table lamp in the front room and laid on the table near the hall entrance from the first floor but was not used.

[Miss Oswald] was found fully dressed even to her hat, strangled to death in her own bed-room, with a cloth belt from one of her own suits in the clothes closet tightly knotted around her neck. A paper bag containing the articles of groceries purchased by Miss Oswald was found on the floor in the rear bedroom, as well as four pennies in money. A bloodspot also appears on the floor in this room and smeared blood can be traced on the floor from this spot through the hall, past the bathroom, and into the front bedroom, where the body of Miss Oswald was found. She had been struck once on the head with a blunt instrument and stran-gled with a cloth belt. Miss Oswald's corset was also found on the floor in the rear bedroom. The fasteners had been torn off, indicating that it had been removed hurriedly.

The clothing of both persons was up over their heads, exposing their persons. Because of the decomposed condition of the bodies, it was not possible to tell whether they had been out-raged or not. The microscopic examination of smears made from these bodies showed nega-tive for human semen. The entire house had been ransacked and several articles of old jewelry were taken. We are unable to get a description of this jewelry.

Three places were set at the kitchen table but only one place had been used and toast and jam were eaten by the person using this place.[11]

We infer from this report that Nelson probably agreed to take the room and board offered by Mrs. May, and then the other roomer, Miss Oswald, suddenly appeared and was eventually sent out for groceries. When she was gone Nelson killed the landlady and then awaited the return of Oswald, killing her when she reappeared, groceries in hand. It seems obvious from the description of the clothing being pulled up "exposing their persons" that a sexual assault of some kind was also involved, even if semen was not later discovered.

∾ ∾ ∾

As we will note below, the focus of the police investigation was on the tangled relationships of Maureen Oswald Atorthy and very little was said in the press about the landlady, Mrs. Fannie May, of whom we have no picture. Fannie Campbell was born in August of 1873 in Belpre, Ohio, just across the Ohio River near Parkersburg, West Virginia.[12] She grew up in Belpre and became a teacher.[13] At the age of 20 in 1894, Fannie Campbell married Patrick J. May, age 26, in Chicago.[14] A son, Edward, was born in March of 1895.[15] Fannie and her husband lived separate and apart for much of their marriage.[16] By 1920, Fannie was listed as a married artist living back in Belpre with her elderly parents, while Patrick May was a boarder in Cleveland, listed as a salesman for photography.[17] Fannie's husband died in Cleveland in June of 1921 of a perforated gastric ulcer and peritonitis. The death certificate listed him as single, age 53, and a salesman.[18]

Shortly after the death of her husband, Fannie moved to Detroit to live with her son on Philadelphia Avenue.[19] Edward, a mechanical engineer, aged 31, got married at the end of June 1926, less than a year before Fannie was murdered.[20] After her son got married, and the couple moved away, Fannie rented some of the rooms in the flat where she subsequently was found murdered.[21] Fannie May was listed as an artist on her death certificate and was buried back in Belpre, Ohio.[22]

∾ ∾ ∾

Returning to the narrative about the Detroit murders, it should be noted that the very useful Frahm report was written several weeks after the murders and does not reflect the initial police investigation. Unlike the police in Buffalo, the police in Detroit did not immediately link the murders to the work of the "gorilla man" strangler, despite the "Room and Board" sign on the premises, the hitting over the head and strangulation of the victims, the apparent sexual assaults, and the theft of jewelry! Instead, over the first days of the investigation, the police focused on suspects thought to have motives to murder Maureen Oswald Atorthy. The police thought that she was the target and that the landlady was the bystander victim, rather than the other way around. This was a crucial mistake on the part of the police. The report of a dark-skinned man entering the premises led to "Hindu" suspects rather than the "dark strangler" from the West Coast.

A picture of Oswald appeared in several local papers.

Of all the victims we have researched for this book, Maureen Oswald is the most mysterious in terms of reliable information on her life. On her death certificate, the informants were ignorant as to her parents, but the certificate stated that she was born in Ireland on January 11, 1899, making her 28 years old upon her death, even though the newspaper reports consistently referred to her as being 29.[23] I have reason to be suspicious that her maiden name was actually Oswald or whether she had previously been married to an Oswald. My search for Irish and English records has been fruitless. Her death certificate listed her as a musician, and Mrs. May's son, Edward, told the police that his mother referred to her boarder as a singer.[24]

The press coverage at the time stated that Maureen Oswald, an Irish beauty, had worked as a nurse in the British Red Cross in the First World War or that she had served in the Women's Auxiliary Army Corps and had been wounded at Vimy Ridge and also saw service on the Belgian front.[25] We have no evidence for any of this.[26] We do not know when Oswald arrived in the United States. According to one report, she first met Dr. Noresh C. Atorthy, a medical doctor of East Indian background, while she was a nurse during the war.[27] Several other reports noted that she first met him in Detroit and had a very fast romance leading to marriage.[28]

Murder victim Maureen Oswald Atorthy (*Detroit Free Press*, June 7, 1927, at 2).

In 1910, Noresh Atorthy was a lodger in Pittsburgh and listed as a veterinarian.[29] By 1917, Atorthy was a medical student at the University of Missouri in Columbia.[30] In 1919 he applied for naturalization, asserting that he was from the Brahman class who had arrived in the United States in 1908. For some reason his application was denied.[31] In 1920 he was a resident physician at Providence Hospital in Detroit.[32] Dr. Atorthy was married at age 37 to Maureen Oswald, age 27, on January 12, 1925.[33] Maureen gave birth to a baby boy, Donald C. Atorthy, in November of that year.

The marriage between Oswald and Atorthy soon ended up in a bitterly contested divorce. During the divorce proceedings, Maureen continued to live at the home she shared with her husband on Jefferson Avenue and then subsequently on Algonquin Avenue. We have various conflicting stories in the press. Dr. Atorthy claimed that his wife was a drug and alcohol addict who had taken large quantities of cocaine from his medical supply and that he had reported her to the federal narcotics department.[34] Initially the police treated Dr. Atorthy as the main suspect until it was proven that he was in England taking a post-graduate course. Then the police focused on the theory that Oswald was indeed a drug addict who was killed by someone in a "dope ring" from whom Oswald obtained a constant supply of narcotics.[35] Apparently police found a hypodermic needle and a half dozen needle points in Oswald's purse, reinforcing the view that she was addicted to drugs.[36] Two "Hindu" men, allegedly drug dealers, were held for questioning, under the theory that she was killed by a "Hindu drug peddler whose attention she scorned."[37] That the man seen by the downstairs boarder was "dark skinned" would, of course, aid this theory.

During the divorce proceeding, Oswald claimed that her husband subjected her to extreme cruelty. During the marriage she complained to neighbors that her husband was regularly beating her.[38] She also was quoted as saying, "After our marriage I found Dr. Atorthy had married me for spite…. He had been going with another girl for four years and when she jilted him, he married me. I realize now that he never loved me…. He forced me to carry 50-pound blocks of ice up two flights of stairs and made me split big junks of coal for the furnace. He seemed to despise me and made patients think I was the scrubwoman."[39] She also claimed he forced her to live on a dollar a week, and after her marriage, just as he snubbed her as inferior, her own family in turn "outlawed" her for marrying a Hindu.[40] The divorce was granted on January 28, 1927.[41]

The whereabouts of the infant child, Donald, post-divorce of his parents and during the period of our narrative is unclear. One report suggested the child had been left in a home by its mother.[42] Another asserted that the child was in a Detroit orphanage.[43] Another report stated that when he was told of the murder, Dr. Atorthy broke down and "announced his intention of returning to Detroit to care for his son, Donald, 18 months old, who is in the Providence Hospital here."[44]

After obtaining her divorce, Maureen Oswald became involved in a romantic relationship with William D. Sinclair, an insurance agent. They were allegedly engaged to be married.[45] For a time Sinclair moved into the Atorthy home where Maureen was living after Dr. Atorthy left to go to England. When Oswald moved to the May rooming house, Sinclair also boarded there, until a week before the murders. The reason for his leaving was said to be that his relationship with Oswald became strained when he discovered that she had kept from him the information that she was a mother.[46] The relationship was not over, however, as Sinclair and Oswald had gone out to a show on Tuesday night, the day before the murders, and after their evening outing, Sinclair had borrowed Oswald's car, promising to return it on Wednesday.[47] When he tried to contact Oswald on Wednesday nobody answered the door. He allegedly tried again on Thursday, Friday, and Saturday.[48] Obviously Sinclair was a suspect, but the police were satisfied upon investigation that he was telling the truth.

≈　≈　≈

After several days of investigating "Hindu" suspects, the police finally linked the murders to the "gorilla man."[49] Detroit detective William Johnson was sent to Buffalo to investigate the similarity of the murder of Mrs. Randolph in that city to the murders in Detroit.[50] Johnson noted that he interviewed a landlady at 878 West Philadelphia Avenue in Detroit who said that a man answering the description of the killer in Buffalo had come to her house seeking a room to rent.[51]

The Detroit police report in the Kansas City police file on the murders included an attached photostat of a finger and palm print found at the scene of the crime.[52] Unfortunately that finger and palm print are not found in the surviving police file. There were a host of fingerprints in the Detroit apartment and the police lifted some finger and palm prints from the table lamp where the cord had been cut to strangle Mrs. May. These were later rushed to Winnipeg and compared with Nelson's prints after he was arrested, but just as had happened with the Portland print, the Detroit prints failed to match Nelson's prints.[53] Again, the police could not say that the print was necessarily that of the killer. However, the police in Winnipeg discovered a knife in the clothes that Nelson had taken from the Patterson house and left at Waldman's store. Mr. Patterson gave evidence that the pocket knife was not his, and therefore we may assume that Nelson must have been carrying it.[54] The blade of the knife was nicked and burned, and Winnipeg chief of detectives George Smith claimed that this was the knife that was likely used to cut the live electrical wire to the table lamp that had been used to strangle Mrs. May in Detroit.[55] The Detroit police could not find a burned knife left at the apartment.[56] One may question the logic that a nicked and burned knife "definitely" linked Nelson with the Detroit murders![57] Furthermore, it would appear that the link to Detroit by way of a nicked knife must have been made without the realization that, as we will see below, the more recent murder in Chicago also involved the cutting of an electrical wire.

Detroit police detectives William Johnson and John Hoffman were reportedly sent to Winnipeg to interview Nelson.[58] Subsequent reports only mention John Hoffman and that his interview with Nelson was useless as Nelson denied ever being in Detroit. "He talked willingly about the weather and current events, but when the conversation turned to the slaying charges, he insisted he was a man of high ideals and would not commit crime."[59] Nelson "talked affably about the weather and Buster Keaton of the movies, but when the discussion turned to the murder charges, Nelson declared he was a Christian man with high ideals."[60] Nevertheless, Detective Hoffman was convinced that Earle Nelson was indeed the "gorilla man" who strangled the two women in Detroit.[61] Hoffman said the police could not be certain that the fingerprints were those of the man who killed the two women, and Nelson's attitude in denying ever being in Winnipeg or Buffalo in the face of overwhelming evidence led Hoffman to say, "Nelson is one of the most cunning criminals I have talked with, and he shows not the slightest trace of an insanity complex of any sort."[62] Nelson's subsequent hanging was so un-newsworthy in Detroit that it was only noted in a few lines on page 9 in one newspaper and on page 42 of another.[63]

≈   ≈   ≈

After the murders, there was a report that the infant child, Donald Atorthy, would be cared for by a friend of Dr. Atorthy until he finished his post-graduate studies in London. It would appear, however, that Dr. Atorthy did not return to London but rather finished his postgraduate work in the United States. In 1928, he was listed in the Detroit City Directory, and in January of that year, a few days before Nelson was hanged in Winnipeg, he was sued by a department store for a $256 debt that Maureen Oswald accumulated in September of 1926 for lingerie and cosmetics. He asserted that he had published a newspaper notice that he was not responsible for her debts after a certain date, and, furthermore, "he had given his wife several land contracts, some furniture and all the money he had in the bank at the time they separated. She sold the land contracts … and squandered the money."[64] We do not know the outcome of the lawsuit. In any case, he eventually became an "eye, ear, and nose" specialist.[65] Dr. Atorthy had another unsuccessful marriage as indicated by the announcement in 1938 that he would no longer be responsible for his wife Irene's debts.[66] He was married a third time at age 52 to a woman named Francis, aged 35,[67] and this marriage appears to have survived, as she was listed as his wife when Dr. Atorthy died at age 86 in 1974.[68]

Donald Atorthy, the son of Dr. Atorthy and Maureen Oswald, died at the age of 96 in 2021.[69] Given privacy concerns for living relatives, I will not outline what the records reveal about his life.

≈   ≈   ≈

While I was speaking at a conference in Windsor, Ontario, several decades ago, I decided to cross the border into Detroit. After utilizing the library at Wayne State University and visiting the Detroit Public Library, I boarded a bus on Woodward Avenue intending to disembark on West Philadelphia. I overshot my destination by quite a bit and thus walked back down Woodward past a whole series of grand churches of various denominations in what had once been a nice neighborhood but was not so nice any longer. Upon reaching West Philadelphia I walked down the street, noticing that there were quite a few empty weed-infested lots where houses had been torn down, but eventually I found an old red brick house now divided into a side by side, one of which had 640 as the house number. I started to take some pictures, but a very irate lady across the street started shouting at me, asking me what I was doing there. I quickly left and made my way to the Wayne County Medical Examiner's Office. Upon being told that I could have no records without a death certificate from the city (and even then, the one-page record would cost $50), I left somewhat frustrated at my lack of success in Detroit, having also failed in receiving any information from the police. I gave up and decided to watch the Tigers play at the attractive baseball stadium I had previously walked past. I bought a ticket and when I sat down in my designated spot a young waiter introduced himself to me. He said, "I am Jesus, and I am here to serve you!" There are not too many, if any, persons named Jesus in Winnipeg, so this was the highlight of my otherwise dismal trip to Detroit.

Chapter 27

Mary Sietsema in Chicago

28. June 2, 1927—Mary Sietsema, 32, Chicago

If Nelson murdered two women in Detroit on the Wednesday afternoon of June 1, he must have wasted no time in traveling to Chicago where Mrs. Mary Sietsema was strangled to death on the Thursday afternoon of June 2, 1927, before the bodies of the victims in Detroit were even discovered. According to the conventional list, this was his last victim in the United States before he crossed the border into Canada less than a week later on June 8. However, as we will note in the next chapter, we believe that there may have been another murder before Nelson hitchhiked into Winnipeg.

Martin Sietsema returned home from work at about five in the evening on Thursday, June 2, and found that Mrs. Maria Lang and her daughter, Vera, were sitting on the rear porch of his house at 7501 South Sangamon Street. Mary Sietsema had invited her good friend Maria Lang to come over for dinner. When nobody had answered the door at about a quarter to four, Mrs. Lang and her daughter assumed Mary must have been out shopping, so they waited on the porch for her to return. Mr. Sietsema found that the front door of his house was locked, so he crawled through a window and found his wife's body lying on the living room floor, with "her clothing ripped away and with three strands of wire twisted about the neck." Her body was smeared with blood, likely that of her attacker, as she put up a "furious struggle."[1]

After making a formal request for a copy of the homicide investigation file by way of freedom of information legislation, I eventually received 34 pages, containing primarily sworn statements from various individuals.[2] Police investigations confirmed that on June 2, 1927, Martin Sietsema had been at his job from eight in the morning till four in the afternoon.[3] The statement of Mrs. Lang provided an interesting narrative as to the discovery of the body:

Mr. Sietsema said he would go and see if his wife left the key underneath the carpet in the front. He then came out and said, "There is no key there." He stood by the gate a few minutes and said, "I'll go up and try the second door, maybe it's unlatched." When he looked in, he could see his wife through the door and came running out and said, "My God, Marie, I think she has fainted." I then ran back in the hall with him up to the door and looked in and said, "Maybe she did faint." He said, "What will I do?" I said, "Aint there some way you can get in?" He said, "I'll try some of the windows." The dining room window on the north side of the house was raised about six inches. He pushed himself up, pushed the screen up and crawled in. He immediately ran into the room in front and came back and said, "My God, Marie, she's dead." He said, "I'll let you in the back door." So he opened the door, and I ran in with him into Mary (his wife). He grabbed her up in his arms and kept on asking her if she was dead. He asked what he should do, and I said I would call the police. After calling the police we both went out on the back porch, and he went up the alley to make inquiries to see if someone had seen anything. A few minutes later the police arrived.[4]

Included in the report from the first officers at the scene was their initial impression that the victim had been sexually assaulted: "We entered the living room and there found Mrs. Sietsema lying on the floor near the southeast corner of the room, on her back, and *her clothes pulled above the hips.* She was fully clothed and had her shoes on, with several lamp cords wound tightly around her neck."[5] Arriving on the scene soon thereafter were sergeants William Egan and Michael Moran who subsequently reported: "Right arm bent at elbow laying across breast; left arm extended full length, palm upward, pointing southwest, body flat on back; wire cord from electric lamp tied around neck; face purple, apron and slip turned up to breast … legs parted."[6]

Again, the obvious implication was that the victim had been sexually assaulted, and the inquest report includes the notation "Moron-Rape."[7] However, it was subsequently reported that Mrs. Sietsema had not been raped.[8] Earle Nelson, whom we firmly believe was the killer, may well have engaged in a sexual assault short of penetration in this case.

Turning now to the press reports, the *Chicago Tribune* presented the death scene as follows:

> Mrs. Sietsema was attacked and then strangled to death with a cord wrenched from a floor lamp in the living room of her home…. Apparently, she had put up a terrific fight against her slayer. Furniture in the room had been overturned, the rugs were in disorder, and her clothing was torn. An examination by Police Physician Joseph E. Springer showed that there were no cuts on Mrs. Sietsema's body and that the blood must have been from cuts she had inflicted on the killer…. A search of the home disclosed two towels tossed behind a radiator in the dining room, apparently by the killer. Bloodstains were found on these.[9]

Later the *Tribune* reported that the police believed that the murderer was "badly cut and bleeding profusely when he left the scene. The living room was spattered with blood and a large metal cigar stand evidently hurled by Mrs. Sietsema was also found to have blood stains on it."[10] Mary Sietsema was described as being five feet, eight inches tall and weighing 180 pounds and "strong enough to put up a terrific fight."[11] Another clue for the police was that the nine strands of electrical cord around the neck of the victim were tied with self-tightening nooses known as sailor's knots.[12]

Following the usual pattern, Nelson stole items. Long after the murder, just before Nelson was hanged, chief of detectives W.E. O'Connor from Chicago wrote a summary of the case found in the Winnipeg police file. He noted that Mr. Sietsema claimed that his wife's diamond ring was missing, as was his overcoat, and $14 in currency was taken from his wife's pocketbook which was left on the dining room table.[13] This was a classic Earle Nelson murder circumstance, especially the taking of an item of clothing. There was also a report that various identification specialists examined a long list of articles and locations in the Sietsema house and found "no fingerprints suitable for identification."[14]

The police believed they could pinpoint the time of the murder as occurring between 2:15 and 2:30 p.m. Mrs. Booth living across the street from the Sietsema house reported that as she walked past, she saw Mrs. Sietsema at 2:15 standing in the dining room talking to someone and she heard a man's voice.[15] Booth claimed the dining room window was open and Mrs. Sietsema was talking in "loud, strained tones."[16]

Several days after the murder, a Mrs. Heck informed the police that her seven-year-old son and several other children while walking down the street found a key in the corner of the yard between the post and sidewalk as they passed the Sietsema house at about 2:35 on June 2. They picked the key up and now Mrs. Heck gave it to the police, who confirmed that it opened the inside front door of the house.[17] Presumably the killer had tossed the key after he had locked and left the house. Thus, the time of death was between the sighting by Mrs. Booth and the finding of the key by the neighborhood children. Locking the door to the house was also a classic Earle Nelson procedure.

While none of the local newspapers mentioned the fact, Chief O'Connor later reported that there was a "For Sale" sign in the front window.[18] Thus, while the murders in Detroit were not yet discovered, everything about the murder of Mrs. Sietsema pointed to the "gorilla man strangler," and yet only the *Herald* mentioned the possible connection. Many newspaper accounts in other cities ran a United Press article which immediately linked the case to the previous murders by the "gorilla man strangler" who had murdered women from one side of United States to the other.[19]

In other cities, Associated Press stories also mentioned the link to the "gorilla man" but then noted that the police had dismissed the link "when they noticed the meat simmering on the stove."[20] Here is where the police investigation got off track as reported in the *Herald*:

> In the kitchen they found an electric iron, still warm, and on the stove a pot containing fresh meat. The meat wrapper, still freshly stained, was on the kitchen table. The same thought occurred to the three police officials coincidently. Exactly twelve years ago all three had worked on the murder case of Mrs. Ella Coppersmith, slain by a degenerate along with her 3-year-old son, Jack. These killings had been at 7100 Lowe Ave., scarcely a mile distant from the Sietsema bungalow. The three officials remembered that those murders had eventually been traced to Russell Pethrick, 20, a butcher shop delivery boy. Martin Sietsema informed the detectives where his wife usually purchased meat.[21]

In the *Tribune* account, the package of meat was found unopened on the table and led to Mr. Hirsch, who had blood on his clothes and shoes and a "small cut on one of his hands."[22] Thus, rather than immediately linking this case to the "dark strangler" from the Pacific Coast, the Chicago police focused on a meat cutter, whose life, and that of his wife, over the next few days became a living hell as he was arrested and put in jail, held incommunicado, and questioned intensively for 36 hours. The story does show how an innocent person can get caught in a web of circumstances that may imperil their freedom and reputation.

Michael Hirsch, 32 years old, worked with his father at the Hirsch and Sons butcher shop at 7021 South Halsted Street.[23] Michael Hirsch readily admitted that he had delivered the meat to Mrs. Sietsema in the morning. Indeed, he had made two deliveries. He had first delivered pork chops in the morning, but Mrs. Sietsema called back and said she wanted pork sausages for her dinner guests, so he took back the chops and returned immediately with the sausages that were found in the kitchen. While he had delivered meat to Mrs. Sietsema, he had certainly not murdered her. However, the police found some electrical wire in Hirsch's pocket, bloodstains on his shoes, a fresh and deep cut on the little finger of his left hand that might have been made by wire, and to top it all off, Hirsch had a key in his pocket that opened the front door of the Sietsema home![24] The police could hardly be faulted for initially taking him into custody.

During the course of the interrogation, Hirsch stated that Mrs. Sietsema had called the shop at 9:30 in the morning and ordered four and a half pounds of corned beef and two one-pound packages of pork sausages. He delivered the items to her at 10:30. Hirsch returned to the store, and about 11, another lady called and while Hirsch was still out on the delivery of that order, his father got a call from Mrs. Sietsema at about 11:45 saying that Hirsch had made a mistake delivering to her pork chops instead of pork sausages. When Michael Hirsch arrived back at the shop, he immediately went back to Mrs. Sietsema with the pork sausages. "I entered through the kitchen door. I received the pork chops and refunded 9 cents, the difference in the price.... The woman mentioned something about the weather and said that she was sorry that she called me back, but that the one pound of the pork sausage was for a friend of hers. I left the house by the back way and returned to the store." Hirsch stated that he got back to the store shortly after the noon hour and that he never left the store for the rest of the day. The police questioned him about the suspicious circumstances, as to the cut on his finger, the blood on his shoes, and wire and the key in his pocket:

> **Q.** How did you get that cut on your left little finger?
> **A.** My dad wanted a bottle to put turpentine in and I went back in the room where we keep sawdust, and I lifted up a butter tub and cut my finger on a flat piece of tin on the butter tub.... I came to the front end of the store where my dad was washing up the counters and tore off a piece of rag.... I wrapped my finger with it and tied a string around it....
> **Q.** How do you account for the blood that was found on your shoes at the time you were arrested?
> **A.** One drop on my left shoe was from my finger, and on the right shoe, light colored blood from the chickens.
> **Q.** Did you repair any lamp cords in your house lately?
> **A.** Yes sir, I did.... Tuesday night.[25]

As to the key that opened the door of the Sietsema house, it was established that the key also opened Hirsch's house by way of a Corbin lock that he had purchased for his back door. The police file includes an investigation report confirming that Hirsch bought a Corbin lock and key and an extra key some time previously at Meyer's hardware store.[26]

Despite his protestations of innocence and verifications of his story, the police continued to hold Mr. Hirsch in jail. The Hirsch family hired lawyer Maxwell Landis who brought a habeas corpus application to court on Friday, June 3.[27] At the hearing on Friday afternoon, Hirsch submitted that the blood on his shoes and clothes were caused when he accidentally cut himself while opening a tub of butter at the butcher shop. Sergeant William Egan testified that indeed he found a tub of butter at the butcher shop, with a jagged edge, and that there was blood in the wash basin where Hirsch claimed he washed his wound. Landis also presented the evidence that the key found on Hirsch was a skeleton key that opened the Hirsch residence. Pieces of wire in Hirsch's pocket did not match the wire found twisted around the victim's neck.[28] Hirsch explained that he had repaired some lamps at his father's home and had stuffed the extra pieces into his pocket.[29] Landis argued that Hirsch was innocent, that he had an excellent reputation, and that neighbors were willing to post a $200,000 bond for his immediate release. Despite the plea and the evidence, the lawyer representing the police argued that the motion should be postponed to the next day so that Hirsch could be detained for another night of questioning. Perhaps due to the lateness of the hour, the judge agreed, and Hirsch was not released until the hearing the next day, Saturday, June 4.[30] Hirsch had been held in custody for about 40 hours, much of it under intense grilling by the police trying to shake him from his story. In the meantime, his name had been published in every newspaper in town as a possible suspect in the murder. As reported, "Meanwhile the butcher's wife, Mrs. Elsie Hirsch, 24 years old, bride of less than a year, is under the care of a physician, having become hysterical when he was taken into custody."[31]

Upon the release of Hirsch, attention had already shifted to various Black suspects who had been arrested.[32] One Black suspect, as described in the *Tribune*, was a man who did not show up for work on Thursday afternoon at the garage that employed him and did not come home on Thursday night either. He had allegedly been seen loitering about the vicinity of the Sietsema house. When he was arrested, he asserted he was simply getting drunk during the time in question.[33] Another Black suspect was a man who neighbors claimed was frequently seen loitering in the area and indecently exposing himself.[34]

The *Chicago Evening Post* put the Hirsch story on the back burner and immediately featured the "negro" garage attendant as the most important suspect. The racism was glaring, as the *Post* reported that the police believed that a Black man was far more likely than someone like Hirsch to be responsible for the death because "a number of pieces of clothing was [*sic*] taken such as a white man would not have bothered with."[35] These included an old overcoat and several pairs of gloves. The second report in the *Post* featured the arrest of the "negro" garage attendant as the most important development in the case.[36]

The *Chicago Daily News* also immediately focused on the Black suspects.[37] Even more racist were the various press stories asserting that after it was determined that Mrs. Sietsema had not been raped, this "more or less eliminates the negroes" as suspects.[38]

There is nothing in the police file as to the possibility that someone might have visited the house because it was for sale. Even after Hirsch was exonerated, the black suspects were released, and the Detroit murders were discovered, the local press said nothing about the "gorilla man strangler" and Captain John Egan proclaimed that the murder was a "tough case" for the police to solve.[39] Really? Weeks after the murder, the police asserted that they believed that someone who knew Mrs. Sietsema was admitted into her house and killed her.[40] Police continued to question Black suspects in relation to the Sietsema murder.[41] In late July of 1927, well after Nelson was in jail in Winnipeg, the Chicago police still apparently hoped to clear up the Sietsema murder by linking it to one or more of four Black men who allegedly acted as a gang of burglars in the neighborhood.[42]

Long after Nelson was safely in jail in Winnipeg, there was a story of a woman in Chicago who had fought off "the gorilla man strangler."[43] When Nelson was hanged in Winnipeg, the *Tribune* did not find it necessary to even mention the fact, while the *Herald* covered the story in two sentences buried on page seven.[44] At least the *Post* carried the Associated Press story which included the "official" list of killings, including the Chicago murder. However, the information given was full of mistakes. The victim's name was misspelled as Mary Sietsoma, her age miscalculated at 67, and her murder was given as June 3, instead of June 2.[45]

It is also noteworthy that when the Winnipeg police made a big deal of the nicked and burned knife that was found in Nelson's clothes as a link to the murders in Detroit where an electrical lamp cord had been cut, they never said anything about the more recent lamp cord cutting in the Chicago murder, leading one to conclude that the Chicago and Winnipeg police were not in communication with each other until well after Nelson was tried and convicted in November 1927. As incredible as it sounds, I can find no report that the police in Chicago ever conceded that Mary Sietsema was murdered by Earle Nelson.

At around the same time that Detective O'Connor was finally communicating with Winnipeg, in December of 1927, the mayor of Winnipeg, Mr. Webb, was communicating with Chicago mayor William Hale Thompson. I am unaware of what remarks Thompson had made that so offended the Winnipeg

Early photograph of murder victim Mary Sietsema presumably at her wedding (*Chicago Tribune*, June 3, 1927, at 44).

mayor, but Webb seemed to mince no words in slamming the "lawlessness and injustice" found in Chicago as compared to the quality of British justice to be found in Canada, and Webb cited the trial, conviction and imminent hanging of Earle Nelson as an example. According to the *Tribune*, Mayor Webb wrote rather condescendingly to the American mayor:

> In England, Canada, and the rest of the British Empire, crime is not tolerated under any consideration.... That is why our laws are respected by people as a whole, and justice is properly meted out to lawbreakers.... If you yourself would adopt the same policy and set the example of encouraging your people to respect the law, especially those who have the idea that law means nothing to them, I believe you could go a long way towards creating a better reputation for Chicago and enlisting the aid of the better citizens there.[46]

∽ ∽ ∽

The newspaper accounts said virtually nothing about the victim, although they provided a few pictures of her.

Murder victim Mary Sietsema (*Chicago Suburbanite Economist*, June 7, 1927, at 3).

Mary (Ward) Sietsema was born on August 26, 1894, in Shamokin, Pennsylvania, the oldest child of a coal mining family.[47] Thus, she was 32 years old when she was murdered in June of 1927. She had numerous siblings and in 1900 the family lived in Garfield, Pennsylvania, where her father was listed as a coal miner.[48] At some stage the family moved to Chicago where the youngest sibling was born in 1903 and where in 1910 her father was listed as a motorman for the streetcars.[49] By 1920, still in Chicago, Mary's father was a carpenter, and the unmarried Mary was listed as a clerk in a commercial establishment.[50] However, at the age of 24, on October 14, 1920, she married Martin Sietsema, age 28, a World War I veteran and a tuck pointer in the bricklaying trade.[51] A friend later told the police that Mary had a millinery store at 1207 West 79th Street and she employed a "colored porter."[52]

Mary Sietsema must have been well known and liked, as it was reported that "crowds of people thronged the streets about her house on the day of the funeral and 300 cars were in the procession to the church, including 2 cars heaped with all the flowers sent for the funeral."[53] After the murder of his wife, Martin Sietsema remarried, and he eventually died in 1954 at the age of 63.[54]

CHAPTER 28

Lena Johannes in Kansas City

29. June 4, 1927—Lena Johannes, 54, Kansas City, Kansas

The murder of Mrs. Sietsema was said to be the last murder in the United States on the conventional list of murders attributed to Nelson. But was it? Nothing was ever said about linking him to the murder that took place in Kansas City, Kansas, on Saturday, June 4, 1927, four days before he arrived in Canada. As noted in a previous chapter, Earle Nelson murdered three people in Kansas City at the end of 1926. Was he now in Kansas City again, perhaps on his way home to California? Did he thereafter change his mind about going home and instead head north to Canada from Kansas City?

This time the murder took place in Kansas City, Kansas, which is part of the larger metropolitan area of Kansas City, Missouri, but is a suburb across the state line in Kansas. It was here that another widow was murdered in the morning of Saturday, June 4. She had boarders in her house, and her house was also for sale. As far as we know, this murder was never solved, and all we have are a few press reports that promptly end a few days after the murder. Our inquiries to the local police have been ignored or misplaced.[1]

Mrs. Lena Johannes, 54, was a recent widow, her husband, Henry, having died in November of 1925 at the age of 57.[2] Lena was described in the press as being rich and living at 611 Ferry Street on a bluff overlooking the Kaw River.[3] Other press reports stated the name of the street as Fowler rather than Ferry.[4] On the fateful Saturday morning, according to the *Kansas City Star*, George Warner and Hines Becker, who roomed at the Johannes house, went to work.[5] Then William Johannes, a married son of Lena who lived nearby and worked at the Armour packing plant, came by on his way to work. William Johannes later reported that "his mother told him of a man calling yesterday to look at her house, which was for sale. The man believed to be a foreigner from Chicago was expected to call again today."[6] William had visited his mother at 7:40 in the morning, and at nine in the morning an ice man arrived at the house to put ice in the refrigerator in the basement.[7]

When the ice man went into the basement, he discovered the body of Mrs. Lena Johannes. The narrative in the *Star* stated, "Her throat had been cut…. Chief McMullan believed Mrs. Johannes was slain for jewelry, including diamond earrings. A small screw from one of the earrings was found on the basement floor."[8] Several days later, Lena's son, William, reported that in addition to the jewelry found missing from the victim's body, the killer had taken "three watches … and a ring set with a large opal."[9]

The most detail as to the finding of the body was given in the *St. Louis Post Dispatch*:

> Mrs. Johannes' throat was slashed, and her skull crushed. A paring knife and a hatchet lay nearby. The body was found in the basement room, but on the first floor were indications of a struggle. A furnace poker, also bearing blood stains, was found near the body.... Diamond earrings and a finger ring valued at $300 are missing. The earrings were slashed from her ears. A dishpan in the kitchen had been used by the murderer to wash his hands.... Police found a sub-basement between the room in which the body was found. The trap door was open, and it is believed the slayer intended to place the body in the sub-basement.[10]

The following day the *Star* reported that

> detectives are working on a theory the man who brutally murdered Mrs. Lena Johannes yesterday ... cut one of his hands severely. They base their opinion on the quantity of blood between the body and the sink, where the murderer apparently washed his hands. No fingerprints were found on either the hatchet or the small knife used in the murder.... The brutality of the crime has led the police to believe it to be the act of a demented person.[11]

Several days later, the *Star* reported that another woman in Kansas City, Kansas, had reported that a man had visited her house on Saturday afternoon, after the murder of Lena Johannes in the morning. The report stated: "This woman told the police today the man who entered her house on the plea he desired to buy a home for his mother tried to drag her into a bedroom. She fought him off and he fled. She described him as about 50 years old, weighing about 175 pounds, as appearing to be a foreigner. She said he had a crippled or injured hand."[12]

The "foreigner" description certainly fits the Earle Nelson narrative, but the age given here is 20 years older than Nelson. However, it is possible that in the stress of being attacked, the woman did not accurately estimate age. We do not know whether it was the same day, but another woman in the neighborhood reported that a man had called upon her as to the sale of her house and asked her if she had money in the bank. He left without molesting her.[13]

The only report we have subsequently is that police discovered a handful of brown hair, presumably in the hand of the victim as she struggled with her assailant, and the Wyandotte County Commissioners offered a reward of $300 for information about the killing.[14] We have no subsequent reports about a medical examination of the body as to whether she had been sexually assaulted or whether the cause of death was actually strangulation. The report of a slashed throat might have been the deep wound caused by something that had been wound around her neck.

This unsolved murder was never linked to Earle Nelson. However, we have many elements of a typical Nelson murder with a house for sale, theft of jewelry, and perhaps an attempt to hide the body. There is no evidence that anybody giving a ride to Nelson into Winnipeg noticed an injured hand, but perhaps in four days Nelson's wounds were sufficiently healed so that no one noticed any wound. As was common with Earle Nelson, money received from pawned jewels or money stolen from the victim would have quickly been squandered, and that Nelson allegedly arrived in Winnipeg with nothing is not surprising even if he was the killer and robber of Mrs. Johannes in Kansas City. One wonders if the police in Kansas City ever presented Nelson's picture to the two women who claimed a visitation from the presumed killer of Mrs. Johannes. We doubt it, given that there was no communication from Kansas City to Winnipeg as to this murder.

∾ ∾ ∾

While we do not know what the maiden name of Lena was, we know that she was born in Germany and came to the United States in 1887.[15] The newspapers stated that she was 54 at the time of her death, and her gravestone says she was born in 1872.[16] We infer that she was married to Henry William Johannes in 1895.[17] Henry was also born in Germany and arrived in the United States in 1882.[18] A son, William Henry Johannes, was born in 1899.[19] Not long after being married, Henry and Lena also took over the responsibility of raising Henry Zimmermann who was the child of Henry's sister, also called Lena, who died in 1899, and whose husband, Karl Zimmermann, died in 1901.[20] Henry Zimmerman at the age of five was already living with Henry and Lena Johannes and one-year-old William in 1900.[21]

For many decades, the family lived at 611 Ferry Street and Henry was listed as a car mechanic.[22] In addition to the son and nephew, there were several boarders living at 611 Ferry Street.[23] Nephew Henry Zimmermann, a machinist, was married in 1917,[24] and son William was married in Leavenworth, Kansas, in 1922 to a divorced woman who already had a son by a previous marriage.[25]

As noted, Lena's husband, Henry, died in November of 1925 at the age of 57.[26] We presume that Lena's move to sell the house had something to do with the premature death of her husband. After the murder of his mother in 1927, William Johannes continued to live with his wife, Marion, in Kansas City, Kansas, and he was listed as working as a machinist in a packing plant.[27] At some stage before 1950,[28] William and Marion were divorced, and William remarried in Florida in 1967.[29] His second wife died in 1984 and he died at age 87 in 1986.[30] They were buried together in Alabama, presumably where the second wife originated.[31] Henry Zimmermann died in Kansas City, Kansas, at the age of 52.[32]

Concluding Reflections

As I have demonstrated, the linking of these 31 murders involves mostly circumstantial evidence. For example, all the murders took place in a rooming house or a house for sale, except perhaps ironically the last murder in Winnipeg, where I have doubts that the house was for sale or a room was for rent despite the police allegation that it was.[1] Aside from similar circumstances, in some cases the eyewitness identification evidence was particularly strong as in the Winnipeg cases and in the cases of Russell, Monks, Myers, and Randolph, where people who spent significant time with the murderer were able to identify Nelson's picture. There were also very positive identifications in other cases involving alleged attempts to murder, like the Murray case in Stockton, or identifications by pawnshop operators, or women who claimed to have encountered Nelson before or after a particular murder.

We are never free of all doubt, and the biggest missing link is the fingerprint evidence. Fingerprint evidence was still not well developed as a forensic science at this point.[2] The fingerprints from the Myers case in Portland and from the Detroit murders do not match Nelson. As we have pointed out, the lack of a match in these two cases could be dismissed because the police were not sure that the print or prints necessarily belonged to the murderer. However, we also have reports from newspaper accounts that fingerprints were apparently found in a further eight cases, and yet we have no evidence as to whether they were ever compared to Nelson. Our task of linking Nelson to various murders would certainly be enhanced if we had even one matching fingerprint from a scene of a murder.

Nelson may have committed all 31 cases we have looked at, but maybe he only committed most of them. As we look at linking the cases, while all are tied together with a degree of circumstantial similarity, I obviously have included some cases that seem suspicious in terms of circumstances but have never been linked to Nelson in the past as far as I know. These would include the Corcoran case, dismissed as a suicide, and the Johannes case, the last case before Nelson arrived in Canada. Furthermore, as noted previously, the three Philadelphia cases in 1925 involved the strangulation murders of landladies, the stealing of clothes, the carrying of the bodies upstairs, and the post-killing sexual assaults, but all three victims were bound and gagged. In no subsequent cases were the victim's hands or feet bound, but perhaps Nelson discovered that there was no need to do so. The similarities outweigh the differences, but we again face a degree of doubt.

Nelson may not have been guilty of every murder I have examined, despite

205

the circumstantial similarities, but, at the same time, he may have been guilty of other murders that were never solved that I have decided not to include in this book because of the early timing or differences in circumstances. However, I cannot dismiss him completely from suspicion in the New York murders of Hoxie in 1920 and Abramowitz in 1927. I also have the murder of Carlson in Piedmont in 1920, the Williams case in San Diego in 1924 and the Wood case in Chicago in 1927. Nelson's name as a possible suspect came up at some stage in all these murders. As noted previously, I have written about most of these murders elsewhere.[3]

By way of conclusion, I will summarize some features of the 31 cases I have presented. In 1925 Nelson's wife would have been 55 years old and we may assume that some of Nelson's murderous anger against women might have been displaced anger at his wife. Twelve of the 31 murders involved women in their 50s or early 60s, like the age of his wife. In terms of elderly victims, we might add Jones and Gallegos, who were in their 70s, bringing the number to 14, amounting to almost half the victims. The other half of the victims were younger. Two victims, the infant and the 14-year-old Cowan teenager, stand out as exceptional. Six victims were in their 20s, another six in their 30s, and only three in their 40s. One might conclude that Nelson killed young women and older women but rarely middle-aged ones. All of this might be coincidence.

If we take out the murder of the infant and the young Cowan girl, we are left with 29 adult women victims, 10 of whom were, or had been at some stage, divorced, while another 10 were married, seven were widowed, and only two were "spinsters." As noted previously, the number of divorced victims seems too high to be a coincidence. Is it possible that Nelson engaged in sufficient conversations with some of his victims to determine their marital status and this may have been an additional trigger for his rage?

When we look at when the murders happened, we are left with 29 days when the murders occurred, given that the Harpin infant murder in Kansas City arose from one incident, as did the double murder in Detroit. Notice that Earle Nelson, assuming he was the guilty party in these cases, never murdered anyone on a Sunday, although there is a slight possibility that Wells might have been murdered on Sunday. Is this just coincidence or should we assume that Nelson avoided that day because a landlady was less likely to be alone? Could there even be a religious angle in terms of Nelson avoiding Sunday? The closest we get to a Sunday is the Randolph murder in Buffalo, but technically she was murdered in the wee hours of Monday morning. Five murders occurred on a Monday, seven on a Tuesday, three on a Wednesday, nine on a Thursday, two on a Friday, and three on a Saturday.

As to the time of day, only two of the murders occurred in the morning, and while I am not sure of the times of the murders of Murray and Wells, they probably happened in the evening or night. There were six murders in the evening category. This means that Nelson on 21 days murdered his victims in the afternoon, usually in the early afternoon, and he seemed to prefer Tuesdays and Thursdays.

When we look at where the victims were found, we note that nine were discovered lying on a bed, but then with the Myers murder, we see a shift to where five of the more recent victims were found under the bed. Perhaps Nelson thought that hiding the bodies would provide more time to escape from the city. Another four victims were found on the floor of a bedroom. Thus, the victims were found on or under the bed or in the bedroom in 18 out of the 31 cases. But in many of these cases the landlady was murdered elsewhere in the house and moved to the bedroom, presumably for purposes of sexual assault. In many of these cases the door to the bedroom was locked, giving Nelson even more time to escape. Four of the victims were found in the basement, three of them behind a furnace. Two victims were found in the attic, one in a trunk in the attic. Two were found in a closet, two in a bathroom, and one each in a kitchen, a radio room, and a living room. A common theme in these cases, wherever the body was found, was the frequency in which the killer locked the door to the room or apartment or house in which the body was found.

Most of the 31 victims, if not all of them, were strangled to death. As we have noted, the medical opinions in relation to Jones, Anderson, Wells, Withers, and Grant disputed the strangulation theory, and in the last American case of Johannes the newspapers reported that the victim had her throat cut. Of the victims that had clearly been strangled, 16 of them were found with some cord, clothing, rag, or wire twisted about their necks, while the others, like the two murders in Winnipeg, involved strangling the victim directly with the murderer's hands without the use of a ligature of some kind. In at least a dozen cases there was evidence that the murderer hit the victim on the head before strangling her. In three cases, Anderson, Wells, and Cowan, the victim was found nude, but in all the rest of the cases the clothing of the victim was torn or disarranged, often raised up, indicating a sexual motive.

If we remove the infant murder, in the 30 remaining cases, how many of the victims were sexually assaulted after death? In eight cases we do not have medical information one way or the other, but the condition of the clothing indicates the likelihood of a sexual encounter with the corpse. In 13 cases we have clear evidence of a sexual assault on the victim and in the remaining nine cases we have reports from the autopsy that the women were not sexually assaulted. However, in most of these nine cases, given the condition of the clothing, we could argue that Nelson did not penetrate the corpse, but he may well have masturbated without leaving a trace on the body. So aside from Gallegos and perhaps Monks, we would argue that necrophilia of some kind was present in at least 28 of the cases.

How about robbery as a secondary motive? In the five murders in 1925 we have some evidence of clothing or jewelry taken in four of the cases, and it may be that in the case of McCoy there was nothing to steal. Then as we get into the murders in 1926, we have noted that Nelson probably stole nothing for the next seven murders, because we assume that he was being supported through his work in Palo Alto or by his relatives. The taking of a hat and the leaving of his own hat at the scene of the Russell murder can be explained in terms of not wanting to wear the hat with the blood spot on it. The motive was not robbery. The evidence is conflicting as to whether there was a robbery of a purse in the Nisbet case. It was in Portland that robbery became a secondary motive in almost all the cases, and this continued right through to Winnipeg. The few cases where there apparently was nothing taken involved victims that perhaps had no jewelry or money or clothing that Nelson was tempted to take away to pawn. The cases where there was no alleged robbery because of the lack of anything to take were the cases of Corcoran, Pace, Harpin, Randolph, and Cowan. Taking items at the scene of the crime was purely instrumental for Nelson in terms of pawning clothes or jewelry to get money. We have no evidence that Nelson took souvenirs from victims to help him remember the event or to arouse his fantasies as an aid to relive the events and become sexually excited by the souvenir.

This book concentrates on the murder narratives, the police investigations, and the victims, rather than on the killer. However, a few observations may be ventured. When we think about a sexual serial killer, we probably think the killer is primarily motivated by the sexual arousal that he gets through his acts of violence or that he kills instrumentally, to obtain a dead victim for sexual pleasure. However, despite Nelson's apparently prodigious sexual appetite, it seems that the murders in our narrative and the necrophilia were less about sexual attraction and sexual release and more about engaging in expressions of contempt and rage toward his female victims. The defilement of the dead was more about loathing and less about lust. Furthermore, it does not seem that Nelson was particularly turned on by some sadistic torturing of the victim, but rather he likely experienced an emotional high simply in the act of strangling a female to death. It makes sense to think of Nelson as a power-control serial killer who was primarily motivated by the great satisfaction he got from having God-like power and control over his victims in compensation for the traumatic loss of control and power in his chaotic and meaningless life.[4] Forensic psychiatrist Gordon Russon noted that Earle Nelson was superbly efficient in one area of his life, namely killing, in contrast to his sense of failures in every other department.[5]

In typical psychopathic fashion, Nelson went to the gallows without ever admitting that he had murdered any of these 31 victims. Rather his self-presentation was that he was a good person, and he was the victim. He was born with the curse of syphilis in his blood, and he had head injuries, and he was put into the insane asylum and thereafter framed by the Winnipeg police. While he attempted to manipulate the narrative in his favor, we also assume that Nelson had an extreme ability to compartmentalize his evil deeds from his conscious self-image as a virtuous person. Perhaps in the end he believed his own lies. However, if it had been possible to make a bargain with him, taking the death penalty off the table in exchange for information as to numbers of victims or unknown victims, would Nelson likely have confessed to save his skin, even if that meant life in prison? Probably.

Serial killers existed long before the 20th century,[6] but there is still a cultural component to the frequency of their existence.[7] Perhaps Earle Nelson serves as an example of the kind of extreme anomie that can happen more frequently in the culture of modernity involving transient and fragmented selves, rootless both geographically and relationally. Nelson could move within various urban environments with complete anonymity and invent various identities for himself.

However, the social environment of the 1920s was still less modern than subsequent decades. Nelson was caught in Canada, partly because he tried to escape through a rural environment where he was instantly recognized as a stranger. But even in the urban settings, while Nelson was not caught, despite Portland and

Chicago being slow at it, the police most often linked the murders together as they happened. This was possible precisely because serial killers were not at all plentiful at the time. The murders of the "dark strangler" were mentioned in newspapers throughout the United States, unlike decades later when murders were so common as to not be newsworthy in most cases beyond the local media. For example, back in the 1920s, a police officer in Buffalo might have read newspaper reports about a strangler murdering and outraging landladies even before he read any bulletin sent by a police department from another city. Therefore, when a landlady was murdered in Buffalo the police might immediately make the link to other cases in other jurisdictions. In more recent decades as serial killing became frequent, various police agencies in the United States and Canada set up some computer databases hoping that local jurisdictions would enter the information on local murders that might then be linked to other cases with the realization that a serial killer was roaming the country.[8]

When it comes to American-born serial killers,[9] Earle Leonard Nelson was likely the most prolific so-called sexual serial killer in the 20th century until at least the 1970s,[10] yet the story of his trail of death and destruction is relatively unknown compared to that of many other subsequent serial killers with lesser body counts. I think that the main reason for this relative obscurity is that the capture, trial, and execution of Nelson took place in Canada, and the American press, while covering the murders, gave very little attention to the subsequent proceedings in Canada, despite Nelson being an American. For example, Nelson was hanged on January 13, 1928, but newspaper headlines throughout the United States carried the story of the execution of Ruth Snyder and her lover, Judd Gray, in the electric chair in New York. This was one of those sensational cases that had received saturated press coverage across the nation as a kind of morality play. In March of 1927, Ruth and Judd had murdered Ruth's husband, making it look like he had been a victim of a home invasion and robbery. They also were expecting to collect the life insurance proceeds. The police immediately saw through the ruse, and the subsequent trial of the "the double indemnity" murder was tabloid fodder, as the sordid sexual escapades of the two lovers cheating on their respective spouses came to light and as they ultimately blamed each other for the crime.[11]

While I have no interest in serial killers as celebrities, the story of Earle Leonard Nelson is an important part of our history of crime and justice.

Chapter Notes

Introduction

1. Alvin A.J. Esau, *The Gorilla Man Strangler Case: Serial Killer Earle Nelson* (Altona, Manitoba: FriesenPress, 2022).

2. For accounts with large doses of fiction added to some factual framework, see, for example, Ryan Green, *Gorilla Killer: A True Story of Betrayal, Brutality and Butchery* (self-published, 2020); Michael Newton, *The Dark Strangler* (Toronto: VP, 2015); and Robert Graysmith, *The Laughing Gorilla: A True Story of Police Corruption and Murder* (New York: Berkley Books, 2009). The Graysmith book is not really about Earle Nelson but rather about other murderers and psychopathic serial killers in the 1930s, interwoven with the corruption of the San Francisco police force and the work of Captain Dullea, who would eventually head the force. A more reliable account of Earle Nelson is found in Harold Schechter, *Bestial: The Savage Trail of a True American Monster* (New York: Pocket Books, 1998), but Schechter also has a layer of fictional reconstruction added to the narrative. When we talk about the considerable amount of misinformation in the existing literature, we do not include the novels that are loosely based on Earle Nelson. We do not expect truth to be told here. For example, there is a sensationalized account in the 1977 book by Robert Olmos and John Howard, *Rooms to Let* (self-published). Another, even more fantastical novel based on the Nelson story is Jay Robert Nash, *The Dark Fountain: A Novel of Horror* (New York: A and W, 1982).

3. Many blogs and podcasts on Earle Nelson have a picture of serial killer Jarvis Catoe staring at his hands instead of a picture of Earle Nelson. Furthermore, they are not based on any original research but simply repeat the same misinformation found in other sources.

4. "Second Murder in City," *Manitoba Free Press*, June 13, 1927, at 1.

5. Edward Smith, Jr., "22 Dead in Path of Dark Strangler," *Oregonian*, July 3, 1927, at 1.

6. Record of Archibald Francis Leonard, from Portland police personnel files, provided to Alvin Esau, July 2008.

7. "City Detective Resigns Post," *Oregonian*, May 1, 1946, at 13; obit for Archie Leonard, *Oregonian*, Oct. 27, 1952, at 17.

8. Police investigative report books, Hyde and Leonard, City of Portland Archives, A 2001–073.

9. Frank W. Anderson, *The Dark Strangler* (Calgary: Frontier, 1974). A shortened version of this book appears as Frank W. Anderson, "The Strangler Who Terrified the Prairies," in *Outlaws and Lawmen of Western Canada: Volume Three* (Surrey, British Columbia: Heritage House, 1987) at 148–158.

10. Harold Schechter, *Bestial: The Savage Trail of a True American Monster* (New York: Pocket Books, 1998).

11. *Ibid.*, at 311–312.

12. Murders at alvinesau.com.

Chapter 1

1. A much more detailed account of the Winnipeg murders and the subsequent manhunt is found in Alvin A.J. Esau, *The Gorilla Man Strangler Case* (Altona, Manitoba: FriesenPress, 2022) [henceforth, *Esau*].

2. *Esau* at 5.

3. *Ibid.*, at 6.

4. *Ibid.*, at 7–8.

5. For a detailed history of the Cowan family, see *Esau* at 9–11, 415–416.

6. Details as to the finding of the body and the condition of the body are found in *Esau* at 49–53.

7. For example, Peter Levins, "What Is Justice?" *The Atlantic Sunday Magazine*, July 25, 1937, at 4 and 20. Levins falsely stated, "The details of the crime were so horrible that they were not made public." H.P. Musson and Fred Allhoff, "Strangler of Twenty Women," *Master Detective* 18 (June, July, and August 1938), falsely state in the August part at 70: "Mutilation had been added to the murderer's other sinister practices." Jay Robert Nash in *Bloodletters and Badmen* (New York: M. Evans, 1973) made the ludicrous statement at 367 that "her body was mutilated almost to the point of obliteration." Robert Graysmith, *The Laughing Gorilla* (New York: Berkley Books, 2009), at 42 stated falsely that "so horribly treated was Lola's body that Chief of Detectives George Smith permanently sealed the record." While not pretending to be necessarily factual, Ryan Green, *Gorilla Killer* (self-published, 2020), at 122–123, has Nelson having sex with

Cowan while she is still half alive, cutting off her fingernails, breaking her bones, and making her suffer like no other previous victims. The literature cited, and much more that could be cited, including information in blogs and podcasts, are replete with numerous errors of fact as to the biography of Earle Nelson and the murders attributed to him.

8. Pictures found in Winnipeg police file.

9. Testimony of Dr. McCowan, inquest transcript at 2; preliminary hearing transcript at 32.

10. Details as to the history of the Patterson family are found in *Esau* at 25–27, 416–417.

11. Winnipeg police circular, June 13 and June 14, 1927. Winnipeg police file.

12. *Esau* at 12–14.

13. Details as to Patterson's discovery of wife's body found in inquest transcript at 35–36 and trial transcript at 57.

14. Dr. McCowan, trial transcript at 95.

15. Details in *Esau* at 18.

16. *Ibid.*, at 19.

17. "Second Murder in City by Same Man," *Manitoba Free Press*, June 13, 1927, at 1.

18. *Esau* at 20–21.

19. *Ibid.*, at 21–23.

20. Details on the Regina sojourn found in *Esau* at 39–41, 44–48.

21. *Ibid.*, at 48.

22. "Description of Wanted Man Received Here," *Regina Leader*, June 13, 1927, at 3.

23. *Esau* at 59, 66–68.

24. *Regina Leader*, June 13, 1927, at 1 and 3. The newspaper was found in "Harcourt's" room by the end of the day.

25. Details as to the Regina transactions found in *Esau* at 59–63.

26. *Ibid.*, at 63–64.

27. Details on "Wilson" with Silverman in *Esau* at 64–66.

28. Details on Wakopa events in *Esau* at 92–95.

29. Details on the capture of "Wilson" in *Esau* at 95–101.

30. Details as to escape from jail and manhunt in Killarney found in *Esau* at 101–110.

31. *Ibid.*, at 110 to 117.

32. Details of the actual capture of Nelson found in the attorney general's files in central registry and also in the trial transcript at 225.

33. *Esau* at 118–120.

34. Original handwriting found in court file, *R. v. Nelson*, Archives of Manitoba, and in the Winnipeg police file.

35. For the problems with eyewitness identification see the classic book by Elizabeth Loftus, *Eyewitness Testimony* (Cambridge: Harvard University Press, 1979).

36. Identification issues are discussed in detail at *Esau* at 197–205.

37. Details on prejudgment and rush to judgment found in *Esau* at 227–245.

38. Information on Graham in *Esau* at 213–215, 419.

39. Information on Stitt and his appointment in *Esau* at 246–261, 421–425.

40. Details on the contentious court proceeding in *Esau* at 263–269.

41. Details on the trial as public entertainment found in *Esau* at 289–303. Details as to jury selection, the case for the prosecution and the defense, the address to the jury by the lawyers and the judge, and the verdict found in *Esau* at 305–369.

42. The classic work on psychopathy is H. Cleckley, *The Mask of Sanity* (St. Louis: C.V. Mosby, 1941). Subsequently the leading work is Robert D. Hare, *Without Conscience: The Disturbing World of Psychopaths Among Us* (New York: Pocket Books, 1993). For literature on the theory that psychopaths might be born with a dysfunctional brain and therefore not criminally responsible, see, for example, Adrian Raine and Andrea Glenn, *Psychopathy: An Introduction to Biological Findings and Their Implications* (New York: New York University Press, 2014). For a contrary view, see, for example, Jarkko Jalava, Michael Mauren, and Stephanie Griffiths, *The Myth of the Born Criminal: Psychopathy, Neurobiology and Creation of the Modern Degenerate* (Toronto: University of Toronto Press, 2015).

43. Details as to Dr. Mathers found in *Esau* at 276–281, 426–429.

44. For the history of capital punishment in Canada, see Frank W. Anderson, *A Concise History of Capital Punishment in Canada* (Calgary: Frontier, 1973); W.E. Morriss, *Watch the Rope* (Winnipeg: Watson and Dwyer, 1996); Ken Leyton-Brown, *The Practice of Execution in Canada* (Vancouver: University of British Columbia Press, 2010); Dale Brawn, *Last Moments: Sentenced to Death in Canada* (Edmonton: Quagmire Press, 2011); and Lorna Poplak, *Drop Dead: The Horrible History of Hanging in Canada* (Toronto: Dundurn, 2017).

45. The literature on the commutation process includes Carolyn Strange, *The Death Penalty and Sex Murder in Canadian History* (Toronto: University of Toronto Press, 2020), and Carolyn Strange, ed., *Qualities of Mercy: Justice, Punishment, and Discretion* (Vancouver: University of British Columbia Press, 1996).

46. Details as to the contents of the Nelson capital case file in the National Archives in Ottawa are found in *Esau* at 381–394.

47. Details as to Webb in *Esau* at 396–397, 402, 430.

48. Most psychopaths are not serial killers. They are usually dysfunctional people, but some are highly successful doctors, lawyers, politicians, business executives, and so forth. See Paul Babiak and Robert Hare, *Snakes in Suits: When Psychopaths Go to Work* (New York: HarperCollins, 2006), and Martha Stout, *The Sociopath Next Door: The Ruthless Versus the Rest of Us* (New York: Broadway, 2005), using the wider category of sociopaths. Some personality traits of psychopaths are even advertised as positive traits. See, for example, Kevin Dutton and Andy McNab, *The Good Psycho-*

path: *Guide to Success* (London: Random House, 2014). Self-confessed psychopaths seek our sympathy even as they treat others in despicable fashion. See, for example, M.E. Thomas, *Confessions of a Sociopath* (New York: Broadway, 2013), and James Fallon, *The Psychopath Inside* (New York: Penguin, 2013).

49. For the details of the hanging and the history of Ellis, see *Esau* at 402–410, 429–430.

50. Details on the hanging and aftermath found in *Esau* at 407–411.

51. The literature is vast, but from my own library, see Kent Roach, *Wrongfully Convicted* (Toronto: Simon & Schuster, 2023); M. Chris Fabricant, *Junk Science and the American Criminal Justice System* (Brooklyn: Akashic Books, 2022); Brandon L. Garrett, *Convicting the Innocent* (Cambridge: Harvard University Press, 2011); and Jim Dwyer, Peter Neufeld, and Barry Scheck, *Actual Innocence* (New York: Signet, 2000). Arguably, the biggest problem in the criminal justice system is not wrongful convictions but the lack of any convictions at all for the majority of murders because they are never solved. See Michael Arntfield, *How to Solve a Cold Case* (Toronto: HarperCollins, 2022).

Chapter 2

1. Oregon Marriage Index, 1885–1919, Vol. 11 at 9. All genealogical information in this book is found on ancestry.com or familysearch.org or findagrave.com, unless otherwise cited. The name Ferrell has various spellings in the documents and press accounts during the life of Earle Nelson.

2. "Births," *S.F. Call*, May 13, 1897, at 11. Earle is often also spelled Earl.

3. "Deaths," *S.F. Chronicle*, March 10, 1898, at 10. Aunt Lillian claimed at the trial that the doctor in Portland had confirmed that James died of syphilis. See trial transcript at 270. It is possible that James contracted syphilis from Fannie. We do not know.

4. "Salvation Army Funeral," *Oregonian*, Oct. 26, 1898, at 10.

5. For example, Harold Schechter, *Bestial: The Savage Trail of a True American Monster* (New York: Pocket Books, 1998) at 20.

6. See Alvin A.J. Esau, *The Gorilla Man Strangler Case* (Altona, Manitoba: FriesenPress, 2022) at 128–131 [henceforth, *Esau*].

7. Most of the previous literature and blogs on Earle Nelson suggest this, as if Nelson had no male adults in the home.

8. Details as to the Nelson family in *Esau* at 131–138, 415–416.

9. U.S. Census of 1900.

10. *Langley's San Francisco Directory 1904.*

11. For example, Frank Anderson, *The Dark Strangler* (Calgary: Frontier, 1974) at 29; Michael Newton, *The Dark Strangler* (Toronto: VP, 2015) at 21; and Schechter, *supra* note 5 at 16 and 19.

12. "Deaths," *S.F. Chronicle*, Dec. 14, 1904, at 15.

13. California Death Index, 1905–1939; "Deaths," *S.F. Call*, July 2, 1907, at 15.

14. Peter Vronsky, *Serial Killers: The Method and Madness of Monsters* (New York: Berkley Books, 2004) at 270.

15. "Married," *S.F. Examiner*, Jan. 5, 1908, at 6.

16. U.S. Census of 1910.

17. Details as to the Willis Nelson family in *Esau* at 134–135, 415–416.

18. California County Marriages, 1850–1952; "Married," *S.F. Call*, March 11, 1906, at 54.

19. Details as to Lillian Fabian family in *Esau* at 135–137, 415–416.

20. Testimony of Lillian Fabian, trial transcript at 276–277 [my emphasis].

21. *Ibid.*, at 271 and 284.

22. Ronald M. Holmes and Stephen T. Holmes, *Serial Murder* (Thousand Oaks, CA: Sage, 3rd ed., 2010) at 55, and James Alan Fox and Jack Levin, *Extreme Killing: Understanding Serial and Mass Murder* (Los Angeles: Sage, 3rd ed., 2015) at 121.

23. "Earle Nelson Talks from Prison Death Cell," *Winnipeg Tribune*, Nov. 30, 1927, at 1.

24. "Affidavit of Arthur West," capital case file.

25. "Dime Novels Inspire Lads," *Alameda Evening Times-Star*, July 19, 1911, at 3. See also "Small Boys Are Jailed as Crooks," *Oakland Tribune*, July 19, 1911, at 3, and similar articles in *Santa Barbara Independent* and *Bakersfield Californian*, *Sacramento Bee* on July 19, 1911, and *Napa Journal* and *Fresno Republican* on July 20, 1911.

26. "Clinical History of Earl Ferrell," June 16, 1921, Napa State Hospital. Capital case file.

27. Trial transcript at 247–248, 273, 278–279.

28. The case details found in *Feather River Bulletin*, July 15, 1915, at 1; July 22, 1915, at 1; July 29, 1915, at 1; and *Plumas Independent*, July 21, 1915, at 1.

29. As to San Quentin prison during this period, see *Esau* at 153–154.

30. *Supra* note 26.

31. We have the official military personnel file for Earle "Ferrel" obtained from the National Personnel Records Center, St. Louis, Missouri [henceforth, *Military Records File*].

32. *Supra* note 26.

33. "Record of Earle Nelson," from S.F. police department to Winnipeg police department. Winnipeg police file.

34. All these proceedings documented in *supra* note 31.

35. "Abstract of Commitment to Napa State Hospital," May 21, 1918. Capital case file.

36. *Ibid.*

37. *Supra* note 23.

38. Lilian Fabian, trial transcript at 281.

39. "Alleged Deserter Jailed After Chase," *Los Angeles Evening Express*, Oct. 28, 1918, at 13; "Sailor Taken in Street Case as Robber," *Los Angeles Herald*, Oct. 28, 1918, at 6.

40. *Supra* note 31.

41. *Supra* note 26.

42. Details on Mary Martin Fuller and the marriage found in *Esau* at 164–172.

43. California Death Records and obit in *Palo Alto Times*, Nov. 8, 1954.

44. Mary Fuller's testimony is in trial transcript at 231–259.

45. *Supra* note 26.

46. Stitt, "Argument for Reprieve," at 5. Capital case file.

47. Fuller, trial transcript at 237.

48. *Ibid.*, at 243.

49. *Ibid.*, at 249.

50. Murders at alvinesau.com.

51. "Police Seek to Link Man to Murder," *Oakland Tribune*, Sept. 13, 1927, at 52.

52. "Gorilla Man Believed Bay Girl's Slayer," *S.F. Examiner*, Sept. 13, 1927, at 12.

53. "Girl Is Strangled to Death," *Oakland Tribune*, March 15, 1920, at 1 and 3; "Strangler in Piedmont," *S.F. Chronicle*, March 15, 1920, at 1 and 3; "Piedmont Girl," *S.F. Examiner*, March 15, 1920, at 13.

54. "Sweetheart of Girl to Avenge Her," *Oakland Tribune*, March 16, 1920, at 13.

55. "Old Suitor of Carlson Girl Sought," *S.F. Examiner*, March 23, 1920, at 1.

56. "Girl Strangled Is Verdict of Coroner's Jury," *S.F. Chronicle*, March 18, 1920, at 2.

57. "Carlson Girl Not Murdered," *S.F. Examiner*, March 19, 1920, at 13.

58. "Scientist Gives Police Clew," *S.F. Chronicle*, March 20, 1920, at 1. [Note: In that era, the word clue was often spelled clew and so when the papers said clew I left it as found.]

59. "Scientist Says Man Slew Girl," *Oakland Tribune*, March 20, 1920, at 7. For an interesting account of Edward Oscar Heinrich, see Kate Winkler Dawson, *American Sherlock: Murder, Forensics, and the Birth of C.S.I.* (New York: G.P. Putman's Sons, 2020).

60. "Writer of Note Purports to Be Girl's Slayer," *S.F. Chronicle*, March 25, 1920, at 1; "Strangler Admits Second Murder in Note," *S.F. Chronicle*, March 29, 1920, at 5; "Strangler in Note Tells of Plan to Kill," *S.F. Chronicle*, April 6, 1920, at 7.

61. "Watson Traced for Murder of Ulla Carlson," *Oakland Tribune*, Oct. 19, 1920, at 16; "Girl Murder Laid at Door of Bluebeard," *S.F. Chronicle*, Oct. 20, 1920, at 13.

62. "Bay Bluebeard Denies Murder," *Oakland Tribune*, May 18, 1926, at 1.

63. "Aunt of Slain Piedmont Girl to Aid Police," *S.F. Chronicle*, March 23, 1920, at 11 [my emphasis].

64. Affidavit of Frank Arnold, Dec. 30, 1927. Capital case file.

65. Jack Carberry, "Phantom Slayer of Cabaret Butterfly Tantalizes Police," *L.A. Express*, Jan. 23, 1930, at 1.

66. Jack Carberry, "Gin and Jazz Girl's Mystery Strangling Still Balks Police," *L.A. Express*, Jan. 28, 1930, at 1.

67. "Find Woman Strangled with Her Own Chemise," *L.A. Times*, March 27, 1920, at 1; "Suspect Held in Strangling Mystery," *L.A. Express*, March 27, 1920, at 1.

68. "Slaying of Pretty Divorcee," *Santa Ana Register*, March 27, 1920, at 1.

69. "Strands of Hair May Hang Women's Slayer," *L.A. Times*, March 28, 1920, at 1; "Seek New Data," *L.A. Times*, March 30, 1920; "Police Puzzled by Strange Slaying as Suspects Released," *L.A. Express*, March 30, 1920, at 1.

70. "Meade Released on Bail," *Salt Lake Tribune*, Sept. 6, 1920, at 18; "Alleged Swindler Is Placed Under Arrest," *Ogden Standard Examiner*, Sept. 6, 1920, at 4.

71. Criminal record sheet of S.F. police department. Winnipeg police file.

72. *Ibid.*

73. "12-Year-Old Girl Attacked by Insane Man," *S.F. Examiner*, May 20, 1921, at 15.

74. Fuller, trial transcript at 274.

75. Fabian, trial transcript at 277.

76. *S.F. Daily News*, May 20, 1921, at 9.

77. *Supra* note 73.

78. "Suspect Held," *S.F. Call and Post*, May 21 at 1 of Sect. 2.

79. "Certificate of Medical Examiners," Superior Court Records. Capital case file.

80. *Supra* note 26.

81. "Abstract of Commitment, Dr. Rogers," July 14, 1921. Winnipeg police file.

82. "Progress Notes," Napa Records. Capital case file.

83. *Ibid.*, June 1, 1922.

84. *Ibid.*, April 2, 1923, July 1, 1923.

85. Trial transcript at 262.

86. *Ibid.*

87. Affidavit of Frank Arnold, Dec. 30, 1927. Capital case file.

88. Los Angeles Police Homicide Records, April 4, 1925. Provided to Alvin Esau by L.A.P.D. in February 2009.

89. "Two Sought," *Madison Journal*, April 6, 1924, at 1; "Mystery in L.A. Murder," *Oakland Post-Enquirer*, April 7, 1924, at 1 and 5.

90. One theory advanced by Jack Jungmeyer, "Vera Stone," *Salt Lake Telegram*, April 23, 1924, at 3.

91. Murders at alvinesau.com.

92. "Canada Strangler Suspect Linked in Local Slaying," *San Diego Sun*, June 22, 1927, at 9.

93. *Ibid.*

94. Murders at alvinesau.com.

95. *Daily Mail*, June 23, 1927, at 1.

96. "Man Held for Hotel Murder," *Boston Post*, June 23, 1925, at 1.

97. "Price Murder Trial Opens," *Boston Globe*, August 17, 1925, at 1.

98. "Corey Is Given Life," *Boston Globe*, March 13, 1926, at 1.

99. "Scharton Makes Apology," *Boston Globe*, March 15, 1926, at 1.

100. *Commonwealth* v. *Crecorian* (1928) 264 Mass 94; 162 N.E. 7 (Mass. S.C.).

101. Murders at alvinesau.com.

Chapter 3

1. "Thug Winds Gems Around Victim's Neck," *S.F. Examiner*, Aug. 24, 1925, at 1 [henceforth, *Examiner*].

2. "Mystery in Aged S.F. Woman's Death," *S.F. Chronicle*, Aug. 24, 1925, at 1 [henceforth, *Chronicle*].

3. *Supra* note 1.

4. *Supra* note 2.

5. "Youth Sought in Death of Aged Woman," *S.F. Call and Post*, Aug. 24, 1925, at 1 [henceforth, *Call and Post*].

6. "Murder Theory Is Scouted," *S.F. Daily News*, Aug. 24, 1925, at 2 [henceforth, *Daily News*].

7. *Ibid.*

8. "Mystery Exploded in Woman's Death," *Chronicle*, Aug. 25, 1925, at 5.

9. "Death Report, Coroner's Office, Elizabeth Jones," 1924. Received from the S.F. Medical Examiner's Office and on file with author.

10. "The New Official," *San Francisco Call*, January 17, 1901, at 12.

11. "Daughter Waits for Law to Get Mother's Slayer," *Bakersfield Californian*, Dec. 9, 1926, at 9.

12. U.S. Census of 1920.

13. Ohio County Marriage Records, 1774–1993.

14. U.S. Census of 1880, 1910 and Ohio Births and Christenings, 1774–1973.

15. U.S. Census of 1910, 1920.

16. He was still alive according to son's draft registration in 1917. See U.S. World War One Draft Registration Cards. However, in the Census of 1920, Elizabeth was listed as a widow.

17. *Call and Post*, Aug. 25, 1925, at 30; *Chronicle*, Aug. 25, 1925, at 6; *Examiner*, Aug. 26, 1925, at 26.

18. "Notice of Sale of Real Estate," *S.F. Recorder*, June 18, 1926, at 7.

19. "Woman Beaten by Pretended Tenant," *Chronicle*, Aug. 29, 1925, at 6.

20. "S.F. Woman Found Strangled to Death: Manager of Apartment Dies Fighting Assailant," *Examiner*, Sept. 16, 1925, at 1.

21. "Landlady Is Found Strangled to Death," *Bakersfield Californian*, Sept. 16, 1925, at 1.

22. "Apartment House Manager at Bay Victim of Slayer," *Fresno Bee*, Sept. 16, 1925, at 2.

23. *Supra* note 20.

24. "Murder Theory in Death of Woman," *Daily News*, Sept. 16, 1925, at 1.

25. "Mystery Hides Death Cause in S.F. Apartment Murder," *S.F. Bulletin*, Sept. 16, 1925, at 1 and 4 [henceforth, *Bulletin*].

26. "Mystery Strangler Kills Woman During Struggle," *Chronicle*, Sept. 16, 1925, at 1.

27. "Police Face Puzzle in Death of Woman," *Call and Post*, Sept. 16, 1925, at 1.

28. *Supra* note 21. See also *Nevada State Journal*, Sept. 16, 1925, at 1, and numerous other accounts.

29. *Supra* note 20.

30. "Death Report, Coroner's Office, Daisy Anderson," 1924. Received from the San Francisco Medical Examiner's Office.

31. *Supra* note 25.

32. "Murder or Pneumonia?" *Examiner*, Sept. 17, 1925, at 17.

33. *Supra* note 26.

34. *Supra* note 27.

35. *Supra* note 24.

36. "Death Mystery," *Bakersfield Morning Echo*, Sept. 17, 1925, at 4.

37. "Death of Woman Laid to Natural Causes," *Bulletin*, Sept. 17, 1925, at 9.

38. *Supra* note 32.

39. *Supra* note 37.

40. *Supra* note 24.

41. *Supra* note 32.

42. *Ibid.*

43. *Ibid.*

44. *Supra* note 30.

45. *Supra* note 27.

46. *Supra* note 24.

47. *Supra* note 25.

48. "Probe of Woman's Death Is Dropped," *Daily News*, Sept. 17, 1925, at 8.

49. *Supra* note 30.

50. Iowa, County Births, 1880–1935; findagrave.com; U.S. Census of 1880.

51. Iowa, County Births, 1880–1935.

52. Kansas Marriage Records.

53. U.S. Census of 1900.

54. U.S. Census of 1910.

55. Findagrave.com.

56. As noted in U.S. Census of 1930. First married at age 19.

57. Ohio, County Marriage Records, 1774–1993. Also see U.S. Census of 1990.

58. *Supra* note 54.

59. "Mrs. Harry Anderson," *Lincoln Republican*, April 20, 1911, at 3.

60. Kansas State Census of 1915.

61. "Mystery Removed in Death of Woman," *Los Angeles Times*, Sept. 17, 1925, at 5.

62. *Supra* note 60. Also, World War I Draft Registration Cards; U.S. Census of 1920.

63. "Death Notice," *Chronicle*, Sept. 17, 1925, at 6.

64. "Joseph P. Griffin Dead," *Ottawa* [Kansas] *Herald*, Feb. 24, 1923, at 1.

65. Findagrave.com.

66. U.S. Census of 1930.

67. Michigan Marriage Records, 1867–1952; U.S. Census of 1950.

68. Findagrave.com.

69. Washington State Marriage Records, 1854–2013.

70. U.S. Census of 1940.

71. See "Leone Christie" obit in *Bellingham Herald*, March 6, 2012, at 5.

72. U.S. Veterans Administration Master Index, 1917–1940.

73. "Jury Demands Strangler Hunt," *Bakersfield Californian*, Dec. 4, 1926, at 2; "Killer Reward Sought," *Oregonian*, Dec. 4, 1926, at 4. See also "Six

Murders in S.F. Laid to Strangler by Coroner Jury," *Chronicle*, Dec. 4, 1926, at 4.

74. "Reward Urged to Spur Search for Strangler," *L.A. Times*, Dec. 4, 1926, at 5.

Chapter 4

1. "Woman Identifies 'Gorilla Man' as Phila. Strangler," *Philadelphia Inquirer*, June 22, 1927, at 1 and 7 [henceforth, *Inquirer*].

2. "Woman Slain by Strangler in Her Home," *Inquirer*, Nov. 11, 1925, at 1.

3. "Woman Strangled as Her Baby Slept," *Harrisburg Telegraph*, Oct. 16, 1925, at 29.

4. "Third Philadelphia Woman," *Hanover Evening Sun*, Nov. 11, 1925, at 8.

5. "Woman Found Strangled to Death in Bed," *Philadelphia Tribune*, Oct. 24, 1925, at 1 [henceforth, *Tribune*].

6. *Ibid.*

7. *Ibid.*

8. *Supra* note 3.

9. "Two Held in Murder Mystery Case Released," *Tribune*, Nov. 7, 1925, at 1.

10. Pennsylvania Death Certificates, 1906–1968.

11. Findagrave.com; U.S. Census of 1900 and 1910.

12. Philadelphia Marriage Index, 1885–1951; findagrave.com re son.

13. According to family tree at ancestry.com.

14. "Policeman Killed in Family Quarrel," *Inquirer*, June 19, 1957, at 7.

15. "When Cops Marry," *Pittsburgh Courier*, Feb. 2, 1957, at 31.

16. "Woman Is Slain, Arrest Boarder," *The Evening Bulletin*, Nov. 7, 1925, at 1 and 2 [henceforth, *Bulletin*].

17. "Woman Is Murdered," *Lowell Sun*, Nov. 7, 1925, at 14.

18. "Women in Fear as Strangler Eludes Police," *Inquirer*, Nov. 12, 1925, at 1 and 10.

19. *Supra* note 16.

20. *Ibid.*

21. "Woman Strangled to Death in Home," *Philadelphia Public Ledger*, Nov. 8, 1925, at 3 [henceforth, *Ledger*].

22. *Supra* note 18.

23. *Supra* note 16.

24. *Ibid.*

25. *Ibid.*

26. "Held on Suspicion of Murdering Woman," *Bulletin*, Nov. 10, 1925, at 25.

27. *Supra* note 2.

28. "Strangler Believed Captured," *Inquirer*, Nov. 14, 1925, at 1 and 4.

29. Pennsylvania Death Certificates, 1906–1968.

30. "Police Net Spread as 'The Strangler' Kills Third Woman," *Bulletin*, Nov. 11, 1925, at 1.

31. *Ibid.*

32. "Maniac Kills Woman Alone in her Home," *Ledger*, Nov. 11, 1925, at 1.

33. *Supra* note 2.

34. *Ibid.*

35. *Supra* note 30.

36. *Ibid.*

37. *Supra* note 32.

38. *Ibid.*

39. *Supra* note 2.

40. *Ibid.*

41. *Ibid.*

42. *Supra* note 30.

43. *Ibid.*

44. *Ibid.*

45. *Supra* note 18.

46. *Ibid.*

47. "Black-Eyed Man Sought as Insane Strangler of Trio," *Wilmington Morning News*, Nov. 12, 1925, at 1 and 7.

48. Findagrave.com.

49. Pennsylvania Death Certificates, 1906–1968.

50. *Supra* note 30.

51. *Ibid.*

52. *Supra* note 3.

53. "Queer Knots Give Clue," *Ledger*, Nov. 12, 1925, at 1 and 5.

54. For example, "Maniac Blamed," *Lebanon Daily News*, Nov. 11, 1925, at 14; "Seek Degenerate," *Steubenville Herald Star*, Nov. 11, 1925, at 1; "Third Philadelphia Woman," *Hanover Evening Sun*, Nov. 11, 1925, at 8.

55. *Supra* note 47.

56. *Supra* note 18.

57. "Quiz Former Boxer in Women's Deaths," *Bulletin*, Nov. 12, 1925, at 1 and 15.

58. "Expect Arrest," *Clearfield Progress*, Nov. 12, 1925, at 1.

59. *Supra* note 57.

60. "New Attack Fans 'Strangler' Terror," *Inquirer*, Nov. 13, 1925, at 1.

61. *Supra* note 53.

62. *Ibid.*

63. "Strangler Clues Lead Searchers to Digger of Subway," *Inquirer*, Nov. 25, 1925, at 1 and 8.

64. "New 'Strangler' Suspect Arrested," *Bulletin*, Nov. 14, 1925, at 2.

65. "New Strangler Suspect Is Held; Pawnbroker Called to See Him," *Ledger*, Nov. 15, 1925, at 1 and 5.

66. For example, *Inquirer*, Nov. 13, 1925, at 1; Nov. 14, 1925, at 1; Nov. 15, 1925, at 1; Nov. 16, 1925, at 1; Nov. 17, 1925, at 2; Nov. 21, 1925, at 2; Nov. 25, 1925, at 1. Also *Bulletin*, Nov. 16, 1925, at 3; Nov. 19, 1925, at 1; Nov. 20, 1925, at 1; Nov. 24, 1925, at 1; Nov. 25, 1925, at 3; Nov. 28, 1925, at 1; Dec. 7, 1925, at 1.

67. "When Other Clues Fail," *Tribune*, Nov. 21, 1925, at 6.

68. "Strangler Scare Pervades South Philadelphia," *Tribune*, Jan. 2, 1926, at 7.

69. "Boy Shot Chasing Girl's Assailant," *Bulletin*, Dec. 5, 1925, at 1; "Youth Fatally Shot Battling Girls' Attacker," *Inquirer*, Dec. 5, 1925, at 1.

70. For example, *Inquirer*, Feb. 1, 1926, at 2;

Aug. 3, 1926, at 1; Nov. 12, 1926, at 1; Nov. 3, 1926, at 2. *Bulletin*, Nov. 2, 1926, at 1; Nov. 3, 1926, at 1; Nov. 8, 1926, at 1; Nov. 12, 1926, at 3.

71. "Strangler Suspect Is Held for Probe," *Inquirer*, Nov. 4, 1926, at 2.

72. "Strangler Foiled Attacking Woman Alone in Kitchen," *Bulletin*, Nov. 2, 1926, at 1.

73. "Norristown Holds Strangler Suspect," *Inquirer*, Dec. 17, 1926, at 3; "Strangler to Face Phila. Witnesses," *Bulletin*, Dec. 17, 1926, at 3.

74. "Boxer Suspect in Stranglings Held by Police," *Inquirer*, Dec. 18, 1926, at 1.

75. "Strangler Held on Murder Charge in Woman's Death," *Bulletin*, Dec. 18, 1926, at 1.

76. *Supra* note 74.

77. "Fail to Identify Man as Strangler," *Bulletin*, Dec. 18, 1926, at 3.

78. "Strangler Suspect Raving Maniac as Alibi Confirmed," *Inquirer*, Dec. 19, 1926, at 1.

79. "'Young Joe Wolcott' Dies of Rheumatism," *Salt Lake Tribune*, Dec. 27, 1933, at 12.

80. "Neighbor Captures Strangler Suspect," *Inquirer*, Jan. 9, 1927, at 7.

81. Communication from David Baugh, Archivist, Philadelphia City Archives.

82. Alvin A.J. Esau, *The Gorilla Man Strangler Case: Serial Killer Earle Nelson* (Altona, Manitoba: FriesenPress, 2022).

83. "Strangler Tours U.S. Say Police," *Bulletin*, June 6, 1927 (page number misplaced).

84. *Ibid.*

85. "Woman Identifies 'Gorilla Man' as Phila. Strangler," *Inquirer*, June 22, 1927, at 1 and 7.

86. "Gorilla Man Now Linked," *Brooklyn Daily Eagle*, June 23, 1927, at 1; "Strangler Is Identified," *Wilmington Journal*, June 22, 1927, at 8; "Gorilla Man May Also Be Strangler," *Hanover Evening Sun*, June 22, 1927, at 10.

87. *Supra* note 85. Also "Identify Photos of Gorilla Man as Phila. Killer," *Bulletin*, June 21, 1927, at 1; "Man in Canada Identified Here As 'Strangler,'" *Ledger*, June 22, 1927, at 1.

88. *Supra* note 87. Also *Bulletin*, June 21, 1927, at 1.

89. *Supra* note 85.

90. "Thirty Cities Want Canada Strangler," *Ledger*, June 23, 1927, at 2.

91. Murders at www.alvinesau.com.

Chapter 5

1. Photo sent to Winnipeg police by San Francisco police, from Winnipeg police file on Nelson.

2. "Death Report, Coroner's Office: Clara M. Newman," Feb. 20, 1926. Provided to me by San Francisco Medical Examiner's Office.

3. 1900 U.S. Census.

4. 1910 U.S. Census.

5. "Obit, Newman," *S.F. Examiner*, Feb. 22, 1926, at 4.

6. 1920 U.S. Census.

7. "Wealthy Woman Choked to Death," *S.F. Examiner*, Feb. 21, 1926, at 1 and 2.

8. *Ibid.*

9. "Workmen to Be Quizzed," *S.F. Chronicle*, Feb. 23, 1926, at 3. Mr. and Mrs. Brown are listed in the coroner's report as being at the scene when the body was found.

10. *Supra* note 7.

11. *Ibid.*

12. "Landlady, 60, Found Choked to Death," *S.F. Chronicle*, Feb. 21, 1926, at 1.

13. Photo of victim sent to Winnipeg police by San Francisco police, from Winnipeg police file on Earle Nelson.

14. "Fingerprints Only Clue in Strangling," *S.F. Examiner*, Feb. 22, 1926, at 3.

15. "Search Opened for Strange Man," *S.F. Bulletin*, Feb. 20, 1926, at 1.

16. *Supra* note 2.

17. *Supra* note 14.

18. *Supra* note 2.

19. *Supra* note 12.

20. "Memo from S.F.P.D. to Philip Stark," June 23, 1927. Winnipeg police file.

21. "Rich S.F. Woman Choked to Death in Attic of Her Home," *S.F. Examiner*, Feb. 21, 1926, at 2.

22. *Supra* note 12.

23. *Supra* note 14.

24. "Crazed Man Sought as Strangler," *S.F. Call and Post*, Feb. 23, 1926, at 6.

25. *Supra* note 14.

26. "Fingerprints May Reveal Strangler," *S.F. Examiner*, Feb. 23, 1926, at 3.

27. "Nude Dancer Sought in Strangling of Woman," *S.F. Daily News*, Feb. 23, 1926, at 2.

28. *Supra* note 9.

29. "Inquest Finds Fiend Slew Miss Newman," *S.F. Examiner*, Feb. 24, 1926, at 11.

30. *Ibid.*

31. *Supra* note 24.

32. "Murder Charges in Stranglings," *L.A. Times*, June 18, 1927, at 9; "S.F. Strangler Is Identified," *S.F. Daily News*, June 22, 1926, at 3.

33. "Suspect Has Record Here," *S.F. Call and Post*, June 17, 1927 (page number misplaced); "Winnipeg Is Certain," *Oregon Journal*, June 18, 1927, at 1 and 9.

34. "S.F. Woman Identifies Strangler," *S.F. Chronicle*, June 18, 1927, at 1 and 5.

35. Duncan Matheson, "International Strangler Captured," *Police Journal* V, no. 9 (1927) at 5, 6, 28 and 29.

36. "Report of Dullea and Frederickson," S.F.P.D., July 5, 1927. Winnipeg police department file on Nelson.

37. Census of 1930 and 1940; Draft Registration Card of April 1942.

38. Obit in *S.F. Examiner* May 3, 1951, at 19. Also findagrave.com.

Chapter 6

1. "Police Have Description," *San Jose Mercury Herald*, March 4, 1926, at 1 and 10 [henceforth, *Mercury Herald*].

2. "Died: Beal," *Mercury Herald*, March 5, 1926, at 34.

3. 1880 U.S. Census.

4. Indiana Marriage Index, 1800–1941.

5. U.S. Census of 1900 and 1910.

6. "Mrs. Laura E. Beal Found Strangled," *Mercury Herald*, March 3, 1926, at 1.

7. "Fiend Murderer Strangles Woman in San Jose Home," *S.F. Chronicle*, March 3, 1926, at 1.

8. "Spouse Finds Rich Woman Strangled," *S.F. Examiner*, March 3, 1926, at 1.

9. "Slaying of 2 Women Laid to Strangler," *S.F. Examiner*, March 4, 1926, at 11.

10. *Supra* note 6.

11. *Supra* note 9.

12. "Strangler of Aged Woman Identified as S.F. Slayer," *S.F. Chronicle*, March 4, 1926, at 6.

13. *Supra* note 1.

14. *Supra* note 9.

15. *Supra* note 13.

16. *Supra* note 9; "Slayer Maniac," *Nevada State Journal*, March 4, 1926, at 1; "Maniac Killer Warning Issued," *S.F. Daily News*, March 4, 1926, at 4; "Hunt Degenerate," *Washington Star*, March 4, 1926, at 23.

17. "San Jose Woman Reports Attack," *Mercury Herald*, March 5, 1926, at 1; "Third Victim of Strangler Is Revealed," *S.F. Daily News*, March 5, 1926, at 19; "Third Woman Found Victim of Strangler," *S.F. Examiner*, March 5, 1926, at 1.

18. "Two New Attempted Attacks," *Mercury Herald*, March 6, 1926, at 1.

19. "Tries to Strangle Woman in Home," *San Diego Union*, March 6, 1926, at 2; "Fifth Victim of Maniac Is Attacked in Her Own Home," *S.F. Examiner*, March 6, 1926, at 1.

20. "Strangler Maniac Attacks Two More San Jose Women," *S.F. Chronicle*, March 6, 1926, at 1.

21. "Attacks Imaginary," *Mercury Herald*, March 7, 1926, at 1.

22. "Strangler Fiend Still at Large," *S.F. Chronicle*, March 9, 1926.

23. "Two Women Beat Off Strangler," *Oakland Herald*, March 6, 1926, at 1; "Murderer Balked by His Sixth Victim," *S.F. Call and Post*, March 6, 1926, at 1.

24. "Woman Twice Routs Fiend," *S.F. Chronicle*, March 13, 1926, at 3; "Tenth Woman Reports Attack by Strangler," *S.F. Chronicle*, March 14, 1926, at 1.

25. "Tells Attack by Strangler," *S.F. Chronicle*, March 18, 1926, at 5; "Fiend Killer Put to Rout 3 Times by S.F. Woman," *S.F. Chronicle*, March 19, 1926, at 7; "Strangler Grabs, Chokes New Victim," *S.F. Examiner*, March 19, 1926, at 5.

26. "Woman Foils Strangler in Apartment House Attack," *S.F. Examiner*, March 14, 1926, at 1 and 4; "Fiend Killer Put to Rout 3 Times by S.F. Woman," *S.F. Chronicle*, March 19, 1926, at 7.

27. For example, "Strangler Trailed in S.F.," *S.F. Call and Post*, March 3, 1926, at 1; "S.F. Woman Foils Fiend," *S.F. Call and Post*, March 6, 1926, at 1.

28. "Strangler Fear Haunts Women," *S.F. Chronicle*, March 20, 1926, at 3.

29. For example, "Dark Strangler Fails to Kill Fourth Victim," *San Diego Union*, April 27, 1926, at 2; "Strangling Beast Flees When Woman Victim Screams," *San Diego Union*, April 28, 1926, at 2; "Woman Chloroformed by Man Seeking Room," *San Diego Union*, April 29, 1926, at 3.

30. "Strangler Maniac Suspect Jailed by San Jose Police," *S.F. Chronicle*, March 7, 1926, at 1.

31. "Man in Custody Not One Wanted," *Mercury Herald*, March 8, 1926, at 1.

32. "Strangler Fiend Suspects Freed," *S.F. Chronicle*, March 16, 1926, at 1.

33. "Suspect Held in Berkeley," *Oakland Post Enquirer*, March 23, 1926, at 1 and 5.

34. "Suspect Freed," *Oakland Tribune*, March 23, 1926, at 35.

35. "Strangler Has Fled Bay City, Police State," *L.A. Times*, March 15, 1926, at 6.

36. "Weddings," *Lafayette Journal and Courier*, Jan. 6, 1927, at 5.

37. California Death Index, 1905–1939; findagrave.com; Indiana Death Certificates, 1899–2017.

38. "Strangler Kills San Jose Woman," *Oakland Post Enquirer*, March 3, 1926, at 1.

39. "Believe Strangler of Local Woman Nabbed," *San Jose News*, June 17, 1927, at 1.

40. "Would Link Murders Here to Strangler," *Newark Evening News*, Nov. 4 at 1 and 4; the original postcards are in the Winnipeg police file.

41. "Newark Hopes to Connect 'Strangler' with Unsolved Murders," *Edmonton Journal*, Nov. 8, 1927, at 21.

42. "Woman Killed by Gag After Being Clubbed," *Newark Evening News*, May 11, 1926, at 1; "Woman of 69, Rich, Clubbed to Death," *Newark Star-Eagle*, May 11, 1926, at 1.

43. "Aged Woman Slain," *Reading Times*, May 12, 1926, at 2.

44. "Woman Killed as She Defends Son from Intruder in Home," *Newark Evening News*, July 3, 1926, at 1; "Mother of Four Slain in Home," *Newark Star-Eagle*, July 3, 1926, at 1.

45. "Four Murders Laid to Killer," *Detroit Free Press*, Dec. 15, 1928, at 4.

46. "Kudzinowski Dies," *Asbury Park Press*, Dec. 21, 1929, at 2.

47. "Aged Woman Slain While Mate Sleeps," *Newark Evening News*, Aug. 9, 1926, at 1; "Newark Wife of 72 Strangled in Sleep," *Newark Star-Eagle*, Aug. 9, 1926, at 1.

48. "Motive Veiled in Murder of Aged Woman," *Newark Evening News*, Aug. 10, 1926, at 1.

49. "Thief Killed Storekeeper," *Lebanon Daily News*, Aug. 9, 1926, at 1.

50. Murders at alvinesau.com.

Chapter 7

1. "'Crusher' Killer Eludes Police," *S.F. Daily News*, June 11, 1926, at 1.

2. Various reports say "Bryan" rather than "Brian."

3. "Third Woman Killed by Strangler," *S.F. Chronicle*, June 11, 1926, at 1.

4. "Conductor on Market Line Gives Clues," *S.F. Chronicle*, June 12, 1926, at 1 and 4.

5. "Strangler Kills S.F. Woman," *Oakland Tribune*, June 11, 1926, at 1.

6. *Supra* note 1.

7. S.F.P.D. letter to Philip Stark, acting chief of Winnipeg police, June 23, 1927. Winnipeg police file.

8. *Supra* note 4.

9. Death Report, Coroner's Office: St. Mary, June 10, 1926. Received by me from S.F. Medical Examiner's Office.

10. *Ibid.*

11. *Supra* note 5.

12. "Third Woman Killed by Strangler," *S.F. Chronicle*, June 11, 1926, at 1; "S.F. Strangler Slays Third Woman," *S.F. Examiner*, June 11, 1926, at 1 and 6: "Third Fiend Slaying," *S.F. Call and Post*, June 11, 1926, at 1; "Strangler Sighted in 3d Killing," *S.F. Bulletin*, June 11, 1926, at 1; "Crusher Killer Eludes Police," *S.F. Daily News*, June 11, 1926, at 1 and 14.

13. "Third Woman Killed by Strangler," *S.F. Chronicle*, June 11, 1926, at 1; "S.F. Strangler Slays Third Woman," *S.F. Examiner*, June 11, 1926, at 1 and 6: "Third Fiend Slaying," *S.F. Call and Post*, June 11, 1926, at 1; "Strangler Sighted in 3d Killing," *S.F. Bulletin*, June 11, 1926, at 1; "Crusher Killer Eludes Police," *S.F. Daily News*, June 11, 1926, at 1 and 14.

14. "Strangler Sighted in 3d Killing," *S.F. Bulletin*, June 11, 1926, at 1 [my emphasis].

15. "Fear Spreads," *S.F. Examiner*, June 13, 1926, at 1 and 2 [my emphasis].

16. "Heavy Set Man Sought," *S.F. Call and Post*, June 11, 1926, at 1 and 10.

17. "Strangler Eludes S.F. Police Net," *S.F. Bulletin*, June 12, 1926, at 1; "Police Net Spread for Strangler," *L.A. Times*, June 12, 1926, at 4.

18. *Supra* note 16.

19. "S.F. Women Warned," *Oakland Tribune*, June 12, 1926, at 13.

20. "Crusher-Strangler Returns to Scene of Crime, Police Told," *S.F. Daily News*, June 12, 1926, at 1 and 2.

21. *Ibid.*

22. "Calls for Aid," *S.F. Examiner*, June 12, 1926, at 1.

23. "'Crusher-Strangler' Psychopath, Say Experts," *S.F. Daily News*, June 12, 1926, at 2.

24. *Ibid.*

25. *Ibid.*

26. "Slayer of 3 Classified as 'Sadist,'" *S.F. Examiner*, June 12, 1926, at 2.

27. "Strangler Kills: Records of Hospitals for Insane Checked," *Oakland Tribune*, June 11, 1927, at 1.

28. "Alameda Girl Attack Brings New Warning," *S.F. Chronicle*, June 13, 1926, at 3; "Ringing of Telephone Foils Girl Attacker," *S.F. Examiner*, June 13, 1926, at 2; "Strangler Attacks Fourth Woman, Escapes," *S.F. Chronicle*, June 14, 1926, at 1; "Woman Foils Strangler," *S.F. Daily News*, June 15, 1926, at 1; "Fiend Routed by Woman's Screams," *S.F. Call and Post*, June 15, 1926, at 1; "'Strangler' at Her Door, Says Woman," S.F. *Examiner*, June 20, 1926, at 3.

29. "'Fiend' Nightmare Stirs Woman to Shoot Own Hand," *S.F. Call and Post*, June 17, 1926. See also "Woman Dreams of Attack," *S.F. Bulletin*, June 17, 1926, at 1; "Dream Ends in Shot," *S.F. Daily News*, June 17, 1926, at 1; "Dreaming of Strangler, Woman Shoots Herself," *S.F. Examiner*, June 18, 1926, at 1.

30. "Dream of Attack by Strangler Causes Woman to Shoot Herself," *San Diego Union*, June 18, 1926, at 1.

31. "Woman Shoots Self in Dream," *S.F. Chronicle*, June 18, 1926, at 1.

32. "Strangler Suspect," *S.F. Bulletin*, June 14, 1926, at 1; "S.F. Butcher Jailed as Strangler Suspect," *S.F. Chronicle*, June 15, 1926, at 1 and 2.

33. "Butcher Held … Freed," *S.F. Chronicle*, June 16, 1926, at 2; "Alleged Slayer to Be Released," *San Diego Union*, June 16, 1926, at 1; "Acquits Suspect," *Bakersfield Californian*, June 15, 1926, at 2.

34. "Mob Menaces Fiend," *S.F. Call and Post*, June 16, 1926, at 1; "Santa Cruz Jails Former Convict as 'Strangler,'" *Oakland Tribune*, June 16, 1926, at 2.

35. "Strangler Fear," *Oakland Post Enquirer*, June 17, 1926, at 1 and 2.

36. "Warnings Sounded," *S.F. Call and Post*, June 12, 1926, at 1.

37. Memo on Nelson investigation by Dullea and Frederickson, sent to Winnipeg police, July 5, 1927. Winnipeg police file.

38. "Fifth Strangler Gets Away," *S.F. Daily News*, Aug. 19, 1926, at 1.

39. "Death Notices," *S.F. Chronicle*, June 13, 1926, at C7.

40. *Supra* note 15.

41. Also confirmed in *supra* note 9.

42. *Supra* note 4.

43. Iowa Census of 1856; U.S. Census of 1870 and 1880. Her original name was Mary Hamilton.

44. As outlined in the will of her mother made in 1905. See California Wills and Probate Records, 1850–1953.

45. Findagrave.com re Modesto Citizens Cemetery.

46. *Ibid.* Brother William Hamilton died at age 62 on April 15, 1926.

47. As inferred from U.S. Census of 1910 where Joseph and Mary are listed as married for eight years.

48. When married to Joseph St. Mary in Nevada on December 8, 1902, her name was listed as Mrs. Lillie Horton.

49. See U.S. Census of 1900. Ironically, Dora St. Mary, listing herself as a widow, became the manager of a large apartment house on Van Ness Avenue.

50. U.S. Census of 1910.

51. U.S. Census of 1920.
52. "S.F. Bay Victim Is Identified," *Oakland Tribune*, March 7, 1928, at 1.

Chapter 8

1. As described by Los Angeles police in a memo sent to Winnipeg police. Winnipeg police file.
2. Franey's account as reported in the local press varied in detail, but probably the most accurate report was Franey's testimony at the inquest as found in "Police Hunt Is Resumed," *Santa Barbara Morning Press,* June 27, 1926, at 1. I have added some details from earlier reports that are consistent with the basic narrative: "Strangler Slays Woman with Cord After Attack," *Santa Barbara Morning Press,* June 25, 1926, at 1 and 2; "Stains on Walls Probed," *Santa Barbara Morning Press,* June 26, 1926, at 1; "Police Combing Entire Coast Line," *Santa Barbara Daily News,* June 25, 1926, at 1 and 3 [henceforth, *S.B. Press* and *S.B. News*].
3. Franey story compiled from sources cited in note 2.
4. Franey story compiled from sources cited in note 2.
5. "Strangler Slays Woman with Cord After Attack," *S.B. Press*, June 25, 1926, at 1 and 2.
6. *Ibid.*
7. As established in the autopsy. "Police Hunt Is Resumed," *S.B. Press,* June 27, 1926, at 1.
8. "Strangler Takes Life of Woman," *L.A. Times,* June 25, 1926, at 9; "Woman Slain, Crime Done Like Work of Strangler," *S.F. Chronicle,* June 25, 1926, at 16; "Strangler Hunted in Santa Barbara," *Oakland Post-Enquirer,* June 25, 1926, at 11; "Strangler Slays Fourth Woman," *S.F. Bulletin,* June 25, 1926, at 5.
9. *Supra* note 5.
10. "Stains on Walls Probed," *S.B. Press,* June 26, 1926, at 1.
11. "Thumbprint on Door Casing Is Slender Clew," *S.B. News,* June 29, 1926, at 1.
12. "Police Hunt Is Resumed," *S.B. Press,* June 27, 1926, at 1.
13. C.B. Pyper, "A Word Sketch of the Accused," *Winnipeg Tribune,* June 17, 1927, at 5.
14. "Detain Two Men," *Bakersfield Californian,* June 26, 1926, at 1.
15. *Supra* note 10.
16. "Officers Pick Holes in Tale," *L.A. Times,* June 26, 1926, at 7.
17. *Supra* note 10.
18. *Supra* note 16.
19. *Ibid.*
20. *Supra* note 10.
21. *Supra* note 12.
22. *Ibid.*
23. *Ibid.*
24. "Strangler Sought by State Experts with Print Clues," *S.B. Press,* June 30, 1926, at 1.
25. It was widely reported that she was 53 years old when she died, but the records show that she was actually a few weeks shy of her 56th birthday.
26. Illinois, Cook County Marriages, 1871–1968.
27. U.S. Census of 1900 and 1910.
28. Los Angles City Directories.
29. California Death Index, 1905–1939.
30. California Wills and Probate Records, 1850–1953.
31. Santa Barbara City Directory, 1923, 1924, 1926.
32. Findagrave.com.
33. "Russell Death Search Centered in L.A.," *S.B. News,* June 30, 1926, at 1.
34. "Police Chief Returns from Los Angeles," *S.B. Press,* July 1, 1926, at 3.
35. "Mystery Cloaks Maniac," *S.B. News,* June 28, 1926, at 1; "Look Out for Murder Suspect," *The Daily Police Bulletin,* police department, Los Angeles, July 1, 1926.
36. "Look Out for Murder Suspect," *The Daily Police Bulletin,* police department, Los Angeles, July 1, 1926.
37. Letter from James E. Davies, chief of police, and H.H. Cline, chief of detectives, Los Angeles police, to Winnipeg police, June 17, 1927. Winnipeg police file.
38. The following account is taken from a letter by James E. Davies and H.H. Cline, chiefs of police and detectives, respectively, of the City of Los Angeles, written to L.V. Jenkins, Portland chief of police, Dec. 3, 1926, outlining all the information they had put together as to the murder on Mrs. Russell in Santa Barbara. The letter is found in the Winnipeg police file.
39. *Ibid.*
40. *Ibid.*
41. *Ibid.*
42. *Ibid.*
43. *Ibid.*
44. *Ibid.*
45. *Ibid.*
46. *Ibid.*
47. *Ibid.*
48. *Ibid.*
49. *Ibid.*
50. "Bay Strangler Suspect Held," *Oakland Post-Enquirer,* July 3, 1926, at 1; "Dark Man Held as Strangler," *Modesto News-Herald,* July 7, 1926, at 1; "Strangler May Be in Custody," *Bakersfield Morning Echo,* July 7, 1926, at 2; "Woman-Strangler Suspect," *Bakersfield Californian,* July 13, 1926, at 1; "Police Assert Suspect Looks Like Strangler," *L.A. Times,* July 14, 1926, at 3; "Suspect Cleared," *Oakland Tribune,* July 15, 1926, at 17; "Strangler Suspect in S.F. Trapped," *Oakland Tribune,* Aug. 2, 1926, at 28.
51. "Man Confesses to Stranglings," *Santa Ana Register,* Aug. 10, 1926, at 1.
52. "Strangler Confesses S.F. Killings," *Oakland Tribune,* Aug. 10, 1926, at 1.
53. "Terror of 'Dark Strangler' Ended," *San Bernardino County Sun,* Aug. 12, 1926, at 1 and 2; "Strangler Confesses," *S.B. News,* Aug. 10, 1926, at 1 and 2.

54. "Stranglings Confessed by Suspect Held in Needles," *S.F. Chronicle*, Aug. 11, 1926, at 1.

55. "Pacific Coast Police Puzzled by Rival Murder Confessions," *Miami Daily Arizona Silver Belt*, Aug. 11, 1926, at 1; "Two 'Fiends' Admit Score of Murders," *Iowa City Press-Citizen*, Aug. 11, 1926, at 1.

56. "Confessed Killer of 14 Peeved at Attention Given to Strangler," *Ogden Standard*, Aug. 12, 1926, at 1.

57. "Dozen Women Victims," *Reno Evening Gazette*, Aug. 11, 1926, at 1; "Confession of Strangler," *S.B. News*, Aug. 14, 1926, at 1.

58. "Strangler's Death Stories Still Checked," *Seattle Post-Inquirer*, Aug. 11, 1926, at 2.

59. "Positive Identification of Strangler Suspect Made," *L.A. Times*, Aug. 12, 1926, at 2.

60. "Say 'Strangler' Identified by Attack Witness," *San Diego Union*, Aug. 12, 1926, at 1 and 2.

61. *Ibid.*

62. "Santa Barbara Man Certain Suspect Slew Mrs. Russell," *S.F. Chronicle*, Aug. 12, 1926, at 1.

63. "Positive Identification of Strangler Suspect Made," *L.A. Times*, August 12, 1926, at 2; "Dark Strangler Partly Identified," *Washington Star*, Aug. 12, 1926, at 4.

64. *Supra* note 60.

65. "Strangler Makes Plea Not Guilty, Wants Trial," *S.B. News*, August 12, 1926, at 1 [my emphasis].

66. "Criminologist Will Examine," *Visalia Daily Times*, Aug. 13, 1926, at 5.

67. "Woman Strangled in Oakland Apartment," *S.F. Chronicle*, Aug. 17, 1926, at 2; "Alleged Strangler's Fate," *Santa Ana Register*, Aug. 14, 1926, at 1.

68. "Sanity Test for Suspect," *L.A. Times*, Aug. 13, 1926, at 4.

69. "Saw Strangler in Action, He Says," *Spokane Spokesman-Review*, Aug. 12, 1926, at 2.

70. "Lack Evidence in Strangling," *L.A. Times*, Aug. 14, 1926, at 6.

71. "Strangler to Face Sanity Examination," *Oakland Post-Enquirer*, Aug. 12, 1926, at 1.

72. "New Crime," *L.A. Times*, August 18, 1926, at 7; "Brown's Connection with S.B. Strangling Mystery Disproved," *S.B. News*, August 17, 1926, at 1.

73. "'Strangler' Said by Alienist to Be Incompetent," *L.A. Times*, Aug. 28, 1926, at 7.

74. "Suspect Held Here to Face Insane Charge," *S.B. News*, Sept. 2, 1926, at 2.

75. "Police in L.A. Jail Suspect as 'Strangler,'" *S.B. News*, Feb. 2, 1927, at 11; "Suspect Held in L.A. Jail Not Strangler," *S.B. News*, Feb. 3, 1927, at 9.

76. "Woman Killer to Be Hanged in Winnipeg," *L.A. Times*, Jan. 13, 1928, at A10.

77. "Police in L.A. Jail Suspect," *S.B. News*, Feb. 2, 1927, at 11.

78. Letter from D. J. O'Brien, San Francisco, to Chris Newton, Winnipeg, Aug. 15, 1927. Winnipeg police file.

79. "Identify Winnipeg Man as Strangler," *Bakersfield Californian*, Aug. 17, 1927, at 1.

80. "Earle Nelson Identified as Man Sought in S.B. Strangle," *S.B. News*, Aug. 17, 1926, at 1.

81. "Canadian Courts Will Try," *S.B. News*, Aug. 18, 1926, at 7.

Chapter 9

1. "Smiling Strangler Sighted at Death," *Oakland Tribune*, Aug. 17, 1926, at 1 [henceforth, *Tribune*].

2. *Ibid.*

3. "Police Seek More Clues," *Oakland Post-Enquirer*, Aug. 19, 1926, at 2 [henceforth, *Post-Enquirer*].

4. *Supra* note 1.

5. "Oakland Woman Strangled," *Post-Enquirer*, Aug. 17, 1926, at 1 and 5.

6. *Supra* note 1.

7. "Towel Used by Fiend to Choke Life from Victim," *S.F. Chronicle*, Aug. 17, 1926, at 1.

8. *Supra* note 1.

9. "State Searched for Stockton Strangler," *Post-Enquirer*, Aug. 19, 1926, at 4; "Woman Put to Torture by Strangler Revelation," *S.F. Chronicle*, Aug. 20, 1926, at 3.

10. "Two Describe Suspect," *S.F. Chronicle*, Aug. 18, 1926, at 1.

11. "Aged Woman at Stockton Murdered," *S.F. Chronicle*, Aug. 19, 1926, at 2.

12. Affidavit of Frank Arnold, Dec. 30, 1927. Capital case file, National Archives of Canada.

13. "Strangler Seen by Mailman," *S.F. Bulletin*, Aug. 17, 1926, at 1 and 2.

14. *Supra* note 1.

15. "East Bay Mail Man Sees Strangler," *S.F. Call and Post*, Aug. 17, 1926, 1 and 2.

16. *Supra* note 1.

17. *Supra* note 10.

18. *Supra* note 13.

19. "Smiling Man Still Hunted," *S.F. Daily News*, Aug. 18, 1926, at 4.

20. "Brute Slays Fourth Victim," *Bakersfield Californian*, Aug. 17, 1926, at 1.

21. "Strangler Trap Set," *Post-Enquirer*, Aug. 18, 1926, at 1 and 4.

22. "Notes Are Clue in Strangler Hunt," *Tribune*, Aug. 18, 1926, at 1 and 2.

23. *Supra* note 21.

24. 1880 U.S. Census.

25. California Marriage Records, 1850–1941.

26. 1900 and 1910 U.S. Census.

27. Findagrave.com. Also, obit in *Tribune*, Dec. 30, 1944, at 13.

28. *Supra* note 25.

29. 1920 U.S. Census.

30. "Wife Gave Love Pledge on Parting for Day," *Tribune*, Aug. 17, 1926, at 1.

31. "Slain Woman's Parents in Critical Condition," *Tribune*, Aug. 17, 1926, at 19.

32. "Moron List of Police Scanned," *Tribune*, Aug. 18, 1926, at 1 and 2.

33. Obit in *Tribune*, Sept. 28, 1953, at 35.

34. "18 Strangler Murders Laid to Suspect," *Tribune*, June 23, 1927, at 5.

35. "New Link in Stranglers Career Seen," *Tribune*, July 19, 1927, at 21.

36. *Ibid.*

Chapter 10

1. "Stockton, Oakland Seeking Murder Fiends," *S.F. Call and Post*, Aug. 19, 1926, at 1 and 10.

2. *Ibid.*

3. *Ibid.*

4. *Ibid.*

5. For example, Associated Press story in *Bakersfield Morning Echo*, Aug. 19, 1926, at 10.

6. "Fifth Woman Strangled," *S.F. Bulletin*, Aug. 18, 1926, at 1.

7. "Strangler Kills Mother," *Modesto News-Herald*, Aug. 19, 1926, at 1.

8. "Fifth Victim of the Strangler," *Santa Rosa Press-Democrat*, Aug. 19, 1926, at 1 and 3.

9. "Strangler Kills Here," *Stockton Independent*, Aug. 19, 1926, at 1 and 4 [henceforth, *Independent*].

10. *Ibid.*

11. "Evidence Shows Same Fiend Strangled Six," *Oakland Tribune*, Aug. 19, 1926, at 2; "Fifth Victim of Maniacal Murderer," *S.F. Examiner*, Aug. 19, 1926, at 1 and 8; "Bay Strangler Is Sought as Stockton Fiend," *Sacramento Bee*, Aug. 19, 1926, at 1; "Bay City Strangler Thought Responsible," *San Diego Union*, Aug. 19, 1926, at 1; "Stockton Landlady Strangled," *Petaluma Morning Courier*, Aug. 19, 1926, at 1.

12. *Supra* note 7.

13. *Ibid.*

14. "Fifth Victim of Maniacal Murderer," *S.F. Examiner*, Aug. 19, 1926, at 1 and 8.

15. "Strangler Enigma," *San Bernardino Sun*, Aug. 20, 1926, at 1; "Strangler Mystery," *L.A. Times*, Aug. 20. 1926, at 5.

16. "New Strangler Kills Stockton Woman," *S.F. Examiner*, Aug. 19, 1926, at 1 and 8; "Fifth Strangler Gets Away," *S.F. Daily News*, Aug. 19, 1926, at 1; "Hunt Stockton Strangler," *Oakland Post-Enquirer*, Aug. 19, 1926, at 1 and 4; "Think Fiend Is Imitator," *Bakersfield Californian*, Aug. 19, 1926, at 1.

17. *Supra* note 1.

18. "Experts Discuss Stranglings," *S.F. Daily News*, Aug. 19, 1926, at 1.

19. "Strangler Is Believed to Have Departed," *Independent*, Aug. 20, 1926, at 1.

20. "Police Hunt in Vain," *S.F. Examiner*, Aug. 20, 1926, at 1.

21. Coroner's Record, Isabelle Gallegos. Kindly sent to the author by Sergeant William Fellers, Deputy Coroner, in May 2005.

22. "Purported Wealth Clue, says Daughter," *S.F. Chronicle*, Aug. 20, 1926, at 3.

23. "Acquaintance of Woman Sought as Slayer," *Independent*, Aug. 21, 1926, at 1 and 4.

24. "Dark Strangler Dies Free of Local Charge," *Independent*, Jan. 13, 1928, at 2.

25. As shown by the cemetery records where her cremated remains are together with her three sons. Findagrave.com.

26. As indicated when one of her sons, Peter Gallegos, was born in 1882. California, County Birth and Death Records, 1800–1994.

27. U.S. Census of 1900, 1910, 1920.

28. California Death Index, 1940–1997; Stockton City Directory for 1893 where Laura and Sophie Drolet are listed as living with Isabella Gallegos; "Kaiser-Drolet," *Stockton Record*, Dec. 1, 1895, at 4, as to marriage of Laura Drolet; Stockton City Directory of 1901 listing Sophie Drolet as employee of Stockton Woolen Mills.

29. His year of birth is confirmed in numerous records including "Obit," *S.F. Chronicle*, June 1, 1899, at 10. John E. Drolet was frequently charged with criminal offences, including several different occurrences of attempted murder. See, for example, "Court Notes," *S.F. Chronicle*, Aug. 2, 1885, at 8; "Mixed Bad Blood," *S.F. Chronicle*, March 7, 1888, at 5; "Stabbing Affray," *Morning Oregonian*, March 8, 1888, at 2; "Morally but Not Legally Guilty," *S.F. Chronicle*, March 15, 1888, at 2.

30. Laura Drolette Kaiser listed her father from Chile and mother from Mexico in the U.S. Census of 1900.

31. U.S. Census of 1880.

32. "Drolet's Child Wife," *S.F. Chronicle*, Feb. 27, 1888, at 8.

33. "An Unnatural Parent," *S.F. Chronicle*, June 27, 1889, at 3.

34. "An Awful Charge," *S.F. Chronicle*, June 27, 1889, at 5.

35. *Supra* note 33. While the implication was that the daughters were prostitutes, at the time of Drolet's death in 1906 all seven of the daughters from his conventional marriage were married. See "Deaths-Drolet," *S.F. Chronicle*, June 30, 1906, at 6.

36. "Quarrelling Attorneys," *S.F. Examiner*, June 29, 1889, at 3.

37. "Drolet Out of Danger," *S.F. Chronicle*, Sept. 6, 1890, at 6; "John Drolet at Liberty," *S.F. Examiner*, Sept. 6, 1890, at 6.

38. *Supra* note 23.

39. Findagrave.com.

40. U.S. Census of 1900, 1910, 1920; Stockton City Directory, 1888, 1899, 1907.

41. The U.S. Census of 1900 has Sophie, George and Peter working in the mill. Also see Stockton City Directory of 1888, 1899.

42. Advertisements, *Stockton Mail*, May 11, 1895, at 1; Sept. 19, 1896, at 8; Oct. 15, 1900, at 6 [hereafter, *Mail*].

43. "Kaiser-Drolet," *Stockton Evening Record*, Dec. 1, 1895, at 4.

44. California Birth, Marriage, and Death Records, 1849–1980.

45. "Exploding Dynamite Deals Death," *Mail*, June 27, 1906, at 1.

46. *Oakland Tribune*, Aug. 19, 1926, at 1.

47. "Stockton Widow Victim," *S.F. Bulletin*, Aug. 18, 1926, at 1.

48. "Shooting at a Hoodlum," *Mail*, April 15, 1881, at 3.

49. "Cut in Hand," *Mail*, Oct. 5, 1885, at 3.

50. "Gallegos," *Mail*, Aug. 30, 1887, at 3.

51. "Gallegos," *Mail*, Aug. 29, 1887, at 3.

52. "Long Waiting," *Mail*, Jan. 30, 1888, at 3.

53. "Arrested for Burglary," *Mail*, April 30, 1892, at 1; "Gallegos Discharged," *Mail*, July 13, 1892, at 1.

54. "Another Dipsomaniac," *Stockton Record*, Aug. 7, 1911, at 3.

55. "Stockton Drug Offender Given Heavy Sentence," *Stockton Record*, Dec. 14, 1920, at 8; U.S. Penitentiary McNeil Island, Photos and Records, 1887–1939, on ancestry.com.

56. "Blas Gallegos Again in Toils," *Stockton Record*, April 19, 1922, at 10; "Sent to Jail, "April 20, 1922, at 11.

57. "Police Notes," *Independent*, Jan. 2, 1923, at 5; "Police Court," *Stockton Record*, Dec. 15, 1923, at 20.

58. *Supra* note 25.

59. "New Theory Offered," *S.F. Chronicle*, Aug. 22, 1926, at 2.

60. "Two Sent to Prison," *Independent*, March 28, 1928, at 12.

61. U.S. Census of 1930.

62. "Union Street Woman Fights Off Strangler," *S.F. Chronicle*, Aug. 20, 1926, at 3; "Fiend Routed in East Bay," *S.F. Call and Post*, Aug. 25, 1926, at 2; "Oakland Woman Flees Attacker," *S.F. Call and Post*, Aug. 27, 1926, at 2; "Cries Rout Attacker of Girl," *Oakland Post-Enquirer*, Aug. 25, 1926, at 1; "Oakland Wife Fights Off Prowler," *Oakland Post-Enquirer*, Aug. 27, 1926, at 1; "Dark Strangler Seeks to Break into Apartment," *S.F. Chronicle*, Aug. 28, 1926, at 1; "Strangler Trailed in Sacramento," *Oakland Tribune*, Aug. 20, 1926, at 51; "Strangler Hits, Chokes Woman Here," *Oakland Tribune*, Aug. 25, 1926, at 1; "Woman Reports 'Strangler' Case," *Oakland Tribune*, Aug. 29, 1926, at 1.

63. For example, "Suspect in Strangler Cases Held," *L.A. Times*, Sept. 9, 1926; "Released," *L.A. Times*, Sept. 10, 1926, at 2, re Winniski.

64. "Suspect in Stranglings," *Oakland Tribune*, Aug. 24, 1926, at 21; "Description of Strangler Fits Suspect in Sacramento," *S.F. Chronicle*, Aug. 21, 1926, at 17; "S.F. Woman Identifies Strangler Photo," *S.F. Chronicle*, Aug. 22, 1926, at 1.

65. "Suspect Held Not Strangler," *S.F. Examiner*, Aug. 23, 1926, at 5.

66. "Two Fail to Identify Fiend," *S.F. Examiner*, Aug. 25, 1926, at 6.

Chapter 11

1. "Death Report, Coroner's Office—Elma Wells, Oct. 1, 1926," provided to me by San Francisco Medical Examiner's Office.

2. For example, "Strangler Suspected," *Los Angeles Times*, Oct. 2, 1926, at 18. Also see reports in *Stockton Independent, Sacramento Bee, San Diego Union*, and numerous others.

3. "Police Hunt Elma Wells' Sister for Murder Clue," *S.F. Inquirer*, Oct. 4, 1926, at 3.

4. San Francisco Area Funeral Home Records, 1895–1985.

5. Washington, State and Territorial Census of 1889. Also see 1900 U.S. Census.

6. 1910 U.S. Census.

7. Washington County Marriages, 1855–2008; Washington Marriage Records, 1854–2013.

8. California, County Birth, Marriage, and Death Records, 1849–1980.

9. Washington County Birth Registers, 1873–1965.

10. Washington Death Certificates, 1907–1960.

11. "Police Seek Friend of Slain Widow," *Oakland Tribune*, Oct. 2, 1926, at 1.

12. "Nude Body of S.F. Divorcee Is Found Strangled," *S.F. Examiner*, Oct. 2, 1926, at 1.

13. "Mystery in Wells Murder," *S.F. Chronicle*, Oct 3. 1926, at 2.

14. "S.F. Divorcee Murdered," *Oakland Post-Enquirer*, Oct. 2, 1926, at 1.

15. *Supra* note 11.

16. S.F. police photo album, p. 85, Bancroft Library, University of California, Berkeley.

17. *Supra* notes 2 and 11.

18. *Supra* note 13.

19. "New Mystery Stirs Probe," *S.F. Examiner*, Oct. 3, 1926, at 2; "Woman Slain, Sweetheart Held," *S.F. Chronicle*, Oct. 2, 1926, at 1 and 4.

20. "Woman Slain, Sweetheart Held," *S.F. Chronicle*, Oct. 2, 1926, at 1 and 4.

21. "Body Is Found in Closet," *S.F. Bulletin*, Oct. 2, 1926, at 1 and 2.

22. *Supra* note 21.

23. "Police Seek Method Used," *S.F. Chronicle*, Oct. 3, 1926, at 1 and 2.

24. For example, *S.F. Examiner*, Sept. 23, 1926, at 28.

25. "New 'Crusher' Murder," *S.F. Daily News*, Oct. 2, 1926, at 1.

26. "Slayer Went Back," *S.F. Chronicle*, Oct. 5, 1926, at 12; "Suitor Sought," *S.F. Call and Post*, Oct. 2, 1926, at 2 and 4.

27. "Inquest Frees Suitor," *S.F. Chronicle*, Oct. 6, 1926, at 10.

28. *Supra* note 21.

29. An amalgam of quotes from *S.F. Chronicle*, Oct. 2, 1926, at 4; *Oakland Tribune*, Oct. 2, 1926, at 1; *S.F. Bulletin*, Oct. 2, 1926, at 1 and 2; *Oakland Post-Enquirer*, Oct. 2, 1926, at 1 and 4; *S.F. Daily News*, Oct. 2, 1926, at 1.

30. "Love Feud," *S.F. Bulletin*, Oct. 2, 1926, at 2.

31. "Friend Says Woman Slain by Strangler," *S.F. Examiner*, Oct. 4, 1926, at 3.

32. *Supra* note 23.

33. "S.F. Murder Puzzles Police," *S.F. Examiner*, Oct. 5, 1926, at 10.

34. "Fingerprints Help Suspect," *San Bernardino County Sun*, Oct. 3, 1926, at 3.

35. *Supra* note 23.

36. "Police Hunt Lover in Woman's Death," *S.F. Bulletin*, Oct. 2, 1926, at 2.

37. These reports by Allison and McDermott are found in the *Oakland Post-Enquirer, S.F. Bulletin*, and *S.F. Chronicle* articles of Oct. 2, 1926.

38. "Woman Slain, Sweetheart Held," *S.F. Chronicle*, Oct. 2, 1926, at 1 and 4.

39. *Supra* note 23.

40. "Autopsy Fails," *Oakland Tribune*, Oct. 5, 1926, at 16.

41. "Suitor Sought," *S.F. Call and Post*, Oct. 2, 1926, at 2 and 4.

42. *Supra* note 1.

43. *Supra* note 21 [my emphasis].

44. *Supra* note 31.

45. "Suitor Sought," *S.F. Call and Post*, Oct. 2, 1926, at 2 and 4.

46. "Fingerprints Help Suspect," *San Bernardino County Sun*, Oct. 3, 1926, at 3.

47. "Inquest Frees Suitor," *S.F. Chronicle*, Oct. 6, 1926, at 10.

48. *Ibid.*

49. "Woman Slain, Sweetheart Held," *S.F. Chronicle*, Oct. 2, 1926, at 1 and 4. That he was half "Indian" was confirmed in U.S. Census of 1910.

50. "Marriages," *S.F. Examiner*, Dec. 9, 1930, at 13; "Legal Notices," *S.F. Examiner*, Aug. 16, 1938, at 25.

51. U.S. Census of 1930, 1940, and 1950.

52. California Marriage Index, 1949–1959.

53. For example, "Dark Killer Strangles," *Oakland Tribune*, Nov. 19. 1926, at 1; "Look for Dark Man," *S.F. Chronicle*, Nov. 23, 1926, at 7.

54. For example, *Pittsburgh Daily Post*, July 31, 1927, at 5; *Birmingham News*, July 24, 1927, at 84; *Oakland Tribune*, June 17, 1927, at 1.

Chapter 12

1. As noted in "Strangled Woman," *Oregon Journal*, Oct. 24, 1926, at 1 and 15 [henceforth, *Journal*].

2. As noted by James Burr Miller, "The Dark Strangler," *Oregonian*, Feb. 27, 1955, at 6. If I had not come across this article and had arrived in Portland with just the original addresses from the newspaper accounts, I would have been unable to locate any of the original residences of murder victims in Portland. In 2007 I found the house at the new address that was undoubtedly the one in which Mrs. Wither's body was found, given that newspapers at the time had shown pictures of this very house. The hedge had grown up and the top floor had skylights that were not there in 1926.

3. "Poetry Inspires Suicide in Trunk," *Oregonian*, Oct. 21, 1926, at 1.

4. *Ibid.*

5. "2 Clews Found in Trunk Death," *Oregonian*, Oct. 23, 1926, at 1 and 6.

6. "Trace Motive in Death Case," *Portland News*, Oct. 21, 1926, at 12 [henceforth, *News*].

7. "'Jake,' New Figure in Trunk Mystery Case,

Now Sought," *Portland Telegram*, Oct. 23, 1926, at 1 and 2 [henceforth, *Telegram*].

8. "Diary Bares Trunk Death Love Tangle," *Journal*, Oct. 22, 1926, at 1 and 13.

9. *Supra* note 7.

10. "Final Withers Fight," *News*, Oct. 21, 1926, at 1.

11. "Seek Coat," *News*, Oct. 22, 1926, at 1.

12. According to Bruce Cuthbertson of the Portland police department writing to me in 2007, no records prior to 1933 are available from the Portland police. I discovered, however, that various police detective notebooks have been preserved at the Portland City Archives. The reference to the door is found in the investigative report book of Moloney and Schulpius.

13. *Oregonian*, Oct. 21, 1926, at 6.

14. "Woman's Death Not Yet Solved," *Telegram*, Oct. 22, 1926, at 1 and 2.

15. "Family Quarrel, Poor Health Cause Worry," *News*, Oct. 21, 1926, at 1 and 12.

16. "Trunk Death Held Suicide by Policemen," *Telegram*, Oct. 21, 1926, at 1 and 2.

17. "Woman Killed Self in Trunk," *Journal*, Oct. 21, 1926, at 1.

18. Diary quotes from *supra* note 5 and "Love Diary of Woman," *S.F. Chronicle*, Oct. 23, 1926.

19. *Supra* note 8.

20. *Supra* note 5.

21. *Supra* note 7.

22. "Girl's Note on Murders," *News*, Oct. 28, 1926, at 1.

23. Archives provided by Mrs. Nancy Salmon, granddaughter of victim, to Alvin Esau, Feb. 23, 2006.

24. Cook County Birth Registers, 1871–1915.

25. Cook County, Illinois, Marriage Index, 1871–1920.

26. 1910 U.S. Census.

27. Listed in Portland City Directory, 1912, 1915, 1916, 1918.

28. 1920 U.S. Census.

29. Boise City Directory of 1921, 1923.

30. 1926 Portland City Directory. See also directory of 1929, 1930.

31. 1930 U.S. Census. Also see Portland City Directory of 1929, 1930, 1931.

32. In the 1931 Seattle City Directory he is listed as investor of securities and living at the Knickerbocker Hotel. Also see Seattle City Directory of 1939, where he is listed as President of Frentzel Manufacturing Co.

33. "Personals and Briefs," *Tacoma Ledger*, Feb. 12, 1931, at 9.

34. "Saindon-Frentzel Wedding," *Chehalis Bee-Nugent*, April 19, 1936. She died in 1997. California Death Index 1940–1997.

35. 1940 U.S. Census; Seattle City Directory of 1940.

36. "New Invention Expands, Deflates Dresses to Fit," *Mendocino Beacon*, Oct. 12, 1940, at 6.

37. "Seek Promoter for Crab Pots," *Seattle Star*,

May 4, 1943, at 16; "2 Deny Charges of Mail Fraud," *Seattle Star*, March 18, 1944, at 3.

38. Seattle city directories of 1953 through 1960.

39. U.S. Genealogy Bank Historical Newspapers Obituaries, 1815–2011. familysearch.org.

40. Washington Death Index, 1940–2017.

41. "Murder Scented in Trunk Death," *Oregonian*, Oct. 22, 1926, at 1.

42. *Ibid.*

43. *Supra* note 5.

44. "Chloroform Is Hinted," *News*, Oct. 23, 1926, at 1.

45. "Trace Motive in Death Case," *News*, Oct. 21, 1926, at 1 and 12.

46. *Supra* note 7.

47. "Reports Upon Deaths," *Telegram*, Oct. 26, 1926, at 1.

48. "Murder View Gains in Withers Case," *Oregonian*, Oct. 24, 1926, at 15.

49. *Ibid.*

50. "Murders Laid to One Man," *Oregonian*, Oct. 24, 1926, at 15.

51. "Chief Issues Warning," *Oregonian*, Oct. 24, 1926, at 15.

52. "Mystery Deepens in Withers Death," *Oregonian*, Oct. 26, 1926, at 5.

53. *Ibid.*

54. "Withers Case Puzzles," *Oregonian*, Oct. 28, 1926, at 3.

55. The coroner's reports were in the Multnomah County Records Center, apparently on reels of microfilm. On application to get these records, I was told that Oregon law exempts disclosure of these records to anybody other than a limited class of family and personal representatives of the deceased, so I could not have them (Dwight Wallis to Alvin Esau, Feb. 6, 2006). Arguing that these women had died more than 80 years ago, and furthermore that the law suggested mandatory disclosure to family, but not mandatory denial to others, especially after a reasonable time had passed in which privacy issues were nonexistent or negligible, I appealed the decision to the district attorney (email appeal of Esau to Deputy D.A. Hoover, Feb. 8, 2006). The opinion of the assistant county attorney was that the law required my denial of the documents (opinion of Assistant County Attorney Jacqueline Weber on ORS 146.03[5] and ORS 146.075[7], Feb. 7, 2006). However, on further appeal, the ruling by the long serving D.A. of Multnomah County, Michael D. Schrunk, was that I should have the records and he so ordered (written opinion of Schrunk, Feb. 14, 2006). I presume from reading Fred Leeson, *Rose City Justice: A Legal History of Portland, Oregon* (Portland: Oregon Historical Society Press, 1998), at 207 that Michael D. Schrunk had been DA since 1981. When I got to the records, I found them to be rather disappointing. The more detailed case files only started in 1933, so I was left with only the coroner's death reports in the four Portland cases. The reports are next to useless in that they do not reveal any information as to what tests, if any, were done. I was hoping to see some evidence as to whether the possibility of sexual assault was even taken seriously.

56. Death Report, Coroner's Office, Beata Withers [my emphasis].

57. Interview with Nancy Salmon, Feb. 23, 2006.

58. Marriage Records for Multnomah County, Case # 14295, Oregon State Archives.

59. Letter from Beata to Vera, Sept. 21, 1926, provided by Nancy Salmon.

60. Letter from Beata to Chuck, Oct. 4, 1926, provided by Nancy Salmon.

61. A typed clipping of information on Charles Withers II, post–1929, which appears to be recollections by Charles Withers III on his father. Provided by Nancy Salmon.

Chapter 13

1. Oregon State Marriages, 1906–1968.

2. "Mabel Fluke's Brother Only Remaining Relative," *The Molalla Bulletin*, April 23, 1980, at 1.

3. Oregon State Deaths, 1864–1968.

4. "Three Women Slain by Strangler," *Oregonian*, Oct. 24, 1926, at 1 and 14.

5. "Police Ask Aid to Hunt Killer," *Oregonian*, Oct. 25, 1926, at 12.

6. *Supra* note 4.

7. *Ibid.* The flashlight reference is from "3 Mysterious Deaths," *Oregon Telegram*, Oct. 25, 1926, at 1 and 2 [henceforth, *Telegram*].

8. "Fiend Linked to Deaths," *Medford Mail Tribune*, Oct. 24, 1926, at 1 and 8.

9. "3 Mysterious Deaths Puzzle Local Sleuths," *Telegram*, Oct. 25, 1926, at 1 and 2.

10. "Strangled Woman," *Oregon Journal*, Oct. 24, 1926, at 1 and 15 [henceforth, *Journal*].

11. Oct. 23, 1926, entry in investigative report book of Hyde and Leonard, Portland City Archives.

12. Investigative report book of Williams and Jewell, Oct. 23, 1926, Portland City Archives.

13. *Ibid.*

14. *Supra* note 4.

15. "Scouts Idea of Foul Play," *Journal*, Oct. 26, 1926, at 1 and 2.

16. "Reports Upon Deaths Do Not Show Murder," *Telegram*, Oct. 26, 1926, at 1.

17. *Supra* note 4.

18. *Supra* note 12.

19. Death Report, Coroner's Office, Mable McDonald Fluke.

20. Death Certificates, Oregon State Deaths, 1864–1968.

21. "Death Inquiry," *Oregonian*, Nov. 15, 1926, at 7.

Chapter 14

1. "Woman Dies; Gems Gone; Quiz Opens," *Oregonian*, Oct. 22, 1926, at 1. After renumbering,

the Grant house at 604 East 22nd Street is now 3106 and 3118 S.E. 22nd Avenue.

2. "2 Clews Indicate Mrs. Grant Slain," *Oregonian*, Oct. 24, 1926, at 16.

3. *Ibid.*

4. *Supra* note 1.

5. "Find Woman Dead; Jewels Missing," *Oregon Journal*, Oct. 22, 1926, at 11 [henceforth, *Journal*].

6. *Ibid.*

7. "California Strangler Suspected," *Journal*, Oct. 25, 1926, at 1 and 6.

8. "Police Hold New Clue in 3 Tragedies," *Portland News*, October 25, 1926, at 1 and 2 [henceforth, *News*].

9. *Ibid.*

10. "Reports Upon Deaths Do Not Show Murder," *Portland Telegram*, Oct. 26, 1926, at 1 [henceforth, *Telegram*].

11. Death Report, Coroner's Office, Virginia A. Grant.

12. Oregon, State Deaths, 1864–1968.

13. *Supra* note 2.

14. Investigative report book of Hyde and Leonard, Portland City Archives.

15. Investigative report book of Thomas and Rockwell, Oct. 23, 1926, Portland City Archives.

16. Nebraska, Select County Marriage Records, 1855–1908.

17. Findagrave.com.

18. U.S. Census of 1900.

19. Colorado Divorce Index, 1851–1902.

20. Inference from U.S. Census of 1910 and 1920.

21. Obit in *Spokane Chronicle*, Feb. 1, 1926, at 19.

22. Inference from U.S. Census of 1910 which states they had been married for seven years.

23. Portland City Directories from 1907 through 1920.

24. Findagrave.com.

25. *Ibid.*

26. *Supra* note 7.

27. "Police Ask Aid to Hunt Killer," *Oregonian*, Oct. 25, 1926, at 12.

28. "Three Women Slain by Strangler," *Oregonian*, Oct. 24, 1926, at 1 and 14.

29. "Fiend Linked to Deaths," *Medford Mail Tribune*, Oct. 24, 1926, at 1 and 8.

30. *Supra* note 8 and 7.

31. "4 Strangled in Bay Cities," *Oregonian*, Oct. 24, 1926, at 15.

32. "Reports Upon Deaths Do Not Show Murder," *Telegram*, Oct. 26, 1926, at 1.

33. *Supra* note 7 and 8.

34. "Death Inquiry Renewed," *Oregonian*, Nov. 15, 1926, at 7.

35. *Supra* note 27.

36. "Weird Deaths Baffle Officials," *Oregonian*, Oct. 27, 1926, at 1.

37. "Physicians and Police Confer on Three Baffling Deaths," *Oregonian*, Oct. 27, 1926, at 15.

38. "3 Mysterious Deaths," *Telegram*, Oct. 25, 1926, at 2.

39. "The Annual Comedy," *The Capital Journal*, April 22, 1927, at 4.

40. "Death Reports Made," *Oregonian*, Nov. 19, 1926, at 1.

41. "Local Police Seek Slayer," *Telegram*, Nov. 26, 1926, at 1.

42. "Annual Report of Bureau of Police, 1926," City of Portland, at 15.

43. "2 More Women Tell of Seeing Strangler Here," *Journal*, June 24, 1927, at 7.

44. Investigative report book of Hyde and Leonard, Portland City Archives. Also, "Woman Foils Fiend Suspect," *News*, Oct. 26, 1926, at 1.

45. *Supra* note 43.

46. "Winnipeg Suspect Recognized Here," *Oregonian*, June 24, 1926, at 10.

47. *Supra* note 44.

48. Confirmed in police notebook, *supra* note 44.

Chapter 15

1. "Apron-String Murder Gives Police Puzzle," *L.A. Times*, Nov. 12, 1926, at 1.

2. "Suicide Clews in Death Case," *L.A. Times*, Nov. 13, 1926, at 2.

3. "Hollywood Wife Is Strangled by Unknown Killer," *Sacramento Bee*, Nov. 12, 1926, at 1; "Strangler in Hollywood Kills Woman," *S.F. Examiner*, Nov. 12, 1926, at 3.

4. "Hollywood Wife Is Strangled by Unknown Killer," *Sacramento Bee*, Nov. 12, 1926, at 1; "Strangler in Hollywood Kills Woman," *S.F. Examiner*, Nov. 12, 1926, at 3.

5. "Hollywood Girl Strangled with Apron Cord," *L.A. Evening Record*, Nov. 12, 1926, at 1.

6. *Supra* note 1.

7. "Former Girl Resident Strangled," *Des Moines Register*, Nov. 13, 1926, at 1.

8. *Supra* note 1.

9. "Hollywood Woman Strangled," *San Diego Union*, Nov. 12, 1926, at 1.

10. *Supra* note 1.

11. For example, in addition to the reports already cited, "Woman Strangled," *S.F. Chronicle*, Nov. 12, 1926, at 1; "Another Murder in Hollywood," *Spokane Spokesman-Review*, Nov. 12, 1926, at 2.

12. "Find Clues in Hunt for Woman's Slayer," *Bakersfield Californian*, Nov. 12, 1926, at 1.

13. *Supra* note 1.

14. *Ibid.*

15. *Supra* note 5.

16. *Supra* note 2.

17. *Ibid.*

18. *Ibid.*

19. "Suicide Theory," *L.A. Record*, Nov. 13, 1926, at 1.

20. "Suicide Verdict Closes Woman's Tragic History," *L.A. Times*, Nov. 16, 1926, at 2.

21. Death Notices—Corcoran, *Hollywood Citizen News*, Nov. 16, 1926, at 11.

22. Kevin Maiberger, LAPD, to Alvin Esau, March 3, 2009.

23. Iowa County Marriages, 1838–1934.

24. While we have no record, a report in 1909 says Mrs. Cravens had been divorced for five years. "Learn of Cravens' Death," *Des Moines Register*, Aug. 7, 1909, at 5.

25. *Ibid*.

26. Iowa County Marriages, 1838–1934.

27. Various press reports on August 6, 1909, include *Indianapolis News*, *Elwood Call Leader*, *Indianapolis Star*, *Alexandria Times-Tribune*, and *Des Moines Register*.

28. Iowa Death Records, 1904–1951.

29. *Des Moines Register*, Nov. 7, 1915, at 41; June 8, 1917, at 17; April 4, 1918, at 9; *Des Moines Tribune*, Aug. 23, 1919, at 3.

30. Iowa, County Marriages, 1838–1934.

31. *Des Moines Register*, May 5, 1921, at 3.

32. *Supra* note 7.

33. Iowa Death Records, 1921–1952.

34. Los Angeles, Birth and Death Records, 1800–1994.

35. California Marriage Records, 1850–1941.

36. "Bankruptcy Filings," *San Francisco Recorder*, June 21, 1928, at 1.

37. California Death Index, 1940–1997.

Chapter 16

1. For example, "Woman Fights Off Madman Who Attacks Her in Home," *S.F. Chronicle*, Oct. 20, 1926, at 1 [henceforth, *Chronicle*]; "Matron Hurt in Struggle with Maniac," *S.F. Examiner*, Oct. 28, 1926, at 1 [henceforth, *Examiner*]; "Strangler Attacks S.F. Woman Lodging House Manager," *S.F. Bulletin*, Oct. 28, 1926, at 3; "Strangler Gags Woman," *Examiner*, Oct. 30, 1926, at 5; "New Strangler Chokes Woman," *Examiner*, Nov. 3, 1926, at 4.

2. "Mate Finds Spouse Near Death from Fiend Attack," *Examiner*, Nov. 5, 1926, at 1.

3. "Police Scout Fiend Attack, Blame Fall," *Examiner*, Nov. 6, 1926, at 17.

4. *Ibid*.

5. "Cultured Man Now Sought as Strangler," *Examiner*, Nov. 22, 1926, at 15.

6. Dullea and Fredrickson to Matheson, July 5, 1927. Winnipeg police file.

7. *Ibid*.

8. "Woman Attacked," *Chronicle*, Nov. 18, 1926, at 1; "Burlingame Woman Foils Attempt," *San Mateo Times*, Nov. 18, 1926, at 1.

9. "Victim Who Battled 'Jack the Strangler,'" *Chronicle*, Nov. 21, 1926, at 1.

10. "Woman Attacked," *Chronicle*, Nov. 18, 1926, at 1.

11. *Ibid*.

12. "Look for Dark Man, Scratched on Face," *Chronicle*, Nov. 23, 1926, at 7.

13. *Supra* note 9.

14. "Strangler Is Identified by Young Matron," *San Mateo Times*, June 18, 1927, at 1.

15. *Ibid*. Also, "2 Stranglers," *S.F. Call and Post*, June 18, 1927, at 2.

16. "S.F. Woman Identifies Strangler," *Chronicle*, June 18, 1927, at 1.

17. "Is This 'Strangler'?" *S.F. Call and Post*, June 17, 1927, at 1; "News in Pictures," *The Bulletin*, June 17, 1927, at 4.

18. "Identified at Burlingame," *Sacramento Bee*, June 18, 1927, at 3; "Strangler's Record Here Bares Crime," *Examiner*, June 18, 1927, at 7.

19. W.J. Quinn to Philip Stark, July 5, 1927. Winnipeg police file.

20. Harper to Quinn, July 3, 1927. Winnipeg police file.

21. "Man Held in Winnipeg Is Identified," *San Mateo Times*, June 25, 1927, at 1.

Chapter 17

1. U.S. Census of 1870.

2. Arkansas, County Marriage Index, 1837–1957.

3. Arkansas, Birth Certificates, 1914–1917.

4. *Arkansas Democrat*, Nov. 26, 1917, at 4.

5. U.S. Census of 1920.

6. Information from his obit found in *Oakland Tribune*, Jan. 3, 1955, at 35.

7. Dullea and Fredrickson to Matheson, July 5, 1927. Winnipeg police file.

8. W.J. Quinn to Philip Stark, July 5, 1927. Winnipeg police file.

9. Death Report, Coroner's Office, Edmond, Nov. 18, 1926.

10. *Ibid*.

11. "Gem Bandit Slays Rich S.F. Widow," *S.F. Chronicle*, Nov. 19, 1926, at 1.

12. "Police, with New Description, Link Strangler in Seven Attacks," *S.F. Chronicle*, Nov. 20, 1926, at 1.

13. "Woman Found Mysteriously Murdered in Locked Room," *S.F. Examiner*, Nov. 19, 1926, at 1.

14. "Slain by Strangler," *S.F. Bulletin*, Nov. 19, 1926, at 1.

15. "Strangler Kills Wealthy S.F. Widow," *Oakland Post-Enquirer*, Nov. 19, 1926, at 1.

16. *Ibid*.

17. *Supra* note 14.

18. "Fiend Murders S.F. Widow," *S.F. Call and Post*, Nov. 19, 1926, at 1; "Dark Killer Strangles S.F. Woman," *Oakland Tribune*, Nov. 19, 1926, at 1.

19. "Look for Dark Man, Scratched on Face," *S.F. Chronicle*, Nov. 23, 1926, at 1 and 7.

20. "Police Sure 'Strangler' Was Slayer," *S.F. Examiner*, Nov. 20, 1926, at 1.

21. "S.F. Strangler Strikes Again," *Stockton Evening Record*, Nov. 19, 1926, at 1.

22. "Strangler Blamed," *Santa Ana Register*, Nov. 19, 1926, at 3.

23. "Frisco Seeks Oregon Fiend," *Tacoma Ledger*, Nov. 22, 1926, at 2.

24. *Supra* note 9.

25. *Supra* note 19.

26. "Strangler's Cunning Baffles," *S.F. Call and Post*, Nov. 20, 1926, at 1.

27. *Supra* note 19.

28. "Extract from Special Order by Chief O'Brien." Winnipeg police file.

29. "Public's Aid Asked," *S.F. Examiner*, Nov. 23, 1926, at 10.

30. "Capture of Dark Fiend Held Near," *S.F. Examiner*, Nov. 21, 1926, at 1.

31. See, for example, "Beaten by Dark Caller," *Oakland Tribune*, Dec. 4, 1926, at 1; "Woman Battles Strangler," *Oakland Post-Enquirer*, Dec. 6, 1926, at 1; "Fiend Renews Activities in San Francisco," *Albany Democratic Herald*, Dec. 6, 1926, at 1; "Screams Over Phone Bring Aid," *S.F. Chronicle*, Dec. 7, 1926, at 1; "S.F. Strangler Attacks Woman," *Oakland Post-Enquirer*, Dec. 30, 1926, at 1.

32. Picture of San Francisco officers with Pacey," *L.A. Times*, Jan. 14, 1927, at 8.

33. "Man Caught Strangling S.F. Woman," *Oakland Tribune*, Jan. 12, 1927, at 1.

34. "Strangler Confesses Crimes," *Oakland Post-Enquirer*, Jan. 13, 1927, at 1.

35. *Supra* note 33.

36. "Police Fail to Link," *Oakland Tribune*, Jan. 18, 1927, at 1.

37. "California Suspect Not 'Dark Strangler,'" *Seattle Times*, Jan. 13, 1927, at 8.

38. "Jail Prisoner Thought to Be Dark Strangler," *L.A. Times*, Feb. 2, 1927, at 3.

39. "Strangler Suspect Freed," *L.A. Times*, Feb. 4, 1927, at 5.

40. *Supra* note 7.

41. Duncan Matheson, "International Strangler Captured," *Police Journal* V, no. 9 (July 1927), at 5.

42. *Supra* note 7.

Chapter 18

1. "Strangler Atrocity Is Similar to Portland's," *Seattle Times*, Nov. 25, 1926, at 1 [henceforth, *Times*]; "Widows Gems Stolen, Deposit Vault Reveals," *Times*, Nov. 28, 1926, at 1 and 8; "Diamonds Clue to Murder," *Seattle Star*, Nov. 26, 1926, at 8 [henceforth, *Star*]; "New Clue in Murder of Widow," *Seattle Union Record*, Nov. 26, 1926, at 1.

2. Deaths and Funerals, *Times*, Nov. 26, 1926, at 25.

3. Findagrave.com.

4. New York City Births, 1846–1909.

5. Family tree on ancestry.com.

6. New York, Kings County Estate Files, 1866–1923.

7. New York Marriage Licenses Indexes, 1907–2018.

8. *Supra* note 3.

9. "Strangler Atrocity Is Similar to Portland's," *Times*, Nov. 25, 1926, at 1 and 8.

10. "Mrs. Monks Scoffed at Fear," *Times*, Nov. 25, 1926, at 8.

11. *Supra* note 9.

12. "Fingerprints Brings Clue," *Times*, Nov. 26, 1926, at 1 and 10.

13. "Nephew, Niece Get Monks Estate," *Seattle Post-Intelligencer*, Nov. 28, 1926, at 6 [henceforth, *Post-Intelligencer*].

14. "Will of Slain Woman," *Times*, Nov. 27, 1926, at 2.

15. *Ibid.*

16. *Supra* note 9.

17. *Supra* note 12.

18. *Ibid.*

19. "Detectives Hampered in Their Hunt for Slayer," *Times*, Nov. 27, 1926, at 1.

20. *Ibid.*

21. *Supra* note 9.

22. *Ibid.*

23. *Ibid.*

24. "Murdered Widow for Jewels," *Star*, Nov. 25, 1926, at 1 and 9.

25. "Rich Seattle Woman Found Slain," *Post-Intelligencer*, Nov. 25, 1926, at 1 and 2.

26. *Supra* note 24.

27. *Supra* note 12.

28. "Fingerprint May Tell Tale," *Spokane Chronicle*, Dec. 4, 1926, at 1.

29. "Widows Gems Stolen, Deposit Vault Reveals," *Times*, Nov. 28, 1926, at 1 and 8.

30. *Supra* note 24; "Safe Deposit Box Clue to Monks Gems," *Post-Intelligencer*, Nov. 28, 1926, at 1; "Hunt Strangler of Rich Seattle Widow," *Seattle Union Record*, Nov. 25, 1926, at 1.

31. *Supra* note 9.

32. "Sleuths Busy Though Tenant Scoffs," *Star*, Nov. 29, 1926, at 1 and 9.

33. "Portland Sleuth Sent to Seattle," *Spokane Chronicle*, Nov. 26, 1926, at 1; "Local Police Seek Strangler," *Portland Telegram*, Nov. 26, 1926, at 1.

34. "New Slaying Suspect," *Post-Intelligencer*, Nov. 26, 1926, at 1 and 2; "Rich Widow Strangled," *L.A. Times*, Nov. 26, 1926, at 5.

35. "Theft Shown Motive for Monks Death," *Post-Intelligencer*, Nov. 27, 1926, at 1 and 2 [my emphasis].

36. "Police Chief Cautions Homeowners," *Times*, Nov. 28, 1926, at 8.

37. *Supra* note 29.

38. "Stranger Asked Whether Widow Lived All Alone," *Times*, Nov. 29, 1926, at 2.

39. "'Strangler' Killed Mrs. Monks, Is Belief," *Times*, Nov. 30, 1927, at 5.

40. "Coast Cities Join Monks Slayer Hunt," *Post-Intelligencer*, Nov. 30, 1926, at 4.

41. *Supra* note 32.

42. "Seek Friend as Beast-Slayer," *Star*, Nov. 30, 1926, at 9.

43. "Monks Inquest Is Planned," *Star*, Dec. 1, 1926, at 1 and 4; "Police Fear 'Dark Killer' Will Return," *Post-Intelligencer*, Dec. 1, 1926, at 1.

44. *Supra* note 19.

45. *Supra* note 29.

46. "Safe Deposit Box Clue to Monks Gems," *Post-Intelligencer*, Nov. 28, 1926, at 1.

47. *Supra* note 29.

48. *Supra* note 46.

49. *Ibid.*

50. "Slain Widow's Funeral," *Times*, Dec. 4, 1926, at 1; "Fingerprints Same in Portland and Seattle," *Times*, Dec. 5, 1926, at 1 and 2.

51. Susan Helf, "Murder at Green Lake: Sylvia Gaines," 2011, at www.historylink.org; Teresa Nordheim, "Murder at Green Lake," in *Murder and Mayhem in Seattle* (Charleston, SC: The History Press, 2016) at 69–73. Also see Harold Schechter, *Bestial: The Savage Trail of a True American Monster* (New York: Pocket Books, 1998) *Bestial: The Savage Trail of a True American Monster* at 88–91.

52. For an overview of the case, see Alan J. Stein, "Whitehall Murder," 2000, at www.historylink.org, essay 2753.

53. Sherry Grindeland, "Kirkland Man Pieces Together Tale of 1926 Killing," *Seattle Times*, Oct. 27, 2004, re the Tom Hitzroth theory that the father may have killed Whitehall after she was raped by someone else.

54. See also J.D. Chandler, *Murder and Mayhem in Portland* (Charleston, SC: The History Press, 2013), who assumes that Nelson was driving a car during his Portland murders.

Chapter 19

1. Findagrave.com.
2. Death Certificate, Oregon Deaths, 1864–1968.
3. Indiana Marriages, 1810–2001.
4. U.S. Veteran's Payment Cards, 1907–1933; U.S. Census of 1900.
5. California Birth Index, 1905–1995.
6. "Slain Woman Once Resident of Redlands," *L.A. Times*, Dec. 2, 1926, at 10; "Room Seeking Fiend Claims Another Life," *San Bernardino County Sun*, Dec. 1, 1926, at 1 and 3.
7. Obit, *Fort Wayne Sentinel*, Sept. 21, 1916, at 1. Also findagrave.com.
8. U.S. Census of 1920.
9. While I had no difficulty finding the houses where Withers, Grant and Fluke had been murdered in Portland, I could not find the Myers house. Writing in 1955, James Burr Miller, "The Dark Strangler," *Oregonian*, Feb. 27, 1955, at 6, stated that the Myers house at 449 10th Street was now numbered 1971 S.W. 10th Avenue. Yet this address only yielded what appeared to be a series of warehouses, so we may assume that the original Myers home is no more.
10. "Widow 48 Slain by Strangler," *Oregon Journal*, Nov. 30, 1926, at 1 and 23 [henceforth, *Journal*].
11. "Ex-Hoosier Woman Strangler Victim," *Indianapolis Star*, Dec. 2, 1926, at 8.
12. Memo of Nov. 30, 1926, from Rockwell and Thomas to Captain Thatcher. Portland City Archives.
13. *Ibid.* Also, notebook of Collins and Goltz, Nov. 30, 1926.
14. "Body of Widow Found Choked," *Portland Telegram*, Nov. 30, 1926, at 1 and 2 [henceforth, *Telegram*].

15. *Ibid.*
16. *Supra* note 12, with additional details from "Coast Cities Join in Strangler Hunt," *Oregonian*, Dec. 1, 1926, at 8.
17. *Supra* note 10.
18. "Photo Brands Man as Slayer," *Seattle Post-Intelligencer*, June 21, 1927, at 5.
19. Investigative report book of Collins and Goltz, Nov. 30, 1926, Portland City Archives.
20. "Strangler Slays Woman in Home," *Oregonian*, Nov. 30, 1926, at 1 and 6.
21. *Supra* note 12.
22. *Supra* note 10.
23. "West Side Matron Is Found Dead," *Portland News*, Nov. 30, 1926, at 1 and 2 [henceforth, *News*]. That he contacted the police around midnight is also stated in *Oregonian, supra* note 20.
24. "Body of Widow Found Choked," *Telegram*, Nov. 30, 1926, at 1 and 2.
25. *Supra* note 10.
26. *Supra* note 24.
27. *Supra* note 10.
28. "Coast Cities Join in Strangler Hunt," *Oregonian*, Dec. 1, 1926, at 1 and 8.
29. *Supra* note 24.
30. *Supra* note 10.
31. *Ibid.*
32. "New Clew in Strangler Case Fails," *Journal*, Dec. 5, 1926, at 1 and 18.
33. *Supra* note 26.
34. "Rewards Offered for Fiend," *Journal*, Dec. 1, 1926, at 1 and 25.
35. *Supra* note 28.
36. "Find Strangler Gems," *News*, Dec. 2, 1926, at 1; "Slain Woman's Funeral Today," *News*, Dec. 3, 1926, at 2.
37. Letter from J.T. Moore to Kansas City chief of police, Jan. 3, 1927. Kansas City Police File on "Adrian Harris" provided to Alvin Esau by Sergeant Kevin Kilkenny of K.C. police.
38. Coroner's report, obtained by Alvin Esau in 2007.
39. *Supra* note 12.
40. *Supra* note 10.
41. *Supra* note 28.
42. *Ibid.*
43. "Police Tighten Strangler Net," *Oregonian*, Dec. 5, 1926, at 1 and 16.
44. *Supra* note 34.
45. "Reward for Killer Increased to $1500," *Oregonian*, Dec. 7, 1926.
46. "Fingerprint Comparison Exonerates Prisoner," *Journal*, Dec. 7, 1926, at 1.
47. "Man at Eugene Not Strangler," *Telegram*, Dec. 7, 1926, at 2.
48. "Portland Man Held in South," *Telegram*, Dec. 8, 1926, at 1.

Chapter 20

1. Unfortunately, James Burr Miller, "The Dark Strangler," *Oregonian*, Feb. 27, 1955, at 6, never gave a contemporary address for this rooming house.

2. "Women Describe Killer's Visit," *Oregonian*, Dec. 3, 1926, at 1 and 10.

3. Investigative notebook of Tackabery and Phillips, Dec. 3, 1926. Portland City Archives.

4. *Supra* note 2.

5. "Find Strangler Gems," *Portland News*, Dec. 2, 1926, at 1 and 2 [henceforth, *News*].

6. "Dragnet Gets Many," *Portland Telegram*, Dec. 3, 1926, at 1 and 2 [henceforth, *Telegram*].

7. Friday is the day given by investigative reports of Collins and Goltz, Dec. 1, 1926. Portland City Archives.

8. *Supra* note 2.

9. *Ibid.*

10. "Net Widens to Capture Strangler," *Oregon Journal*, Dec. 3, 1926, at 1 and 2 [henceforth, *Journal*].

11. "2 Murders Are Linked by Jewelry," *Journal*, Dec. 2, 1926, at 1 and 2; "Gems Offer Clew to Dark Strangler," *Oregonian*, Dec. 2, 1926, at 1 and 6.

12. "Monks Killer Fingerprints Arrive Here," *Seattle Post-Intelligencer*, Nov. 4, 1926, at 7.

13. *Supra* note 2. Also, "Jewels Found in Portland," *Seattle Times*, Dec. 2, 1926, at 1 and 2; "Slain Widow's Gems Identified," *Seattle Times*, Dec. 3, 1926, at 1 and 2 [henceforth, *Times*].

14. *Supra* note 11.

15. "Pencil Adds Link in Killer Chain," *Oregonian*, Dec. 3, 1926, at 10.

16. *Supra* note 11.

17. "Portland Women Shed More Light on 'Strangler,'" *Times*, Dec. 3, 1926, at 2.

18. "Crime Here Found to Be by Portland Strangler," *Times*, Dec. 5, 1926, at 1.

19. *Ibid.*

20. "Portland's Strangler Monks Killer," *Seattle Post-Intelligencer*, Dec. 5, 1926, at 12.

21. "Lose Trail of the Strangler," *Seattle Star*, Dec. 4, 1926, at 1.

22. *Supra* note 3.

23. "Dual Personality of Killer Bared," *Oregonian*, Dec. 4, 1926, at 1.

24. "Strangler Is Believed in Disguise," *Journal*, Dec. 4, 1926, at 1 and 2.

25. "New Clew in Strangler Case Fails," *Journal*, Dec. 5, 1926, at 1 and 18.

26. *Supra* note 23.

27. "Fingerprints Same in Portland and Seattle," *Times*, Dec. 5, 1926, at 1 and 2.

28. *Supra* note 11.

29. "Clerk Sure Suspect Is Portland Strangler," *Times*, June 19, 1927, at 1 and 8.

30. "Police Tighten Strangler Net," *Oregonian*, Dec. 5, 1926, at 1 and 16.

31. "Portland 'Killer' Sets Grim Record," *Oregonian*, Dec. 6, 1926, at 20.

32. "Net Closing on Strangler!" *News*, Dec. 1, 1926.

33. "Strangler Feared to Be Here," *Vancouver Columbian*, Dec. 2, 1926, at 1.

34. "Suspect Is Strangler, Police Think," *Journal*, Dec. 6, 1926, at 1 and 18.

35. "Fingerprints Exonerate," *Journal*, Dec. 7, 1926, at 1.

36. "Portland Man Held in South as Strangler," *Telegram*, Dec. 8, 1926, at 1.

37. "Indian Held," *Oakland Post-Enquirer*, Dec. 14, 1926, at 3.

38. *Supra* note 24.

39. *Ibid.*

40. *Supra* note 23.

41. *Supra* note 31.

42. "Slain Woman's Funeral," *Times*, Dec. 4, 1926, at 1.

43. *Supra* note 10.

44. Winnipeg police file on Nelson.

45. "New Clew in Strangler Case Fails," *Journal*, Dec. 5, 1926, at 1 and 18. (The failure refers not to the fingerprints, but to a suspect held in Salem and then released.) "Suspect Is Strangler, Police Think," *Journal*, Dec. 6, 1926, at 1 and 18; "Fingerprints Same in Portland and Seattle," *Times*, Dec. 5, 1926, at 1 and 2; "Portland's Strangler Monks Killer," *Seattle Post-Intelligencer*, Dec. 5, 1926, at 12; "Police Tighten Strangler Net," *Oregonian*, Dec. 5, 1926, at 1 and 6.

46. *Supra* note 30.

47. "Identification of Strangler Made," *Journal*, June 17, 1927, at 1 and 11.

48. "Strangler Taken Police Informed," *Oregonian*, June 17, 1927, at 1 and 8; "Fingerprints Link Convict with Slayer," *Seattle Post-Intelligencer*, June 19, 1926, at 1.

49. "Winnipeg Certain It Has Strangler," *Journal*, June 18, 1927, at 1 and 9.

50. Fingerprint analysis submitted through the auspices of John Burchell, Winnipeg police, 2008.

51. "Identity of Man Held in Winnipeg Now Determined," *Journal*, June 19, 1927, at 7.

52. "Canada Prisoner's Picture Recognized," *Oregonian*, June 10, 1927, at 17.

53. "Identity of Man Held in Winnipeg Now Determined," *Journal*, June 19, 1927, at 7.

54. *Ibid.*

55. *Ibid.* Also, *supra* note 52.

56. "Dark Strangler Proven," *Journal*, June 21, 1927, at 1.

57. "Net Closes Further on Strangler," *Journal*, June 21, 1927, at 1 and 21.

58. *Ibid.*

59. *Ibid.*

60. "2 Women Identify Winnipeg Suspect," *Oregonian*, June 25, 1927, at 9.

61. "Fate Saves Woman From 'Strangler,'" *Journal*, June 22, 1927, at 1 and 2; "2 More Women Tell of Seeing Strangler Here," *Journal*, June 24, 1927, at 7.

62. "2 More Women Tell of Seeing Strangler Here," *Journal*, June 24, 1927, at 7.

63. "Sleuth Collins Sure Strangler in Canadian Jail," *Journal*, July 4, 1927, at 4.

Chapter 21

1. Biographical details from "Mrs. John Berard, Former Hennessey Woman, Murdered," *Hennessey Clipper*, Dec. 30, 1926, at 1 and 8; "Hennessey Woman," *Kingfisher Free Press*, Dec. 30, 1926, at 1.

2. Oklahoma Marriage Records, 1890–1995.

3. U.S. Census of 1910.

4. In the U.S. Census of 1920, the Berard family was listed as living in Maxwell, but in the Iowa State Census of 1925, they were in Council Bluffs.

5. "Council Bluffs, the City of Depots," *Omaha World-Herald*, Oct. 2, 1927, Magazine Section at 2 [henceforth, *World-Herald*].

6. "Strangler Deals Death in Iowa," *Oregonian*, Dec. 25, 1926, at 3.

7. "Mrs. John Berard, Former Hennessey Woman, Murdered," *Hennessey Clipper*, Dec. 30, 1926, at 1 and 8.

8. "Take Up Murder Theories," *Kansas City Star*, Dec. 29, 1926, at 1.

9. "Mystery Veils Woman's Death," *The Idaho Daily Statesmen*, Dec. 25, 1926, at 1 and 2.

10. "Woman Is Slain in Own Cellar," *Wisconsin Rapids Daily Tribune*, Dec. 24, 1926, at 1.

11. "Find Woman Dead," *Lincoln Star Journal*, Dec. 24, 1926, at 3; "Iowa Murder Mystery," *Sioux City Journal*, Dec. 25, 1926, at 1.

12. "Strangler of Iowa Woman Still Free," *Burlington Hawk Eye*, Dec. 26, 1926, at 1.

13. "Mrs. John Berard, Former Hennessey Woman, Murdered," *Hennessey Clipper*, Dec. 30, 1926, at 1 and 8.

14. "Bluffs Woman Found Strangled," *Omaha Daily News*, Dec. 24, 1926, at 1 and 3 [henceforth, *News*].

15. "Woman Is Found Mysteriously Strangled," *Council Bluffs Nonpareil*, Dec. 24, 1926, at 1 [henceforth, *Nonpareil*].

16. "Slain Bluffs Woman's Body Found Behind Furnace," *Omaha Evening Bee*, Dec. 24, 1926, at 1 and 2 [henceforth, *Bee*].

17. "Strangler Sought for Death of Iowa Woman," *Seattle Times*, Dec. 25, 1926, at 2.

18. "Police Seek Man in Bluffs Murder Probe," *World Herald*, Dec. 25, 1926, at 4.

19. *Supra* note 15; "Police Are Mystified," *Creston Daily Advertiser*, Dec. 24, 1926, at 1.

20. "Police Seek Stranger in Iowa," *New York Times*, Dec. 25, 1926, at 14: "Stranger Sought," *Washington Star*, Dec. 25, 1926, at 7.

21. *Supra* note 18.

22. *Supra* note 15.

23. "Berard Killer Believed Frisco 'Strangler,'" *Nonpareil*, Dec. 26, 1926, at 1.

24. *Supra* note 18.

25. *Supra* note 15.

26. *Supra* note 16.

27. *Supra* note 9.

28. *Supra* note 15.

29. *Supra* note 18.

30. "Mystery in the Murder of Woman," *Davenport Democrat*, Dec. 24, 1926, at 1.

31. "Mrs. John Berard, Former Hennessey Woman, Murdered," *Hennessey Clipper*, Dec. 30, 1926, at 1 and 8.

32. "Berard Collapses," *Nonpareil*, Dec. 31, 1926, at 1; "Strangled Wife's Mate Goes Insane," *Bee*, Dec. 31, 1926, at 1; "Slain Woman's Husband Is Ill," *News*, Dec. 31, 1926, at 1; "Husband of Slain Woman Insane," *Kansas City Star*, Dec. 31, 1926, at 3; "Goes Insane as He Talks," *Reno Evening Gazette*, Dec. 31, 1926, at 1.

33. *Supra* note 23.

34. *Supra* note 18.

35. *Supra* note 23.

36. "Shirt Murder Still Baffles Bluffs Police," *Des Moines Sunday Register*, Dec. 26, 1926, at G7.

37. *Supra* note 23.

38. *Supra* note 18.

39. *Supra* note 23.

40. *Ibid.*

41. *Ibid.*

42. "Moore Is Positive," *Nonpareil*, Dec. 27, 1926, at 1.

43. *Supra* notes 6, 14 and 17.

44. *Supra* note 23.

45. Investigative notebook of Hyde and Leonard, Dec. 25, 1926. Portland City Archives.

46. "Strangler Slays 3 in Kansas City," *Bee*, Dec. 28, 1926, at 1; 'Murder Striking Parallel," *Nonpareil*, Dec. 28, 1927, at 1; "Case Like Local Death," *Nonpareil*, Dec. 29, 1927, at 1.

47. "Murder Suspect Held by Police at Creston," *World-Herald*, Dec. 27, 1926, at 1 and 2; "Unable to Identify 'Strangler' Suspect," *World-Herald*, Dec. 28, 1926, at 2; "Strangler Held in Indiana Town, Sherriff Beliefs," *World-Herald*, Jan. 17, 1927, at 1.

48. "O'Brien Is Not Strangler," *Lincoln State Journal*, Dec. 27, 1926, at 14; "Suspect Not Strangler," *News*, Dec. 28, 1926, at 12.

49. "Police Embrace Suicide Theory," *Bee*, Jan. 30, 1927, at 1.

50. "Relative Fails to Throw Light on Berard Case," *Bee*, Jan. 2, 1927, at 16.

51. "Probe of Wife's Death Reopened," *Bee*, Feb. 20. 1927, at 1.

52. "Winnipeg Has No Berard Data," *Nonpareil*, June 21, 1927, at 7.

53. Email to author from Lt. Robert L Miller, Council Bluffs police, March 7, 2008.

54. "Identification by Mrs. Brown," *Nonpareil*, June 20, 1927, at 1.

55. "Strangler Suspect Not Berard Killer," *Nonpareil*, July 3, 1927, at 13.

56. "Dark Strangler Hanged in Winnipeg," *World-Herald*, Jan. 14, 1928, at 4.

57. Gorilla Not Council Bluffs Strangler," *Waterloo Evening Courier*, July 2, 1927, at 2; also, *Cedar Rapids Gazette*, July 2, 1927, at 1.

58. "Not Iowa Strangler," *Lincoln Journal Star*, June 23, 1926, at 15.

59. "Strangler May Have Been Here," *Nonpareil*, Nov. 23, 1927, at 9; "Believe He Is Iowa Strangler," *Sioux County Index*, Dec. 2, 1927, at 2.

60. U.S. Census of 1930 and 1940.

61. Iowa Marriage Records, 1880–1945. Also see "Miss Berard and Mr. Williams Are Wed," *Nonpareil*, Nov. 19, 1933, at 12.

62. *Des Moines Register*, Feb. 8, 1961, at 7.

63. "Dedicates Life to Find Slayer," *News*, Jan. 2, 1927, at 1.

64. "Bachelor Rail Engineer," *Nonpareil*, Feb. 5, 1956, at 25.

65. "Nelson's Body Passes Through," *Nonpareil*, Jan. 16, 1928, at 7.

Chapter 22

1. Findagrave.com.

2. Missouri Marriage Records, 1805–2002.

3. *Supra* note 1.

4. Ben Simmons, "Case Study: 'The Dark Strangler': Kansas City's First Serial Killer," *CSI Forensic Forum, Quarterly Newsletter* 14 (April–June 2004), Kansas City Crime Lab, 8 to 11.

5. "Woman Found Strangled to Death in Home," *Kansas City Journal*, Dec. 28, 1926, at 1 and 2 [hereinafter, *Journal*].

6. *Ibid.*

7. "Finds Wife Slain in Home," *Kansas City Times*, Dec. 28, 1926, at 2 [hereinafter, *Times*].

8. *Ibid.*

9. "Take Up Murder Theories," *Kansas City Star*, Dec. 29, 1926, at 1 [hereinafter, *Star*].

10. "A Woman Slain in Home," *Star*, Dec. 27, 1926, at 1.

11. Police report of Shumway and Bendure, Kansas City police file provided to author by Sergeant Kevin Kilkenny, June 2009.

12. *Supra* note 5.

13. *Supra* note 11.

14. *Ibid.*

15. "Friend Held in Murder," *Star*, Dec. 28, 1926, at 13.

16. *Ibid.*

17. "Pacific Coast Fiend Sought in Deaths Here," *Journal*, Dec. 30, 1926, at 1and 2.

18. *Supra* note 10.

19. *Supra* note 15.

20. *Supra* note 7.

21. "Only Murder Witness Dies," *Star*, Jan. 18, 1927, at 1.

22. Victor Ray Pace, Death Certificates 1910–1957, County of Jackson, online at Missouri State Archives.

23. "Son of Strangler's Victim Is Dead," *Ogden Standard Examiner*, Jan. 19, 1927, at 1.

24. According to his obit, "Raymond Pace Rites," *Clinton Eye*, May 26, 1964, at 5.

25. Missouri Death Certificates, 1910–1969.

26. Missouri Marriage Records, 1805–2002.

27. *Supra* note 24.

28. U.S. Social Security Death Index, 1935–2014.

29. "Fiend Strangles Mother and Baby," *Journal*, Dec. 29, 1926, at 1 and 2.

30. *Ibid.*

31. *Supra* note 9.

32. "Strangler Murders Second Kansas City Woman, with Infant," *The Billings Gazette*, Dec. 29, 1926, at 1.

33. *Supra* note 9.

34. *Supra* note 4.

35. "A Mother and Baby Slain," *Times*, Dec. 29, 1926, at 1.

36. *Supra* note 29.

37. Police Report of Bendure and Shumway, date unreadable in my copy, Metropolitan Police Department, Kansas City.

38. *Supra* note 35.

39. *Supra* note 9.

40. Statement of Harpin, sworn on Dec. 28, 1926, Kansas City police file.

41. *Supra* note 29.

42. *Ibid.*

43. *Ibid.*

44. *Ibid.*

45. *Supra* note 9.

46. Letter from Toyne to chief of detectives in Detroit, June 21, 1927; to Moore in Seattle, January 11, 1927; to Lane, Wilmington, January 21, 1927. Kansas City police file.

47. Germaine Harpin, Missouri State Board of Health, Certificate of Death, online at Missouri State Archives.

48. Robert Harpin, Missouri State Board of Health, Certificate of Death, online at Missouri State Archives.

49. Letter from Toyne to James Davis, chief of Los Angeles Police, July 1, 1927. Kansas City Police File.

50. "Scenes and Principles in Slaying of Mother and Child," *Journal*, Dec. 29, 1926, at 3.

51. *Supra* note 9.

52. "Strangler Trail in Blind Alley," *Journal*, Dec. 31, 1926, at 1.

53. *Supra* note 9; Also see, "Strangler in East Believed One Who Slew 5 Women Here," *S.F. Chronicle*, Dec. 30, 1926, at 4.

54. "Pacific Coast Fiend Sought in Deaths Here," *Journal*, Dec. 30, 1926, at 1 and 2.

55. For example, "Find a Strangler," *Times*, Dec. 30, 1926, at 2.

56. "Phantom Strangler Terrorizes," *Sandusky Register*, Jan. 2, 1927, at 1.

57. Western Union Cable, June 25, 1927, from Toyne to Winnipeg. Kansas City police file.

58. *Supra* note 35.

59. U.S. Census of 1930; U.S. Naturalization Records, 1791–1992.

60. France, Social Security Death Index, 1970–2019.

Chapter 23

1. See Alvin A. J. Esau, *The Gorilla Man Strangler Case* (Altona, Manitoba: FriesenPress, 2022).

2. "Libelous to Call Nelson Gorilla Man," *Winnipeg Tribune*, Dec. 1, 1927, at 1.

3. "Gorilla Man in Prison," *De Kalb Chronicle*, Jan. 20, 1910, at 14.

4. "Gorilla Man Sought," *Richmond Palladium-Item*, March 27, 1917, at 1; "Gorilla Man Freed," *Detroit Free Press*, June 20, 1917, at 10; "Gorilla Man Is Nabbed; Attacked 15 Girls," *L.A.*

Evening Post-Record, May 24, 1918, at 13; "Quest for Slayer of Catherine Dunn," *Brooklyn Daily Eagle*, Dec. 22, 1919, at 1 (called gorilla man); "Mob Hunts Gorilla Man," *Passaic News*, July 24, 1926, at 2; "Gorilla Man Lodged in Jail," *Indiana Gazette*, Oct. 22, 1926, at 12.

5. "'Gorilla Man' Reformed by Brain Operation," *Buffalo Times*, March 9, 1922, at 1.

6. "Prison Guard at Canon City Sought as Killer of 'Gorilla Man,'" *Santa Fe New Mexican*, Aug. 26, 1924, at 3.

7. "Benner's Acts," *Elmira Star-Gazette*, Dec. 31, 1923, at 11; "Confessed Girl Slayer Shocks Sleuths," *Richmond Item*, Dec. 30. 1923, at 1.

8. "Six Murders Credited to Gorilla Man," *Santa Rosa Republican*, Dec. 28, 1923, at 1.

9. "Benner, Woman Slayer, Dodges Electric Chair," *N.Y. Daily News*, March 15, 1924, at 6.

10. For example, "Gorilla Man Who Slew 24 to be Killed," *Sacramento Star*, Dec. 19, 1924, at 1.

11. "Held in Strangler Case," *Kansas City Star*, Jan. 3, 1927, at 1: "On Woman's Charges," *Kansas City Star*, Jan. 7, 1927, at 1.

12. "Strangler in Custody in Helena?" *Helena Independent*, Jan. 3, 1927, at 1 and 5; "Haug Adjudged Insane," *Helena Independent*, Jan. 5, 1927, at 5.

13. "Man Caught Strangling S.F. Woman," *Oakland Tribune*, Jan. 12, 1927, at 1.

14. "Police Fail to Link," *Oakland Tribune*, Jan. 13, 1927, at 2; "Pacey's Record," *Napa Journal*, Jan. 13, 1927, at 1 and 8.

15. For example, "Strangler Is Eluding Police," *Redwood City Tribune*, June 12, 1926, at 5; and *Palo Alto Peninsula Times*, June 12, 1926, at 1.

16. "Gorilla Man Who Killed 15 Women, Believed Caught," *Brooklyn Daily Eagle*, Jan. 17, 1927, at 20; "Sheriff Seeks to Prove Ojers Is Gorilla Man," *Evansville Courier and Press*, Jan. 18, 1927, at 1 and 2; "Gorilla Man Suspect Held," *Tampa Bay Times*, Jan. 17, 1927, at 1 and 2; "Gorilla Man Captured in Indiana Town," *Capital Journal*, Jan. 16, 1927, at 1: "Strangler Caught in Indiana," *Billings Gazette*, Jan. 17, 1927, at 1.

17. "Check Stories of Gorilla Man," *Princeton Clarion*, Jan. 17, 1927, at 1.

18. "Indiana Strangler Is Not San Francisco Slayer," *S.F. Examiner*, Jan. 18, 1927, at 15.

19. For example, "Gorilla Man Picked Up By Police," *Davenport Democrat*, Jan. 18, 1927, at 15; "Two Jailed As Strangler Suspects," *Oakland Tribune*, Feb. 2, 1927, at 32; "May Be Dark Strangler," *Eugene Morning Register*, Feb. 3, 1927, at 1; "Strangler Suspect Is Arrested in Portland," *San Mateo Times*, Feb. 7, 1927, at 2; "Strangler Suspect Held," *Spokane Spokesman-Review*, Feb. 9, 1927, at 5; "Strangler Suspect Arrested," *Santa Cruz News*, Feb. 15, 1927 at 2; "Strangler Suspect Held in Oakland," *S.F. Examiner*, Feb. 21, 1927, at 13; "May Be Dark Strangler," *Eugene Morning Register*, May 6, 1927, at 1.

20. "Protests He Is Not 'Gorilla Man,'" *Elyria Chronicle-Telegram*, March 5, 1927, at 5.

21. Winnipeg police department File on Nelson.

22. "Wife Claims," *San Francisco Examiner*, June 19, 1927, at 14.

23. Trial transcript at 285.

24. "Woman Found Dead in Tub," *Fairfield Ledger*, March 1, 1927, at 4; 'Woman Found Dying in a Bathtub Strangled," *Sedalia Democrat*, March 1, 1927, at 3.

25. "Mystery in Body in Tub," *Greensburg News*, March 1, 1927, at 1; "Mystery Veils Bride's Death," *Sioux City Journal*, March 2, 1927, at 9; "Renew Search for Clews," *Chicago Southtown Economist*, March 4, 1927, at 1.

26. "Police Hunt for Slayer," *Bismarck Tribune*, March 1, 1927, at 3; "Match Box Is Clue," *Kokomo Tribune*, March 4, 1927, at 1; "Woman Found Dying," *Sedalia Democrat*, March 4, 1927, at 18.

27. 'Match Box May Trap Murderer," *Dubuque Telegraph Herald*, March 4, 1927, at 1.

28. "Police Hunt for Slayer," *Bismarck Tribune*, March 1, 1927, at 3.

29. "Mystery Veils Bride's Death," *Sioux City Journal*, March 2, 1927, at 9.

30. "Boonville Girl Is Slain," *Boonville Enquirer*, March 4, 1927, at 1.

31. "Killer of Young Bride Believed Murderer of 15," *Salt Lake Telegram*, March 2, 1927, at 1; "Hint of 'Gorilla' in Bride's Death," *Indianapolis Times*, March 2, 1927, at 9; "Gorilla Man Is Suspected," *Sheboygan Press*, March 2, 1927, at 1: "Gorilla Man May Be Slayer," *Fairfield Daily Ledger*, April 2, 1927, at 12; "Gorilla Man Strangler May Be Involved," *Portsmouth Times*, March 2, 1927, at 1; "Gorilla Man May Be Cause," *Oelwein Register*, March 2, 1927, at 1; "Chicago Officials Apparently Have Given Up," *Owensboro Messenger-Inquirer*, March 20, 1927, at 2.

32. See Murders at alvinesau.com.

Chapter 24

1. Pennsylvania Death Certificates, 1906–1968.

2. According to U.S. Census of 1900.

3. Born to William R. and Mary McConnell, baptized on March 14, 1894, in Church of the Mediator, Philadelphia. Pennsylvania Church Records.

4. U.S. Census of 1900 and 1910.

5. Findagrave.com. Also, family tree for Alice Nicholson Donovan on ancestry.com.

6. U.S. Census of 1900 and 1910.

7. Pennsylvania Marriages, 1852–1968.

8. "Strangler Beats Woman to Death and Steals Gems," *Philadelphia Public Ledger*, April 28, 1927, at 1 and 16 [hereinafter *Ledger*].

9. "Strangler Kills Woman and Hides Body Under Bed," *Philadelphia Evening Bulletin*, April 28, 1927, at 1 and 20 [hereinafter *Bulletin*]. The same quote is found in "Fiend Suspect Tries to Enter W. Phila. Home," *Philadelphia Inquirer*, April 29, 1927, at 1 and 10 [hereinafter *Inquirer*].

10. *Bulletin*, *supra* note 9.

11. *Supra* note 8.

12. "Woman Found Strangled to Death in Home," *Inquirer*, April 28, 1927, at 1 and 7.

13. Also see "No Signs of Fight Found by Police," *Lancaster News Journal*, April 29, 1927, at 2.

14. *Supra* note 9.

15. "Strangler Death Remains a Mystery," *Bulletin*, June 1, 1927, at 3.

16. "Buys Newspaper and Finds Wife Was Murdered," *Wilkes-Barre Times-Leader*, April 29, 1927, at 15.

17. *Inquirer, supra* note 9.

18. "Strangler-Robber Theory Advanced," *Inquirer*, May 2, 1927, at 3.

19. Copy of Philadelphia police circular, dated April 29, 1927, in Winnipeg police file.

20. *Supra* notes 9 and 12. See also "Like Crimes on Both Coasts Laid to Choker," *Scranton Times-Tribune*, April 28, 1927, at 2.

21. "Strangler," *Eugene Morning Register,* April 29, 1927, at 1.

22. "Dark Strangler Is in the East," *Oakland Tribune*, May 14, 1927, at 1.

23. "Strangling Recalls Series of Killings in Fall of 1925," *Ledger*, April 28, 1927, at 16. However, the paper did note that in 1925 the police thought a Black man was the killer and here the strangler of McConnell was described as a swarthy white man. Also, see *Inquirer, supra* note 9.

24. "Strangler Traced to Delaware County," *Bulletin*, April 29, 1927, at 1.

25. *Inquirer, supra* note 9.

26. "Strangler Clue in N.Y.," *Bulletin*, May 3, 1927, at 48; "Seek Strangler in N.Y.," *Inquirer*, May 4, 1927, at 6.

27. *Supra* notes 9 and 12.

28. *Inquirer, supra* note 1.

29. *Ibid.*

30. *Supra* note 8.

31. *Supra* note 12.

32. *Supra* notes 9 and 12.

33. *Inquirer* at *supra* notes 9 and 12. Also "Strangler Traced to Delaware County," *Bulletin*, April 29, 1927, at 1; "Detectives Trail Strangler Suspect," *Inquirer*, April 30, 1927, at 2; "Police Grill Prisoner Who Questioned Women at Homes 'For Sale,'" *Inquirer*, May 21, 1927, at 1.

34. "Girl, 15, Choked, Beaten on Head by Strangler," *Ledger*, April 29, 1927, at 1 and 5; "Woman's Ruse Routs Strangler," *Ledger*, May 5, 1927, at 1; "Police Seeking Man in Attack on Woman, 63," *Inquirer*, May 9, 1927, at 1 and 5; "Woman Beaten, Left for Dead by Strangler," *Ledger*, May 9, 1927, at 1; "Woman Is Attacked," *Inquirer*, May 12, 1927, at 1 and 8; "Strangler Binds Woman in N. Phila.," *Ledger*, May 12, 1927, at 1; "Strangler Attack Foiled by Husband," *Inquirer*, May 14, 1927, at 2; "Woman, 64, Beaten, Skull Fractured," *Bulletin*, May 9, 1927, at 1; "Strangler Beats Woman Insensible," *Bulletin*, May 12, 1927, at 3; "Woman Choked By Strangler Is Saved by Police," *Ledger*, May 26, 1927, at 1; "Band Routs Wife's Strangler," *Ledger*, May 30, 1927, at 2.

35. "Strangler Alarm Frightens Women," *Bulletin*, May 5, 1927, at 1; "Another Strangler Scare," *Bulletin*, May 18, 1927, at 1; "Strangler Flees as Woman Shouts," *Bulletin*, June 2, 1927, at 1.

36. "Suspect Not 'Strangler,'" *Ledger*, May 2, 1927, at 2; "Fail to Identify Man as Strangler," *Bulletin*, May 14, 1927, at 2; "New Strangler Suspect Seized in Upper Darby," *Ledger*, May 14, 1927, at 1; "Causes Strangler Scare," *Bulletin*, May 16, 1927, at 1.

37. "Strangler Tours U.S. Say Police," *Bulletin*, June 6, 1927, at 1; see earlier story, "Woman Beaten, Robbed of $293," *Ledger*, May 2, 1927, at 2.

38. "Woman Can Break 'Strangler's' Hold," *Inquirer*, May 1, 1927, at 1.

39. *Ibid.*

40. *Inquirer, supra* note 9. Also, "Detectives Trail Strangler Suspect," *Inquirer*, April 30, 1927, at 2; "Ex-Convict Sought Now as Strangler," *Ledger*, May 1, 1927, at 1; "Ex Convict Sought," *Inquirer*, May 1, 1927, at 3; "Strangler Traced to Delaware Co.," *Bulletin*, April 29, 1927, at 1 and 2; "Nab Suspect as 'Strangler,'" *Chester Times*, May 14, 1927, at 1; "Women Exonerate Strangler Suspect," *Inquirer*, May 15, 1927, at 2.

41. "Strangler Death Remains Mystery," *Bulletin*, June 1, 1927, at A3; "W. Phila. Strangler Still at Liberty," *Inquirer*, June 1, 1927, at 2.

42. *Supra* note 12.

43. "Get 'Gorilla Man' Who Escaped Jail," *Bulletin*, June 16, 1927, at 1.

44. "Send 'Stranglers' Photo," *Bulletin*, June 18, 1927, at 3.

45. "Woman Identifies 'Gorilla' Man as Phila. Strangler," *Inquirer*, June 22, 1927, at 1 and 7.

46. *Ibid.*

47. "Identify Photos of Gorilla Man as Phila. Killer," *Ledger*, June 21, 1927, at 2.

48. *Ibid.*

49. *Supra* note 45.

50. "Canada Strangler Suspect Was Here," *Bulletin*, June 23, 1927, at 2.

51. Letter of William Lahey to Chief Newton, Oct. 13, 1927. Winnipeg police file.

52. "Suspect Identified," *Inquirer*, June 30, 1927, at 4; "Strangler Placed on Trial in Canada," *Bulletin*, Nov. 2, 1927, at 2.

53. *Supra* note 47.

54. "Ask Warrant Here for Canada Slayer," *Bulletin*, June 22, 1927, at 1; "Warrant Issued for 'Gorilla Man,'" *Inquirer*, June 23, 1927, at 2.

55. "Delay 'Strangler' Warrant," *Bulletin*, June 24, 1927, at 2.

56. "Two Strangling Charges Await Nelson Here," *Inquirer*, Nov. 2, 1927, at 4.

57. "To View 'Gorilla Man,'" *Inquirer*, July 27, 1927, at 2.

58. "Man Sees Accused Strangler of Wife," *Bulletin*, Jan. 12, 1928, at 3.

59. *Ibid.* See also "Phila. Man Quizzes Canada Strangler," *Ledger*, Jan. 12, 1928, at 2.

60. "Nelson, Strangler, Dies on Scaffold," *Bulletin*, Late Edition, Jan. 13, 1928, at 2.

61. "Strangler Hangs, Denies Crime Here," *Ledger*, Jan. 14, 1928, at 2.

62. "Thinks Nelson Is the Man," *Manitoba Free Press*, Jan. 13, 1928, at 1.

63. "Strangler Hangs," *Ledger*, Jan. 14, 1928, at 2.

64. Phone call to author from Officer Bell, Philadelphia police department, April 15, 2009.

65. According to email to author from David Baugh, Archivist, Philadelphia City Archives, June 16, 2008.

66. U.S. Census of 1930, 1940 and 1950.

67. Pennsylvania Death Certificates, See also deaths, *Inquirer*, March 1, 1938, at 31.

68. Findagrave.com.

Chapter 25

1. On a sweltering hot Columbus Day in 2007, before the Buffalo Bills lost a close game to Dallas, I visited the Buffalo police headquarters and was given the homicide investigation file on the Randolph case from Captain Mark Antonio.

2. As noted in a memo from John Marnon, deputy chief of Buffalo police, to Edward Fox, chief of Detroit detectives, June 7, 1927. Buffalo police file.

3. "Sworn Statement of Gideon Gillett," May 30, 1927. Buffalo police file.

4. "Memo from Madigan to Roche," June 2, 1927. Buffalo police file.

5. "Report of Officers Quigley and Holz," May 30, 1927. Buffalo police file.

6. "Adrian Harris Sought," *Buffalo Evening Times*, June 1, 1927, at 8 [henceforth, *Times*].

7. "Sworn Statement of Fred Merritt," May 30, 1927. Buffalo police file.

8. "Roomer Sought After Murder of Landlady," *Buffalo Evening News*, May 31, 1927, at 1 [henceforth, *News*].

9. "Woman Slain in Plymouth," *Buffalo Courier Express*, May 31, 1927, at 1 [henceforth, *Express*].

10. *Supra* note 3.

11. *Supra* note 7.

12. *Supra* note 9.

13. *Supra* note 2.

14. *Supra* note 8. The same expression is used in *supra* note 6.

15. "Report of Officers Quigley and Holz," to Deputy Chief Marmon, May 31, 1927. Buffalo police file.

16. "Memo on Murder of Mrs. Jennie Randolph in Buffalo," compiled by Detective William Johnson of the Detroit police and dated June 15, 1927. Found in the Winnipeg police file. The memo is full of factual errors as to the murder of Randolph, but the coroner's report is in quotations. When I applied to the County of Erie Medical Examiner to confirm the report, I was informed that, unlike most other jurisdictions, coroner's reports were not open to the public. "Letter from Costantino to Esau," July 16, 2007.

17. "Plymouth Ave. Woman Is Slain," *Buffalo Evening Times*, May 31, 1927, at 1 and 2 [henceforth, *Times*].

18. "Letter from Higgins to Chief of Police of Kansas City," June 16, 1927. Kansas City police file.

19. *Supra* note 9.

20. *Ibid.* Indeed on the very day of the murder, the first police memo names the suspect as Charles Harrison, alias Adrian Harris. See "Memo of Madigan and Carroll," to chief of detectives, Austin Roche, May 30, 1927. Buffalo police file.

21. "Fiend Sought for Murders in Five Cities," *Express*, June 1, 1927, at 1.

22. *Supra* note 17.

23. "Circular of James Higgins, Chief of Police," May 30, 1927. Buffalo police file.

24. See "Buffalo Police Cannot Find," *Dunkirk Observer*, May 31, 1927, at 17; "Search for Slayer," *Salamanca Republican*, May 31, 1927, at 1; "Nation-Wide Hunt," *News*, June 1, 1927, at 1.

25. Pawn cards found in Buffalo police file.

26. "Think Killer Sold Clothes," *News*, June 3, 1927, at 1; "Police Receive Wearing Apparel," *Express*, June 3, 1927, at 1; "Harris May Still Be in City," *Times*, June 3, 1927, at 13.

27. "Think Killer Sold Clothes," *News*, June 3, 1927, at 1; "Police Receive Wearing Apparel," *Express*, June 3, 1927, at 1; "Harris May Still be in City," *Times*, June 3, 1927, at 13.

28. "Evidence Receipt from Madigan to Pawn Broker," June 4, 1927. Buffalo police file.

29. "Hold for Evidence Order," June 4, 1927. Buffalo police file.

30. Letter submitted from the lab of Dr. Hill, Aug. 12, 1927. Buffalo police file. Dr. Hill had died shortly after completing this assignment, which accounted for the lateness of the report based on his handwritten notes.

31. "Memo to Chief Roche from Madigan," June 2, 1927. Buffalo police file.

32. Circular of John S. Marnon, deputy chief of police, Buffalo, dated June 2, 1927, and found in the Winnipeg police file and found in the Buffalo police file.

33. "Whitwell and Fingerprint Police Squad," *Times*, June 12, 1927, at 70.

34. Various memos found in Buffalo police file.

35. "Memo from Officer Madigan," June 2, 1927. Buffalo police file.

36. "Memo from Flynn and Madigan," June 3, 1927. Buffalo police file.

37. Numerous memos on the investigation of Winey are found in the police file. See also "Slayer Roams Central New York," *Syracuse Herald*, June 3, 1927, at 1; "Woman's Murderer Sought in Syracuse," *News*, June 2, 1927, at 3; "Think Randolph Murder Suspect Now in Syracuse," *Times*, June 2, 1927, at 1; "Syracuse Suspect Not Adrian Harris," *Express*, June 5, 1927, at 1.

38. "Not Buffalo Slayer," *News*, June 13, 1927, at 3.

39. Telegram to Winnipeg by Marnon, June 17, 1927; Letter to Winnipeg by Marnon, June 17, 1927. Buffalo police file.

40. Various items from Chief Constable Stark of Winnipeg found in Buffalo police file.

41. "Memo to Roche from Madigan," June 20, 1927. Buffalo police file.

42. "Nelson Is Identified as Buffalo Strangler," *Times*, June 20, 1927, at 1.

43. "Memo to Roche from Carroll," June 20, 1927. Buffalo police file.

44. *Supra* note 42; also, "Prosecutor to Ask Murder Indictment," *News*, June 20, 1927, at 1.

45. "Buffalo Unlikely to Try Strangler," *News*, June 21, 1927, at 1.

46. "To Indict Strangler Suspect Today," *Express*, June 21, 1927, at 11.

47. "Memo from Carroll to Roche," June 20, 1927. Buffalo police file.

48. *Supra* note 46.

49. "Telegram from Marnon to Winnipeg Police," June 21, 1927. Buffalo police file.

50. Documents found in the Buffalo police file.

51. *Supra* note 45 and 46.

52. "Strangler to Face Noose," *Express*, Nov. 6, 1927, at 1; 'Dark Strangler Guilty of Murder," *News*, Nov. 5, 1927, at 1. The rival paper had the news on the back page, "Dark Strangler Is Found Guilty," *Times*, Nov. 6, 1927, at 54.

53. U.S. Census of 1870 and 1880. Dates of birth are given in U.S. Census of 1900.

54. "Gideon B. Gillet Dead," *Courier*, April 15, 1903, at 2; New York State Census of 1892; U.S. Census of 1900.

55. New York State, Marriage Index, 1881–1967. Age of husband based on U.S. Census of 1880 and U.S. Headstone Applications for Military Veterans, 1925–1970. He was born on April 15, 1876.

56. U.S. Census of 1900.

57. There was publicity as to his service in various press reports: *Rochester Democrat*, Sept. 29, 1898, at 4; *Elmira Star-Gazette*, Oct. 3, 1898, at 5; *News*, Nov. 5, 1898, at 6.

58. *Buffalo Commercial*, May 23, 1899, at 12.

59. "Olean Wants Him," *Courier*, Oct. 11, 1900, at 7; "Looking for Randolph," *Express*, Oct. 11, 1900, at 2.

60. "Looking for Randolph," *Express*, Oct. 11, 1900, at 2.

61. "Arrested in Iroquois Lobby," *Buffalo Review*, Nov. 21, 1902, at 6.

62. *Ibid.*

63. Information from World War One Draft Registration Cards, 1917–18; Indiana Marriages, 1810–2001; U.S. Census of 1920, 1930, 1940, 1950; U.S. Headstone Applications for Military Veterans, 1925–1970.

64. Jennie called herself a widow in the Buffalo City Directory and the U.S. Census of 1910.

65. *Supra* note 54.

66. New York State Census of 1905.

67. New York State Census of 1915; U.S. Census of 1920; New York State Census of 1925.

68. "Died," *News*, Sept. 22, 1913, at 3.

69. "Orville Gillett Randolph," *News*, Oct. 12, 1913, at 43.

70. *Supra* note 17.

71. "Neighbors, Friends Grieve Over Death," *Express*, June 2, 1927, at 11.

72. "Mrs. Gillett Dead at 91," *Buffalo Enquirer*, Jan. 30, 1924, at 8.

73. U.S. Census of 1930.

74. Pennsylvania Death Certificates, 1906–1968.

75. New York State Death Index, 1957–1970.

Chapter 26

1. "Intensive Search Reveals no Clue," *Buffalo Courier Express*, June 2, 1927, at 22.

2. "Neighbors, Friends, Grieve," *Buffalo Courier Express*, June 2, 1927, at 11.

3. "2 Women Slain by Strangler," *Detroit News*, June 6, 1927, at 1 and 2 [henceforth *News*].

4. *Ibid.*

5. "Hindu Sought in Death of Women," *Detroit Evening Times*, June 6, 1927, at 1 [henceforth, *Times*].

6. *Supra* note 3.

7. "Hunt Strangler in Killing of 2," *News*, June 8, 1927, at 37.

8. "Clues Lacking in Dual Killing," *Detroit Free Press*, June 7, 1927, at 1 [henceforth, *Free Press*].

9. Letter of Fox, Detroit, June 17, 1927. Kansas City police file.

10. Memo from Frahm, Detroit, June 13, 1927. Kansas City police file.

11. *Ibid.*

12. Michigan Death Certificates, 1921–1952.

13. U.S. Census of 1880. Her teaching certificate in 1892 is found in one of the family trees on ancestry.com.

14. Cook County Marriage Index, 1871–1920.

15. U.S. Census of 1900.

16. U.S. Census of 1900 and 1910. Also, various city directories indicate husband living in East Liverpool and Akron while wife is in Belpre.

17. U.S. Census of 1920.

18. Ohio Deaths, 1908–1953.

19. *Supra* note 5 at 2.

20. Michigan Marriage Records, 1867–1952.

21. As noted in her death certificate, *supra* note 12.

22. Findagrave.com.

23. Michigan Death Records, 1867–1952.

24. *Supra* note 3.

25. *Supra* note 3 and 5.

26. There is no record of any Oswald in the British Red Cross, and the only woman with an Oswald last name who served in the WAAC was born in Scotland in 1896 and died in Australia in 1993. U.K. Army Auxiliary Corps Service Records, 1917–1920.

27. *Supra* note 3.

28. *Supra* note 5.

29. U.S. Census of 1910.

30. U.S. World War I Draft Registration Cards.

31. U.S. Naturalization Records.

32. U.S. Census of 1920.

33. Michigan Marriage Records, 1867–1952.

34. "Police Seeking Physician to Question Him,"

Free Press, June 6, 1927, at 1 and 3; also, *News*, *supra* note 3.

35. "Dual Murder Balks Police," *Free Press*, June 8, 1927, at 1.

36. *Ibid.*

37. "2 Hindus Held in Double Slaying," *Times*, June 7, 1927, at 1 and 2.

38. *Supra* note 3.

39. *Ibid.*

40. "Outlawed by Marriage," *Saint Joseph Herald Press*, Sept. 16, 1926, at 5.

41. Michigan Divorce Records, 1897–1959.

42. *Supra* note 5.

43. *Supra* note 34.

44. *Supra* note 7.

45. *Supra* note 5.

46. *Ibid.*

47. *Supra* note 34.

48. *Supra* note 37.

49. "Gorilla Sought in Slayings," *Times*, June 8, 1927, at 1 and 13.

50. "Buffalo Strangler Is Now Wanted Here," *News*, June 15, 1927, at 1.

51. "Memo from Johnson to Frahm," June 15, 1927. Winnipeg police file on Nelson.

52. *Supra* note 10.

53. "Detroit Officers to See Strangler," *News*, June 20, 1927; "Police to Question Gorilla," *Times*, June 20, 1927, at 1.

54. Testimony of William Patterson, inquest transcript at 38.

55. "Knife a Clue in 2 Murders," *Free Press*, June 24, 1927, at 4.

56. "Believes Man Held Is Detroit Slayer," *News*, June 24, 1927, at 2.

57. "Knife Links Gorilla," *Times*, June 24, 1927, at 7.

58. *Supra* note 53.

59. "Thinks Nelson Killed 2 Here," *News*, June 25, 1927, at 2.

60. "Positive Captive Man Wanted as Strangler," *Buffalo Courier-Express*, June 25, 1927, at 20.

61. "Sleuth Calls Gorilla Guilty," *Times*, June 30, 1927, at 2.

62. *Supra* note 59.

63. "Dark Strangler Dies on Gallows," *Free Press*, Jan. 14, 1928, at 9; "Canada Hangs Slayer of 22," *News*, Jan. 13, 1928, at 42.

64. "Suit Recalls the Atorthy Case," *Free Press*, Jan. 8, 1928, at 4.

65. U.S. Census of 1940.

66. "Notice," *Free Press*, Aug. 22, 1938, at 17.

67. Michigan Marriage Records.

68. "Death Notice," *Free Press*, March 21, 1974, at 15; also see U.S. Social Security Death Index.

69. California Cemetery and Funeral Home Collection.

Chapter 27

1. "Strangler Slays Woman," *Chicago Herald and Examiner*, June 3, 1927, at 1 and 4 [henceforth *Herald*].

2. Chicago police file received from Rory P. O'Brien, Chicago police department, Oct. 1, 2009.

3. Report of Michael McFadden, June 3, 1927. Chicago police file.

4. Statement of Marie Lang, June 2, 1927. Chicago police file.

5. Statement of Polzin and Crowley. Chicago police file [my emphasis].

6. Memo of Egan, Moran, and Fitzsimmons, July 7, 1927. Chicago police file.

7. Homicide Bureau, File No. 891, Inquest, June 3, 1927. Chicago police file.

8. Letter from W.E. O'Connor of Chicago to Chief Newton of Winnipeg, December 14, 1927. Winnipeg police file.

9. "Woman Strangled in Home by Moron," *Chicago Tribune*, June 3, 1927, at 1 [henceforth, *Tribune*].

10. "Hunt Wounded Man as Killer of Housewife," *Tribune*, June 4, 1927, at 3.

11. "Find Key," *Chicago Suburbanite Economist*, June 7, 1927, at 1 [henceforth, *Economist*].

12. "Police in Raid Nab Negro Suspect," *Chicago Evening Post*, June 4, 1927, at 4; "Trail Strangler by Sailor-Knot," *Herald*, June 4, 1927, at 1.

13. *Supra* note 8.

14. Report of Bureau of Identification, June 3, 1927. Chicago police file.

15. Statement of Evelyn Booth, June 3, 1927. Chicago police file.

16. "Trail Strangler by Sailor-Knot," *Herald*, June 4, 1927, at 1.

17. Report on Key, June 5, 1927. Chicago police file.

18. *Supra* note 8.

19. For example, "Strangler Is at Work Again," *Dayton Herald*, June 3, 1927, at 1; "Think Chicago Murderer Is Notorious Strangler," *Visalia Times*, June 3, 1927, at 1; "Believe 'Strangler' Who Terrorized West, Person Who Killed Chicago Woman," *Decatur Herald*, June 3, 1927, at 1; "Strangler Kills Another Woman," *Bakersfield Californian*, June 3, 1927, at 1.

20. For example, "Woman in Chicago Found Strangled," *Nebraska State Journal*, June 3, 1927, at 12; "Butcher's Helper Quizzed in Slaying," *Washington Star*, June 3, 1927, at 17; "Clues Sought in Murder," *Lima News*, June 3, 1927, at 25; "Woman Loses Life," *Albert Lea Tribune*, June 3, 1927, at 1.

21. *Supra* note 1.

22. *Supra* note 9.

23. *Supra* note 1.

24. *Supra* note 9.

25. Statement of Michael Hirsch, June 2, 1927. Chicago police file.

26. Memo of McNamara and Parrish, June 3, 1927. Chicago police file.

27. *Supra* note 10.

28. "Hunt Continues for Strangler of Housewife," *Tribune*, June 5, 1927, at 20.

29. "Murder Case Suspect Seeks Release Writ," *Sioux City Journal*, June 4, 1927, at 1.

30. *Supra* note 28.

31. "Dead Woman's Marks Clew to Strangler," *Chicago Daily Journal*, June 3, 1927, at 1.

32. *Supra* note 28.

33. *Ibid.*

34. *Ibid.*

35. "Police Hunt Negro Garage Worker in Sietsema Murder," *Chicago Evening Post*, June 3, 1927, at 1.

36. "Police in Raid Nab Negro Suspect," *Chicago Evening Post*, June 4, 1927, at 2.

37. "Nab 2 on Clew," *Chicago Daily News*, June 3, 1927, at 1.

38. For example, "Chicago Police Baffled," *Abilene News*, June 5, 1927, at 1.

39. "Police Begin Fresh Search for Strangler," *Herald*, June 5, 1927, at 4.

40. "Sietsema Murder Remains Mystery After Two Weeks," *Chicago Suburbanite Economist*, June 14, 1927, at 1.

41. "Negro Raids Beverly Hills," *Tribune*, July 18, 1927, at 1.

42. "Flashlight Gang Believed Broken as One Is Shot," *Tribune*, July 21, 1927, at 3.

43. "Woman's Cries Frighten Off Gorilla Man," *Herald*, Aug. 23, 1927, at 3.

44. "Nelson, Strangler of Women, Is Hanged," *Herald*, Jan. 14, 1928, at 7.

45. "Dark Strangler, Murderer of 22, Dies on Gallows," *Chicago Evening Post*, Jan. 13, 1928, at 5.

46. "Winnipeg Mayor Urges Big Bill to Be Reformer," *Tribune*, Dec. 6, 1927, at 21; also see "Winnipeg Mayor Writes to Big Bill Thompson on Chicago, Crime and Justice," *Winnipeg Free Press*, Dec. 6, 1927, at 6.

47. Illinois Death and Stillborn Index, 1916–1947.

48. U.S. Census of 1900.

49. U.S. Census of 1910.

50. U.S. Census of 1920.

51. Cook County Marriage Index, 1871–1920. See his obit in the *Tribune*, May 14, 1954, at 12.

52. Statement of Maggie Mitchell, June 3, 1927. Chicago police file.

53. *Supra* note 11.

54. Death notice, *Tribune*, May 14, 1954, at 34.

Chapter 28

1. Alvin Esau to Kansas City police, May 30, 2008.

2. "Johannes," *Kansas City Times*, Nov. 11, 1925, at 19.

3. "Cops Think Bandit Slew Rich Widow," *Wichita Beacon*, June 4, 1927, at 12.

4. The local press stated that she lived at 611 Fowler Street, but census records consistently mention 611 Ferry as her address.

5. "Woman Slain in Home," *Kansas City Star*, June 4, 1927, at 3.

6. *Ibid.*

7. "Widow Killed in Home on Kaw River with Hatchet," *St. Louis Post-Dispatch*, June 5, 1927, at 91.

8. *Supra* note 5.

9. "A Robbery Clew in Murder," *Kansas City Star*, June 9, 1927, at 2.

10. *Supra* note 7.

11. 'Wounded Hand Murder Clew," *Kansas City Star*, June 5, 1927, at 22.

12. "A Johannes Murder Clew," *Kansas City Star*, June 6, 1927, at 16.

13. "Called at Homes for Sale," *Kansas City Star*, June 7, 1927, at 2.

14. "Hair a Clew in a Murder," *Kansas City Times*, June 7, 1927, at 3.

15. Census records consistently say so.

16. "Death Notice," *Kansas City Star*, June 5, 1927, at 26. Gravestone on findagrave.com.

17. U.S. Census of 1910 notes that Henry and Lena had been married for 15 years.

18. U.S. Census of 1900.

19. *Ibid.*

20. See findagrave.com. Oak Grove Cemetery, Kansas City.

21. *Supra* note 18.

22. U.S. Census of 1910 and 1920.

23. *Ibid.*

24. Kansas Marriages, 1840–1935.

25. Marriage licenses, *Leavenworth Times*, Feb. 17, 1922, at 4. U.S. Census of 1930 re stepson, Jack Gilbert.

26. "Johannes," death notice, *Kansas City Times*, Nov. 11, 1925, at 19.

27. U.S. Census of 1930 and 1940.

28. In the U.S. Census of 1950, Marion was listed as divorced and living with her mother and married son, Jack Gilbert.

29. Florida Marriage Index, 1927–2001.

30. Florida Death Index, 1877–1998.

31. Findagrave.com.

32. Death Notice in *Kansas City Star*, March 1, 1947, at 2.

Concluding Reflections

1. For the argument that it might not have been for sale, see Esau, *The Gorilla Man Strangler Case* at 12–14, 34–35.

2. For a history, see Colin Beavan, *Fingerprints: The Origins of Crime Detection and the Murder Case That Launched Forensic Science* (New York: Hyperion, 2001).

3. Murders at alvinesau.com.

4. For the trauma-control theory of serial killers, see Eric Hickey, *Serial Murderers and Their Victims* (Belmont, CA: Wadsworth, 6th ed., 2013). Also see James Alan Fox and Jack Levin, *The Will to Kill: Explaining Senseless Murder* (Boston: Pearson Educational, 2006).

5. Gordon W. Russon, "A Psychiatric Viewpoint," in Frank Anderson, *The Dark Strangler* (Calgary: Frontier, 1974) at i–iv.

6. Peter Vronsky, *Sons of Cain: A History of Serial Killers from the Stone Age to the Present* (New York: Berkley, 2018); Katherine Ramsland, *The Human Predator: A Historical Chronicle of*

Serial Murder and Forensic Investigation (New York: Berkley Books, 2005); Harold Schechter, *The Serial Killer Files* (New York: Ballantine, 2003).

7. Elliott Leyton, *Men of Blood: Murder in Everyday Life* (Toronto: McClelland and Stewart, 1995).

8. For the development of the Canadian version, see Doug Clark, *Dark Paths, Cold Trails: How a Mountie Led to the Quest to Link Serial Killers to Their Victims* (Toronto: HarperCollins, 2002).

9. One crime writer speculates that a German immigrant, Paul Mueller, was a serial killer responsible for a host of axe murders of families across the United States in the early part of the 20th century. He may have murdered around 100 people, which is obviously a higher number than Earle Nelson in the 20s. See Bill James with Rachel McCarthy James, *The Man from the Train* (New York: Scribner, 2017).

10. Another axe murderer was Jake Bird who also traveled across the country during the decades of the 1930s and '40s and killed a dozen women, but he allegedly confessed to murdering many more. However, the confession may have been unreliable, motivated by an attempt to buy time before execution. The next serial killer that came close to Nelson in the number of infamous deeds was Carroll Edward Cole, who strangled women in the 1970s. While he had a body count of 16 confirmed cases, he may have been responsible for up to 35, which puts him in the Nelson category. See Michael Newton, *Silent Rage* (New York: Dell, 1994).

11. See Landis MacKellar, The *"Double Indemnity" Murder: Ruth Snyder, Judd Gray, and New York's Crime of the Century* (Syracuse: Syracuse University Press, 2006).

Bibliography

Primary Materials

Attorney General of Manitoba. Central registry file on *R* v. *Nelson*. Archives of Manitoba.
> [This file includes the transcript of the inquest and numerous memos and affidavits dealing with the arrest, escape, recapture, reward allocation and prosecution of Earle Nelson.]

Buffalo police file on murder of Randolph.

Capital case file on Earle Nelson. Library and Archives Canada.
> [This file includes the transcript of the preliminary hearing and trial transcript and numerous submissions and affidavits on the history of Earle Nelson, including the asylum records.]

Chicago police file on murder of Sietsema.

Kansas City police file on murders of Pace and Harpin.

Los Angeles Police Homicide Ledger confirming Corcoran case dismissed as suicide.

Los Angeles police reports on murder of Russell in Santa Barbara. Winnipeg police file.

Military file of Earle Leonard Ferrell. National Personnel Records Center, St. Louis.
> [This file deals with the enlistment, desertion, court martial, jail and various insanity hearings involving "Ferrell."]

Portland coroner's reports. Multnomah County Records Center.

Portland police investigative report books on murders of Withers, Fluke, Grant, and Myers. Portland City Archives (formerly Stanley Parr Archives and Research Center).

San Francisco autopsy reports. San Francisco Medical Examiner's Office.

San Francisco police reports on murders of Newman, St. Mary and Edmonds and criminal history of Earle Nelson. Winnipeg police file.

Victim biographies found at Ancestry.com, family search.org, and findagrave.com.
> [Census records, birth, marriage, death records, city directories, and so forth.]

Winnipeg police file on Earle Nelson.
> [This file deals with the investigation of the murders of Cowan and Patterson, the arrest of Nelson and various materials from police forces in the United States, including the criminal record of Nelson.]

Newspapers

NOTE: These are only the primary newspapers consulted, not all the newspapers cited in the book.

California

Alameda Times-Star
Bakersfield Californian
Bakersfield Echo
Feather River Bulletin
Fresno Bee
Los Angeles Express
Los Angeles Herald
Los Angeles Post-Record
Los Angeles Times
Modesto News-Herald
Oakland Post-Enquirer
Oakland Tribune
Palo Alto Times
Plumas Independent
Sacramento Bee
Sacramento Star
San Bernardino Sun
San Diego Sun
San Diego Union
San Francisco Bulletin
San Francisco Call and Post
San Francisco Chronicle
San Francisco Examiner
San Francisco News
San Francisco Recorder
San Jose Mercury Herald
San Jose News
San Mateo Times
Santa Ana Register
Santa Barbara News
Santa Barbara Press
Santa Rosa Press-Democrat
Stockton Independent
Stockton Mail
Stockton Record

Canada

Manitoba Free Press
Regina Leader
Winnipeg Tribune

Illinois

Chicago Herald and Examiner
Chicago Journal
Chicago Post
Chicago Southtown Economist
Chicago Suburbanite Economist
Chicago Tribune

Iowa

Council Bluffs Nonpareil

Des Moines Register
Dubuque Telegraph Herald
Sioux City Journal

Michigan

Detroit Free Press
Detroit News
Detroit Times

Missouri

Kansas City Journal
Kansas City Star
Kansas City Times
St. Louis Post-Dispatch

Nebraska

Omaha Bee
Omaha News
Omaha World-Herald

New Jersey

Newark News
Newark Star-Eagle

New York

Buffalo Commercial
Buffalo Courier
Buffalo Enquirer
Buffalo Express
Buffalo News
Buffalo Times
New York News
New York Times
Syracuse Herald

Oregon

Eugene Guard
Eugene Register
Oregon Journal
Oregonian

Portland News
Portland Telegram
Salem Capital Journal
Tacoma Ledger

Pennsylvania

Philadelphia Bulletin
Philadelphia Inquirer
Philadelphia Public Ledger
Philadelphia Tribune
Pittsburgh Courier
Pittsburgh Post

Washington State

Seattle Post-Intelligencer
Seattle Star
Seattle Times
Seattle Union Record
Spokane Chronicle
Spokane Spokesman-Review

Secondary Sources

On Earle Nelson

NOTE: Some of the literature on Earle Nelson is fictional or has added fictional elements and errors of fact.

Anderson, Frank W. *The Dark Strangler*. Calgary: Frontier, 1974.

Douthwaite, A.C. *Mass Murder*. New York: Henry Holt, 1929.

Esau, Alvin A.J. *The Gorilla Man Strangler Case: Serial Killer Earle Nelson*. Altona, Manitoba: FriesenPress, 2022.

Graham, R.B. Recollections of Graham. Archives of Manitoba.

Graysmith, Robert. *The Laughing Gorilla*. New York: Berkley Books, 2009.

Green, Ryan. *Gorilla Killer: A True Story of Betrayal, Brutality and Butchery*. Self-published, 2020.

Levins, Peter. "What Is Justice?" *The Atlantic Sunday Magazine*, July 25, 1937.

Matheson, Duncan. "International Strangler Captured." *Police Journal* V, no. 9 (1927).

Miller, James Burr. "The Dark Strangler." *Oregonian*, Feb. 27, 1956.

Musson, H.P., and Fred Allhoff. "Strangler of Twenty Women." *Master Detective* 18 (June, July, and August 1938).

Nash, Robert. *The Dark Fountain: A Novel of Horror*. New York: A and W, 1982.

Newton, Michael. *The Dark Strangler*. Toronto: VP, 2015.

Olmos, Robert, and John Howard. *Rooms to Let*. Self-published, 1977.

Redekop, Bill. *Crimes of the Century: More of Manitoba's Most Notorious Crimes*. Winnipeg: Great Plains, 2004.

Russon, Gordon W. "A Psychiatric Viewpoint," in Frank Anderson, *The Dark Strangler* (Calgary: Frontier, 1974) at i–iv.

Schechter, Harold. *Bestial: The Savage Trail of a True American Monster*. New York: Pocket Books, 1998.

Simmons, Ben. "Case Study: The Dark Strangler: Kansas City's First Serial Killer." *CSI Forensic Forum, Quarterly Newsletter* 14 (April–June 2004).

Smith, Edward, Jr. "22 Dead in Path of Dark Strangler." *Oregonian*, July 3, 1927.

Smith, George. "How we Trapped Strangler Nelson." *Winnipeg Tribune*, March 15, 1952.

On Legal Process/Forensics/Other

Anderson, Frank W. *A Concise History of Capital Punishment in Canada*. Calgary: Frontier, 1973.

Arntfield, Michael. *How to Solve a Cold Case*. Toronto: HarperCollins, 2022.

Babiak, Paul, and Robert Hare. *Snakes in Suits: When Psychopaths Go to Work*. New York: HarperCollins, 2006.

Beavan, Colin. *Fingerprints: The Origins of Crime Detection and the Murder Case That Launched Forensic Science*. New York: Hyperion, 2001.

Brawn, Dale. *Last Moments: Sentenced to Death in Canada*. Edmonton: Quagmire Press, 2011.

Burchill, John. *Pioneer Policemen: The History of the Manitoba Provincial Police, 1920–32*. Winnipeg: Themis, 2020.

Chandler, J.D. *Murder and Mayhem in Portland*. Charleston, SC: The History Press, 2013.

Clark, Doug. *Dark Paths, Cold Trails: How a Mountie Led to the Quest to Link Serial Killers to Their Victims*. Toronto: HarperCollins, 2002.

Cleckley, Hervey. *The Mask of Sanity*. St. Louis: C.V. Mosby, 1941.

Dawson, Kate Winkler. *American Sherlock: Murder, Forensics, and the Birth of C.S.I.* New York: G.P. Putman's Sons, 2020.

Dutton, Kevin, and Andy McNab. *The Good Psychopath: Guide to Success*. London: Random House, 2014.

Dwyer, Jim, Peter Neufeld, and Barry Scheck. *Actual Innocence*. New York: Signet, 2000.

Fabricant, M. Chris, *Junk Science and the American Criminal Justice System*. Brooklyn: Akashic Books, 2022.

Fox, James Alan, and Jack Levin. *Extreme Killing: Understanding Serial and Mass Murder*. Los Angeles: Sage, 3rd ed., 2015.

Fox, James Alan, and Jack Levin. *The Will to Kill: Explaining Senseless Murder*. Boston: Pearson Educational, 2006.

Garrett, Brandon L. *Convicting the Innocent*. Cambridge: Harvard University Press, 2011.

Grindeland, Sherry. "Kirkland Man Pieces Together Tale of 1926 Killing." *Seattle Times*, Oct. 27, 2004.

Hare, Robert. *Without Conscience: The Disturbing World of Psychopaths Among Us*. New York: Pocket Books, 1993.

Hickey, Eric W. *Serial Murderers and Their Victims*. Belmont, CA: Wadsworth, 6th ed., 2013.

Holmes, Ronald M., and Stephen T. Holmes. *Serial Murder*. Thousand Oaks, CA: Sage, 3rd ed., 2010.

Jalava, Jarkko, Michael Mauren, and Stephanie Griffiths. *The Myth of the Born Criminal: Psychopathy, Neurobiology and the Creation of the Modern Degenerate*. Toronto: University of Toronto Press, 2015.

James, Bill, with Rachel McCarthy James. *The Man from the Train*. New York: Scribner's, 2017.

Kiehl, Kent. *Psychopath Whisperer: The Science of Those Without Conscience*. New York: Crown, 2014.

Leeson, Fred. *Rose City Justice: A Legal History of Portland, Oregon*. Portland: Oregon Historical Society Press, 1998.

Leyton, Elliott. *Men of Blood: Murder in Everyday Life*. Toronto: McClelland and Stewart, 1995.

Leyton-Brown, Ken. *The Practice of Execution in Canada*. Vancouver: University of British Columbia Press, 2010.

Loftus, Elizabeth. *Eyewitness Testimony*. Cambridge: Harvard University Press, 1979.

MacKellar, Landis. *The "Double Indemnity" Murder: Ruth Snyder, Judd Gray, and New York's Crime of the Century*. Syracuse: Syracuse University Press, 2006.

Morriss, W.E. *Watch the Rope*. Winnipeg: Watson and Dwyer, 1996.

Nordheim, Teresa. *Murder and Mayhem in Seattle*. Charleston, SC: The History Press, 2016.

Poplak, Lorna. *Drop Dead: The Horrible History of Hanging in Canada*. Toronto: Dundurn, 2017.

Raine, Adrian, and Andrea Glenn. *Psychopathy: An Introduction to Biological Findings and Their Implications*. New York: New York University Press, 2014.

Ramsland, Katherine. *The Human Predator: A Historical Chronicle of Serial Murder and Forensic Investigation*. New York: Berkley Books, 2005.

Roach, Kent. *Wrongfully Convicted*. Toronto: Simon & Schuster, 2023.

Schechter, Harold. *The Serial Killer Files*. New York: Ballantine, 2003.

Stout, Martha. *The Sociopath Next Door: The Ruthless Versus the Rest of Us*. New York: Broadway, 2005.

Strange, Carolyn. *The Death Penalty and Sex Murder in Canadian History*. Toronto: University of Toronto Press, 2020.

Strange, Carolyn, ed. *Qualities of Mercy: Justice, Punishment, and Discretion*. Vancouver: University of British Columbia Press, 1996.

Vronsky, Peter. *Serial Killers: The Method and Madness of Monsters*. New York: Berkley Books, 2004.

Vronsky, Peter. *Sons of Cain: A History of Serial Killers from the Stone Age to the Present*. New York: Berkley Books, 2018.

Index

Printed by BoD™in Norderstedt, Germany